S0-AHS-395

ONE
PRESENTS

モブサイコ100

MOB PSYCHO
100

VOLUME 4

DARK HORSE MANGA

MOB PSYCHO 100
VOLUME 4
Translated by
KUMAR SIVASUBRAMANIAN
Lettering and Retouch by
JOHN CLARK
Edited by
CARL GUSTAV HORN

CHAPTER 25: RIGHT/WRONG RELATIONSHIPS

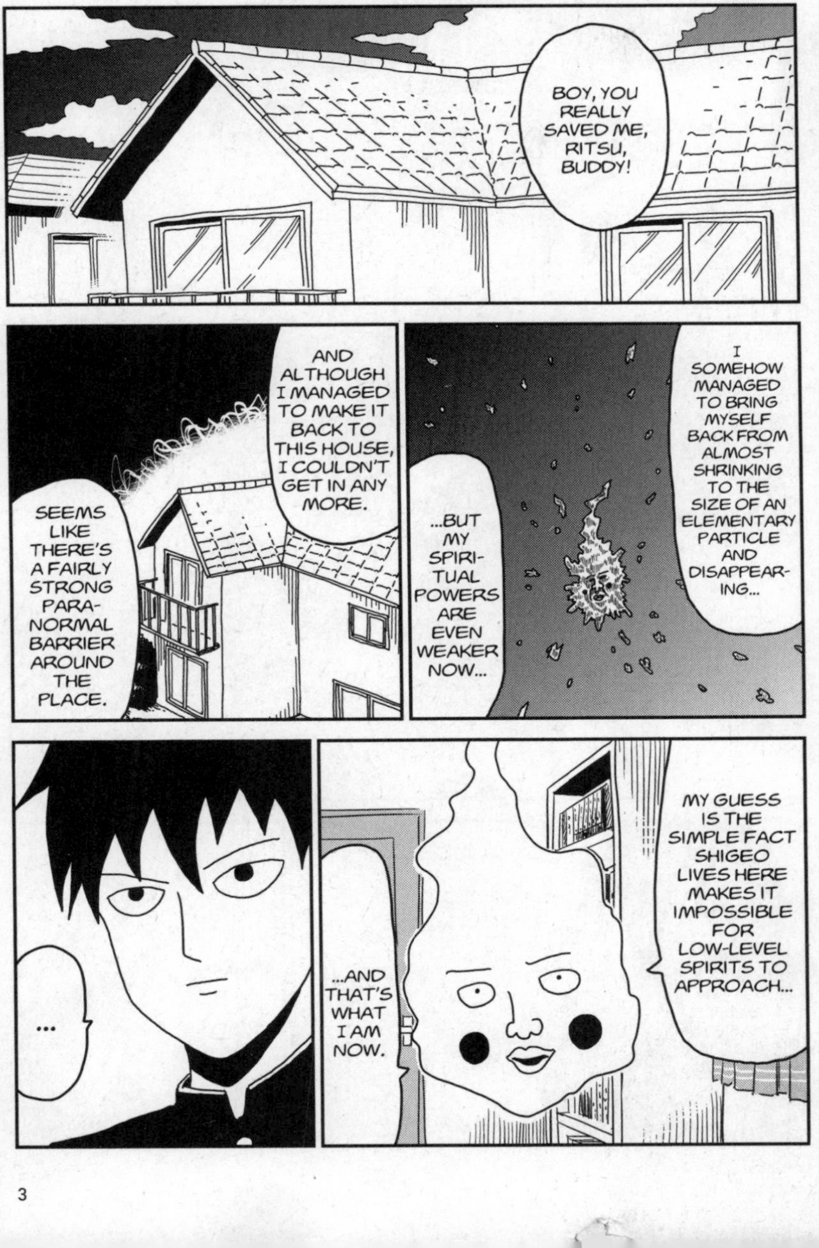
BOY, YOU REALLY SAVED ME, RITSU, BUDDY!
I SOMEHOW MANAGED TO BRING MYSELF BACK FROM ALMOST SHRINKING TO THE SIZE OF AN ELEMENTARY PARTICLE AND DISAPPEARING...
...BUT MY SPIRITUAL POWERS ARE EVEN WEAKER NOW...
AND ALTHOUGH I MANAGED TO MAKE IT BACK TO THIS HOUSE, I COULDN'T GET IN ANY MORE.
SEEMS LIKE THERE'S A FAIRLY STRONG PARANORMAL BARRIER AROUND THE PLACE.
MY GUESS IS THE SIMPLE FACT SHIGEO LIVES HERE MAKES IT IMPOSSIBLE FOR LOW-LEVEL SPIRITS TO APPROACH...
...AND THAT'S WHAT I AM NOW.
...

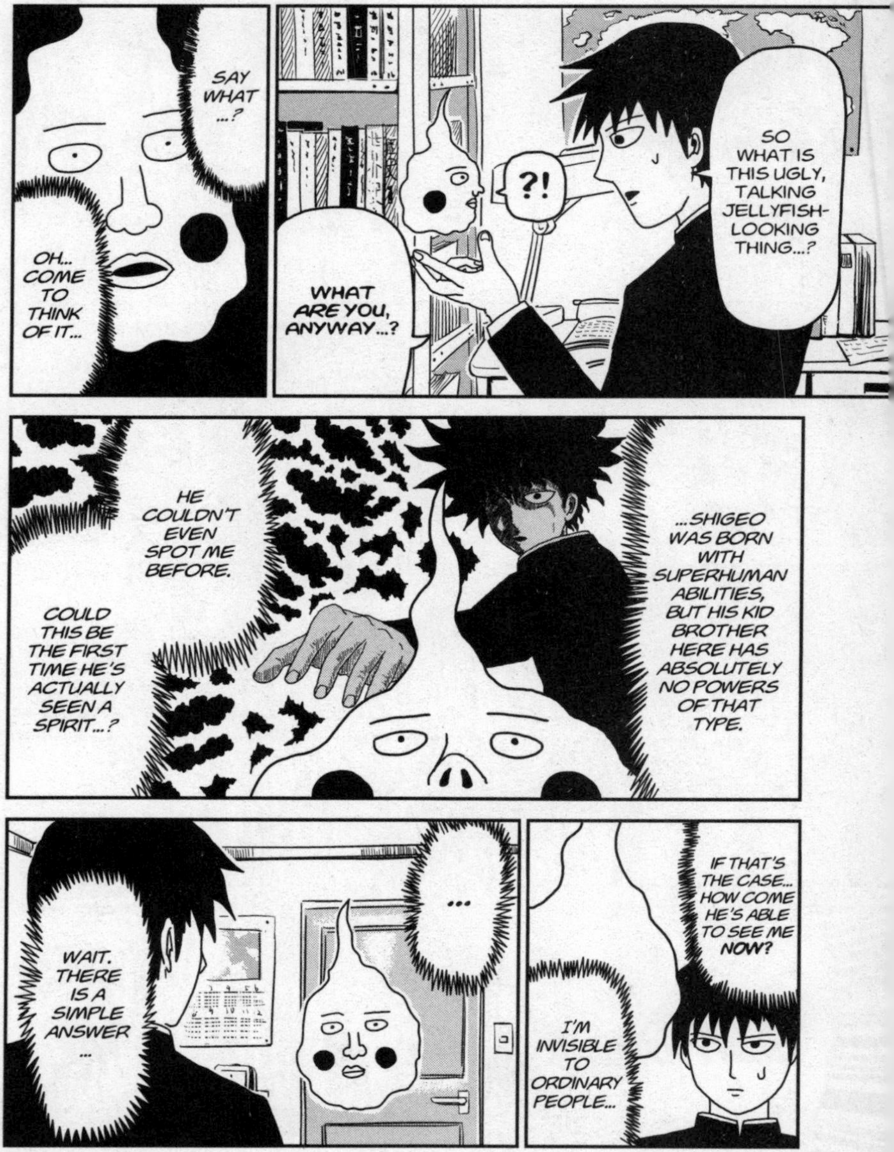
SO WHAT IS THIS UGLY, TALKING JELLYFISH-LOOKING THING...?
?!
WHAT ARE YOU, ANYWAY...?
SAY WHAT ...?
OH... COME TO THINK OF IT...
...SHIGEO WAS BORN WITH SUPERHUMAN ABILITIES, BUT HIS KID BROTHER HERE HAS ABSOLUTELY NO POWERS OF THAT TYPE.
HE COULDN'T EVEN SPOT ME BEFORE.
COULD THIS BE THE FIRST TIME HE'S ACTUALLY SEEN A SPIRIT...?
IF THAT'S THE CASE... HOW COME HE'S ABLE TO SEE ME **NOW**?
I'M INVISIBLE TO ORDINARY PEOPLE...
...
WAIT. THERE IS A SIMPLE ANSWER ...

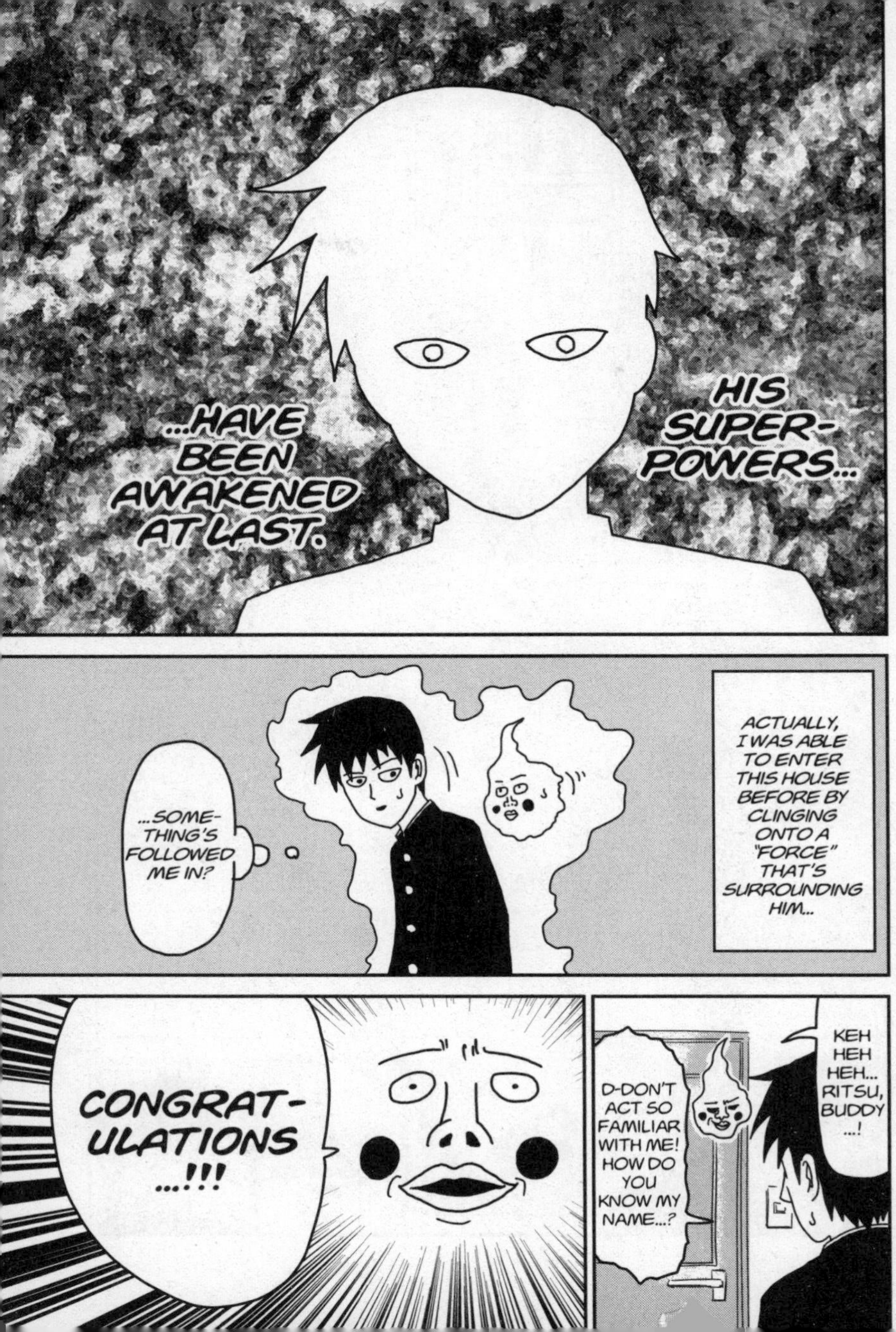
HIS SUPER-POWERS...
...HAVE BEEN AWAKENED AT LAST.
ACTUALLY, I WAS ABLE TO ENTER THIS HOUSE BEFORE BY CLINGING ONTO A "FORCE" THAT'S SURROUNDING HIM...
...SOME-THING'S FOLLOWED ME IN?
KEH HEH HEH... RITSU, BUDDY ...!
D-DON'T ACT SO FAMILIAR WITH ME! HOW DO YOU KNOW MY NAME...?
CONGRAT-ULATIONS ...!!!

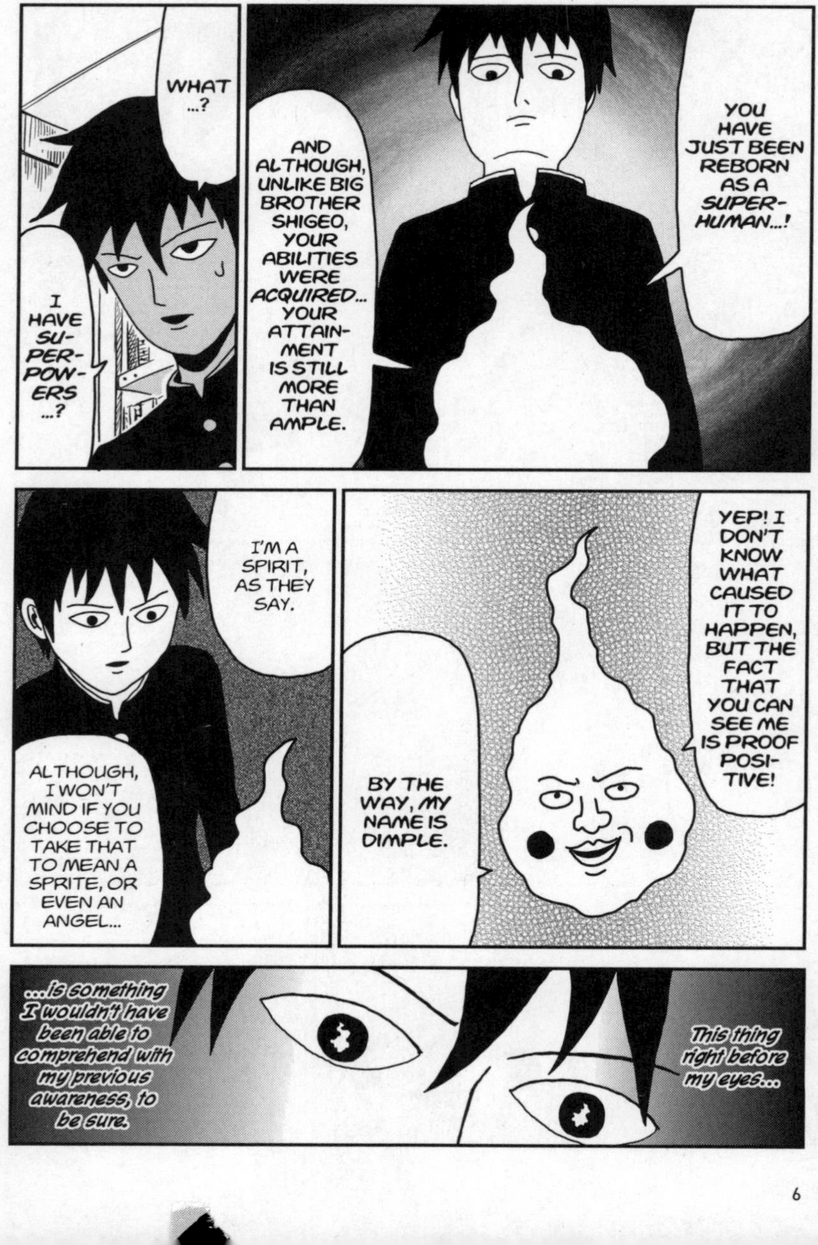
YOU HAVE JUST BEEN REBORN AS A SUPER-HUMAN...!
AND ALTHOUGH, UNLIKE BIG BROTHER SHIGEO, YOUR ABILITIES WERE ACQUIRED... YOUR ATTAINMENT IS STILL MORE THAN AMPLE.
WHAT ...?
I HAVE SUPERPOWERS ...?
YEP! I DON'T KNOW WHAT CAUSED IT TO HAPPEN, BUT THE FACT THAT YOU CAN SEE ME IS PROOF POSITIVE!
BY THE WAY, MY NAME IS DIMPLE.
I'M A SPIRIT, AS THEY SAY.
ALTHOUGH, I WON'T MIND IF YOU CHOOSE TO TAKE THAT TO MEAN A SPRITE, OR EVEN AN ANGEL...
This thing right before my eyes...
...is something I wouldn't have been able to comprehend with my previous awareness, to be sure.

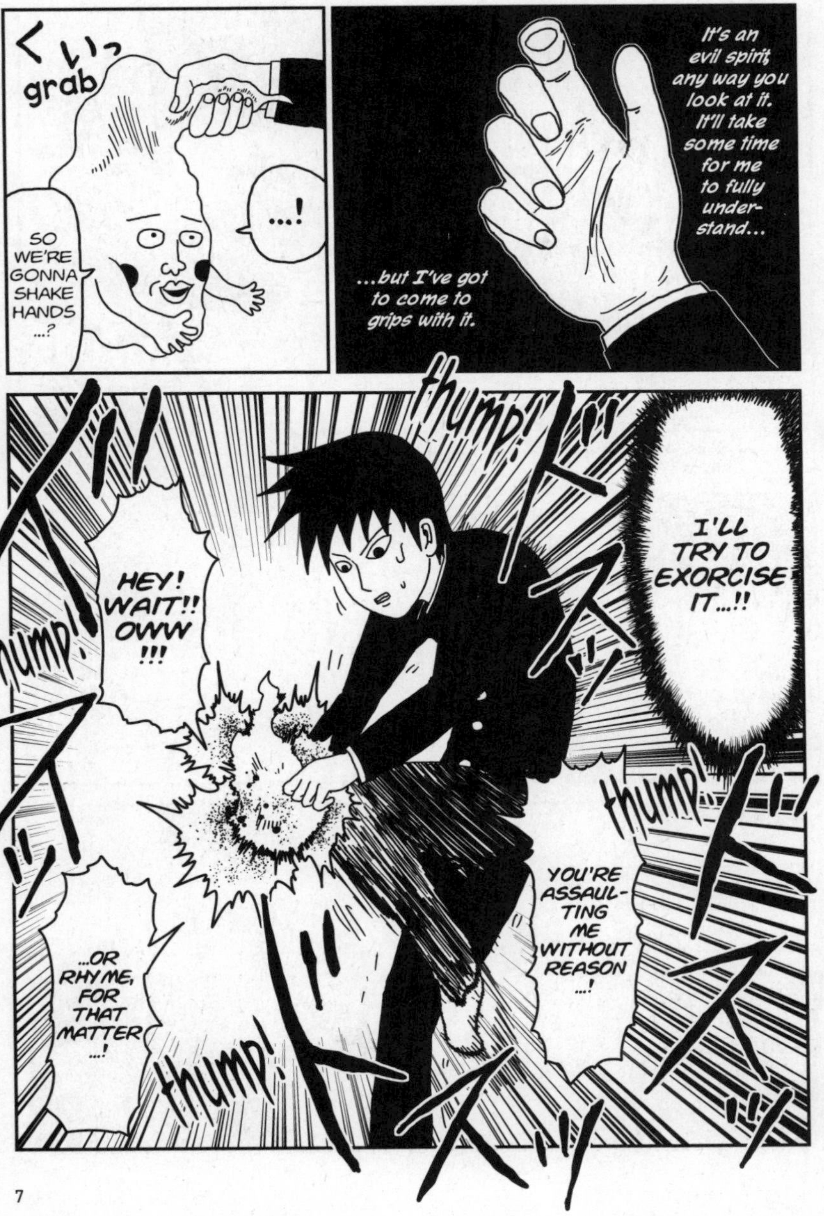
It's an evil spirit, any way you look at it. It'll take some time for me to fully under-stand...
...but I've got to come to grips with it.
くいっ
grab
...!
SO WE'RE GONNA SHAKE HANDS ...?
thump!
I'LL TRY TO EXORCISE IT...!!
HEY! WAIT!! OWW !!!
thump!
thump!
YOU'RE ASSAUL-TING ME WITHOUT REASON ...!
...OR RHYME, FOR THAT MATTER ...!
thump!

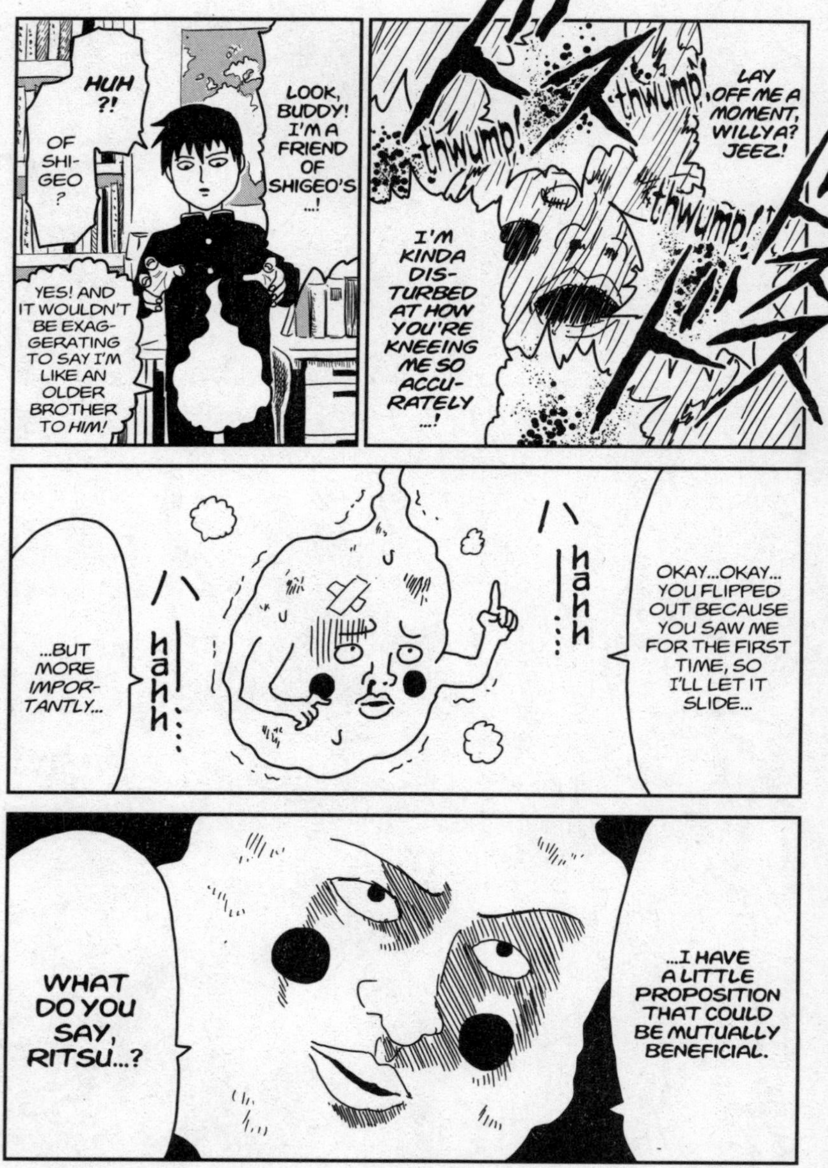

LAY OFF ME A MOMENT, WILLYA? JEEZ!
thwump!
thwump!
thwump!
I'M KINDA DISTURBED AT HOW YOU'RE KNEEING ME SO ACCURATELY...!
LOOK, BUDDY! I'M A FRIEND OF SHIGEO'S...!
HUH?!
OF SHIGEO?
YES! AND IT WOULDN'T BE EXAGGERATING TO SAY I'M LIKE AN OLDER BROTHER TO HIM!
OKAY...OKAY... YOU FLIPPED OUT BECAUSE YOU SAW ME FOR THE FIRST TIME, SO I'LL LET IT SLIDE...
hahh...
hahh...
...BUT MORE IMPORTANTLY...
...I HAVE A LITTLE PROPOSITION THAT COULD BE MUTUALLY BENEFICIAL.
WHAT DO YOU SAY, RITSU...?

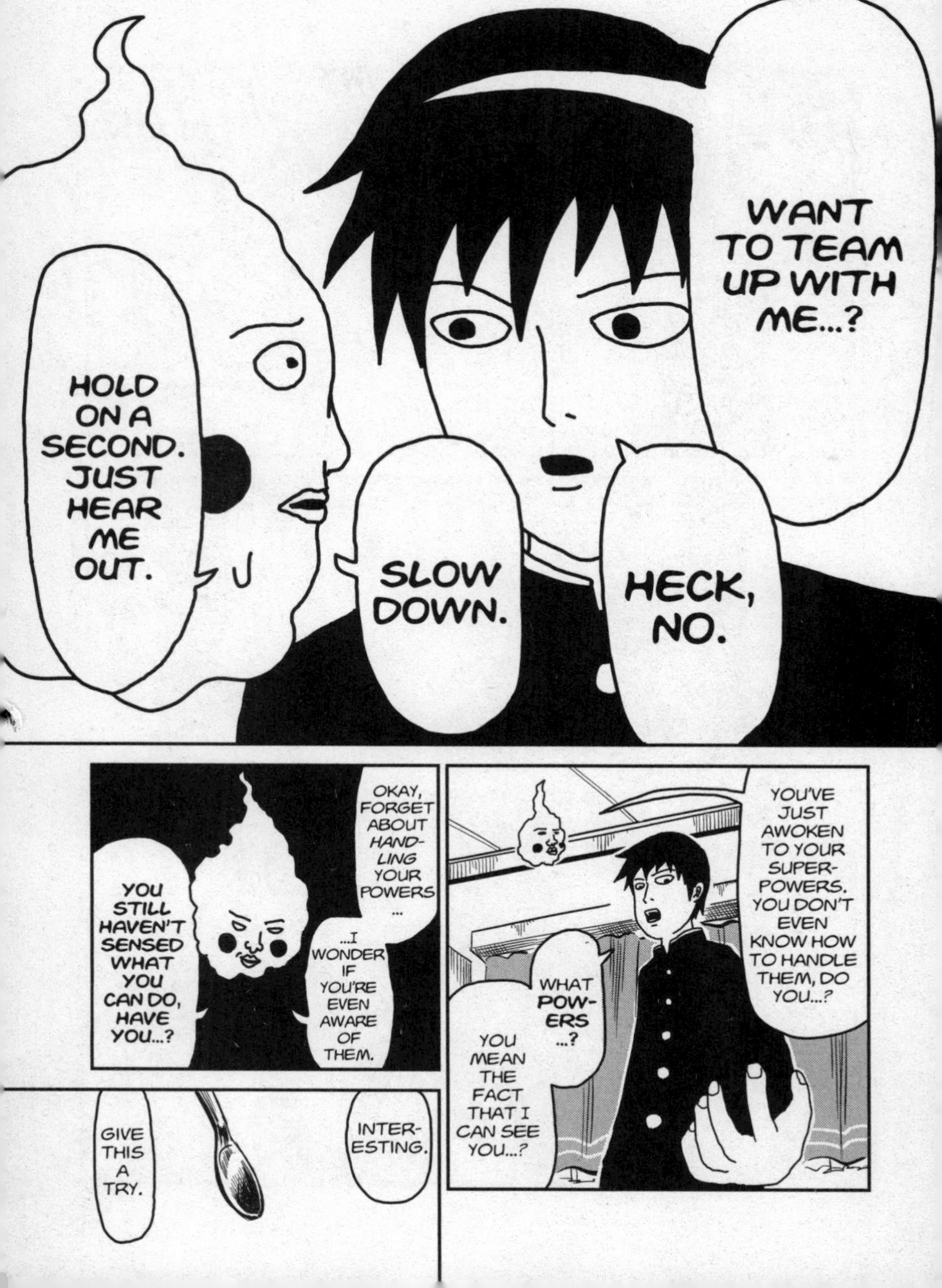
WANT TO TEAM UP WITH ME...?
HECK, NO.
SLOW DOWN.
HOLD ON A SECOND. JUST HEAR ME OUT.
YOU'VE JUST AWOKEN TO YOUR SUPER-POWERS. YOU DON'T EVEN KNOW HOW TO HANDLE THEM, DO YOU...?
WHAT POW-ERS...?
YOU MEAN THE FACT THAT I CAN SEE YOU...?
OKAY, FORGET ABOUT HAND-LING YOUR POWERS...
...I WONDER IF YOU'RE EVEN AWARE OF THEM.
YOU STILL HAVEN'T SENSED WHAT YOU CAN DO, HAVE YOU...?
INTER-ESTING.
GIVE THIS A TRY.

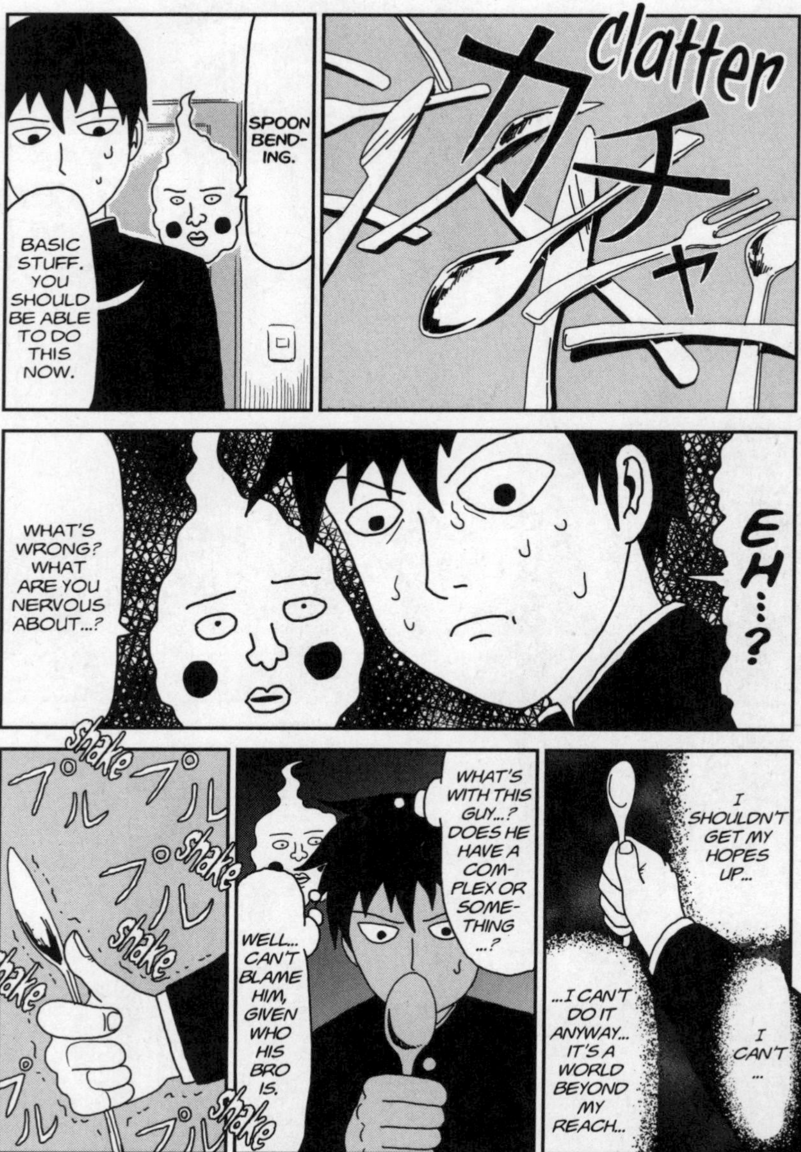
clatter
カチャ
SPOON BENDING.
BASIC STUFF. YOU SHOULD BE ABLE TO DO THIS NOW.
EH...?
WHAT'S WRONG? WHAT ARE YOU NERVOUS ABOUT...?
I SHOULDN'T GET MY HOPES UP...
I CAN'T...
...I CAN'T DO IT ANYWAY... IT'S A WORLD BEYOND MY REACH...
WHAT'S WITH THIS GUY...? DOES HE HAVE A COMPLEX OR SOMETHING...?
WELL... CAN'T BLAME HIM, GIVEN WHO HIS BRO IS.
shake
プルプル
shake
プルプル
shake
shake
プルプル
shake

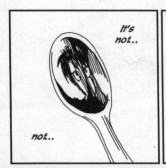

It's
not..

not..

It's
not..

It..

Not...

...bending.

...YOU
LIED
TO
ME!

THIS
SPOON IS
NEVER
GOING TO
BEND...!

D...

DIIIIIIIMPLE!!

...

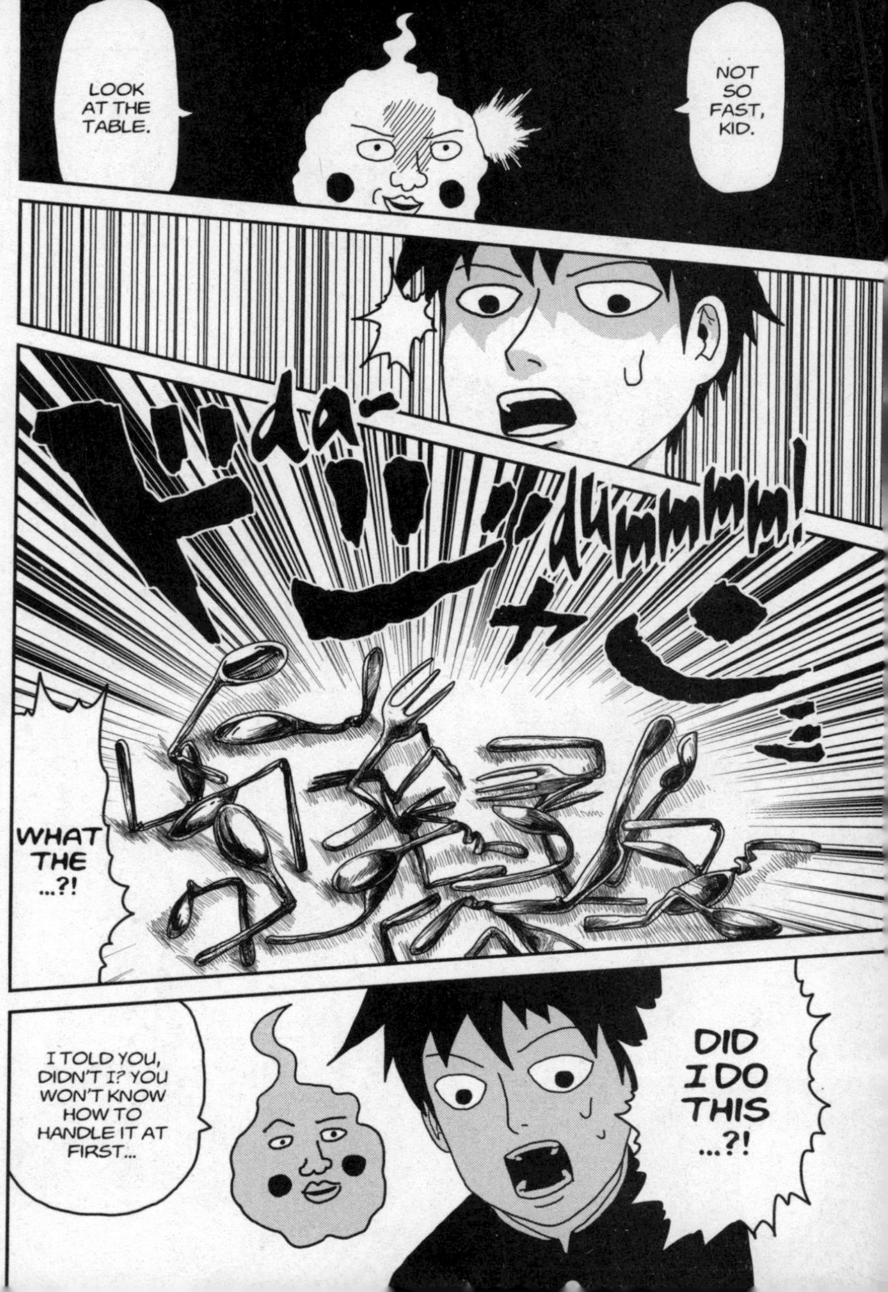
NOT SO FAST, KID.
LOOK AT THE TABLE.
da-
dummmmm!
WHAT THE ...?!
DID I DO THIS ...?!
I TOLD YOU, DIDN'T I? YOU WON'T KNOW HOW TO HANDLE IT AT FIRST...

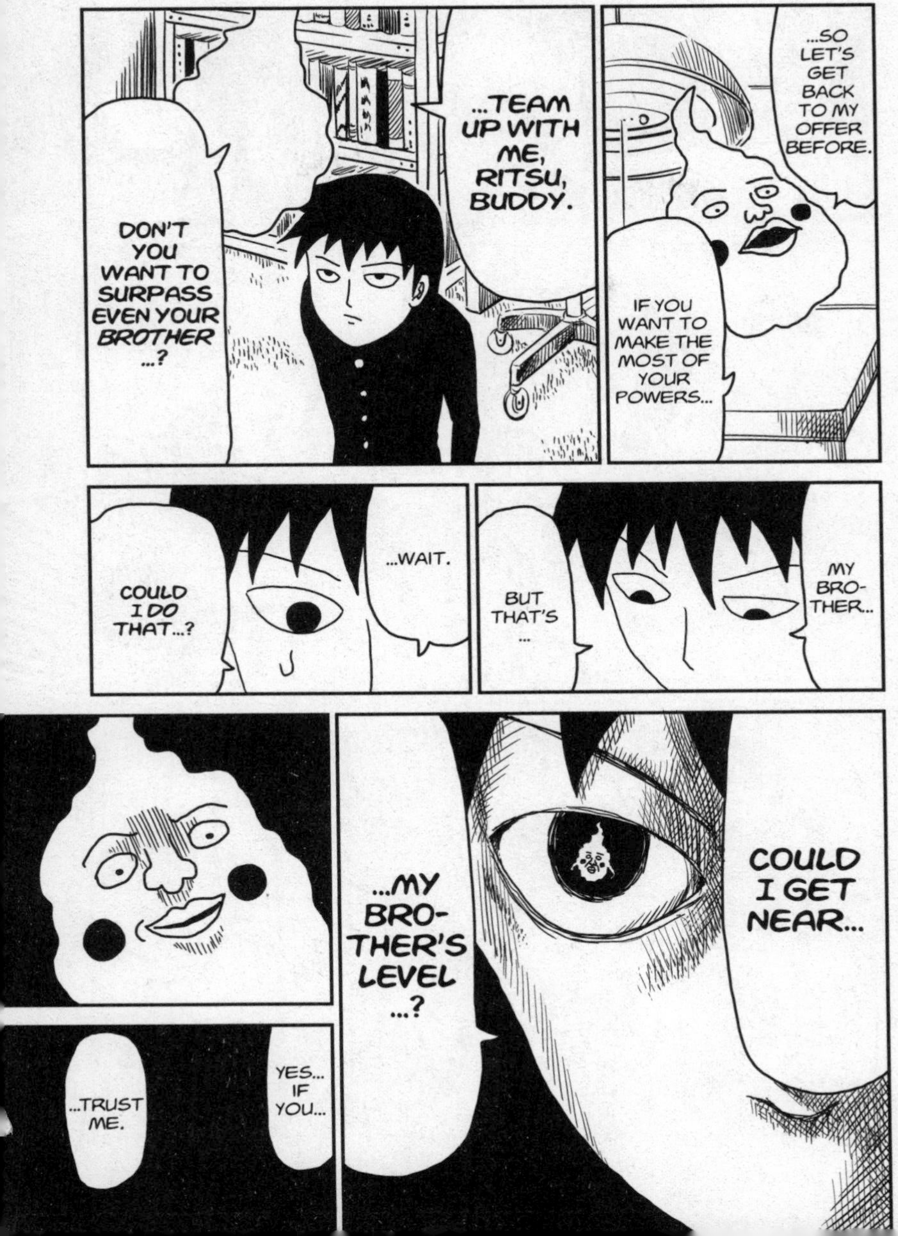
...SO LET'S GET BACK TO MY OFFER BEFORE.
IF YOU WANT TO MAKE THE MOST OF YOUR POWERS...
...TEAM UP WITH ME, RITSU, BUDDY.
DON'T YOU WANT TO SURPASS EVEN YOUR BROTHER ...?
MY BRO-THER...
BUT THAT'S ...
...WAIT.
COULD I DO THAT...?
COULD I GET NEAR...
...MY BRO-THER'S LEVEL ...?
YES... IF YOU...
...TRUST ME.

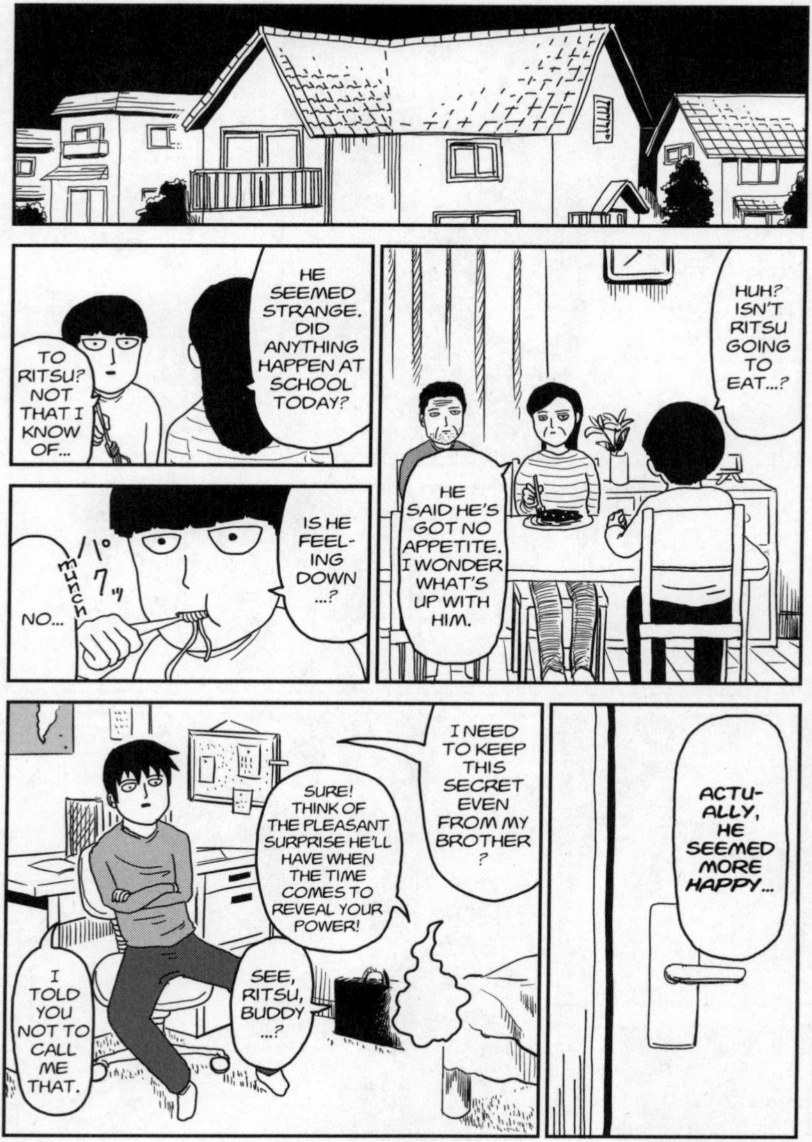
HUH? ISN'T RITSU GOING TO EAT...?
HE SAID HE'S GOT NO APPETITE. I WONDER WHAT'S UP WITH HIM.
HE SEEMED STRANGE. DID ANYTHING HAPPEN AT SCHOOL TODAY?
TO RITSU? NOT THAT I KNOW OF...
IS HE FEELING DOWN ...?
パクッ
munch
NO...
ACTUALLY, HE SEEMED MORE HAPPY...
I NEED TO KEEP THIS SECRET EVEN FROM MY BROTHER ?
SURE! THINK OF THE PLEASANT SURPRISE HE'LL HAVE WHEN THE TIME COMES TO REVEAL YOUR POWER!
SEE, RITSU, BUDDY ...?
I TOLD YOU NOT TO CALL ME THAT.

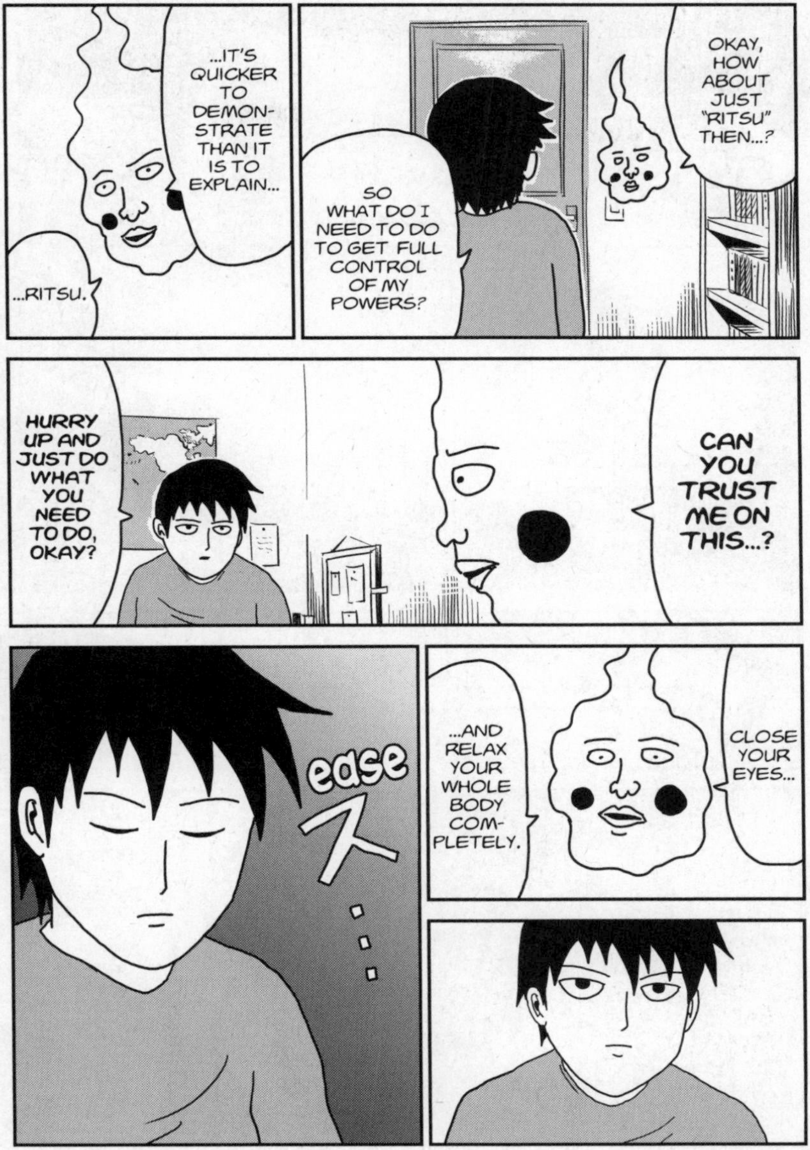
OKAY, HOW ABOUT JUST "RITSU" THEN...?
SO WHAT DO I NEED TO DO TO GET FULL CONTROL OF MY POWERS?
...IT'S QUICKER TO DEMON-STRATE THAN IT IS TO EXPLAIN...
...RITSU.
CAN YOU TRUST ME ON THIS...?
HURRY UP AND JUST DO WHAT YOU NEED TO DO, OKAY?
CLOSE YOUR EYES...
...AND RELAX YOUR WHOLE BODY COM-PLETELY.
ease
ス

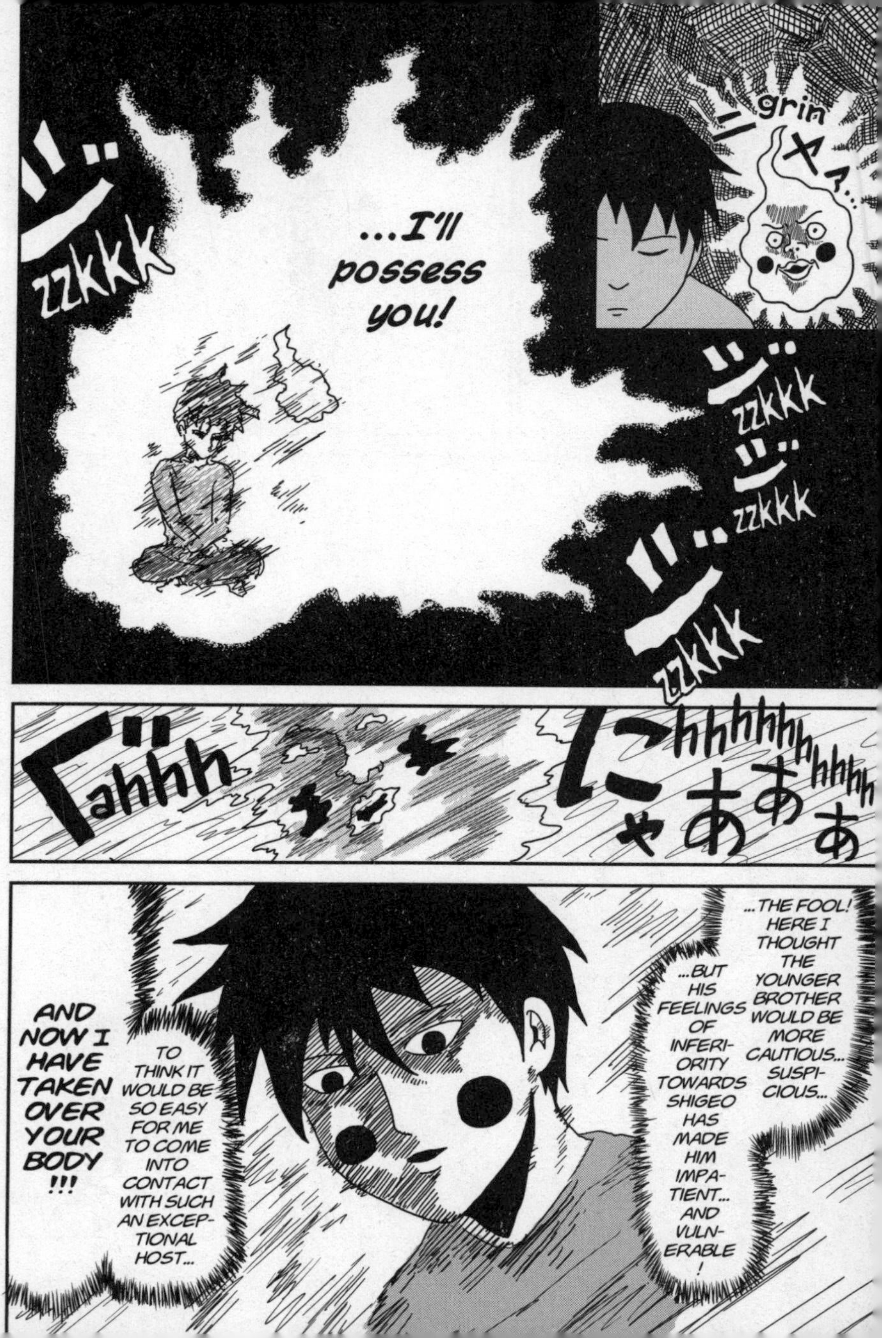

ニヤァ…
grin
...I'll possess you!
ジジジ
zzkkk
zzkkk
zzkkk
zzkkk
にゃあああ
ahhhh
...THE FOOL! HERE I THOUGHT THE YOUNGER BROTHER WOULD BE MORE CAUTIOUS... SUSPICIOUS...
...BUT HIS FEELINGS OF INFERIORITY TOWARDS SHIGEO HAS MADE HIM IMPATIENT... AND VULNERABLE!
TO THINK IT WOULD BE SO EASY FOR ME TO COME INTO CONTACT WITH SUCH AN EXCEPTIONAL HOST...
AND NOW I HAVE TAKEN OVER YOUR BODY!!!

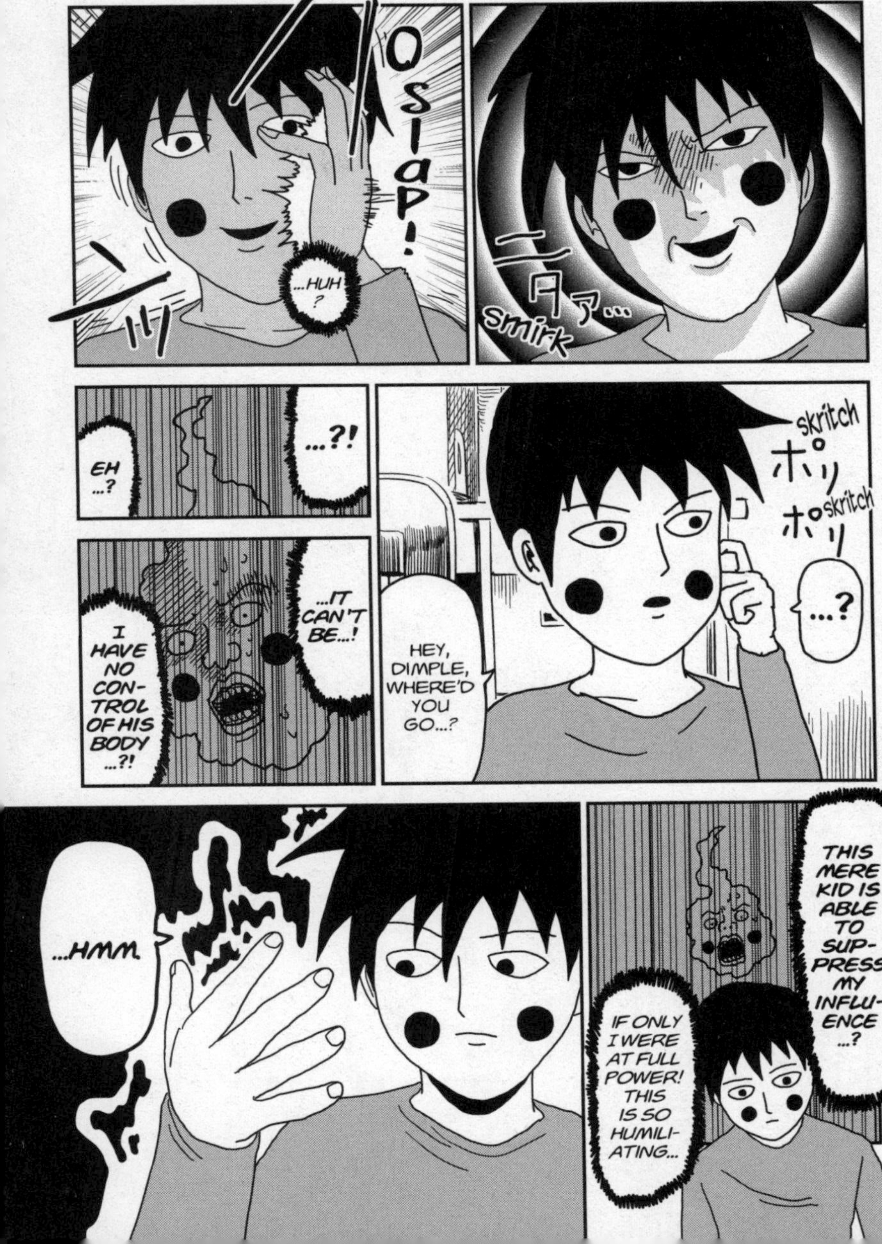
ニタァ…
smirk
slap!
...HUH?
skritch
ポリ
skritch
ポリ
...?
HEY, DIMPLE, WHERE'D YOU GO...?
...?!
EH...?
...IT CAN'T BE...!
I HAVE NO CONTROL OF HIS BODY...?!
THIS MERE KID IS ABLE TO SUPPRESS MY INFLUENCE...?
IF ONLY I WERE AT FULL POWER! THIS IS SO HUMILIATING...
...HMM.

CHAPTER 26: THRILL

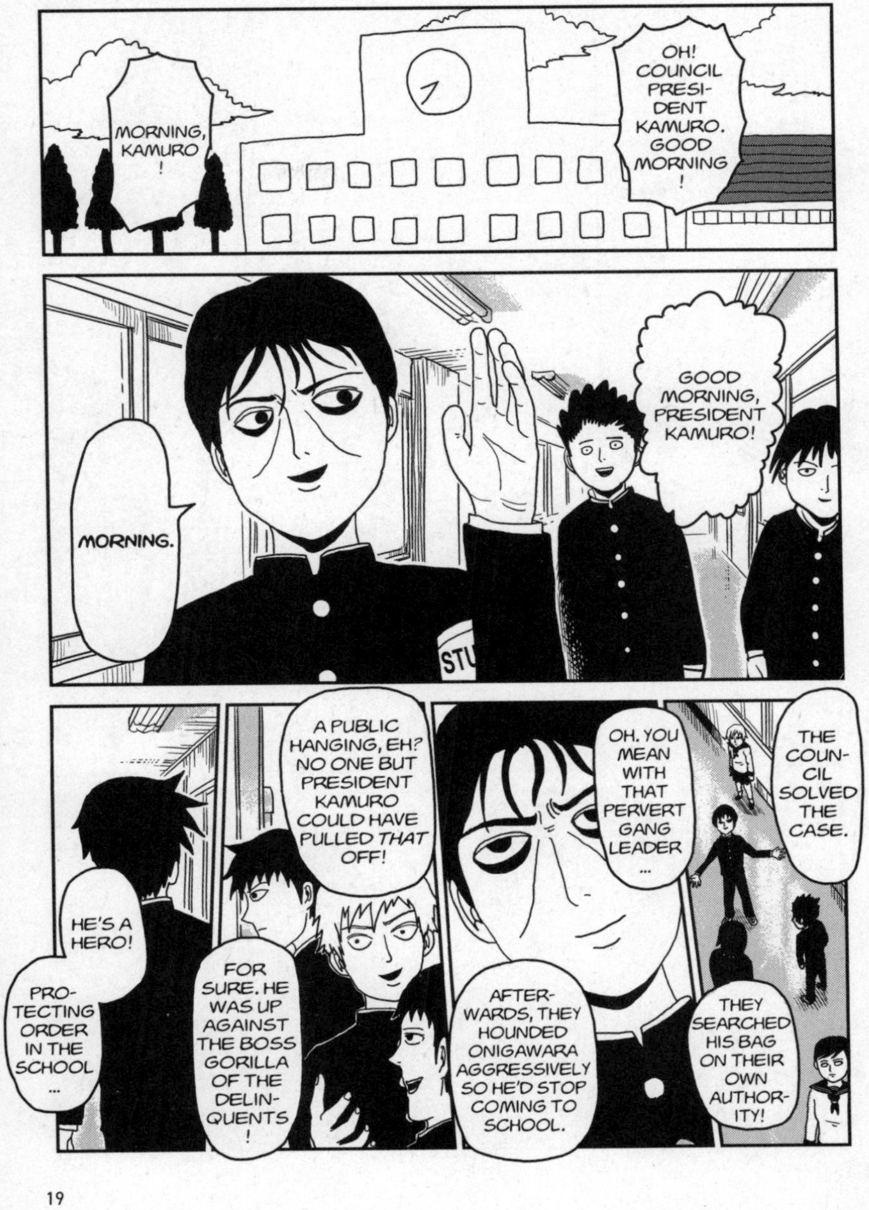
OH! COUNCIL PRESIDENT KAMURO. GOOD MORNING!
MORNING, KAMURO!
GOOD MORNING, PRESIDENT KAMURO!
MORNING.
THE COUNCIL SOLVED THE CASE.
THEY SEARCHED HIS BAG ON THEIR OWN AUTHORITY!
OH. YOU MEAN WITH THAT PERVERT GANG LEADER...
AFTERWARDS, THEY HOUNDED ONIGAWARA AGGRESSIVELY SO HE'D STOP COMING TO SCHOOL.
A PUBLIC HANGING, EH? NO ONE BUT PRESIDENT KAMURO COULD HAVE PULLED *THAT* OFF!
FOR SURE. HE WAS UP AGAINST THE BOSS GORILLA OF THE DELINQUENTS!
HE'S A HERO!
PROTECTING ORDER IN THE SCHOOL...

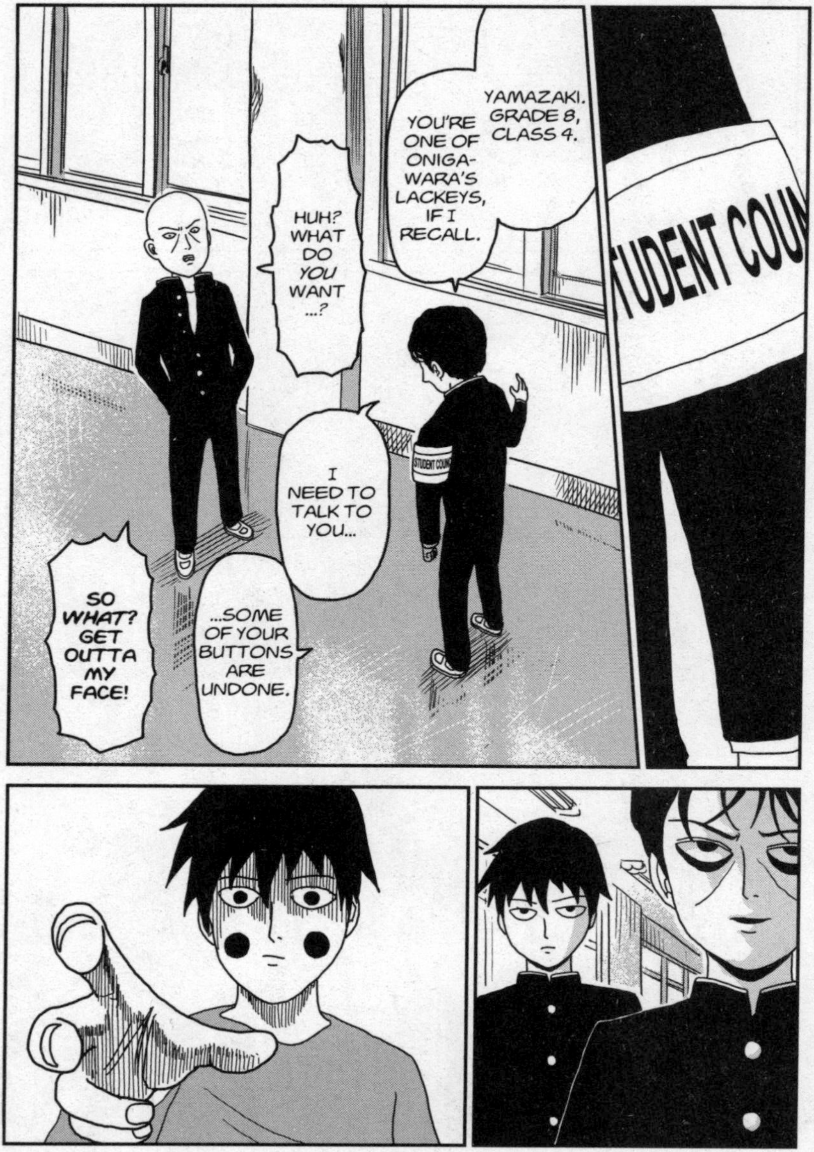
TUDENT COUN
YAMAZAKI. GRADE 8, CLASS 4.
YOU'RE ONE OF ONIGA-WARA'S LACKEYS, IF I RECALL.
HUH? WHAT DO *YOU* WANT ...?
I NEED TO TALK TO YOU...
...SOME OF YOUR BUTTONS ARE UNDONE.
SO *WHAT?* GET OUTTA MY FACE!

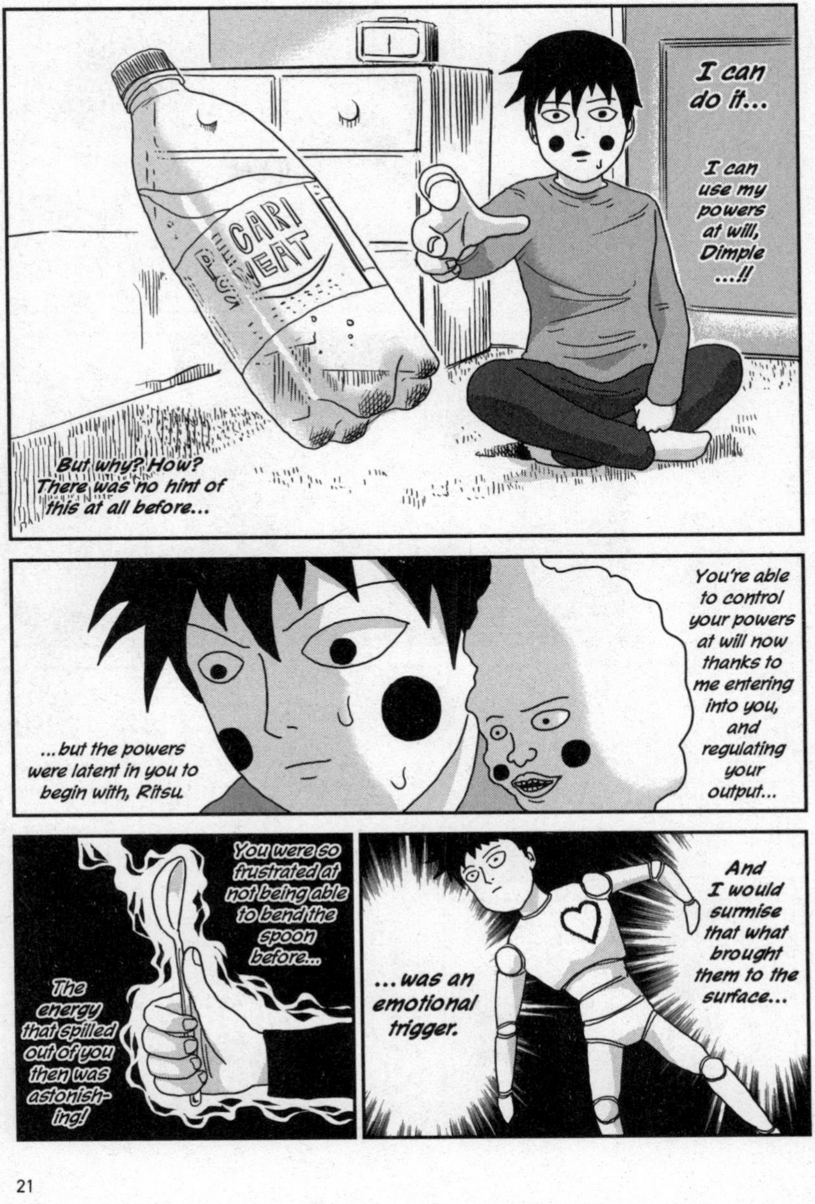
I can do it...
I can use my powers at will, Dimple ...!!
But why? How? There was no hint of this at all before...
You're able to control your powers at will now thanks to me entering into you, and regulating your output...
...but the powers were latent in you to begin with, Ritsu.
And I would surmise that what brought them to the surface...
...was an emotional trigger.
You were so frustrated at not being able to bend the spoon before...
The energy that spilled out of you then was astonish-ing!

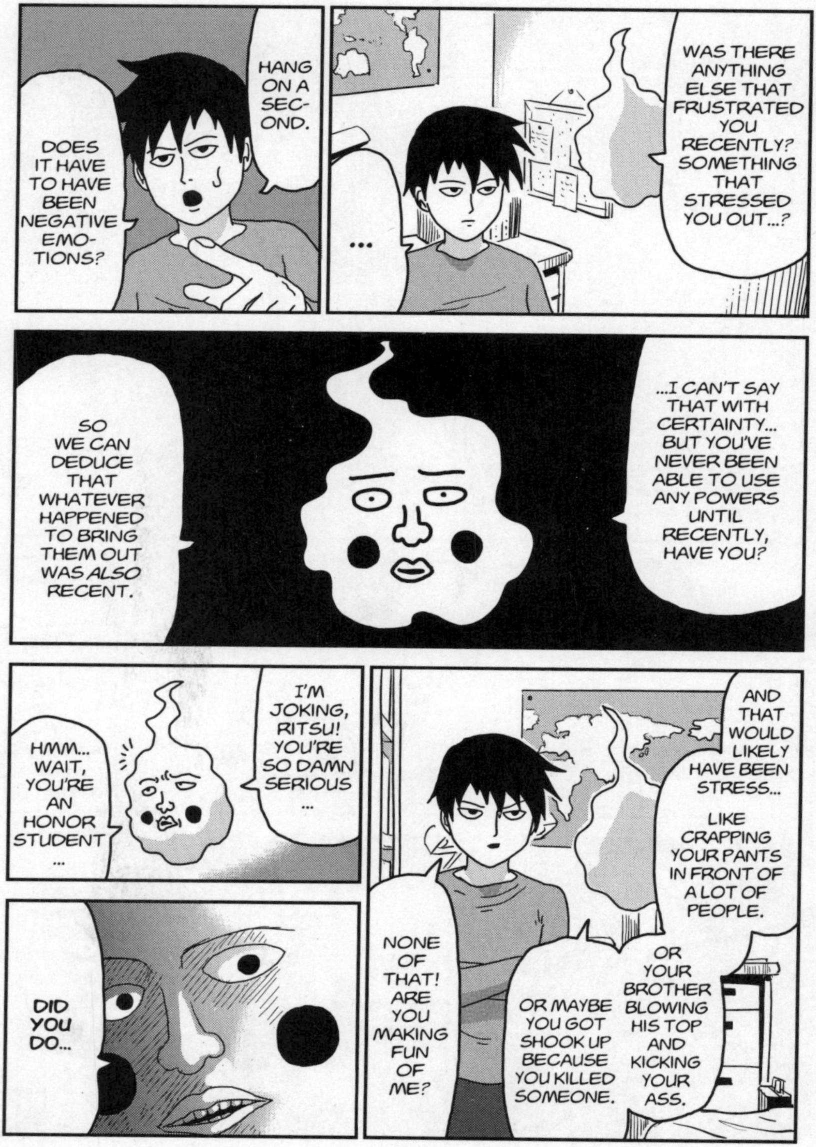
WAS THERE ANYTHING ELSE THAT FRUSTRATED YOU RECENTLY? SOMETHING THAT STRESSED YOU OUT...?
...
HANG ON A SECOND.
DOES IT HAVE TO HAVE BEEN NEGATIVE EMOTIONS?
...I CAN'T SAY THAT WITH CERTAINTY... BUT YOU'VE NEVER BEEN ABLE TO USE ANY POWERS UNTIL RECENTLY, HAVE YOU?
SO WE CAN DEDUCE THAT WHATEVER HAPPENED TO BRING THEM OUT WAS *ALSO* RECENT.
AND THAT WOULD LIKELY HAVE BEEN STRESS...
LIKE CRAPPING YOUR PANTS IN FRONT OF A LOT OF PEOPLE.
OR YOUR BROTHER BLOWING HIS TOP AND KICKING YOUR ASS.
OR MAYBE YOU GOT SHOOK UP BECAUSE YOU KILLED SOMEONE.
NONE OF THAT! ARE YOU MAKING FUN OF ME?
I'M JOKING, RITSU! YOU'RE SO DAMN SERIOUS ...
HMM... WAIT, YOU'RE AN HONOR STUDENT ...
DID YOU DO...

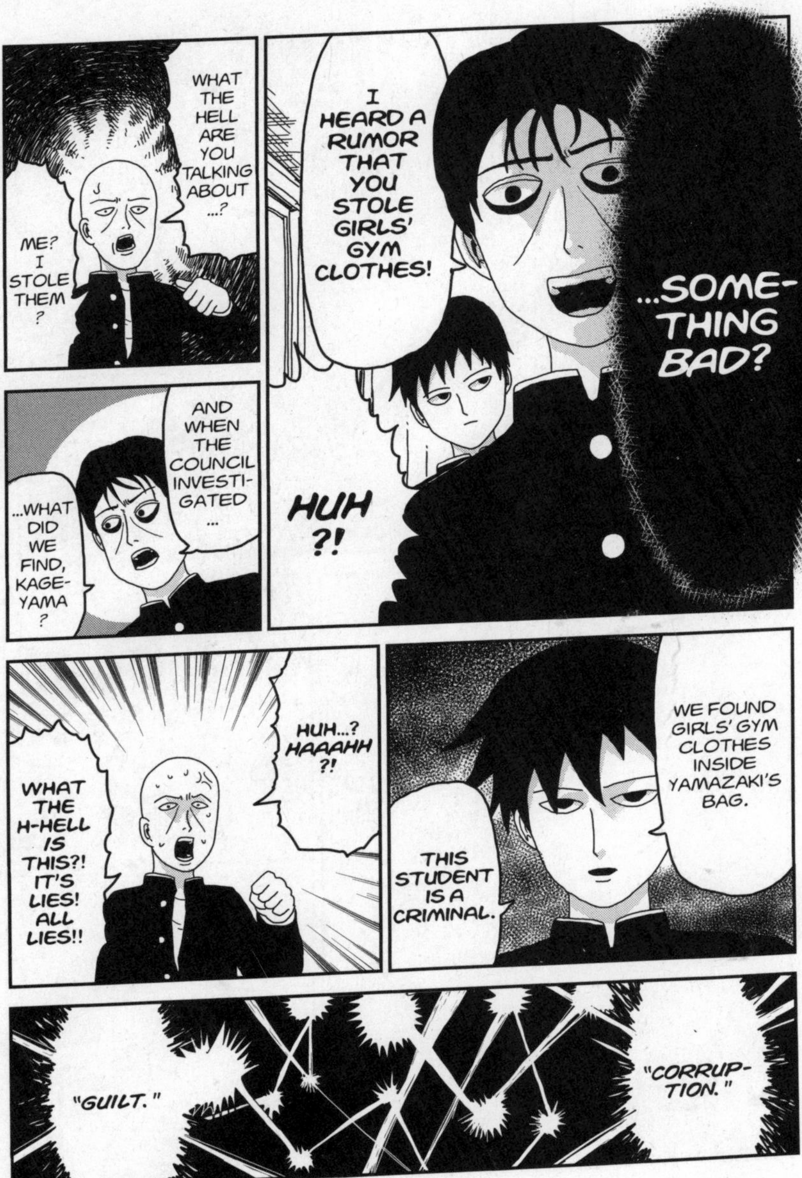
I HEARD A RUMOR THAT YOU STOLE GIRLS' GYM CLOTHES!
...SOMETHING BAD?
HUH ?!
WHAT THE HELL ARE YOU TALKING ABOUT ...?
ME? I STOLE THEM ?
AND WHEN THE COUNCIL INVESTIGATED ...
...WHAT DID WE FIND, KAGEYAMA ?
WE FOUND GIRLS' GYM CLOTHES INSIDE YAMAZAKI'S BAG.
THIS STUDENT IS A CRIMINAL.
HUH...? HAAAHH ?!
WHAT THE H-HELL IS THIS?! IT'S LIES! ALL LIES!!
"CORRUPTION."
"GUILT."

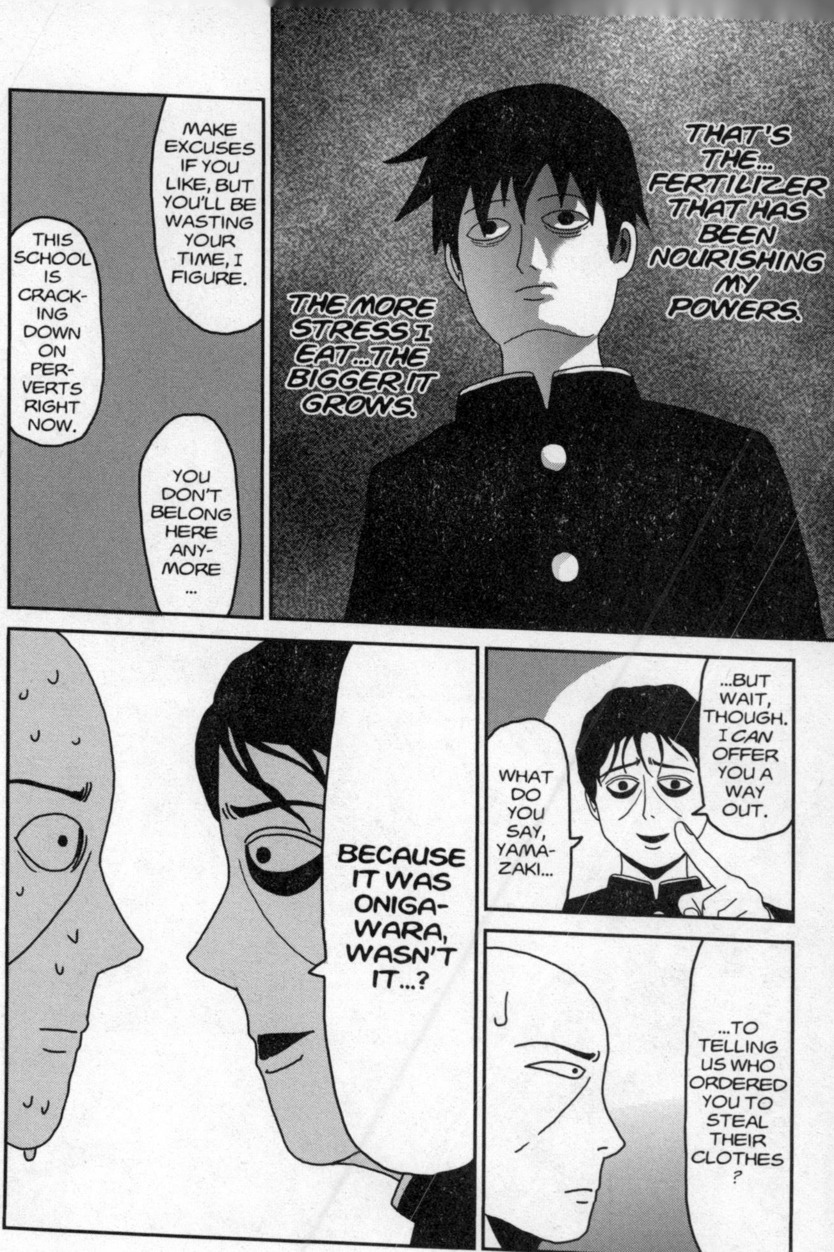
THAT'S THE... FERTILIZER THAT HAS BEEN NOURISHING MY POWERS.
THE MORE STRESS I EAT...THE BIGGER IT GROWS.
MAKE EXCUSES IF YOU LIKE, BUT YOU'LL BE WASTING YOUR TIME, I FIGURE.
THIS SCHOOL IS CRACKING DOWN ON PERVERTS RIGHT NOW.
YOU DON'T BELONG HERE ANYMORE...
...BUT WAIT, THOUGH. I CAN OFFER YOU A WAY OUT.
WHAT DO YOU SAY, YAMAZAKI...
...TO TELLING US WHO ORDERED YOU TO STEAL THEIR CLOTHES?
BECAUSE IT WAS ONIGAWARA, WASN'T IT...?

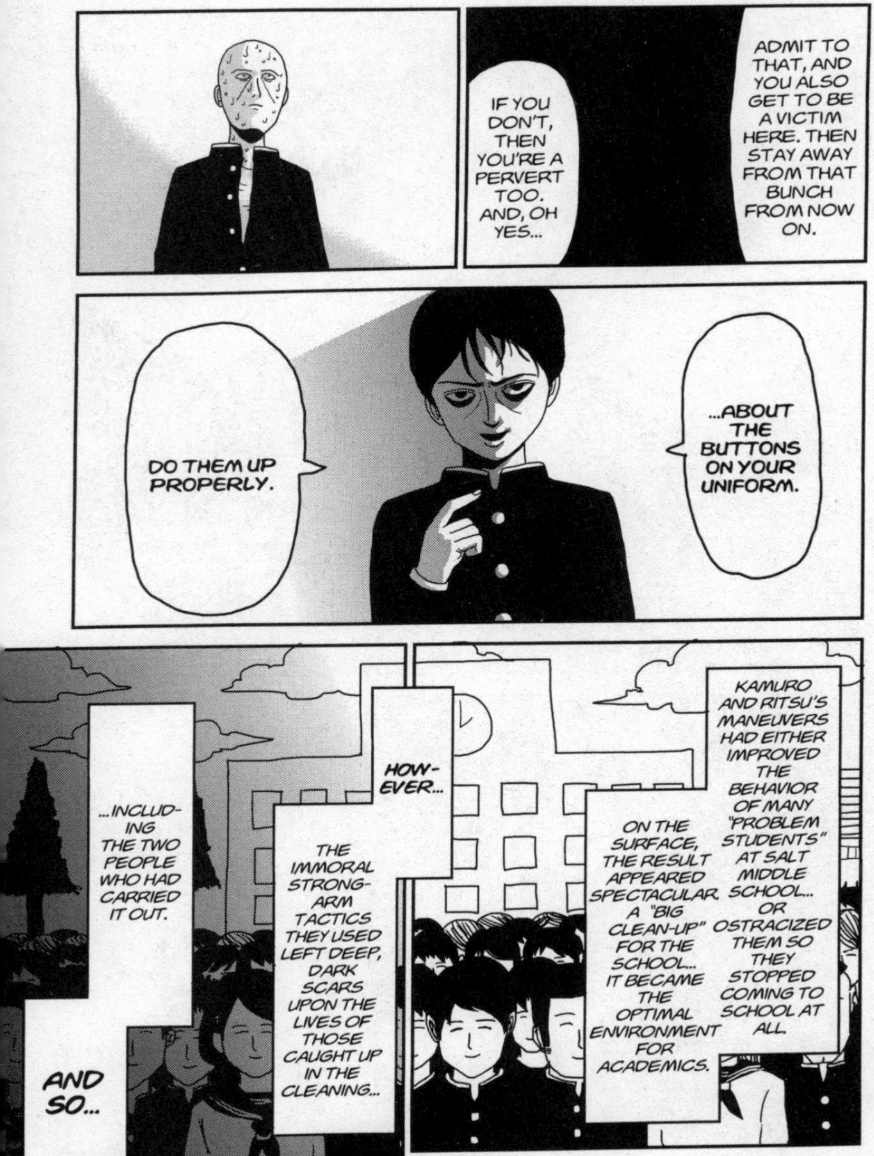
ADMIT TO THAT, AND YOU ALSO GET TO BE A VICTIM HERE. THEN STAY AWAY FROM THAT BUNCH FROM NOW ON.
IF YOU DON'T, THEN YOU'RE A PERVERT TOO. AND, OH YES...
...ABOUT THE BUTTONS ON YOUR UNIFORM.
DO THEM UP PROPERLY.
KAMURO AND RITSU'S MANEUVERS HAD EITHER IMPROVED THE BEHAVIOR OF MANY "PROBLEM STUDENTS" AT SALT MIDDLE SCHOOL... OR OSTRACIZED THEM SO THEY STOPPED COMING TO SCHOOL AT ALL.
ON THE SURFACE, THE RESULT APPEARED SPECTACULAR. A "BIG CLEAN-UP" FOR THE SCHOOL... IT BECAME THE OPTIMAL ENVIRONMENT FOR ACADEMICS.
HOW-EVER...
THE IMMORAL STRONG-ARM TACTICS THEY USED LEFT DEEP, DARK SCARS UPON THE LIVES OF THOSE CAUGHT UP IN THE CLEANING...
...INCLUD-ING THE TWO PEOPLE WHO HAD CARRIED IT OUT.
AND SO...

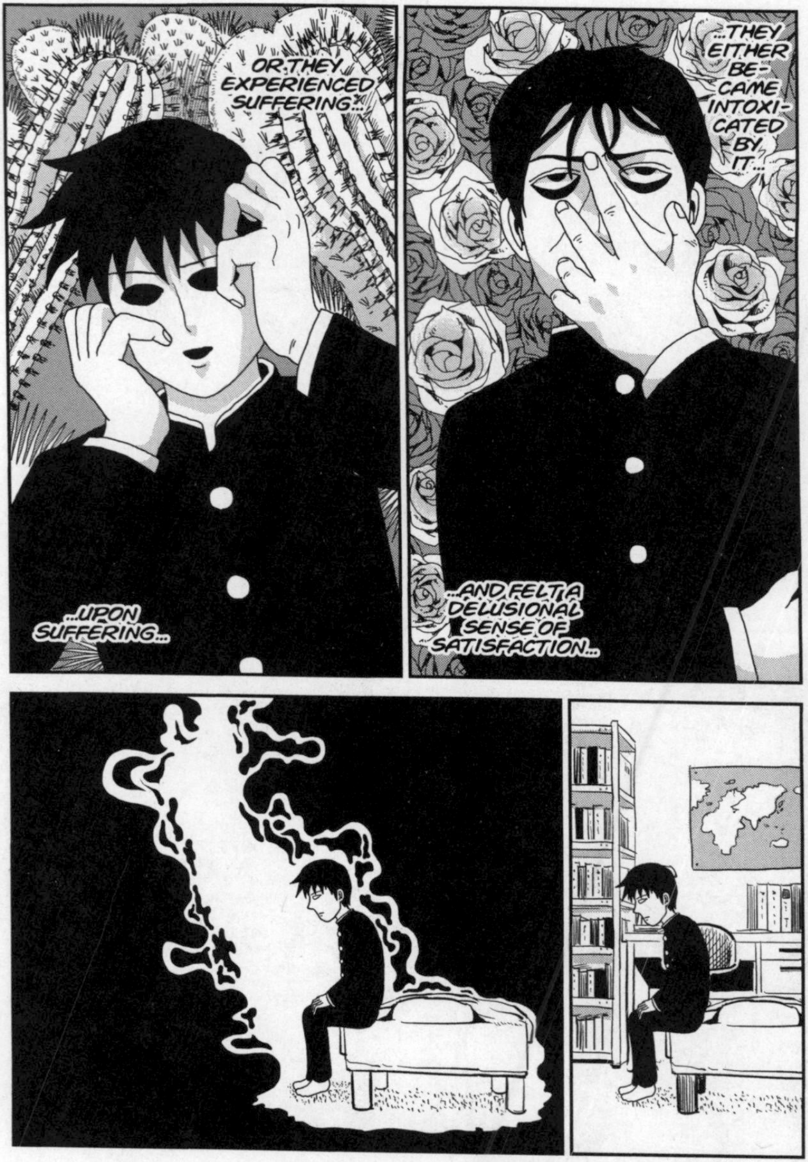
...THEY EITHER BE-CAME INTOXI-CATED BY IT...
...AND FELT A DELUSIONAL SENSE OF SATISFACTION...
OR THEY EXPERIENCED SUFFERING...
...UPON SUFFERING...

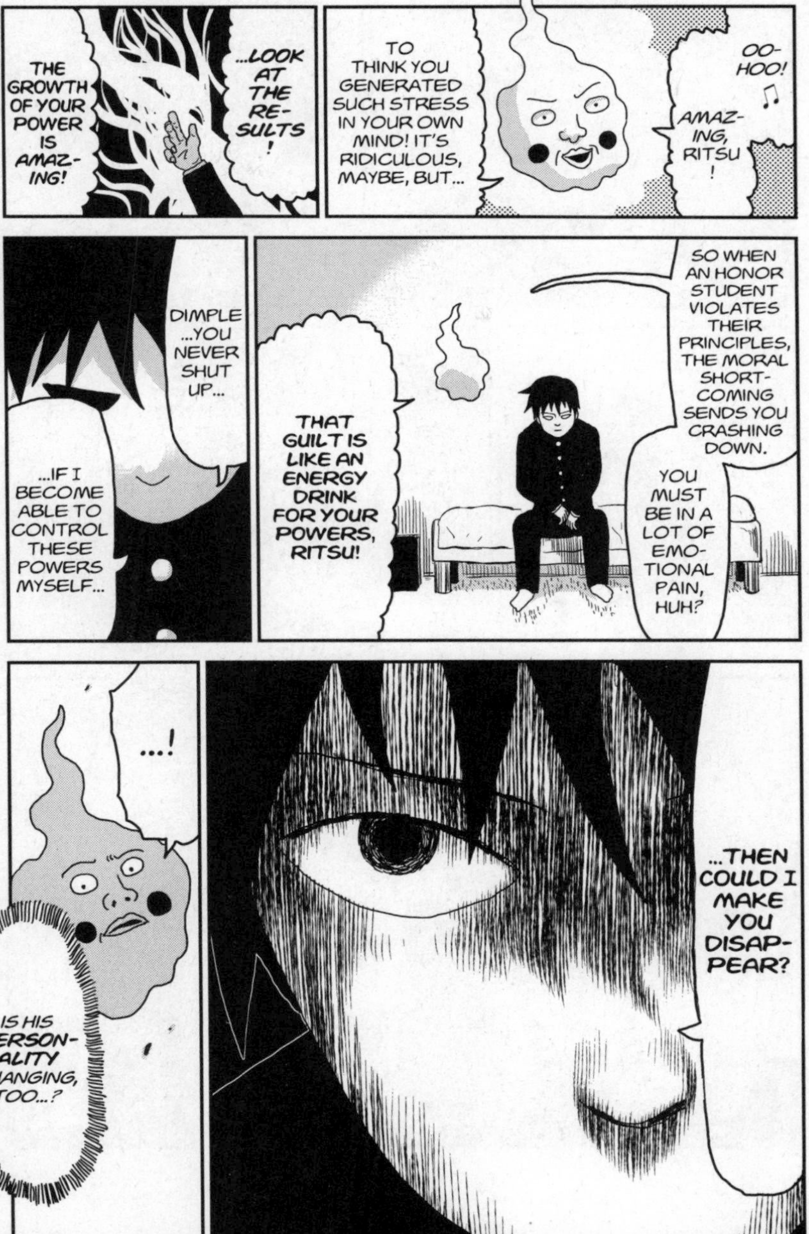
OO-HOO! ♫
AMAZ-ING, RITSU!
TO THINK YOU GENERATED SUCH STRESS IN YOUR OWN MIND! IT'S RIDICULOUS, MAYBE, BUT...
...LOOK AT THE RE-SULTS!
THE GROWTH OF YOUR POWER IS AMAZ-ING!
SO WHEN AN HONOR STUDENT VIOLATES THEIR PRINCIPLES, THE MORAL SHORT-COMING SENDS YOU CRASHING DOWN.
YOU MUST BE IN A LOT OF EMO-TIONAL PAIN, HUH?
THAT GUILT IS LIKE AN ENERGY DRINK FOR YOUR POWERS, RITSU!
DIMPLE ...YOU NEVER SHUT UP...
...IF I BECOME ABLE TO CONTROL THESE POWERS MYSELF...
...THEN COULD I MAKE YOU DISAP-PEAR?
...!
IS HIS PERSON-ALITY CHANGING, TOO...?

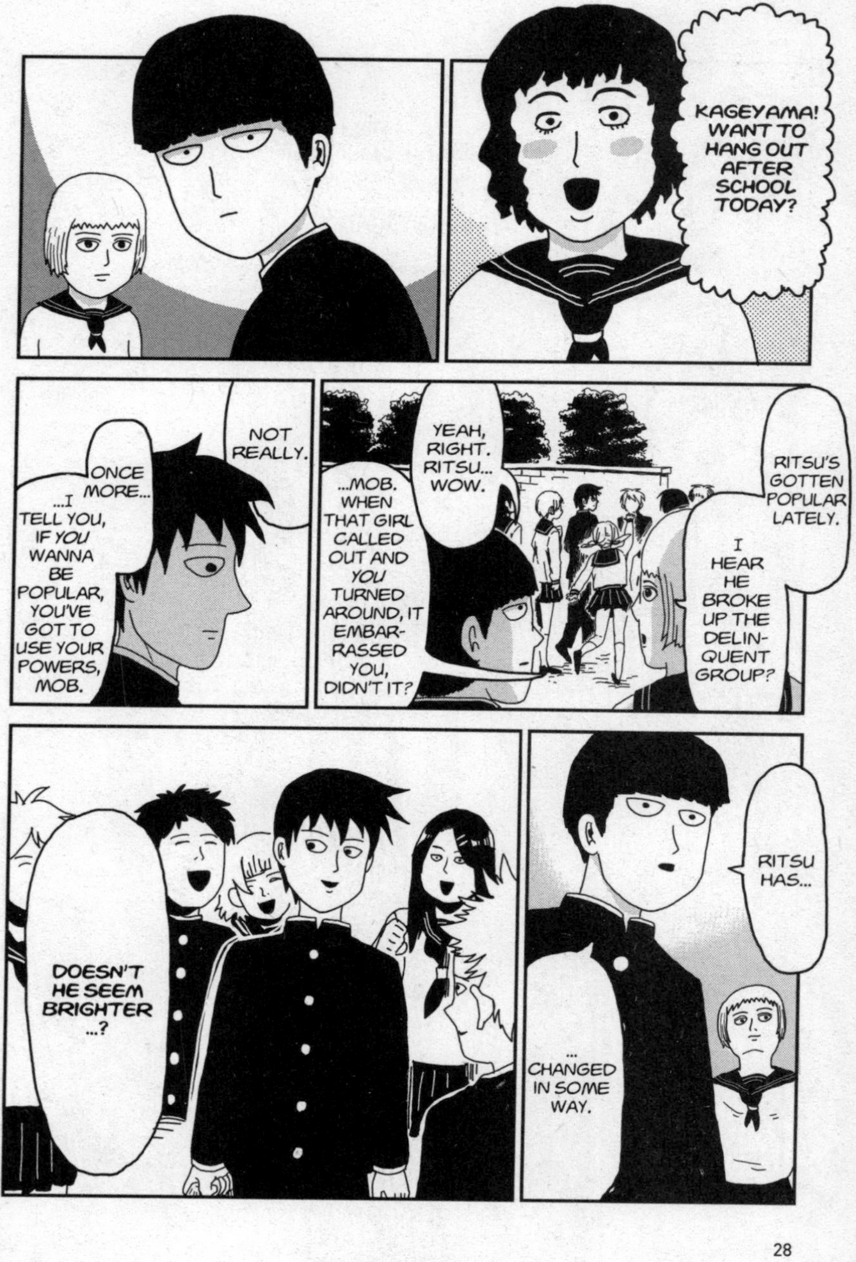
KAGEYAMA! WANT TO HANG OUT AFTER SCHOOL TODAY?
RITSU'S GOTTEN POPULAR LATELY.
I HEAR HE BROKE UP THE DELINQUENT GROUP?
YEAH, RIGHT. RITSU... WOW.
...MOB. WHEN THAT GIRL CALLED OUT AND *YOU* TURNED AROUND, IT EMBARRASSED YOU, DIDN'T IT?
NOT REALLY.
ONCE MORE...
...I TELL YOU, IF *YOU* WANNA BE POPULAR, YOU'VE GOT TO USE YOUR POWERS, MOB.
RITSU HAS...
...CHANGED IN SOME WAY.
DOESN'T HE SEEM BRIGHTER...?

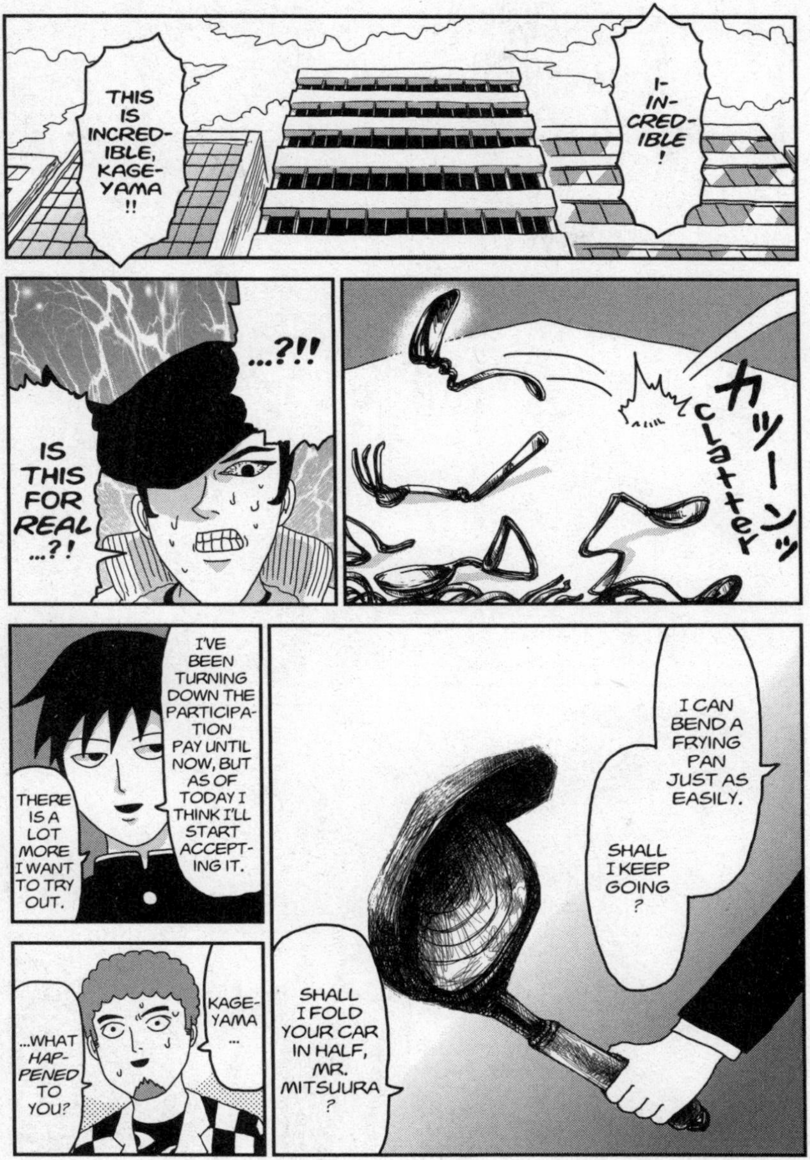
I-INCREDIBLE!
THIS IS INCREDIBLE, KAGEYAMA!!
カッーンッ
Clatter
...?!!
IS THIS FOR REAL...?!
I CAN BEND A FRYING PAN JUST AS EASILY.
SHALL I KEEP GOING?
SHALL I FOLD YOUR CAR IN HALF, MR. MITSUURA?
I'VE BEEN TURNING DOWN THE PARTICIPATION PAY UNTIL NOW, BUT AS OF TODAY I THINK I'LL START ACCEPTING IT.
THERE IS A LOT MORE I WANT TO TRY OUT.
KAGEYAMA...
...WHAT HAPPENED TO YOU?

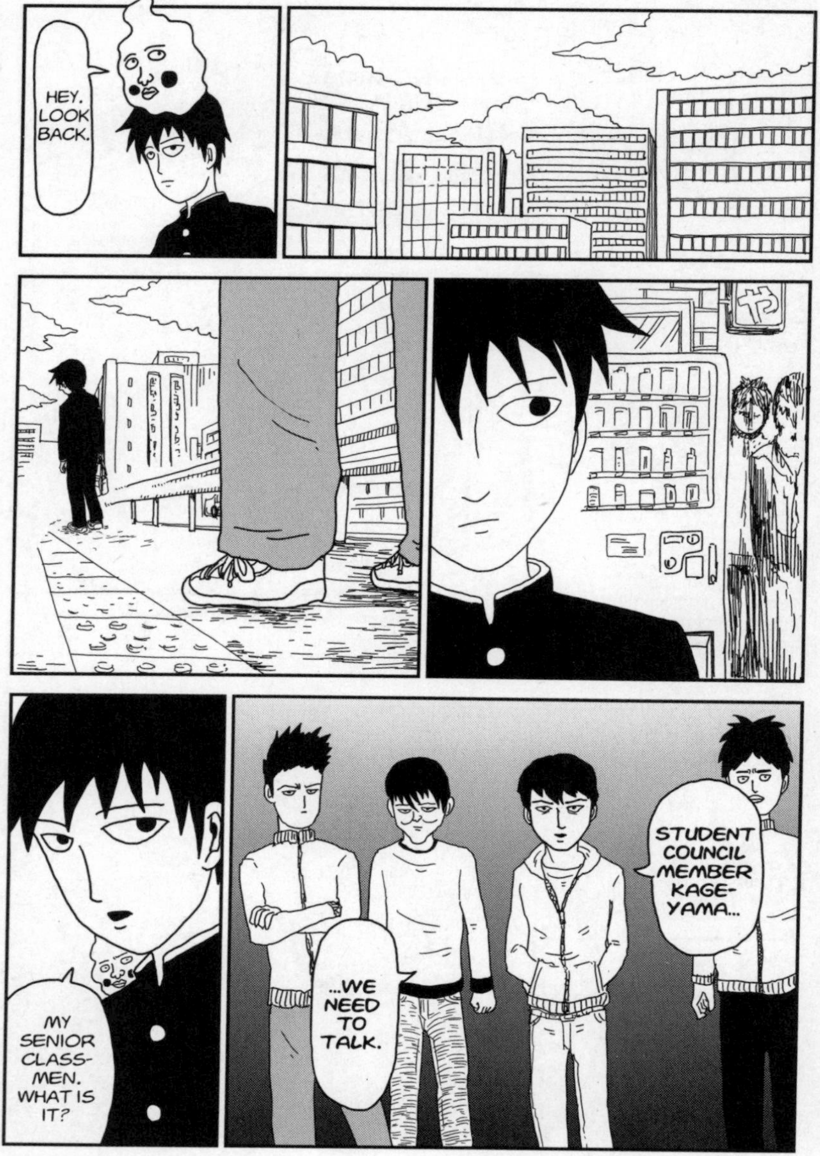
HEY. LOOK BACK.
や
STUDENT COUNCIL MEMBER KAGE-YAMA...
...WE NEED TO TALK.
MY SENIOR CLASS-MEN. WHAT IS IT?

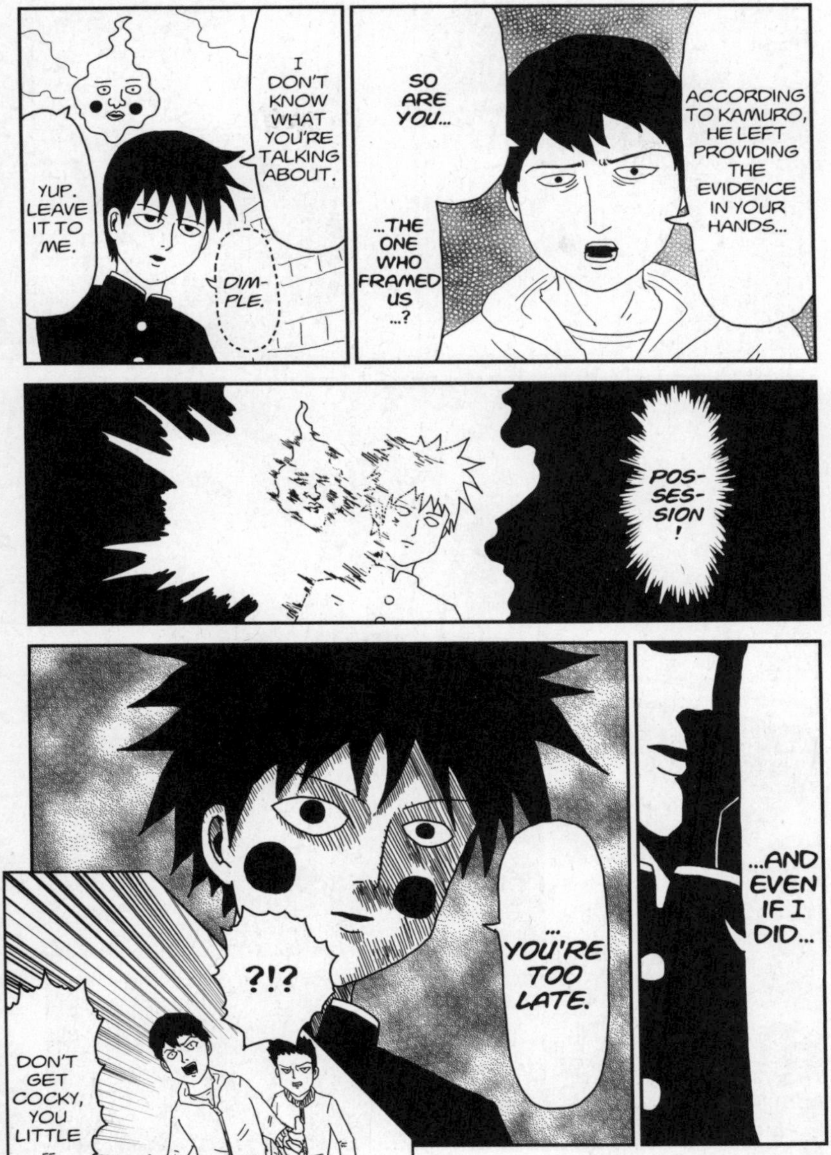
ACCORDING TO KAMURO, HE LEFT PROVIDING THE EVIDENCE IN YOUR HANDS...
SO ARE YOU...
...THE ONE WHO FRAMED US ...?
I DON'T KNOW WHAT YOU'RE TALKING ABOUT.
YUP. LEAVE IT TO ME.
DIM-PLE.
POS-SES-SION!
...AND EVEN IF I DID...
...YOU'RE TOO LATE.
?!?
DON'T GET COCKY, YOU LITTLE --

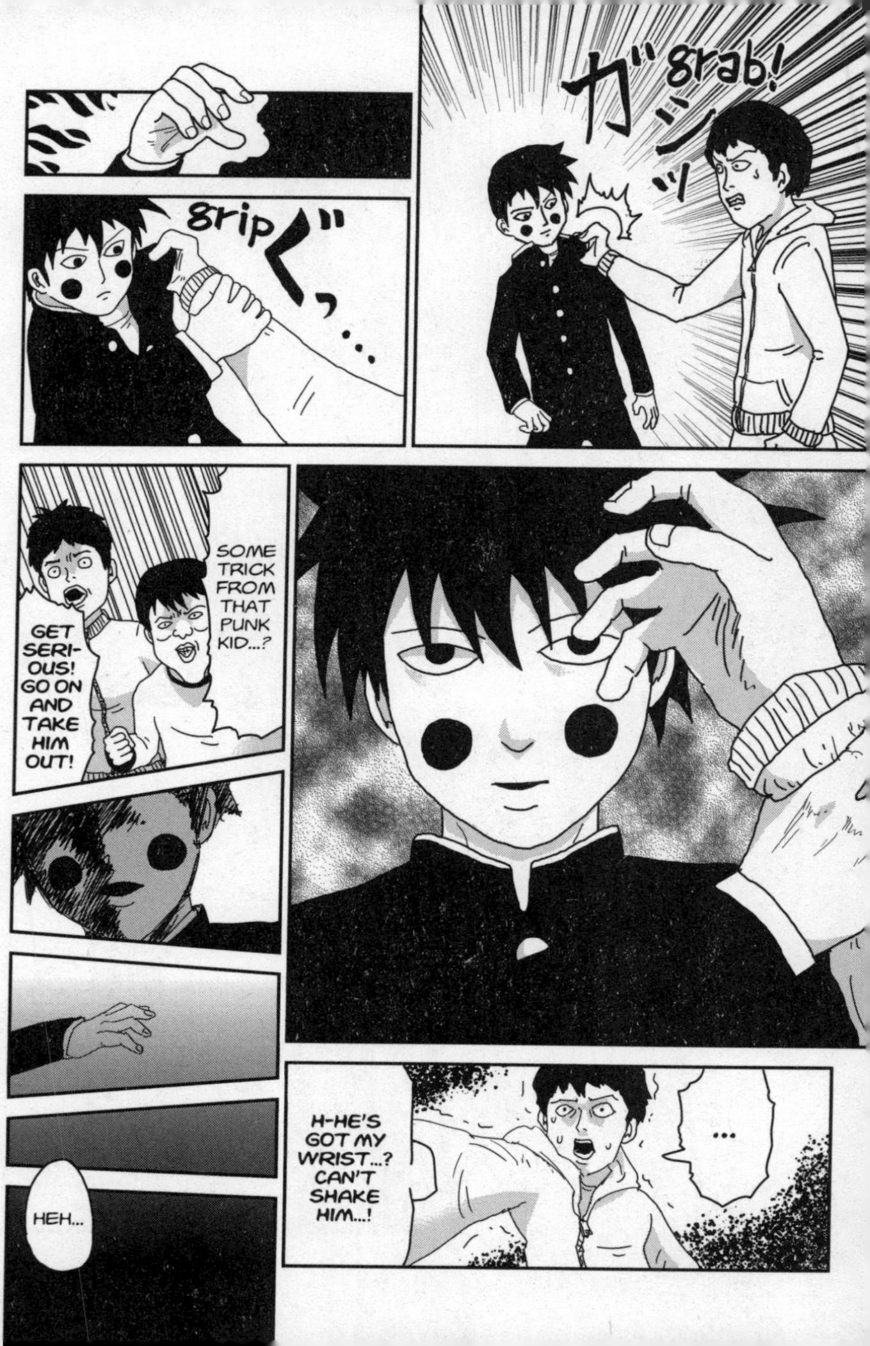

ガシッ
grab!
grip
ぐっ
...
SOME TRICK FROM THAT PUNK KID...?
GET SERI-OUS! GO ON AND TAKE HIM OUT!
H-HE'S GOT MY WRIST...? CAN'T SHAKE HIM...!
...
HEH...

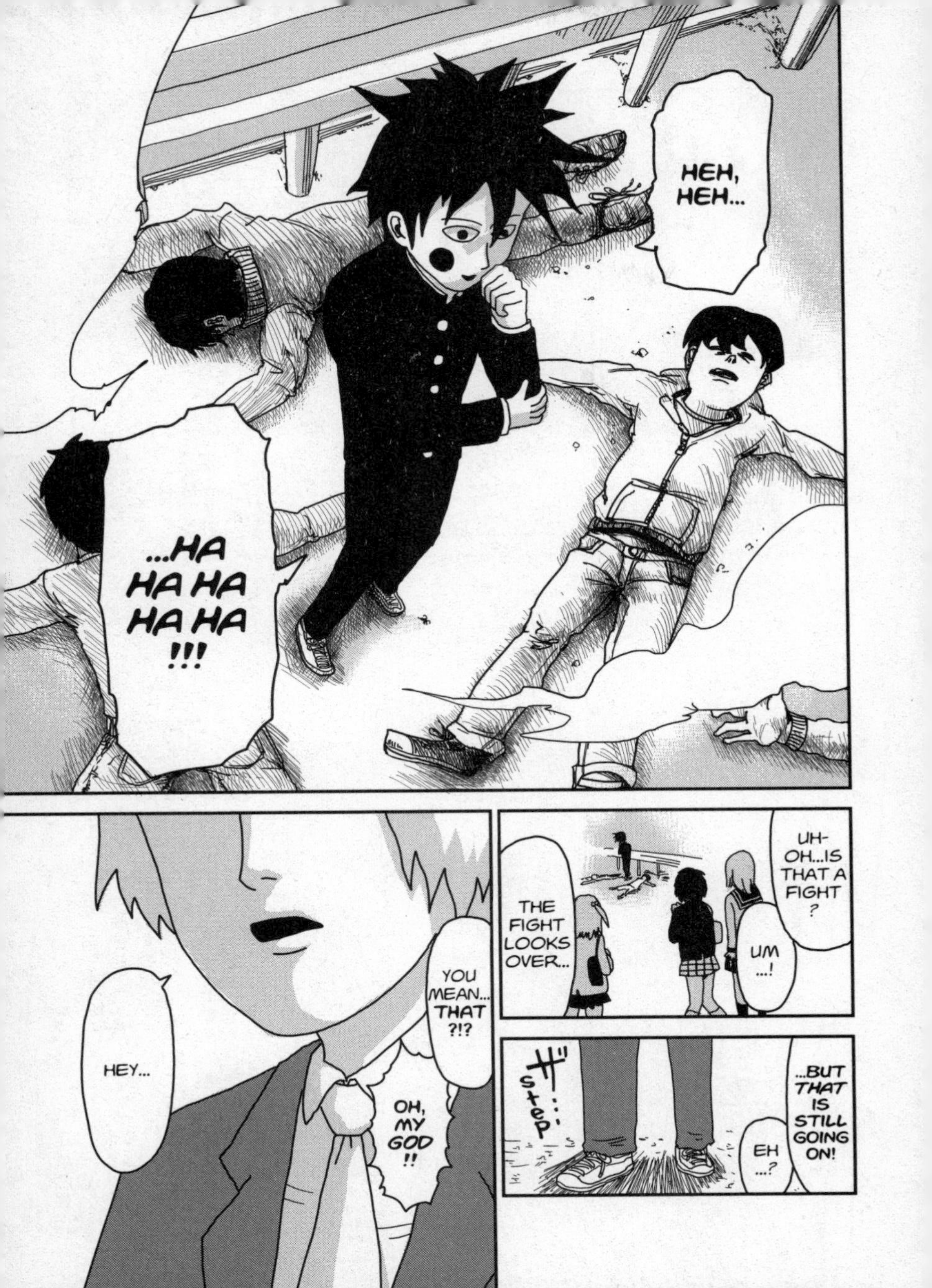
HEH, HEH...
...HA HA HA HA HA !!!
UH-OH...IS THAT A FIGHT ?
UM ...!
THE FIGHT LOOKS OVER...
...BUT THAT IS STILL GOING ON!
EH ...?
step
YOU MEAN... THAT ?!?
OH, MY GOD !!
HEY...

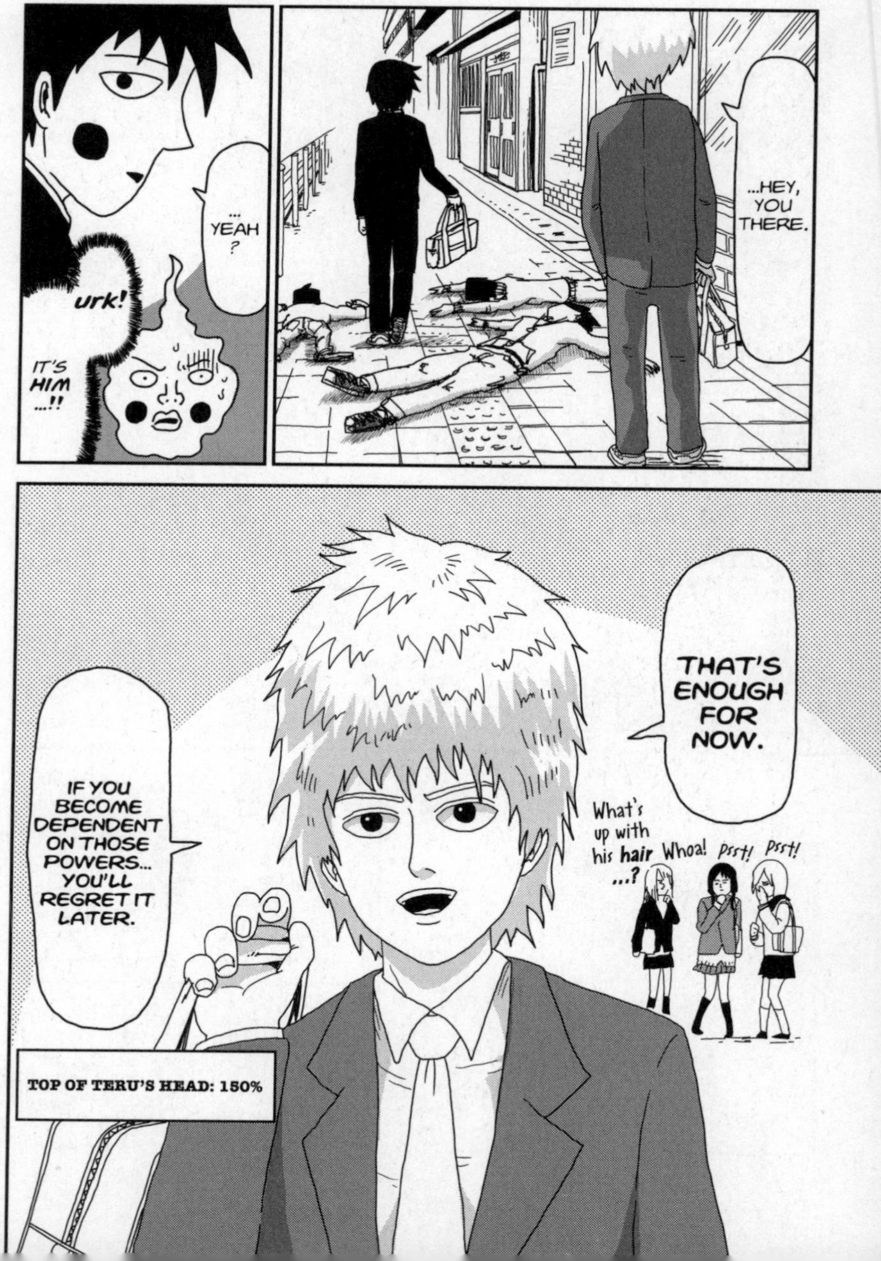
...HEY, YOU THERE.
...YEAH?
urk!
IT'S HIM...!!
THAT'S ENOUGH FOR NOW.
Psst! Psst!
Whoa!
What's up with his hair...?
IF YOU BECOME DEPENDENT ON THOSE POWERS... YOU'LL REGRET IT LATER.
TOP OF TERU'S HEAD: 150%

CHAPTER 27: DISCORD

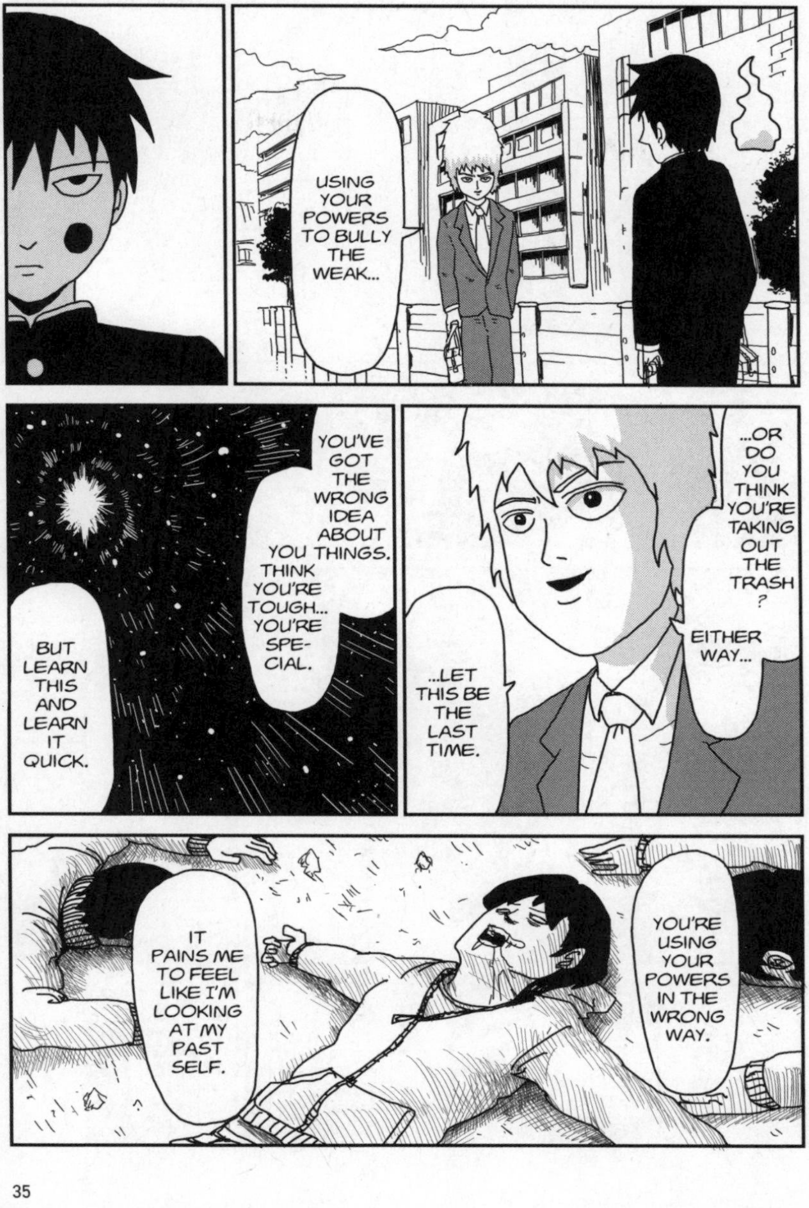
USING YOUR POWERS TO BULLY THE WEAK...
...OR DO YOU THINK YOU'RE TAKING OUT THE TRASH?
EITHER WAY...
...LET THIS BE THE LAST TIME.
YOU'VE GOT THE WRONG IDEA ABOUT THINGS.
YOU THINK YOU'RE TOUGH... YOU'RE SPE-CIAL.
BUT LEARN THIS AND LEARN IT QUICK.
YOU'RE USING YOUR POWERS IN THE WRONG WAY.
IT PAINS ME TO FEEL LIKE I'M LOOKING AT MY PAST SELF.

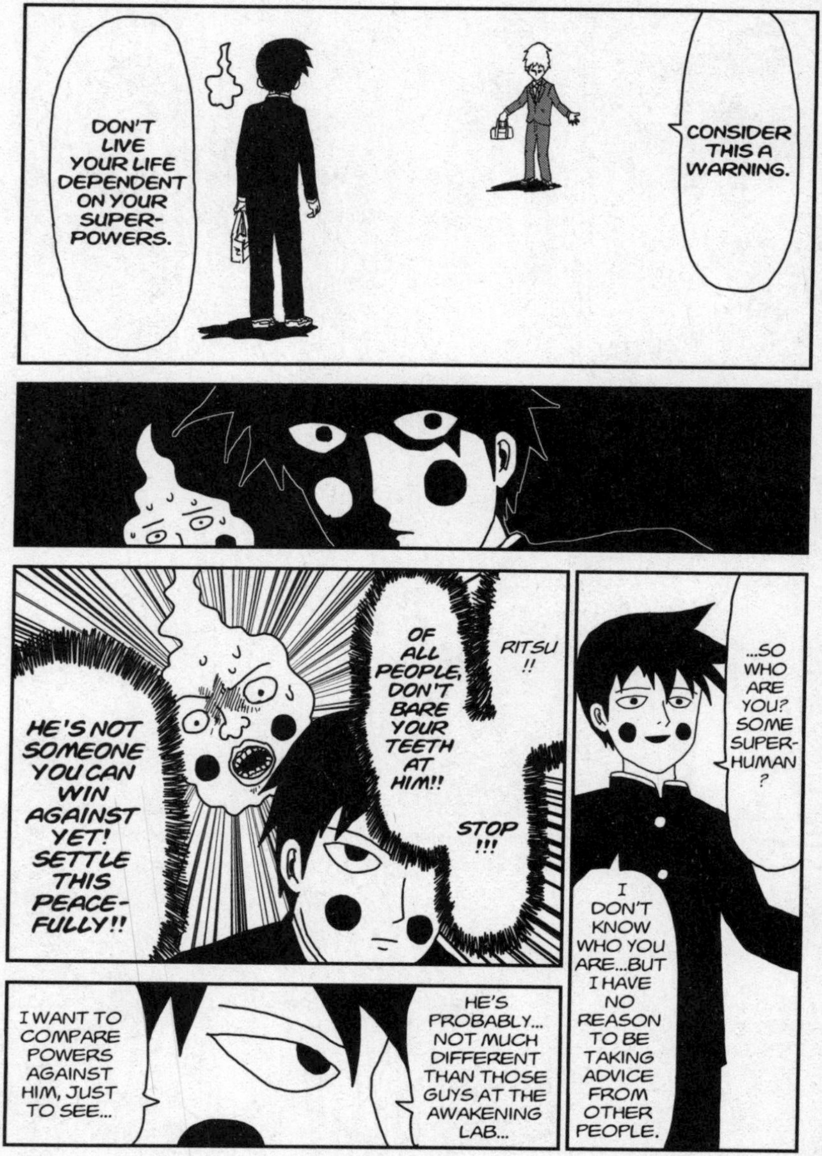
CONSIDER THIS A WARNING.
DON'T LIVE YOUR LIFE DEPENDENT ON YOUR SUPER-POWERS.
...SO WHO ARE YOU? SOME SUPER-HUMAN?
I DON'T KNOW WHO YOU ARE...BUT I HAVE NO REASON TO BE TAKING ADVICE FROM OTHER PEOPLE.
RITSU!!
OF ALL PEOPLE, DON'T BARE YOUR TEETH AT HIM!!
STOP!!!
HE'S NOT SOMEONE YOU CAN WIN AGAINST YET! SETTLE THIS PEACE-FULLY!!
HE'S PROBABLY... NOT MUCH DIFFERENT THAN THOSE GUYS AT THE AWAKENING LAB...
I WANT TO COMPARE POWERS AGAINST HIM, JUST TO SEE...

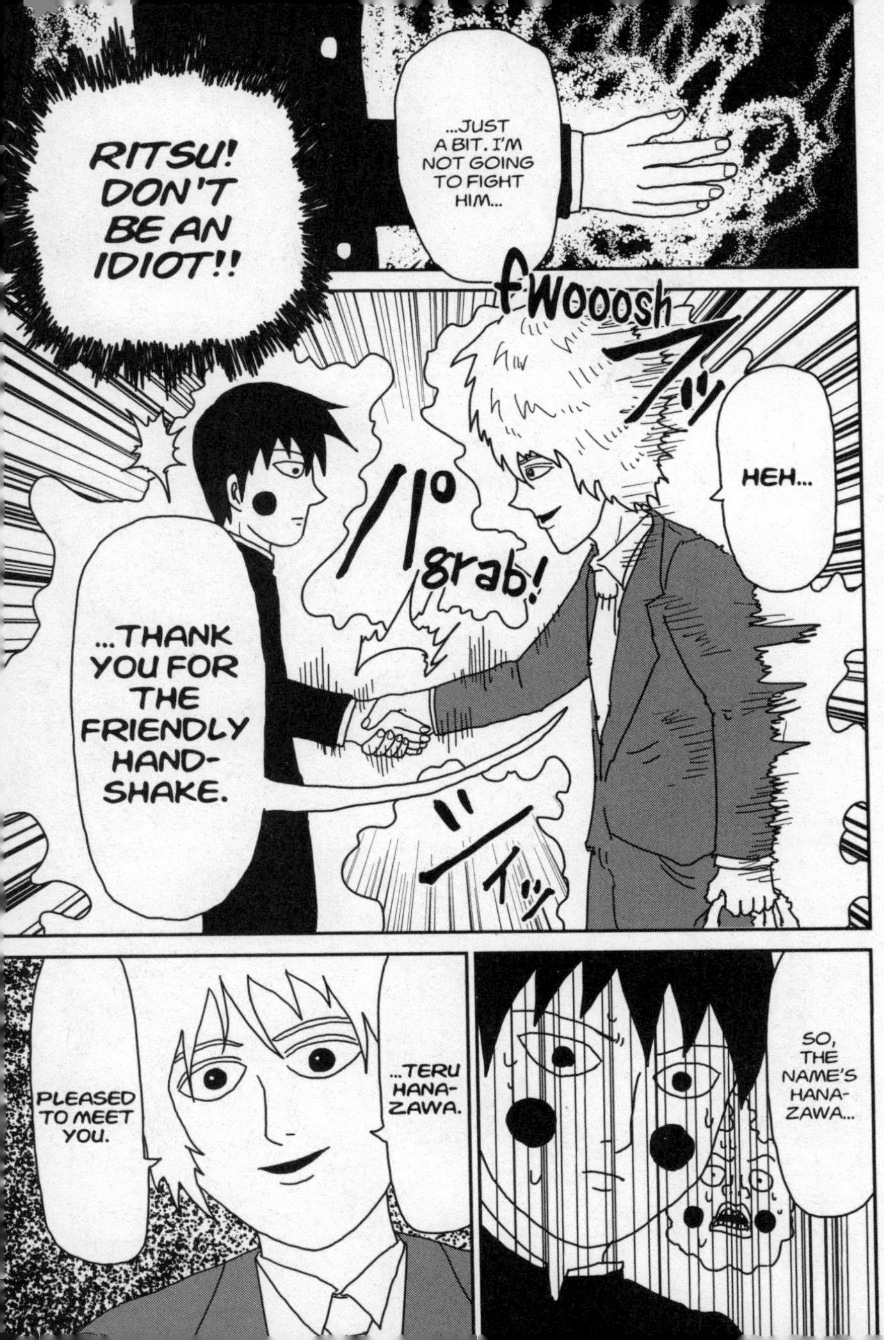
...JUST A BIT. I'M NOT GOING TO FIGHT HIM...
RITSU! DON'T BE AN IDIOT!!
fwooosh
HEH...
grab!
...THANK YOU FOR THE FRIENDLY HAND-SHAKE.
SO, THE NAME'S HANA-ZAWA...
...TERU HANA-ZAWA.
PLEASED TO MEET YOU.

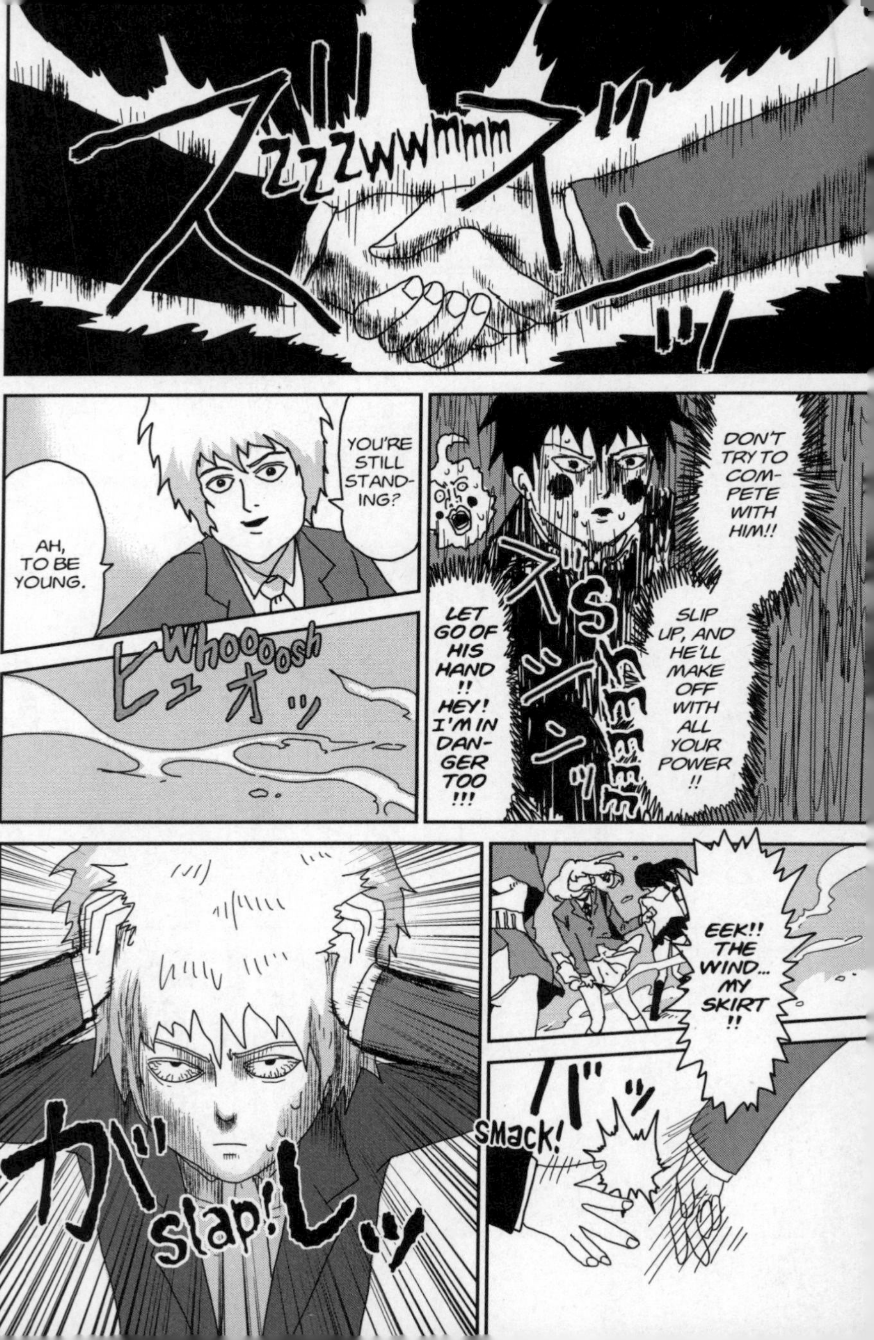
zzzzwwmmm
DON'T TRY TO COMPETE WITH HIM!!
SLIP UP, AND HE'LL MAKE OFF WITH ALL YOUR POWER!!
LET GO OF HIS HAND!! HEY! I'M IN DANGER TOO!!!
YOU'RE STILL STANDING?
AH, TO BE YOUNG.
Whoooosh
EEK!! THE WIND... MY SKIRT!!
SMACK!
slap!

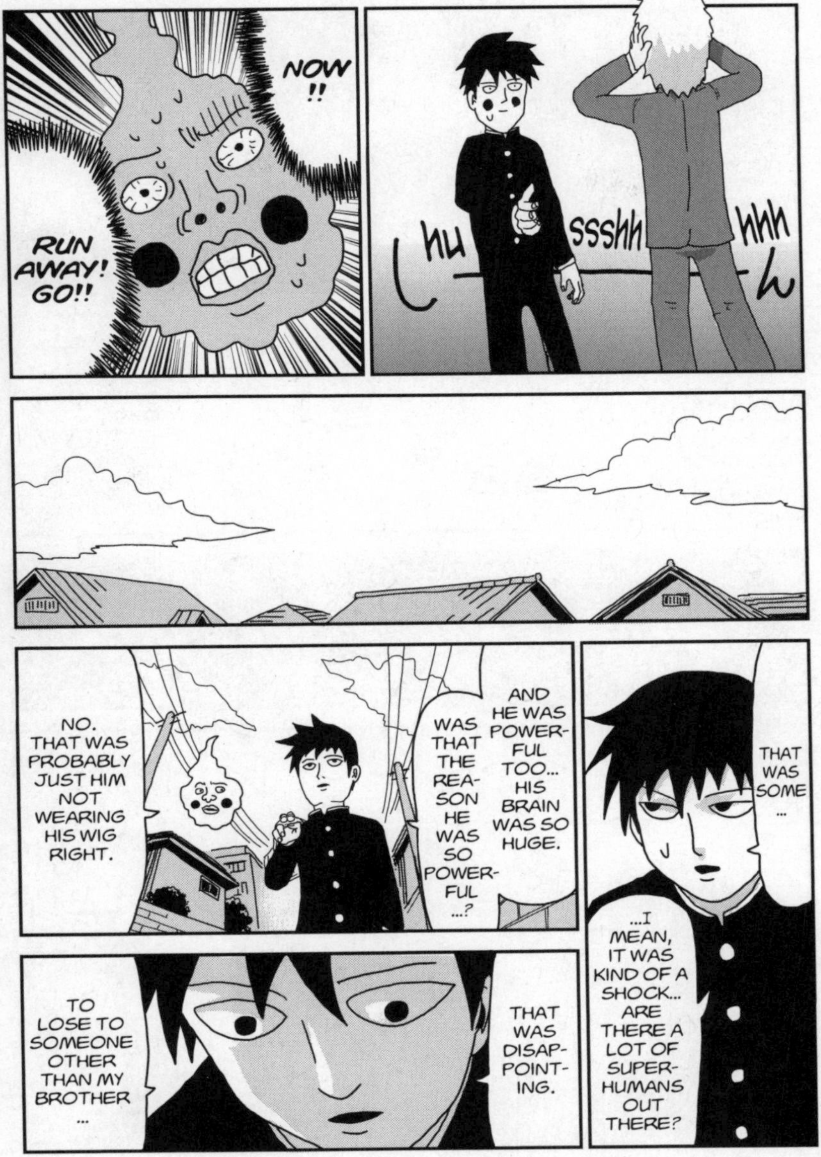
hu ssshh hhh
NOW !!
RUN AWAY! GO!!
THAT WAS SOME ...
...I MEAN, IT WAS KIND OF A SHOCK... ARE THERE A LOT OF SUPER-HUMANS OUT THERE?
AND HE WAS POWER-FUL TOO... HIS BRAIN WAS SO HUGE.
WAS THAT THE REA-SON HE WAS SO POWER-FUL ...?
NO. THAT WAS PROBABLY JUST HIM NOT WEARING HIS WIG RIGHT.
THAT WAS DISAP-POINT-ING.
TO LOSE TO SOMEONE OTHER THAN MY BROTHER ...

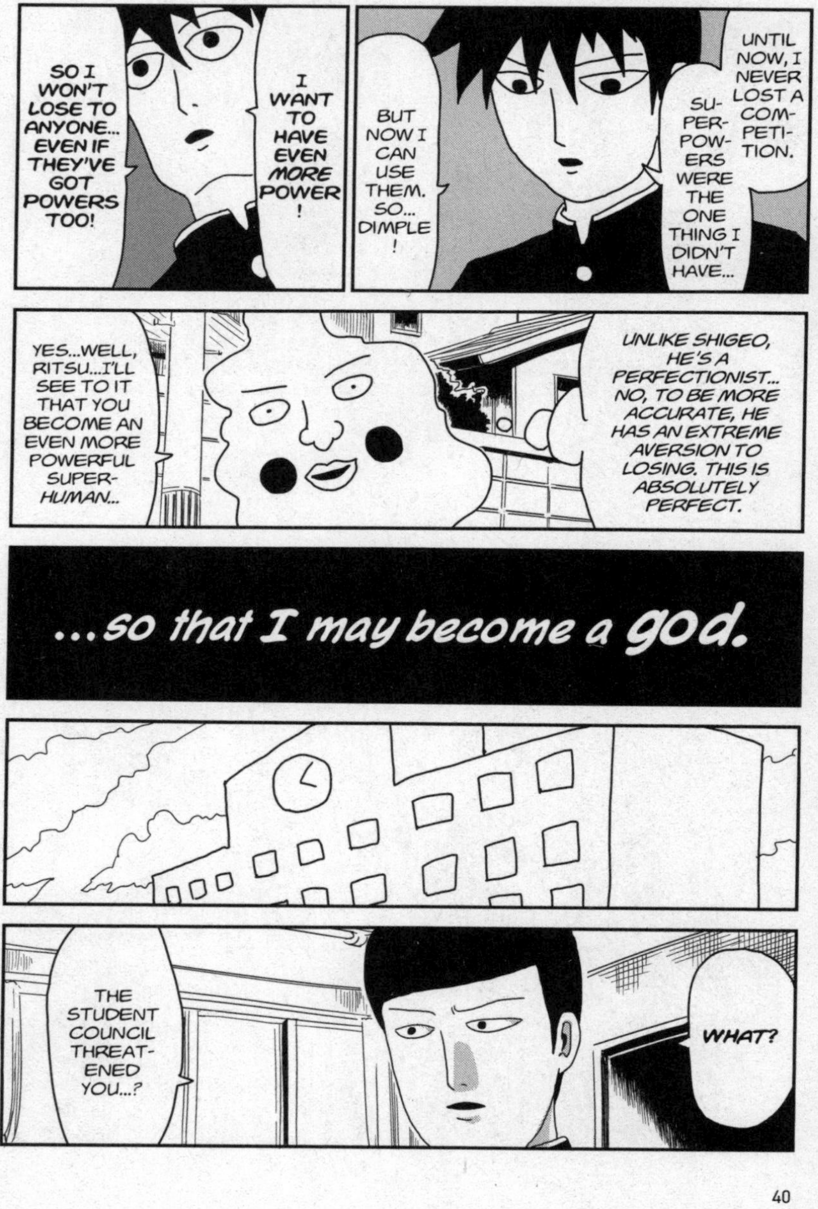
UNTIL NOW, I NEVER LOST A COMPETITION.
SUPERPOWERS WERE THE ONE THING I DIDN'T HAVE...
BUT NOW I CAN USE THEM. SO... DIMPLE!
I WANT TO HAVE EVEN MORE POWER!
SO I WON'T LOSE TO ANYONE... EVEN IF THEY'VE GOT POWERS TOO!
UNLIKE SHIGEO, HE'S A PERFECTIONIST... NO, TO BE MORE ACCURATE, HE HAS AN EXTREME AVERSION TO LOSING. THIS IS ABSOLUTELY PERFECT.
YES...WELL, RITSU...I'LL SEE TO IT THAT YOU BECOME AN EVEN MORE POWERFUL SUPERHUMAN...
...so that I may become a god.
WHAT?
THE STUDENT COUNCIL THREATENED YOU...?

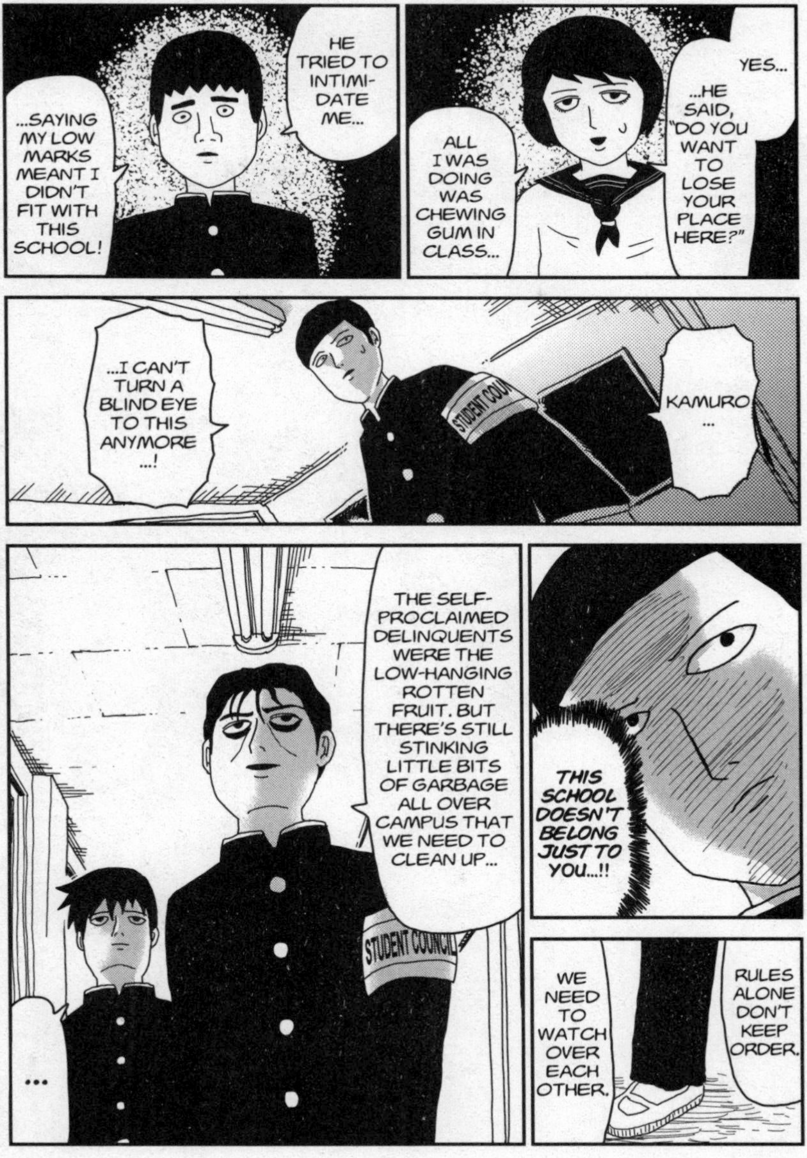
YES...
...HE SAID, "DO YOU WANT TO LOSE YOUR PLACE HERE?"
ALL I WAS DOING WAS CHEWING GUM IN CLASS...
HE TRIED TO INTIMIDATE ME...
...SAYING MY LOW MARKS MEANT I DIDN'T FIT WITH THIS SCHOOL!
KAMURO...
STUDENT COU
...I CAN'T TURN A BLIND EYE TO THIS ANYMORE...!
THIS SCHOOL DOESN'T BELONG JUST TO YOU...!!
RULES ALONE DON'T KEEP ORDER.
WE NEED TO WATCH OVER EACH OTHER.
THE SELF-PROCLAIMED DELINQUENTS WERE THE LOW-HANGING ROTTEN FRUIT. BUT THERE'S STILL STINKING LITTLE BITS OF GARBAGE ALL OVER CAMPUS THAT WE NEED TO CLEAN UP...
STUDENT COUNCIL
...

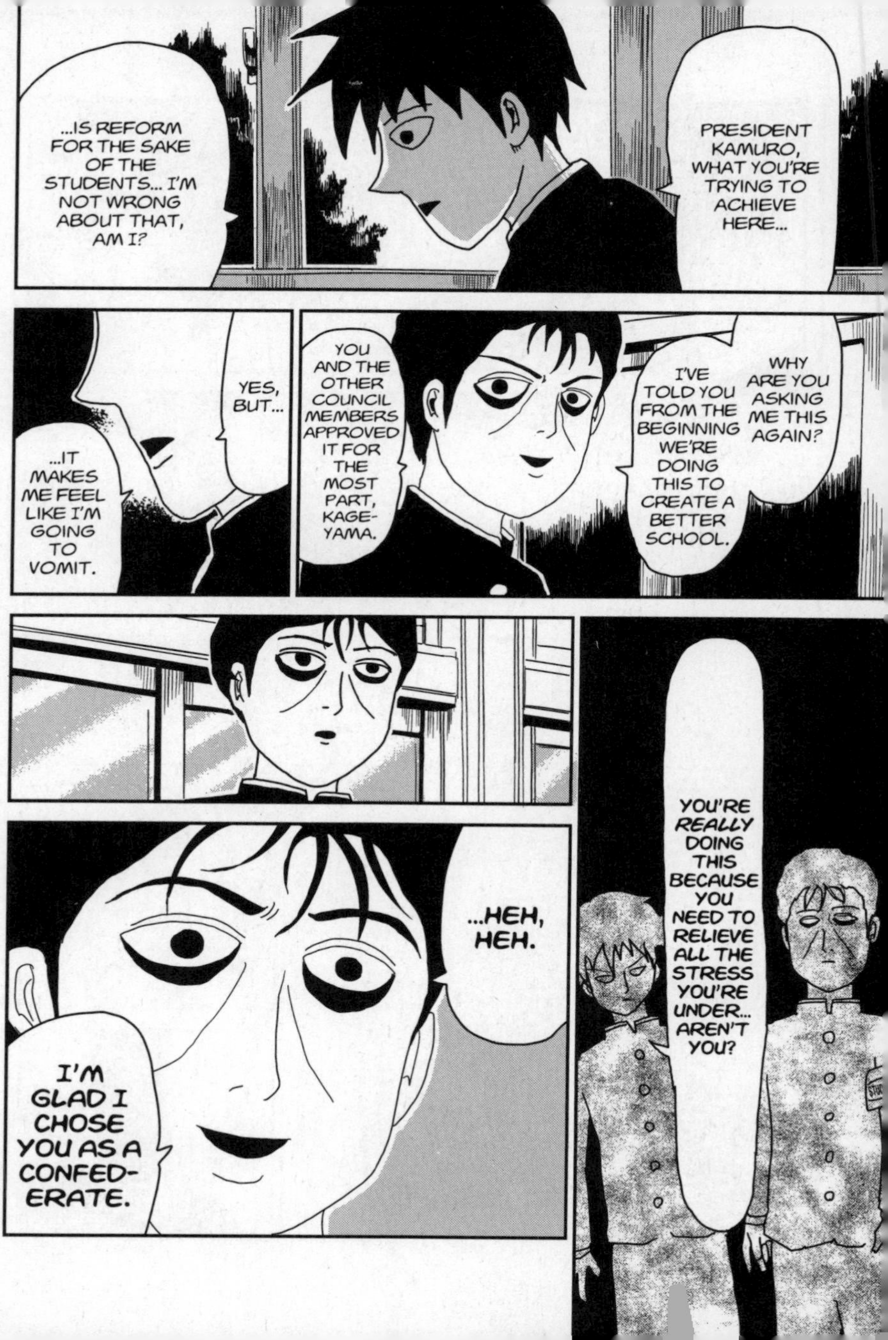
PRESIDENT KAMURO, WHAT YOU'RE TRYING TO ACHIEVE HERE...
...IS REFORM FOR THE SAKE OF THE STUDENTS... I'M NOT WRONG ABOUT THAT, AM I?
WHY ARE YOU ASKING ME THIS AGAIN?
I'VE TOLD YOU FROM THE BEGINNING WE'RE DOING THIS TO CREATE A BETTER SCHOOL.
YOU AND THE OTHER COUNCIL MEMBERS APPROVED IT FOR THE MOST PART, KAGE-YAMA.
YES, BUT...
...IT MAKES ME FEEL LIKE I'M GOING TO VOMIT.
YOU'RE *REALLY* DOING THIS BECAUSE YOU NEED TO RELIEVE ALL THE STRESS YOU'RE UNDER... AREN'T YOU?
...HEH, HEH.
I'M GLAD I CHOSE YOU AS A CONFED-ERATE.

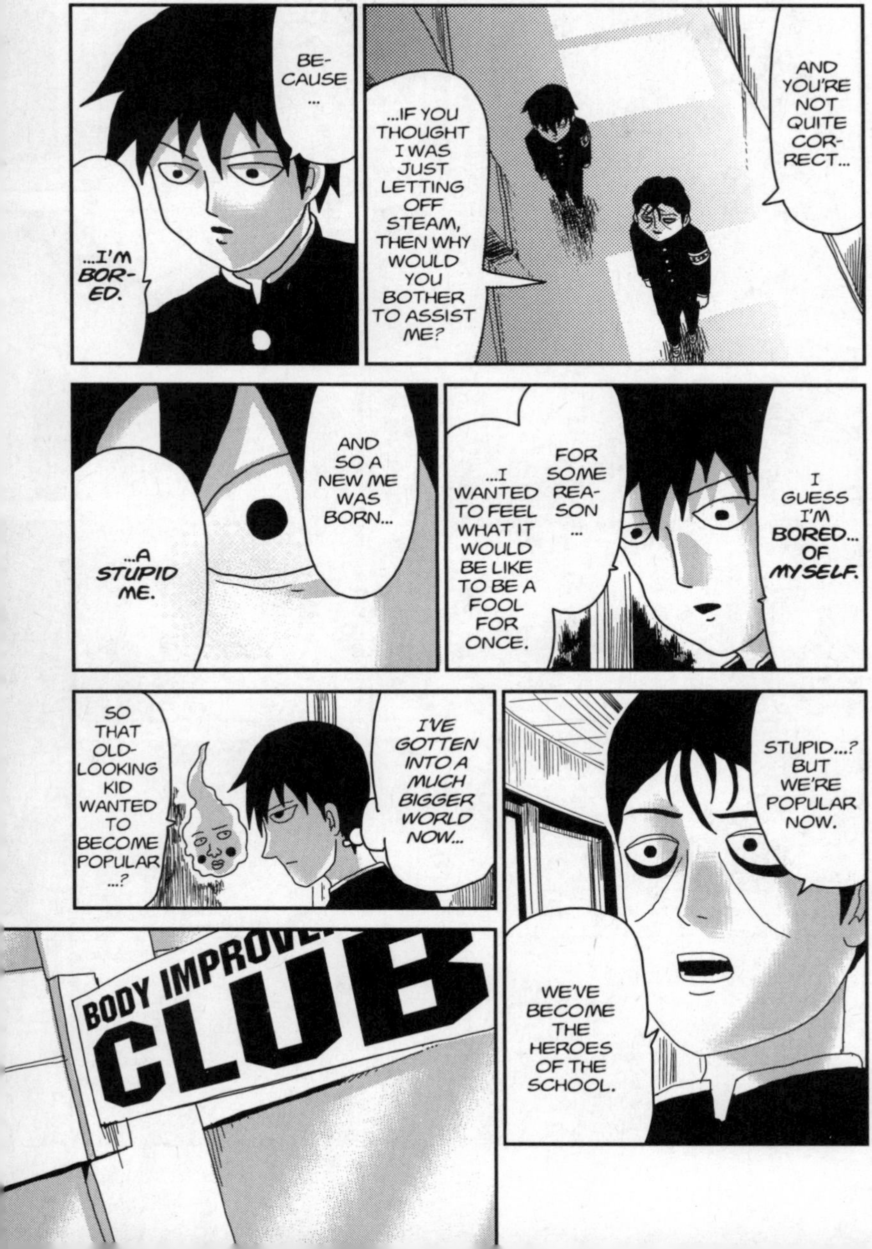
AND YOU'RE NOT QUITE COR-RECT...
...IF YOU THOUGHT I WAS JUST LETTING OFF STEAM, THEN WHY WOULD YOU BOTHER TO ASSIST ME?
BE-CAUSE ...
...I'M *BOR-ED.*
I GUESS I'M **BORED...** OF ***MYSELF.***
FOR SOME REA-SON ...
...I WANTED TO FEEL WHAT IT WOULD BE LIKE TO BE A FOOL FOR ONCE.
AND SO A NEW ME WAS BORN...
...A ***STUPID*** ***ME.***
STUPID...? BUT WE'RE POPULAR NOW.
WE'VE BECOME THE HEROES OF THE SCHOOL.
I'VE GOTTEN INTO A MUCH BIGGER WORLD NOW...
SO THAT OLD-LOOKING KID WANTED TO BECOME POPULAR ...?
BODY IMPROV
CLUB

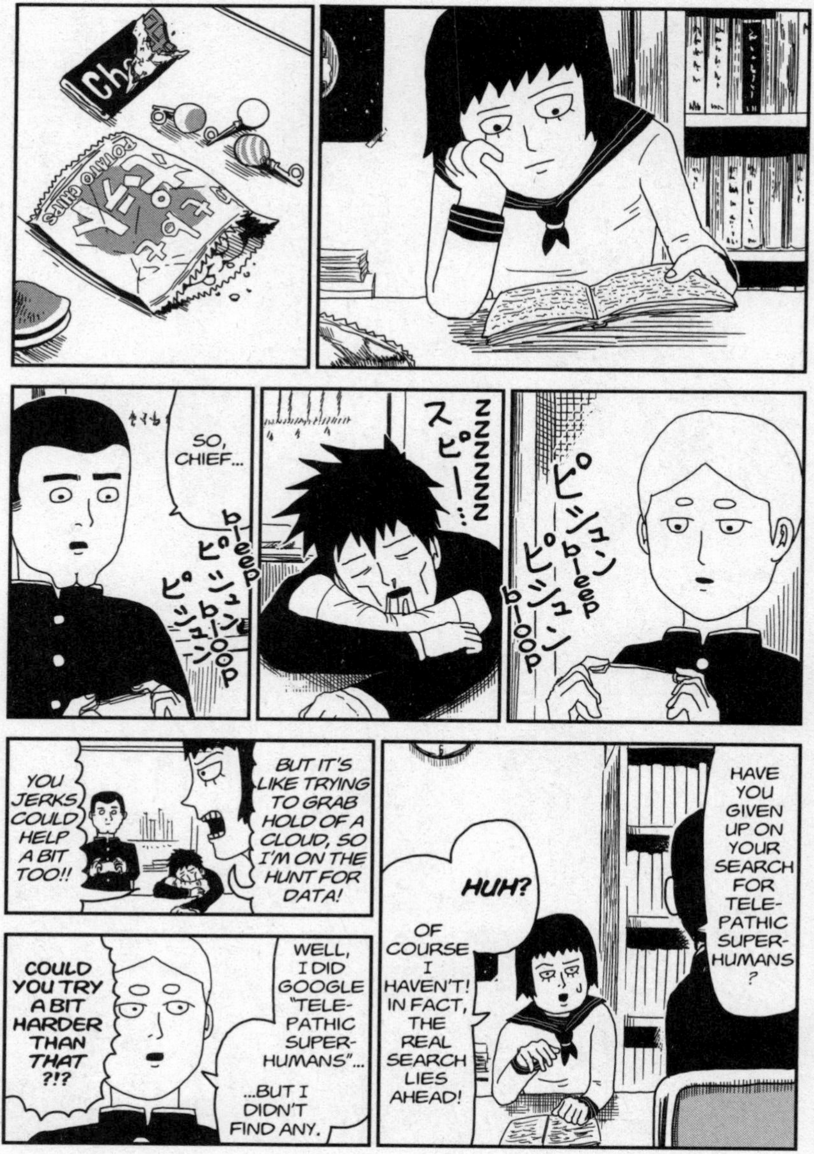
Ch
POTATO CHIPS
ピシュン bleep ピシュン bloop
ZZZZZZ スピー…
SO, CHIEF…
bleep ピシュ ピシュン bloop
HAVE YOU GIVEN UP ON YOUR SEARCH FOR TELE-PATHIC SUPER-HUMANS?
HUH?
OF COURSE I HAVEN'T! IN FACT, THE REAL SEARCH LIES AHEAD!
BUT IT'S LIKE TRYING TO GRAB HOLD OF A CLOUD, SO I'M ON THE HUNT FOR DATA!
YOU JERKS COULD HELP A BIT TOO!!
WELL, I DID GOOGLE "TELE-PATHIC SUPER-HUMANS"…
…BUT I DIDN'T FIND ANY.
COULD YOU TRY A BIT HARDER THAN THAT?!?

KURATA...
...COULD YOU KEEP IT DOWN, PLEASE?
OH! SORRY.
THANKS. I'M STILL NOT DONE TALKING TO THIS GUY YET.
C'MON! I'VE HAD ENOUGH, MUSASHI!
YOU HAVEN'T HAD NEARLY ENOUGH!
DON'T BE SO GUTLESS!!
GET YOURSELF BACK TO CLASS, ONIGAWARA!
I DON'T BELONG THERE ANYMORE...
MY FRIENDS WON'T EVEN TALK TO ME NOW...
CRAP...! AND THE GANGS AT THE OTHER SCHOOLS HAVE STARTED BUZZING AROUND TOO...
IT'S ALL OVER...
IF ONLY WE HAD WHITE T POISON ON OUR SIDE...
YOU'RE STILL OBSESSING ABOUT BRAWLING?
SPEND THAT ENERGY ON GETTING TO CLASS!
ガラッ rrrattle

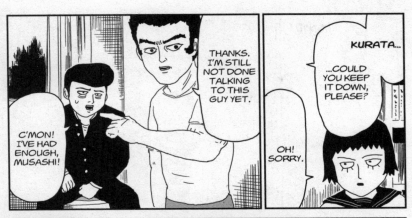

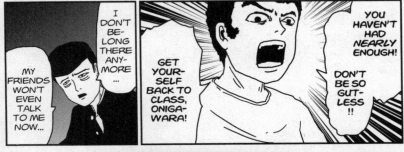

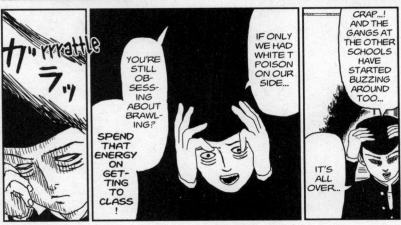

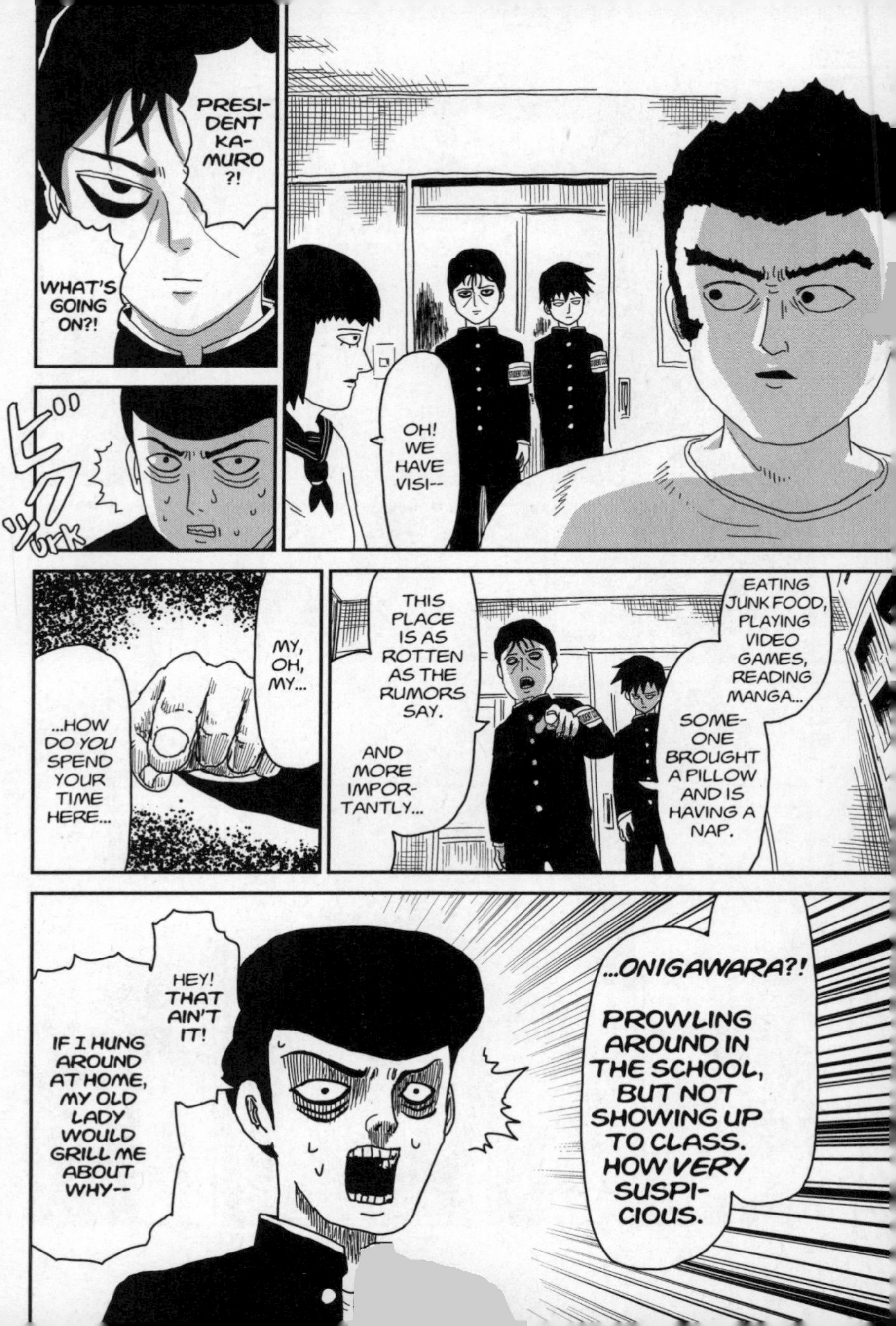
OH! WE HAVE VISI--
PRESIDENT KAMURO?!
WHAT'S GOING ON?!
ヒク
YURK
EATING JUNK FOOD, PLAYING VIDEO GAMES, READING MANGA...
SOMEONE BROUGHT A PILLOW AND IS HAVING A NAP.
THIS PLACE IS AS ROTTEN AS THE RUMORS SAY.
AND MORE IMPORTANTLY...
MY, OH, MY...
...HOW DO YOU SPEND YOUR TIME HERE...
...ONIGAWARA?!
PROWLING AROUND IN THE SCHOOL, BUT NOT SHOWING UP TO CLASS. HOW VERY SUSPICIOUS.
HEY! THAT AIN'T IT!
IF I HUNG AROUND AT HOME, MY OLD LADY WOULD GRILL ME ABOUT WHY--

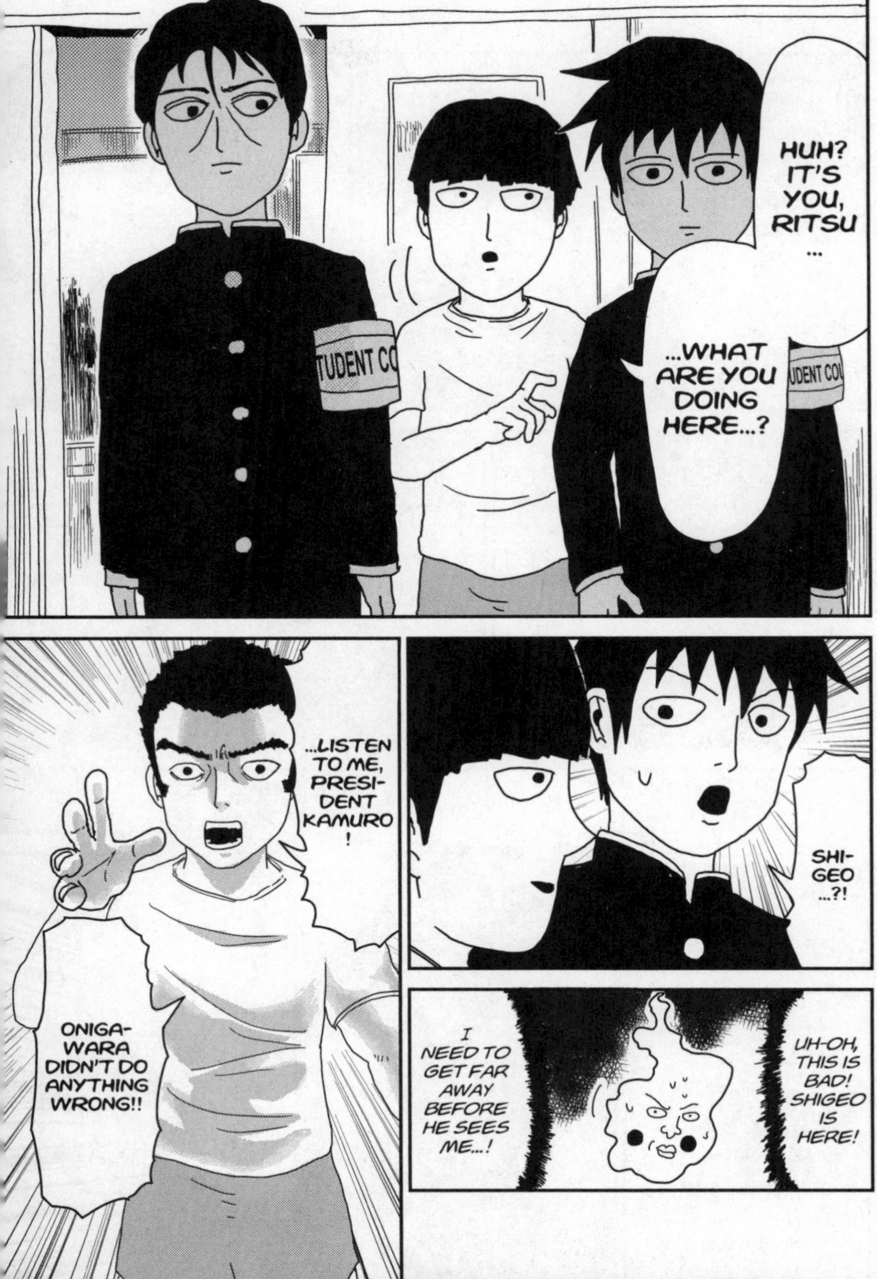
HUH? IT'S YOU, RITSU ...
...WHAT ARE YOU DOING HERE...?
TUDENT CO
UDENT CO
SHI-GEO ...?!
UH-OH, THIS IS BAD! SHIGEO IS HERE!
I NEED TO GET FAR AWAY BEFORE HE SEES ME...!
...LISTEN TO ME, PRESI-DENT KAMURO!
ONIGA-WARA DIDN'T DO ANYTHING WRONG!!

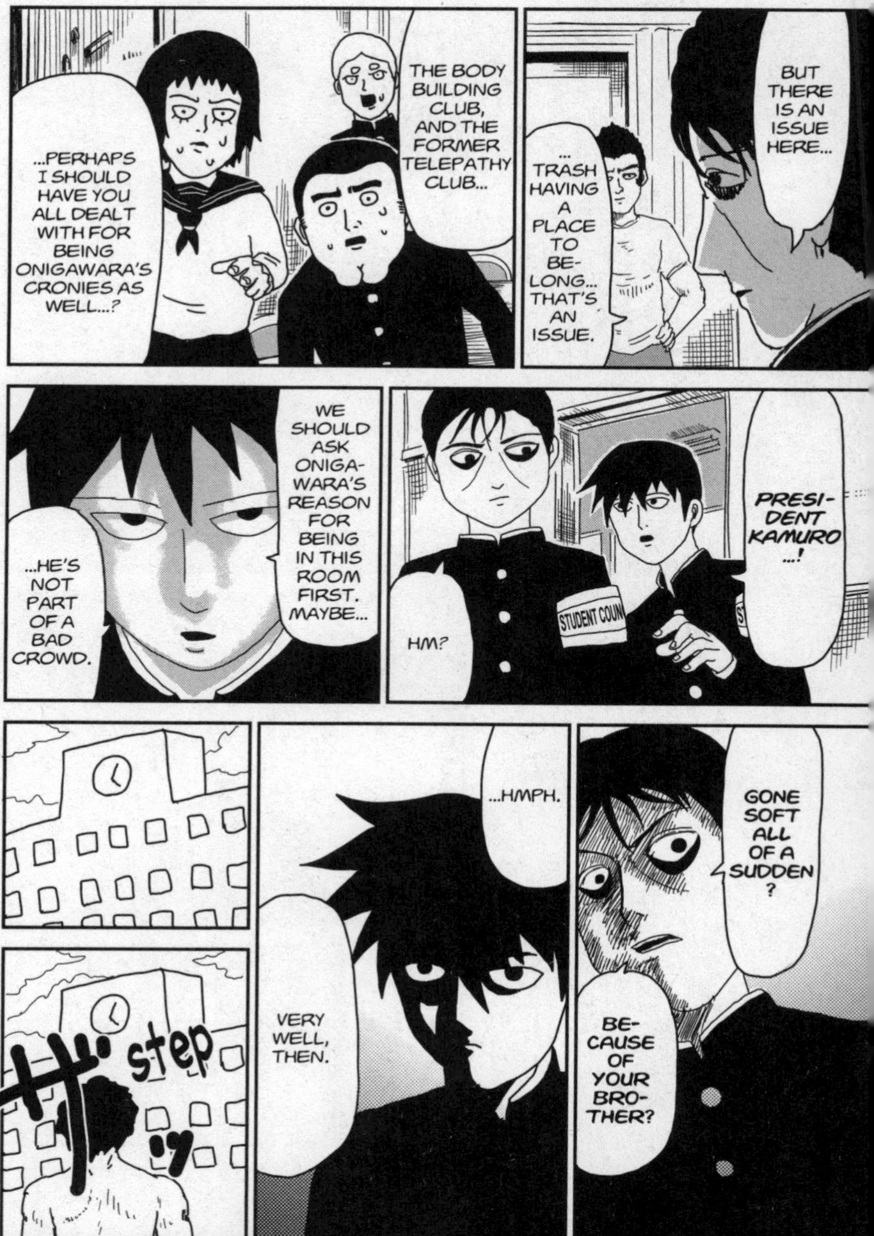
BUT THERE IS AN ISSUE HERE...
...TRASH HAVING A PLACE TO BE-LONG... THAT'S AN ISSUE.
THE BODY BUILDING CLUB, AND THE FORMER TELEPATHY CLUB...
...PERHAPS I SHOULD HAVE YOU ALL DEALT WITH FOR BEING ONIGAWARA'S CRONIES AS WELL...?
PRESI-DENT KAMURO ...!
STUDENT COUN
HM?
WE SHOULD ASK ONIGA-WARA'S REASON FOR BEING IN THIS ROOM FIRST. MAYBE...
...HE'S NOT PART OF A BAD CROWD.
GONE SOFT ALL OF A SUDDEN?
BE-CAUSE OF YOUR BRO-THER?
...HMPH.
VERY WELL, THEN.
step

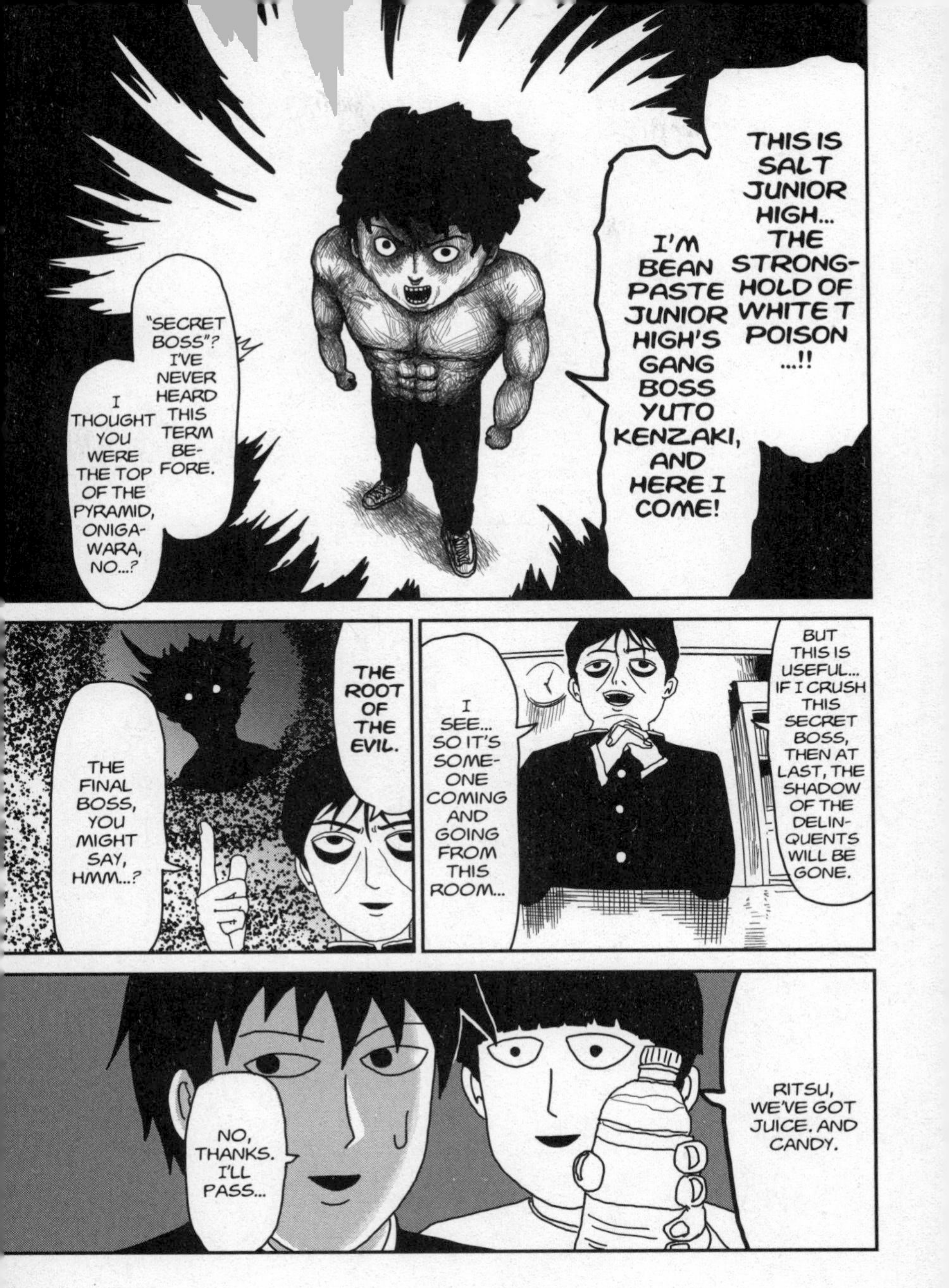
THIS IS SALT JUNIOR HIGH... THE STRONGHOLD OF WHITE T POISON ...!!
I'M BEAN PASTE JUNIOR HIGH'S GANG BOSS YUTO KENZAKI, AND HERE I COME!
"SECRET BOSS"? I'VE NEVER HEARD THIS TERM BEFORE.
I THOUGHT YOU WERE THE TOP OF THE PYRAMID, ONIGAWARA, NO...?
BUT THIS IS USEFUL... IF I CRUSH THIS SECRET BOSS, THEN AT LAST, THE SHADOW OF THE DELINQUENTS WILL BE GONE.
I SEE... SO IT'S SOMEONE COMING AND GOING FROM THIS ROOM...
THE ROOT OF THE EVIL.
THE FINAL BOSS, YOU MIGHT SAY, HMM...?
RITSU, WE'VE GOT JUICE. AND CANDY.
NO, THANKS. I'LL PASS...

That can't be it... can it?

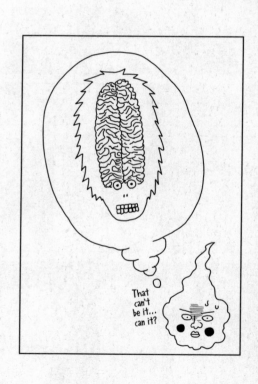

CHAPTER 28: CHANGE

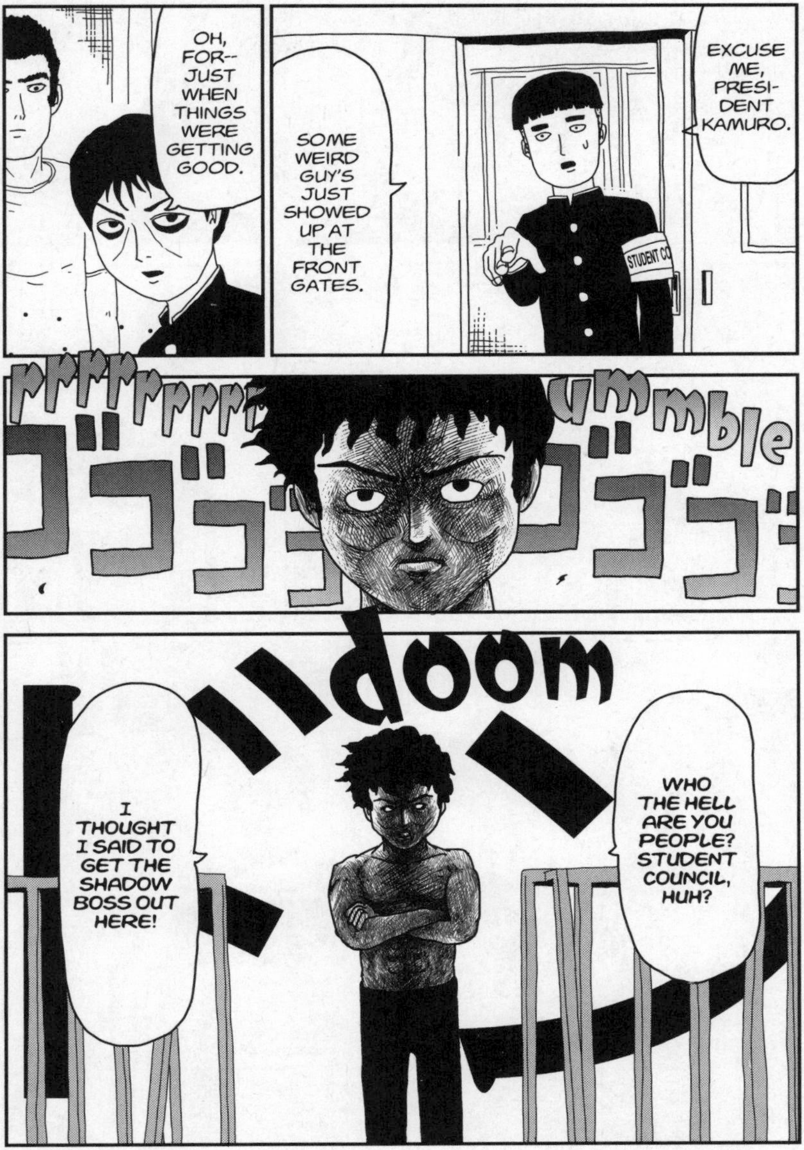
EXCUSE ME, PRESIDENT KAMURO.
STUDENT CO
SOME WEIRD GUY'S JUST SHOWED UP AT THE FRONT GATES.
OH, FOR-- JUST WHEN THINGS WERE GETTING GOOD.
ummble
ゴゴゴ
rrrrrrrrrr
ゴゴゴ
doom
WHO THE HELL ARE YOU PEOPLE? STUDENT COUNCIL, HUH?
I THOUGHT I SAID TO GET THE SHADOW BOSS OUT HERE!

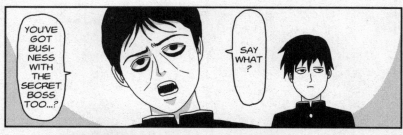

SAY WHAT?
YOU'VE GOT BUSINESS WITH THE SECRET BOSS TOO...?
WELL, STEP AWAY FROM THE GATE.
LET'S HAVE A CHAT.
IT'S NOT JUST ME. THE GANGS ALL OVER TOWN ARE TALKING ABOUT HIM.
THEY SAY IF YOU WANNA BE THE TOP OF THEM ALL, YOU GOTTA TAKE DOWN SALT'S WHITE T POISON.
HM. WHAT A PAIN.
AS LONG AS THIS SECRET BOSS OR WHATEVER IS AT OUR SCHOOL, THEN THIS TYPE OF RIFFRAFF IS GOING TO KEEP SHOWING UP, HMM...?
BUT IF WE PLAY THIS RIGHT... THEY COULD WIPE EACH OTHER OUT AT THE SAME TIME.
WHAT DO YOU THINK, KAGEYAMA?
COULD WE PLEASE STOP WITH THESE TWISTED SCHEMES?

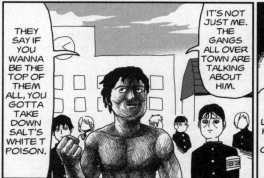

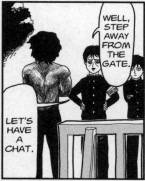

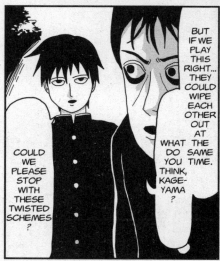

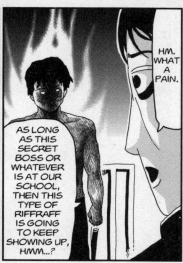

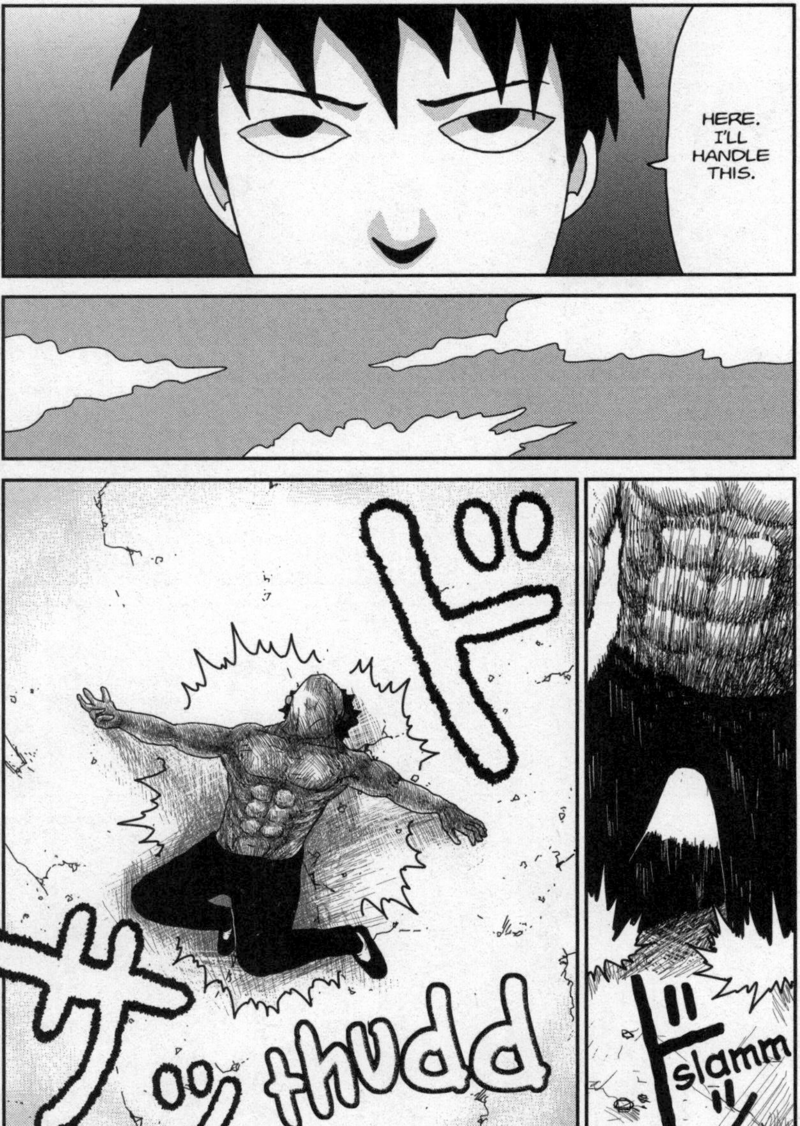
HERE. I'LL HANDLE THIS.
slamm
thudd

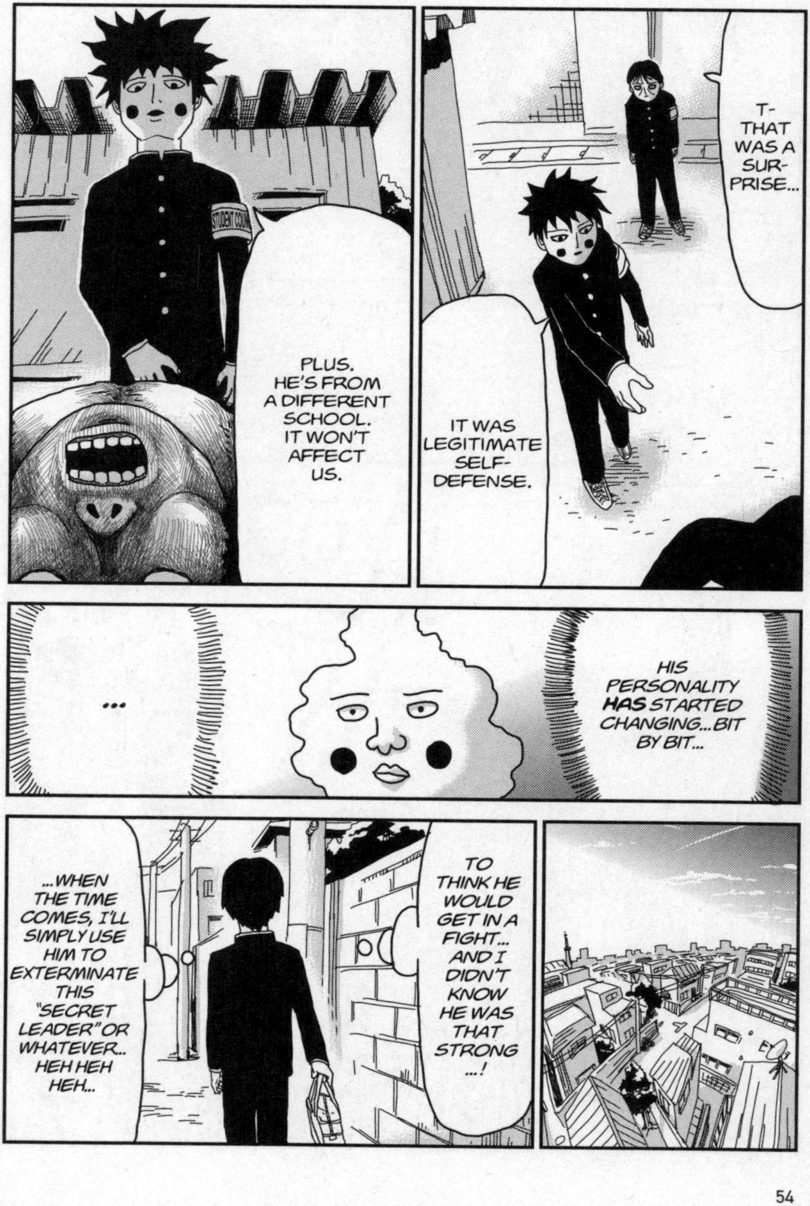
T-THAT WAS A SURPRISE...
IT WAS LEGITIMATE SELF-DEFENSE.
PLUS. HE'S FROM A DIFFERENT SCHOOL. IT WON'T AFFECT US.
HIS PERSONALITY **HAS** STARTED CHANGING...BIT BY BIT...
...
TO THINK HE WOULD GET IN A FIGHT... AND I DIDN'T KNOW HE WAS THAT STRONG ...!
...WHEN THE TIME COMES, I'LL SIMPLY USE HIM TO EXTERMINATE THIS "SECRET LEADER" OR WHATEVER... HEH HEH HEH...

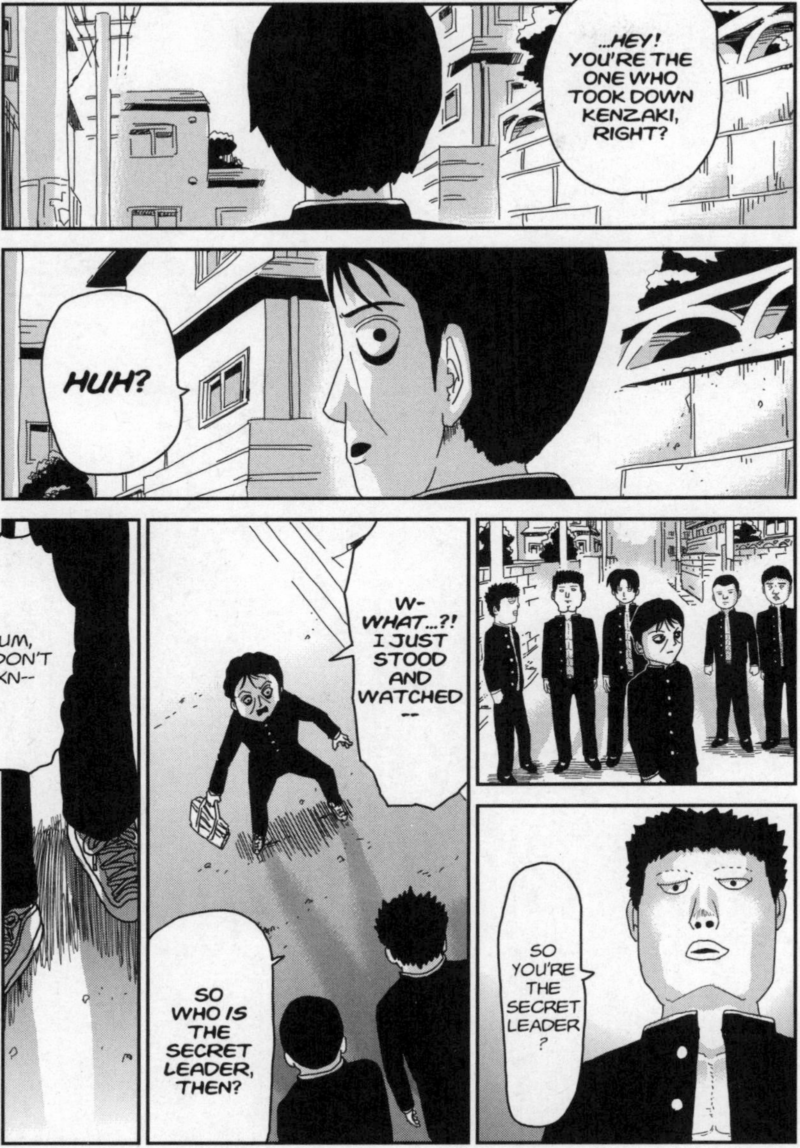
...HEY! YOU'RE THE ONE WHO TOOK DOWN KENZAKI, RIGHT?
HUH?
SO YOU'RE THE SECRET LEADER?
W-WHAT...?! I JUST STOOD AND WATCHED --
SO WHO IS THE SECRET LEADER, THEN?
UM, I DON'T KN--

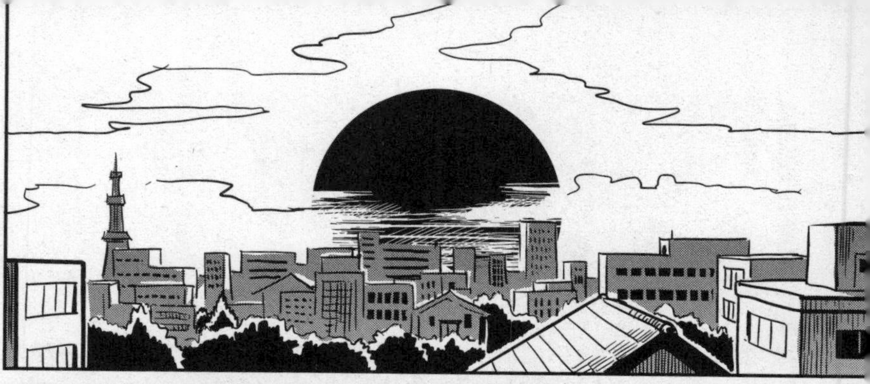
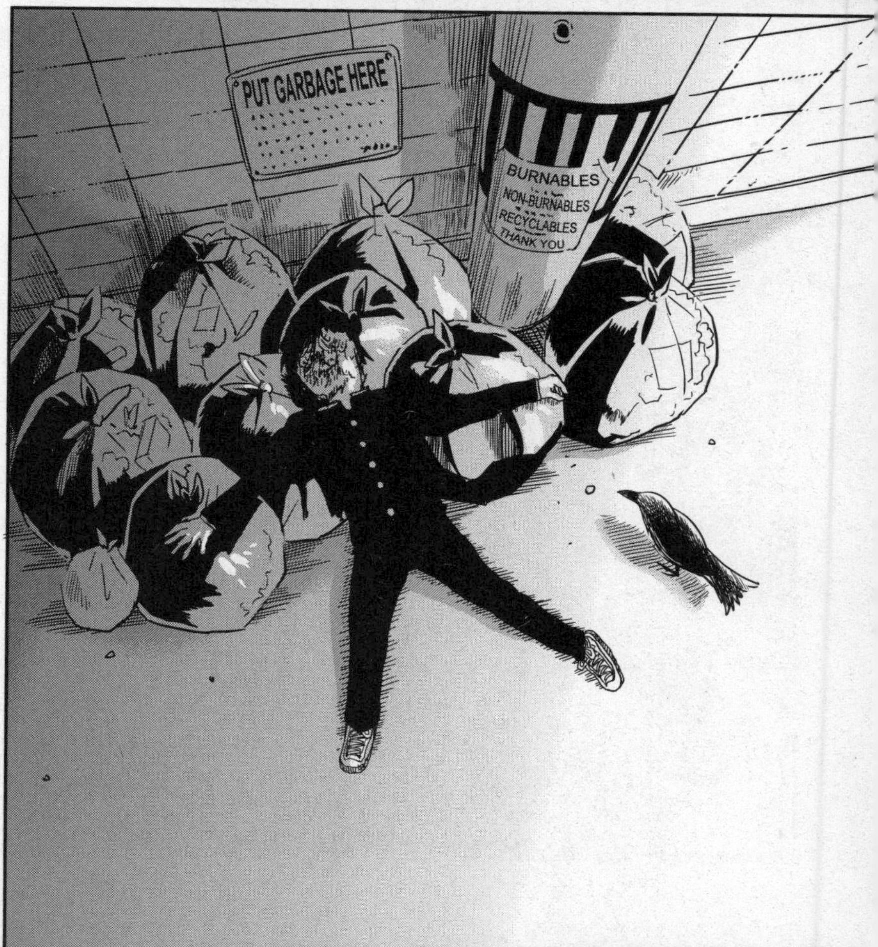
PUT GARBAGE HERE
BURNABLES
NON-BURNABLES
RECYCLABLES
THANK YOU

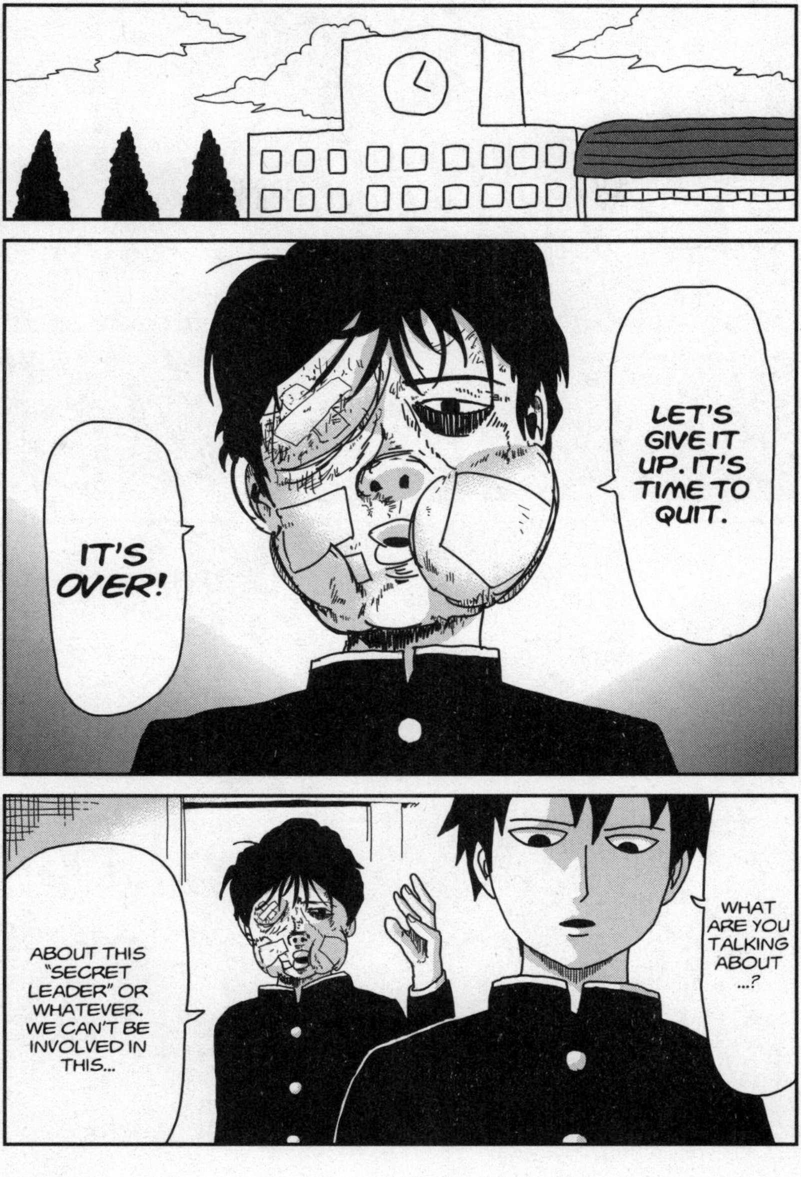
LET'S GIVE IT UP. IT'S TIME TO QUIT.
IT'S OVER!
WHAT ARE YOU TALKING ABOUT ...?
ABOUT THIS "SECRET LEADER" OR WHATEVER. WE CAN'T BE INVOLVED IN THIS...

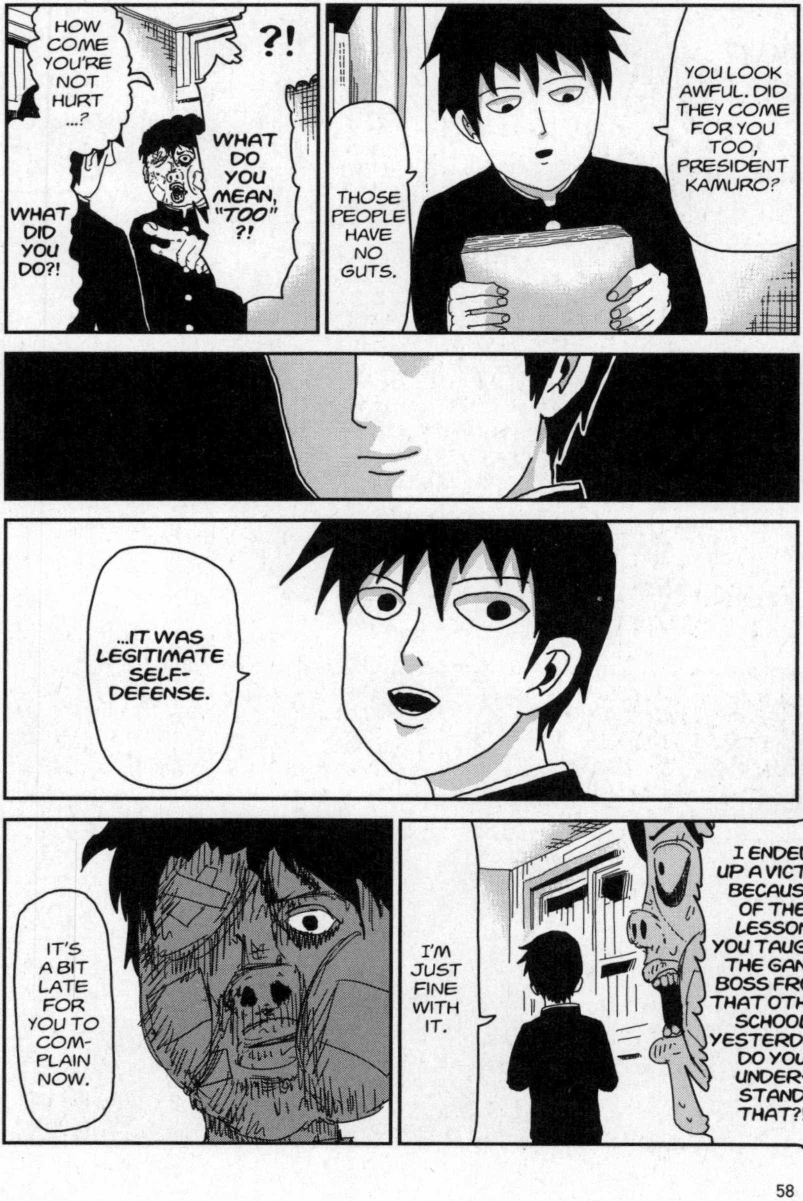
YOU LOOK AWFUL. DID THEY COME FOR YOU TOO, PRESIDENT KAMURO?
THOSE PEOPLE HAVE NO GUTS.
?!
WHAT DO YOU MEAN, "TOO"?!
HOW COME YOU'RE NOT HURT ...?
WHAT DID YOU DO?!
...IT WAS LEGITIMATE SELF-DEFENSE.
I ENDED UP A VICTIM BECAUSE OF THE LESSON YOU TAUGHT THE GANG BOSS FROM THAT OTHER SCHOOL YESTERDAY! DO YOU UNDER-STAND THAT?!
I'M JUST FINE WITH IT.
IT'S A BIT LATE FOR YOU TO COM-PLAIN NOW.

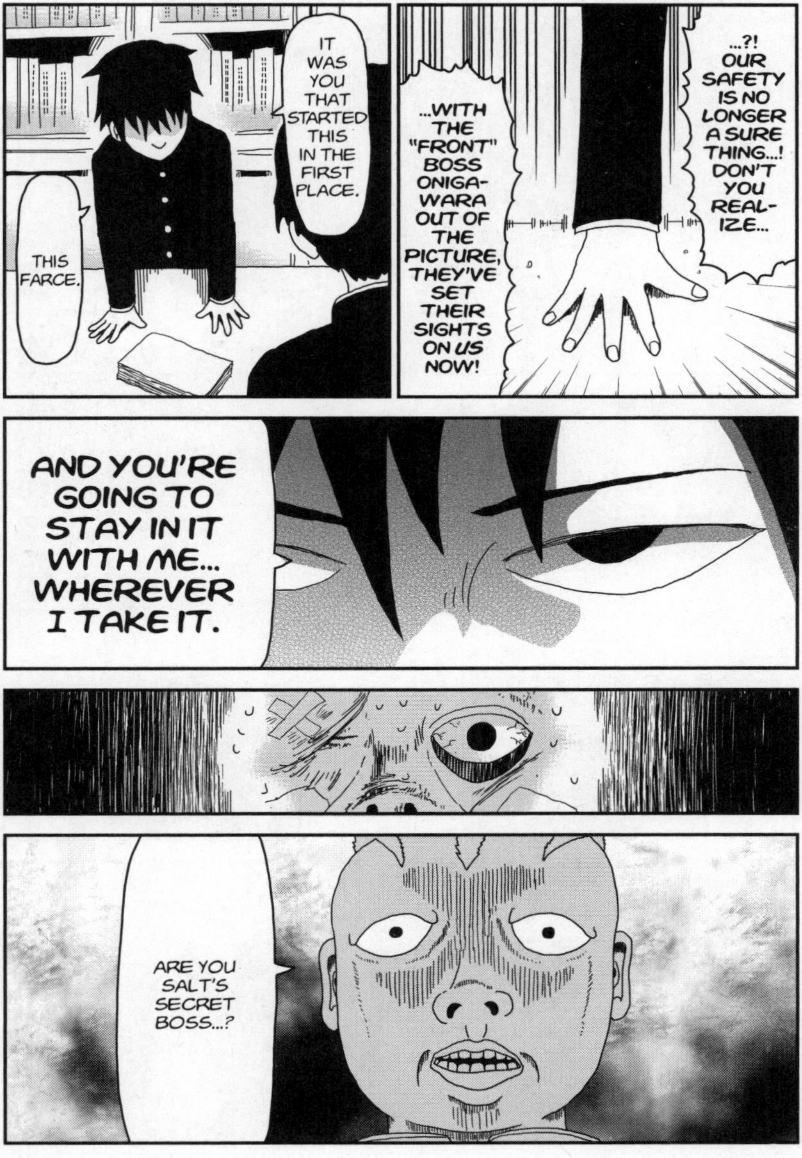
...?! OUR SAFETY IS NO LONGER A SURE THING...! DON'T YOU REALIZE...
...WITH THE "FRONT" BOSS ONIGAWARA OUT OF THE PICTURE, THEY'VE SET THEIR SIGHTS ON US NOW!
IT WAS YOU THAT STARTED THIS IN THE FIRST PLACE.
THIS FARCE.
AND YOU'RE GOING TO STAY IN IT WITH ME... WHEREVER I TAKE IT.
ARE YOU SALT'S SECRET BOSS...?

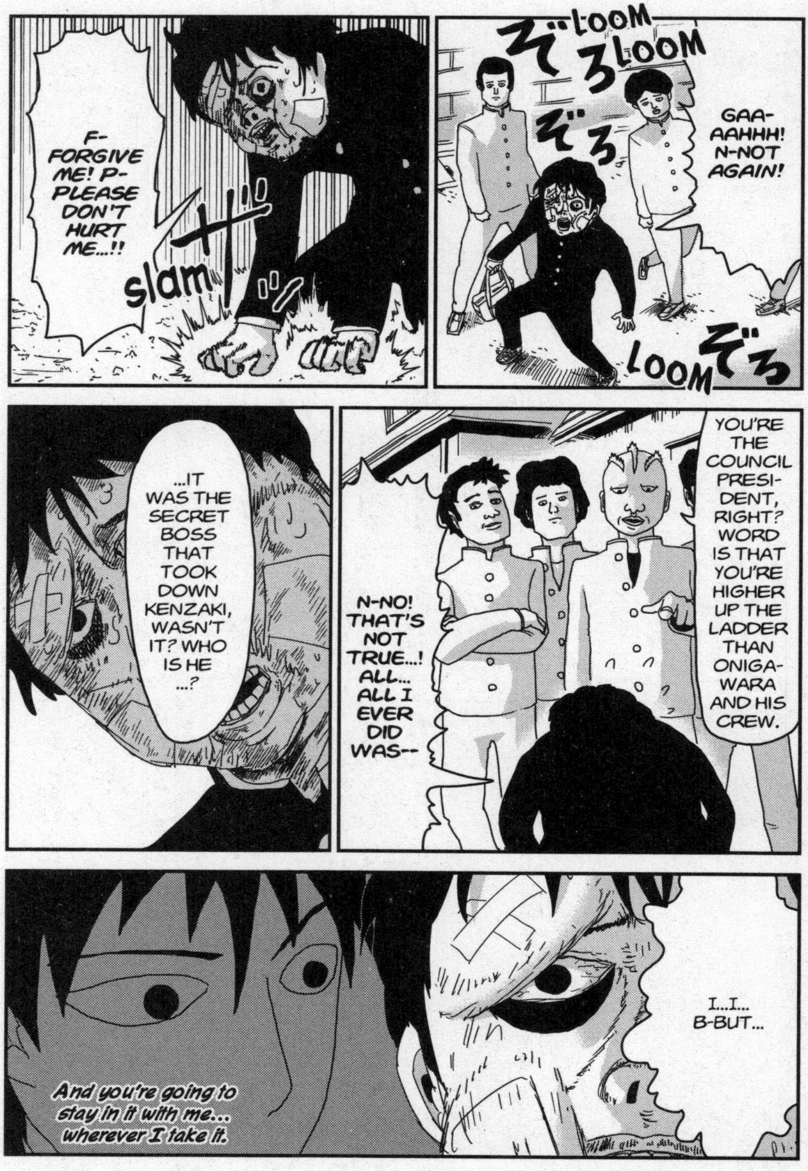

LOOM
ぞろ LOOM
ぞろ
GAA-AAHHH! N-NOT AGAIN!
ぞろ LOOM
F-FORGIVE ME! P-PLEASE DON'T HURT ME...!!
slam
YOU'RE THE COUNCIL PRESIDENT, RIGHT? WORD IS THAT YOU'RE HIGHER UP THE LADDER THAN ONIGAWARA AND HIS CREW.
N-NO! THAT'S NOT TRUE...! ALL... ALL I EVER DID WAS--
...IT WAS THE SECRET BOSS THAT TOOK DOWN KENZAKI, WASN'T IT? WHO IS HE ...?
I...I... B-BUT...
And you're going to stay in it with me... wherever I take it.

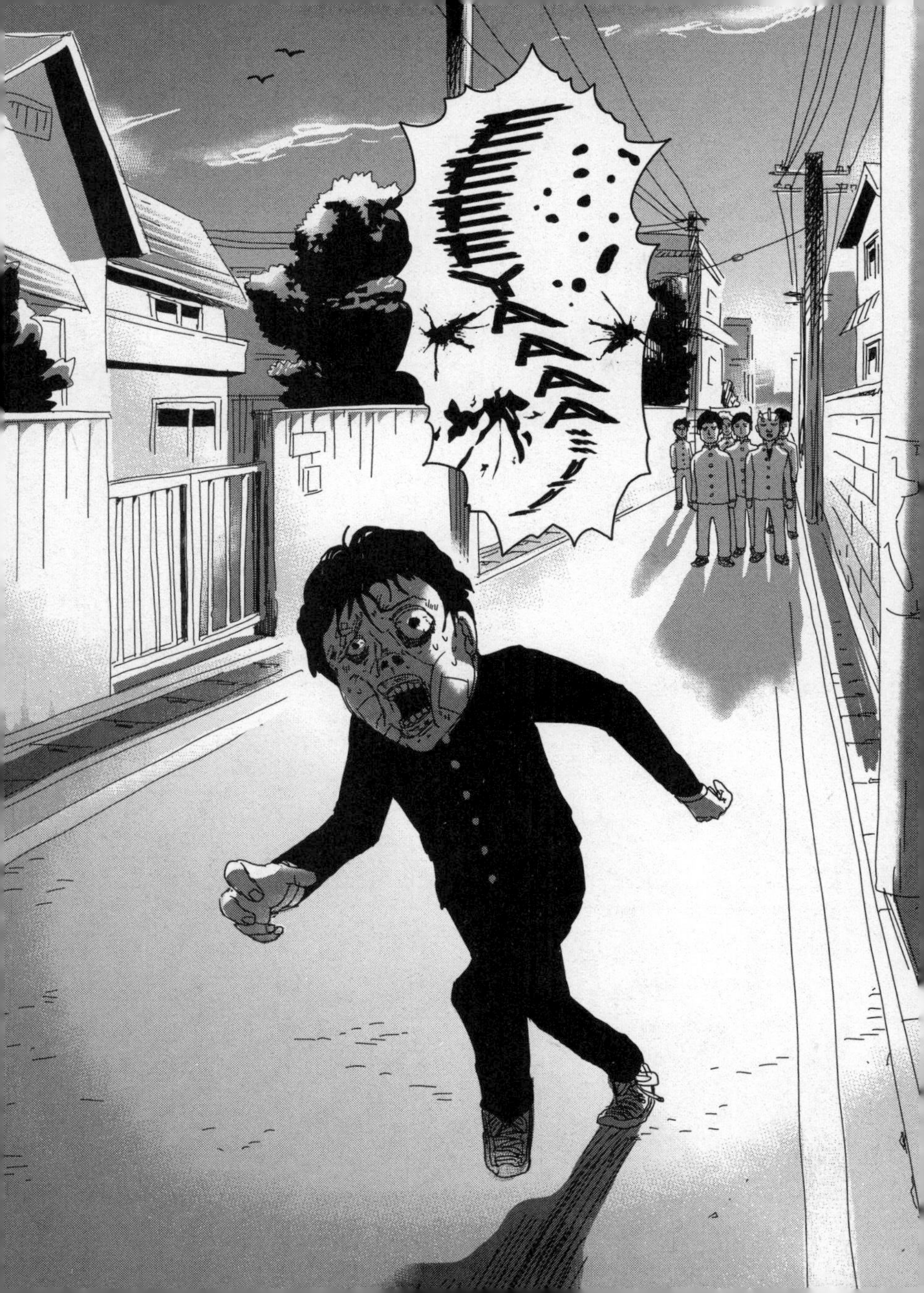
EEEEYAAAA

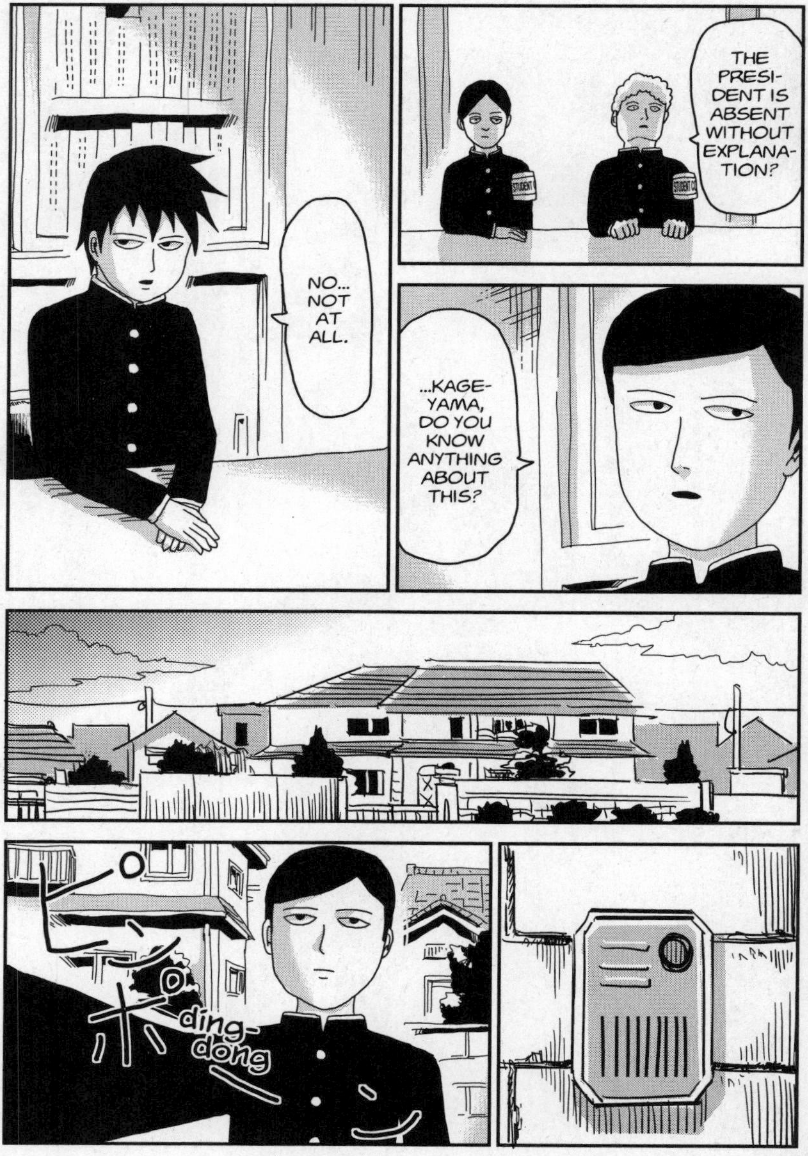
THE PRESIDENT IS ABSENT WITHOUT EXPLANATION?
...KAGEYAMA, DO YOU KNOW ANYTHING ABOUT THIS?
NO... NOT AT ALL.
ding-dong

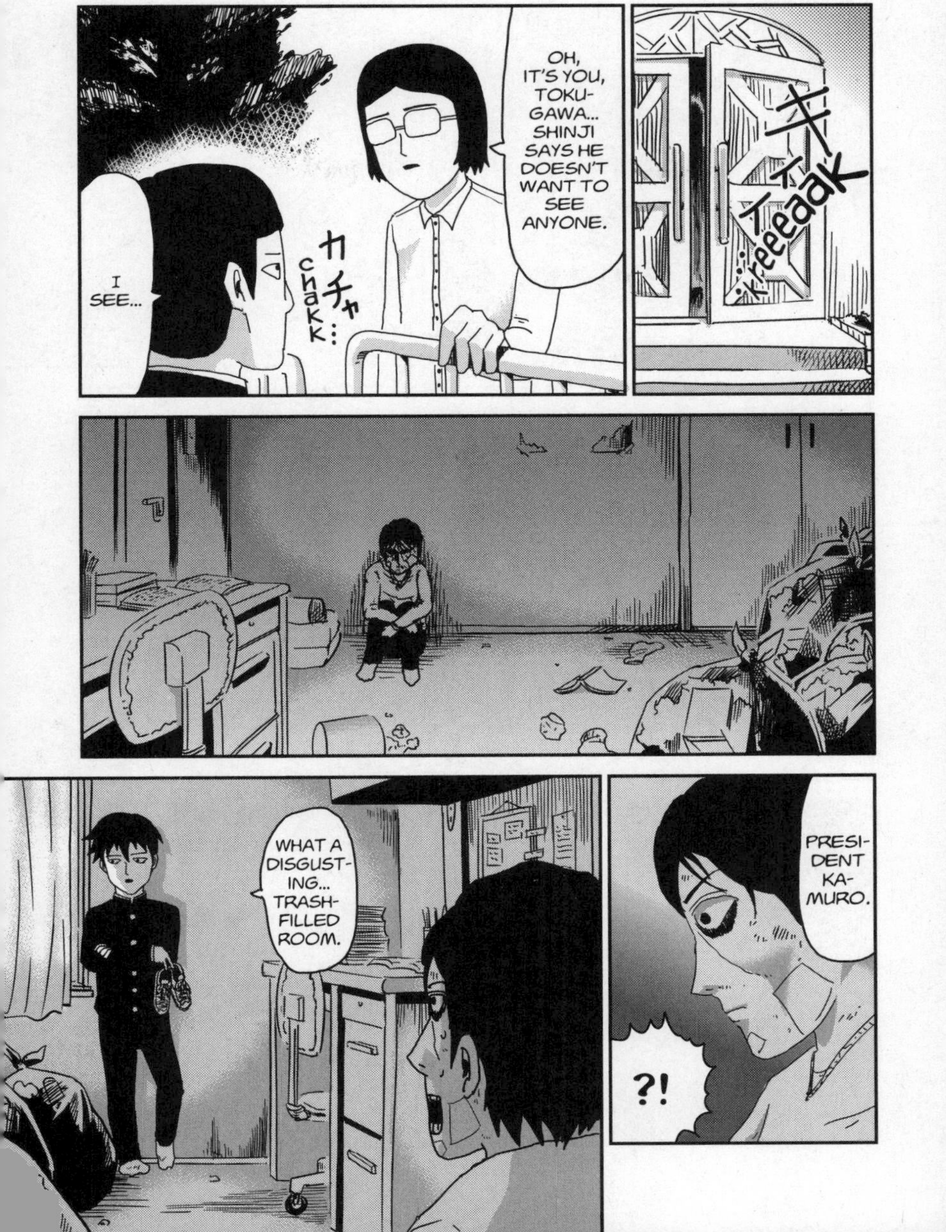

キィィ
kreeeaak...
OH, IT'S YOU, TOKU-GAWA... SHINJI SAYS HE DOESN'T WANT TO SEE ANYONE.
カチャ
chakk...
I SEE...
PRESI-DENT KA-MURO.
?!
WHAT A DISGUST-ING... TRASH-FILLED ROOM.

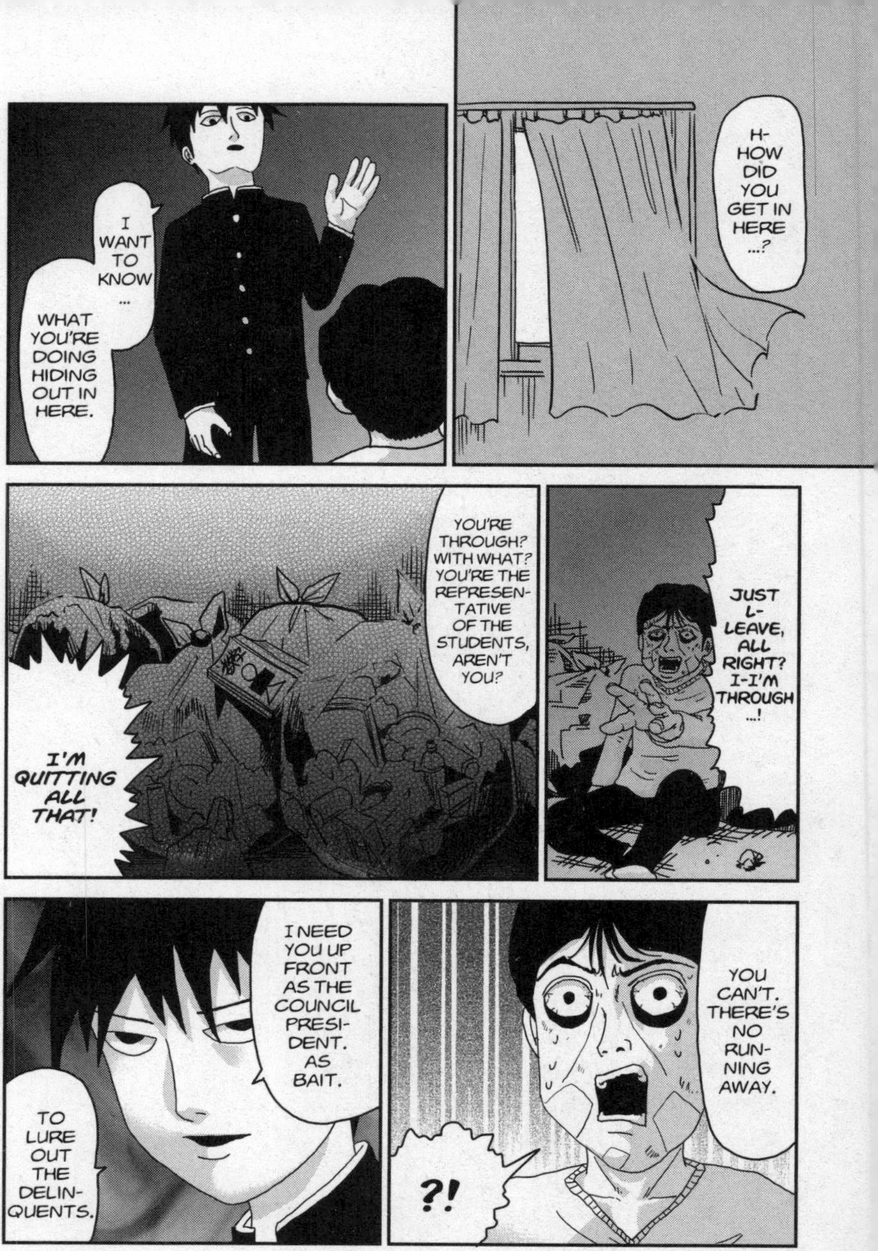

H-HOW DID YOU GET IN HERE ...?
I WANT TO KNOW ... WHAT YOU'RE DOING HIDING OUT IN HERE.
JUST L-LEAVE, ALL RIGHT? I-I'M THROUGH ...!
YOU'RE THROUGH? WITH WHAT? YOU'RE THE REPRESENTATIVE OF THE STUDENTS, AREN'T YOU?
I'M QUITTING ALL THAT!
YOU CAN'T. THERE'S NO RUNNING AWAY.
?!
I NEED YOU UP FRONT AS THE COUNCIL PRESIDENT. AS BAIT.
TO LURE OUT THE DELINQUENTS.

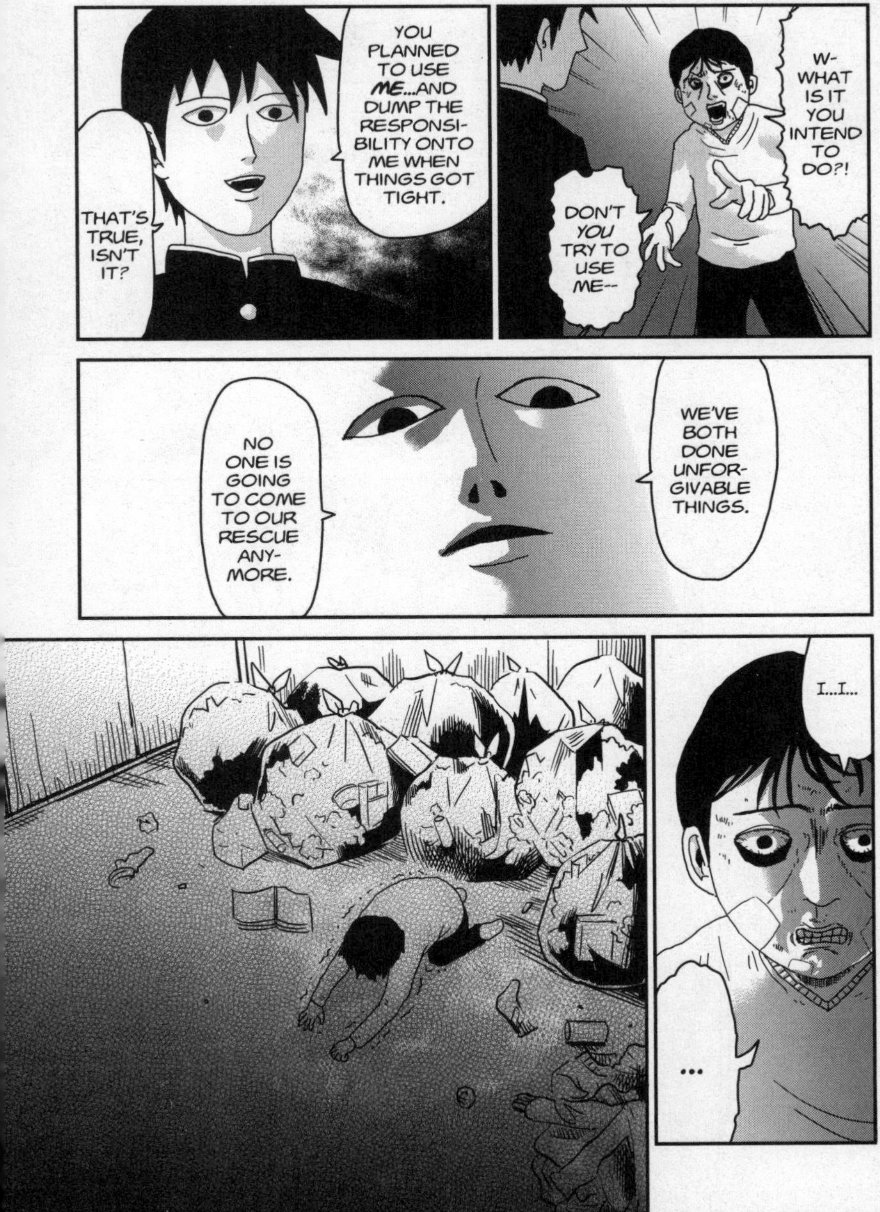
W-WHAT IS IT YOU INTEND TO DO?!
DON'T *YOU* TRY TO USE ME--
YOU PLANNED TO USE *ME*...AND DUMP THE RESPONSIBILITY ONTO ME WHEN THINGS GOT TIGHT.
THAT'S TRUE, ISN'T IT?
WE'VE BOTH DONE UNFORGIVABLE THINGS.
NO ONE IS GOING TO COME TO OUR RESCUE ANYMORE.
I...I...
...

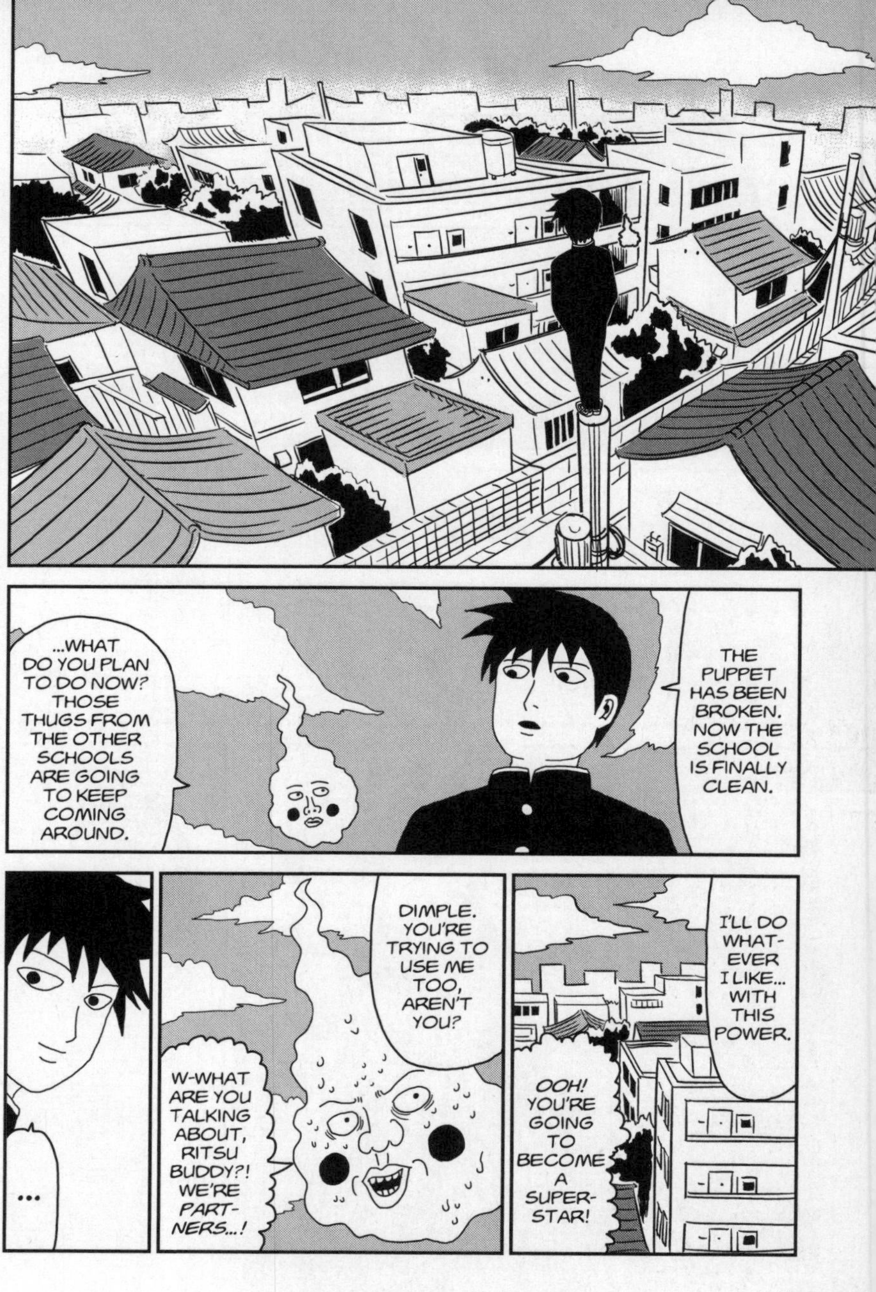
THE PUPPET HAS BEEN BROKEN. NOW THE SCHOOL IS FINALLY CLEAN.
...WHAT DO YOU PLAN TO DO NOW? THOSE THUGS FROM THE OTHER SCHOOLS ARE GOING TO KEEP COMING AROUND.
I'LL DO WHATEVER I LIKE... WITH THIS POWER.
OOH! YOU'RE GOING TO BECOME A SUPERSTAR!
DIMPLE. YOU'RE TRYING TO USE ME TOO, AREN'T YOU?
W-WHAT ARE YOU TALKING ABOUT, RITSU BUDDY?! WE'RE PARTNERS...!
...

CHAPTER 29: WHAT HAVE YOU DONE?!

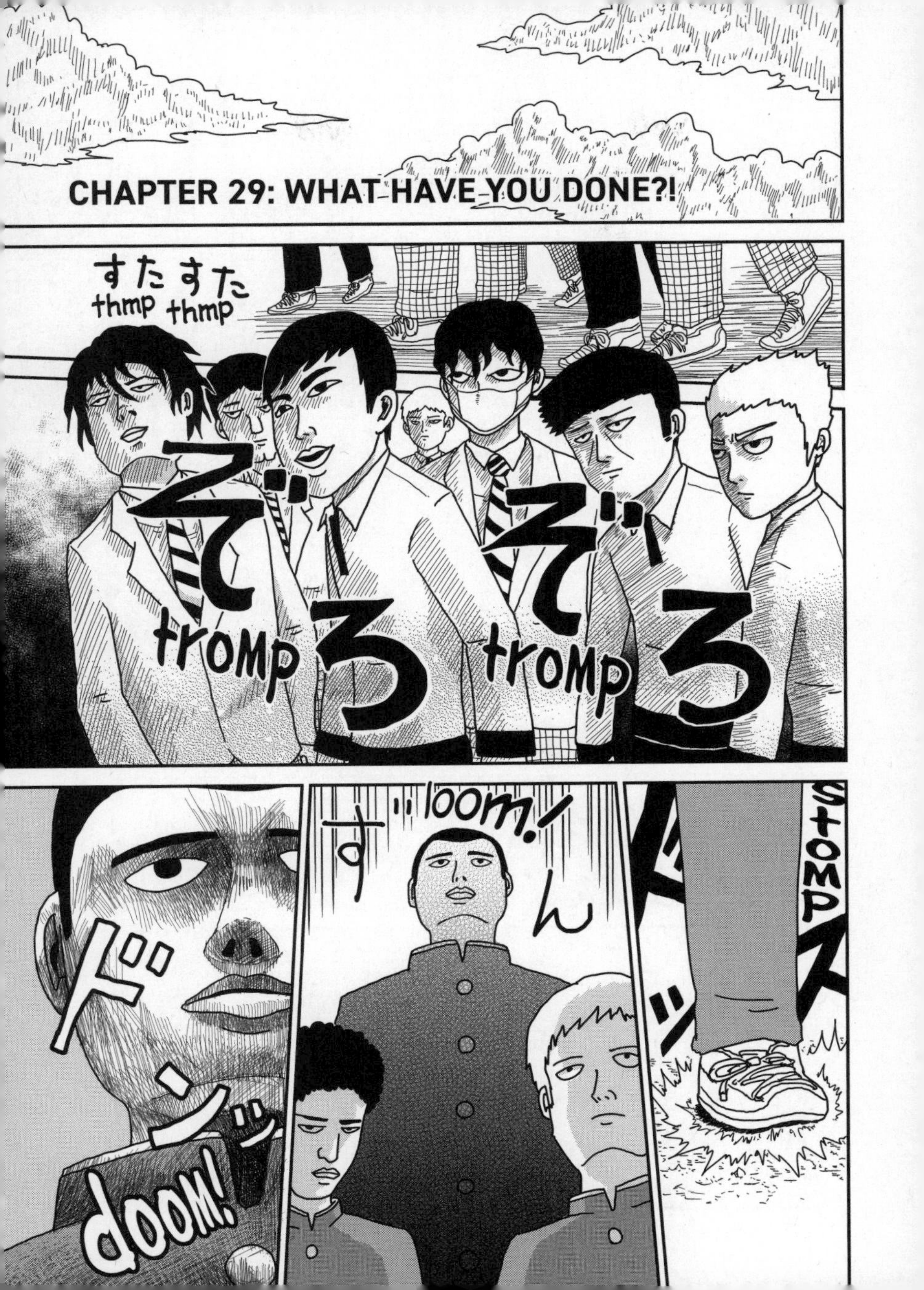
すたすた
thmp thmp
ぞろぞろ
tromp tromp
ズ
STOMP
すん
loom!
ドン
doom!

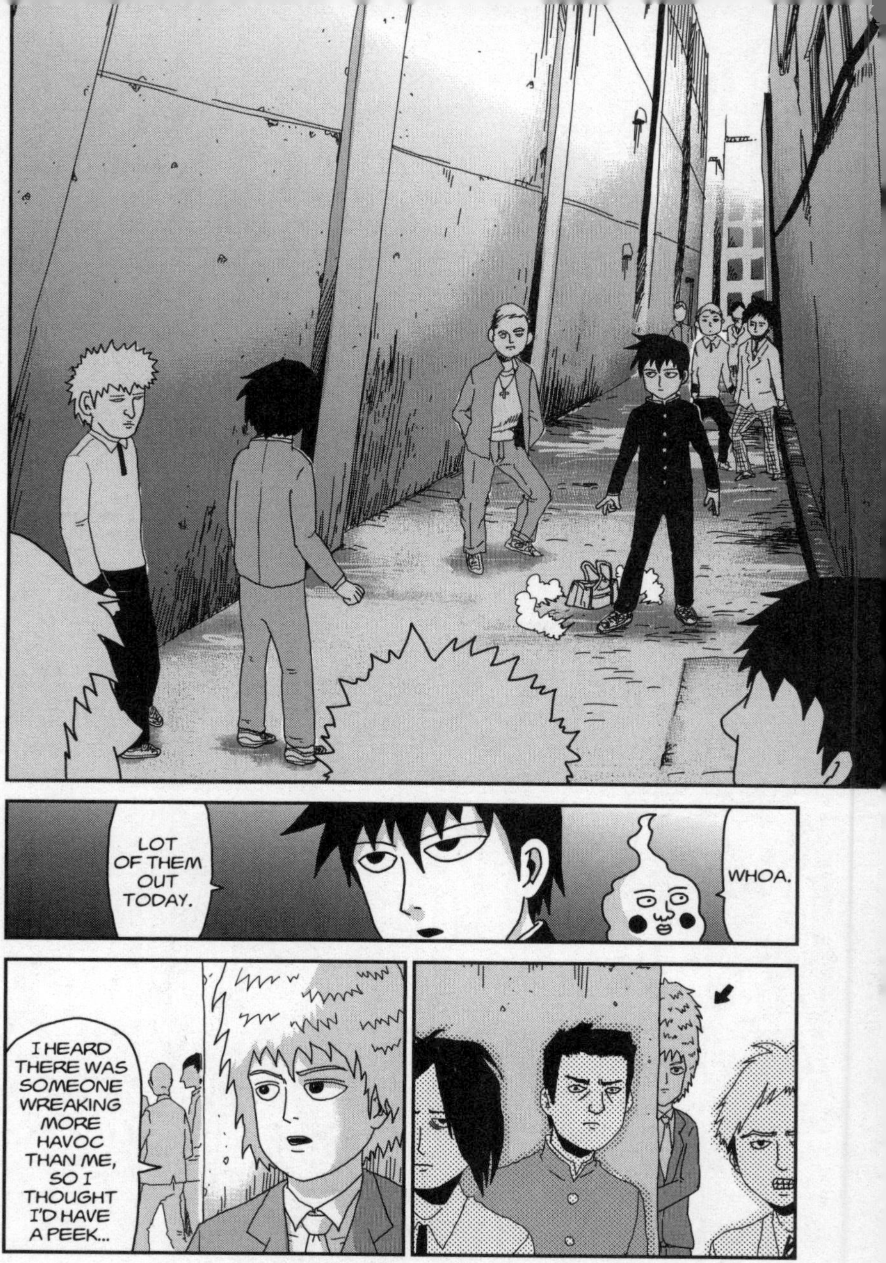
WHOA.
LOT OF THEM OUT TODAY.
I HEARD THERE WAS SOMEONE WREAKING MORE HAVOC THAN ME, SO I THOUGHT I'D HAVE A PEEK...

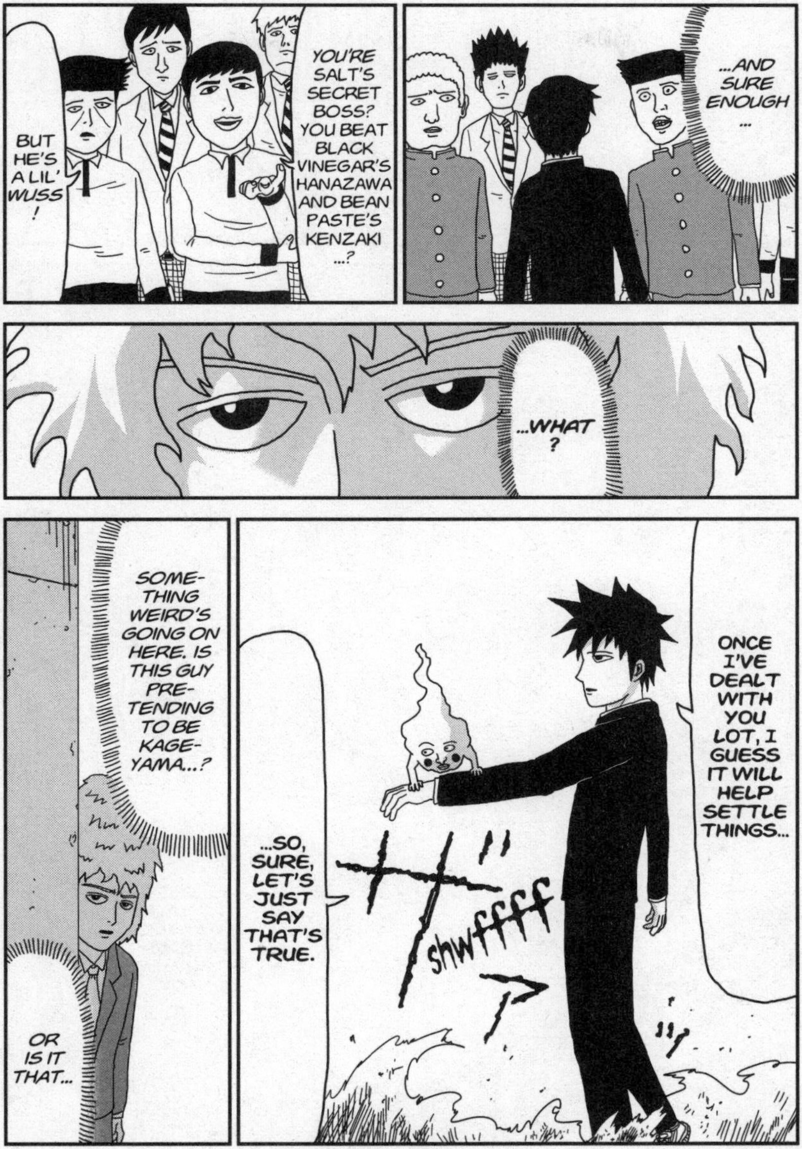
...AND SURE ENOUGH ...
YOU'RE SALT'S SECRET BOSS? YOU BEAT BLACK VINEGAR'S HANAZAWA AND BEAN PASTE'S KENZAKI ...?
BUT HE'S A LIL' WUSS!
...WHAT?
ONCE I'VE DEALT WITH YOU LOT, I GUESS IT WILL HELP SETTLE THINGS...
...SO, SURE, LET'S JUST SAY THAT'S TRUE.
shwffff
SOME-THING WEIRD'S GOING ON HERE. IS THIS GUY PRE-TENDING TO BE KAGE-YAMA...?
OR IS IT THAT...

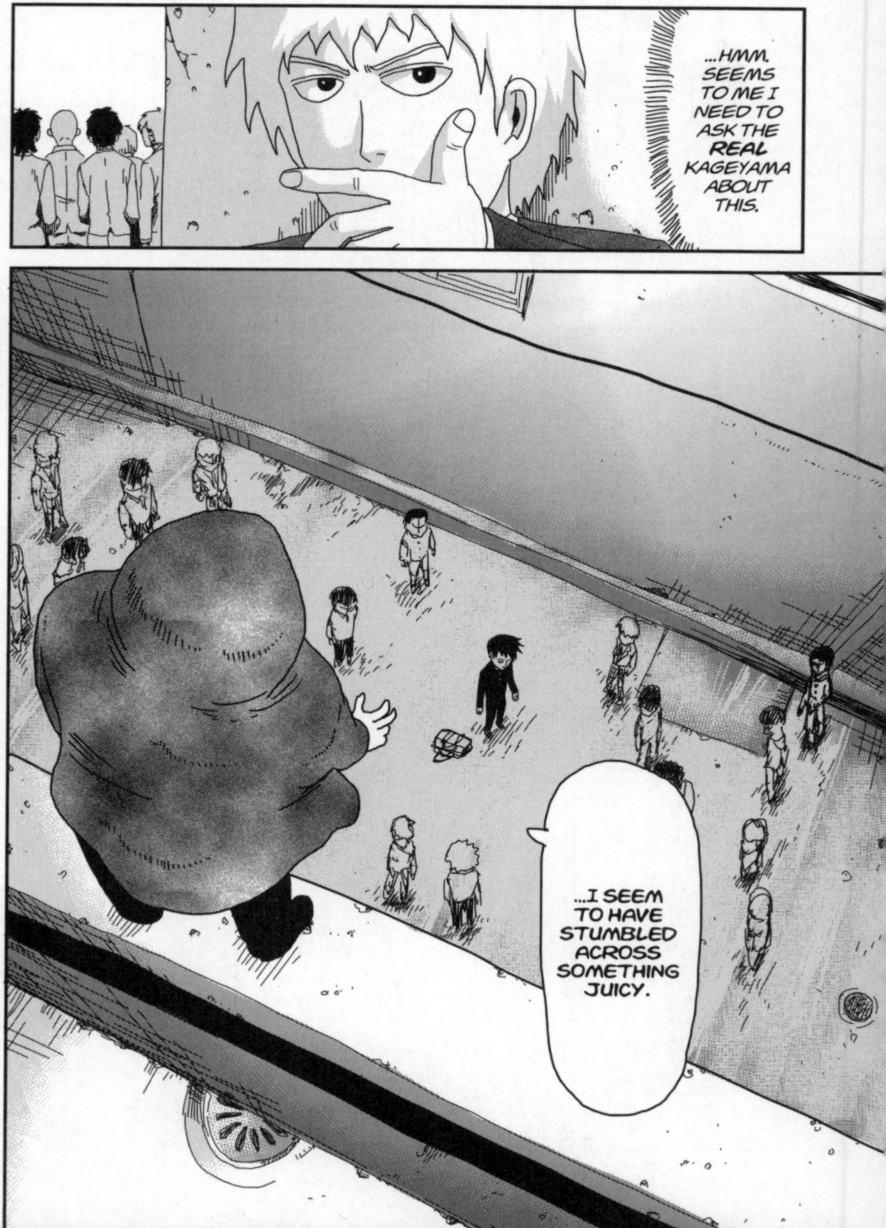
...HMM. SEEMS TO ME I NEED TO ASK THE REAL KAGEYAMA ABOUT THIS.
...I SEEM TO HAVE STUMBLED ACROSS SOMETHING JUICY.

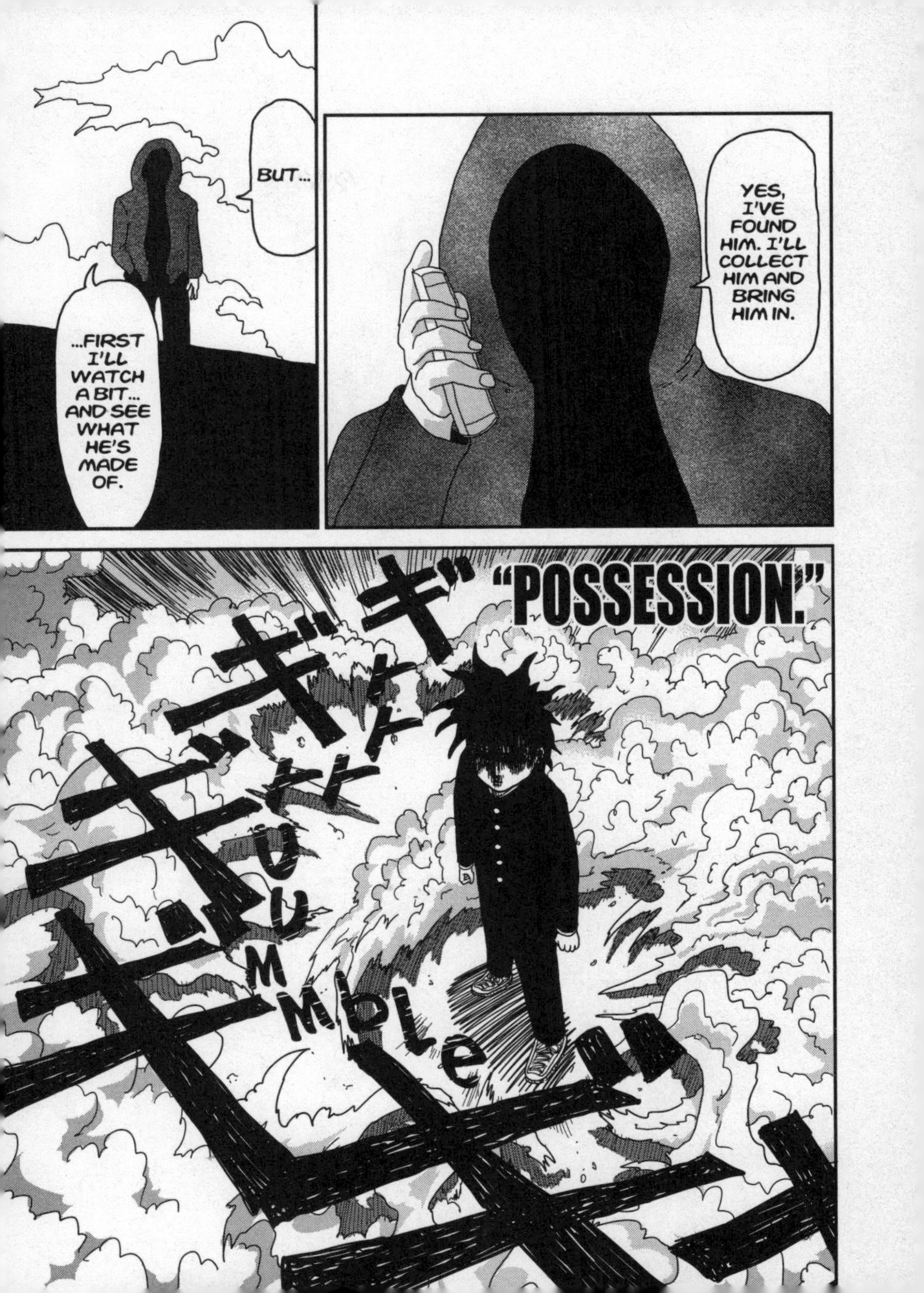
YES, I'VE FOUND HIM. I'LL COLLECT HIM AND BRING HIM IN.
BUT...
...FIRST I'LL WATCH A BIT... AND SEE WHAT HE'S MADE OF.
"POSSESSION."
UUMMbLe

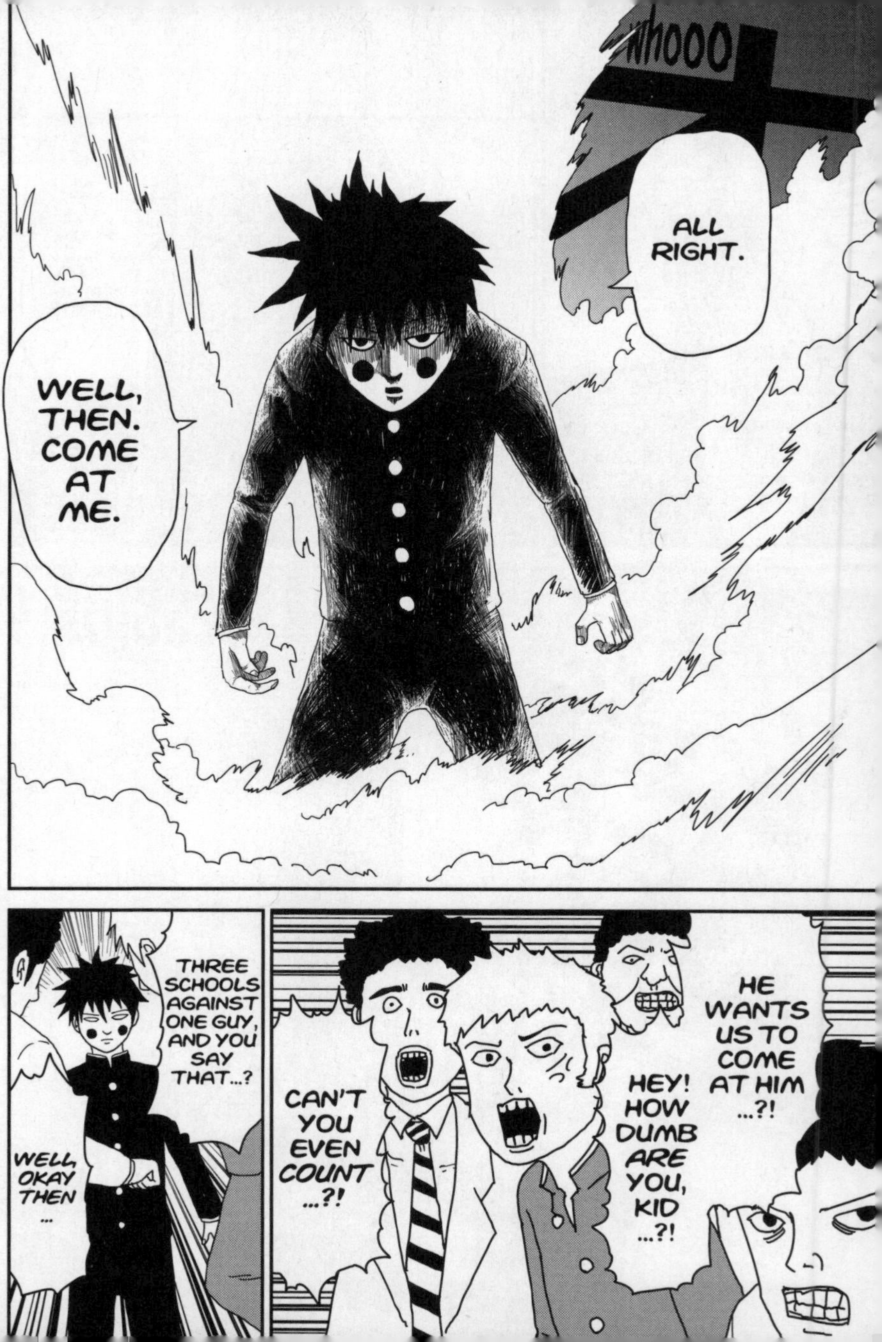
WHOOO
ALL RIGHT.
WELL, THEN. COME AT ME.
HE WANTS US TO COME AT HIM ...?!
HEY! HOW DUMB ARE YOU, KID ...?!
CAN'T YOU EVEN COUNT ...?!
THREE SCHOOLS AGAINST ONE GUY, AND YOU SAY THAT...?
WELL, OKAY THEN ...

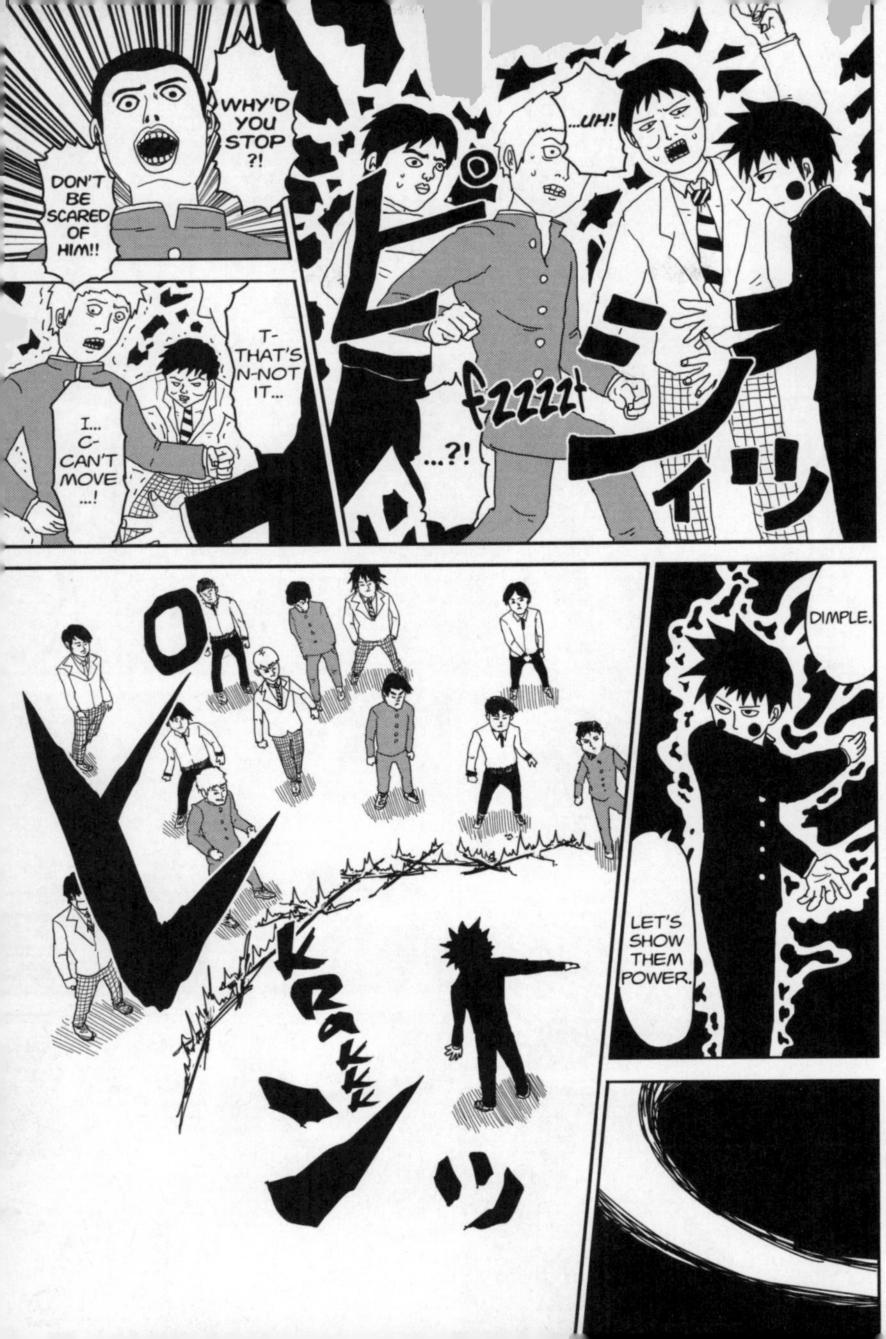
...UH!
fzzzzt
...?!
WHY'D YOU STOP?!
DON'T BE SCARED OF HIM!!
T-THAT'S N-NOT IT...
I... C-CAN'T MOVE...!
DIMPLE.
LET'S SHOW THEM POWER.
KRAKKK

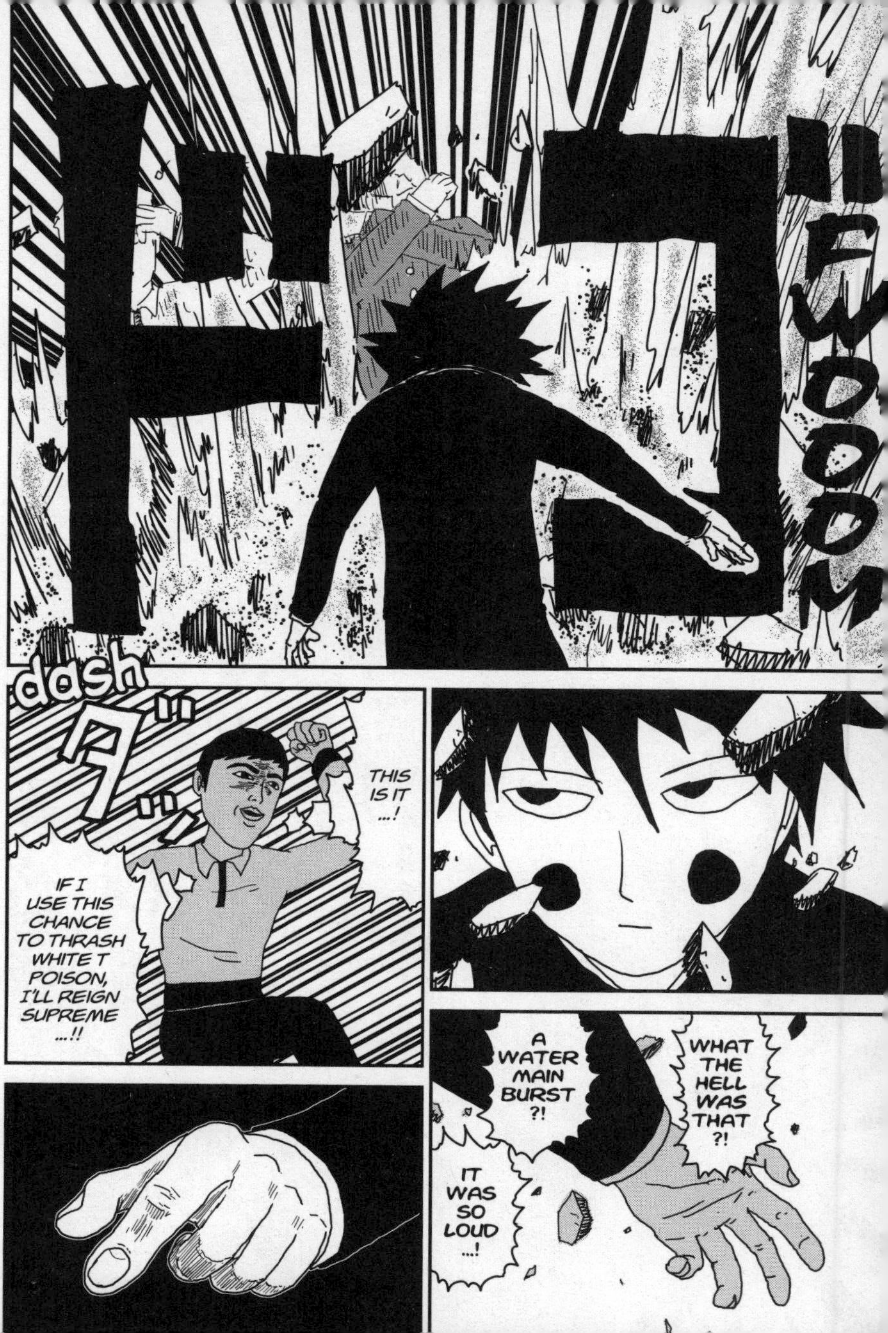
ドゴ
FWOOOM
dash
ダッ
THIS IS IT ...!
IF I USE THIS CHANCE TO THRASH WHITE T POISON, I'LL REIGN SUPREME ...!!
WHAT THE HELL WAS THAT?!
A WATER MAIN BURST?!
IT WAS SO LOUD ...!

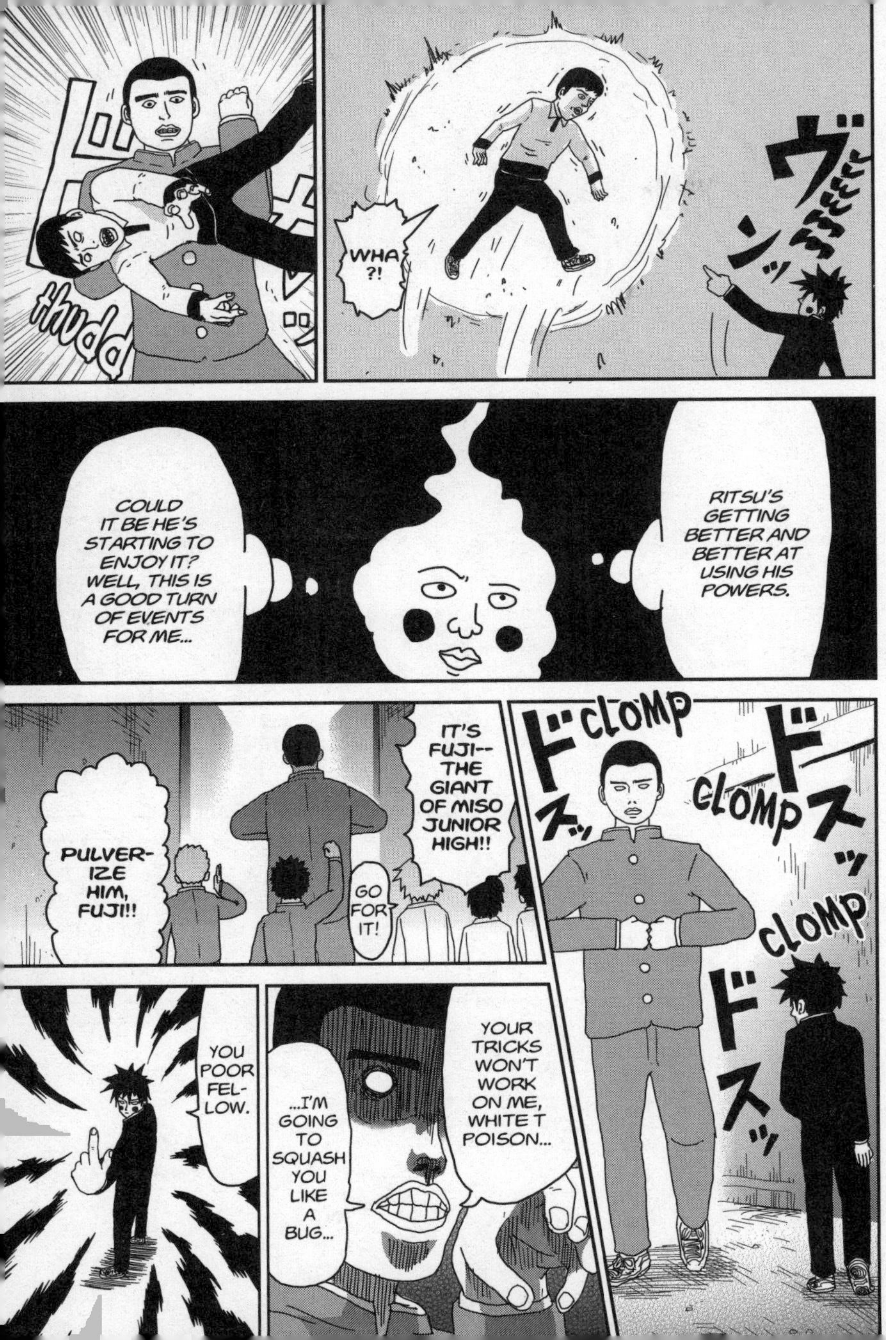
WHA ?!
thudd
RITSU'S GETTING BETTER AND BETTER AT USING HIS POWERS.
COULD IT BE HE'S STARTING TO ENJOY IT? WELL, THIS IS A GOOD TURN OF EVENTS FOR ME...
CLOMP
CLOMP
CLOMP
IT'S FUJI-- THE GIANT OF MISO JUNIOR HIGH!!
GO FOR IT!
PULVER- IZE HIM, FUJI!!
YOUR TRICKS WON'T WORK ON ME, WHITE T POISON...
...I'M GOING TO SQUASH YOU LIKE A BUG...
YOU POOR FEL- LOW.

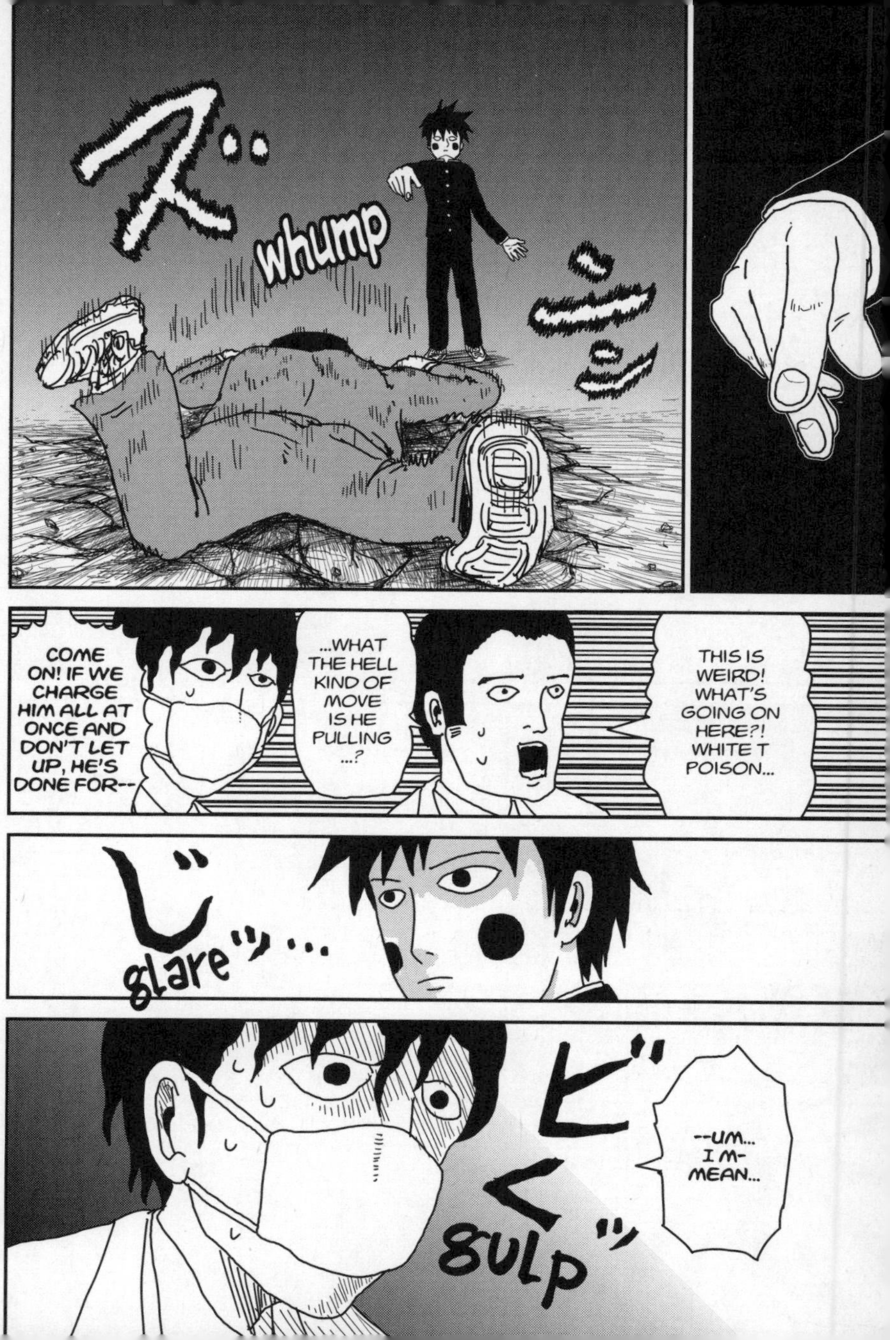
ズ..
whump
THIS IS WEIRD! WHAT'S GOING ON HERE?! WHITE T POISON...
...WHAT THE HELL KIND OF MOVE IS HE PULLING ...?
COME ON! IF WE CHARGE HIM ALL AT ONCE AND DON'T LET UP, HE'S DONE FOR--
じッ...
glare
--UM... I M-MEAN...
ビくッ
gulp

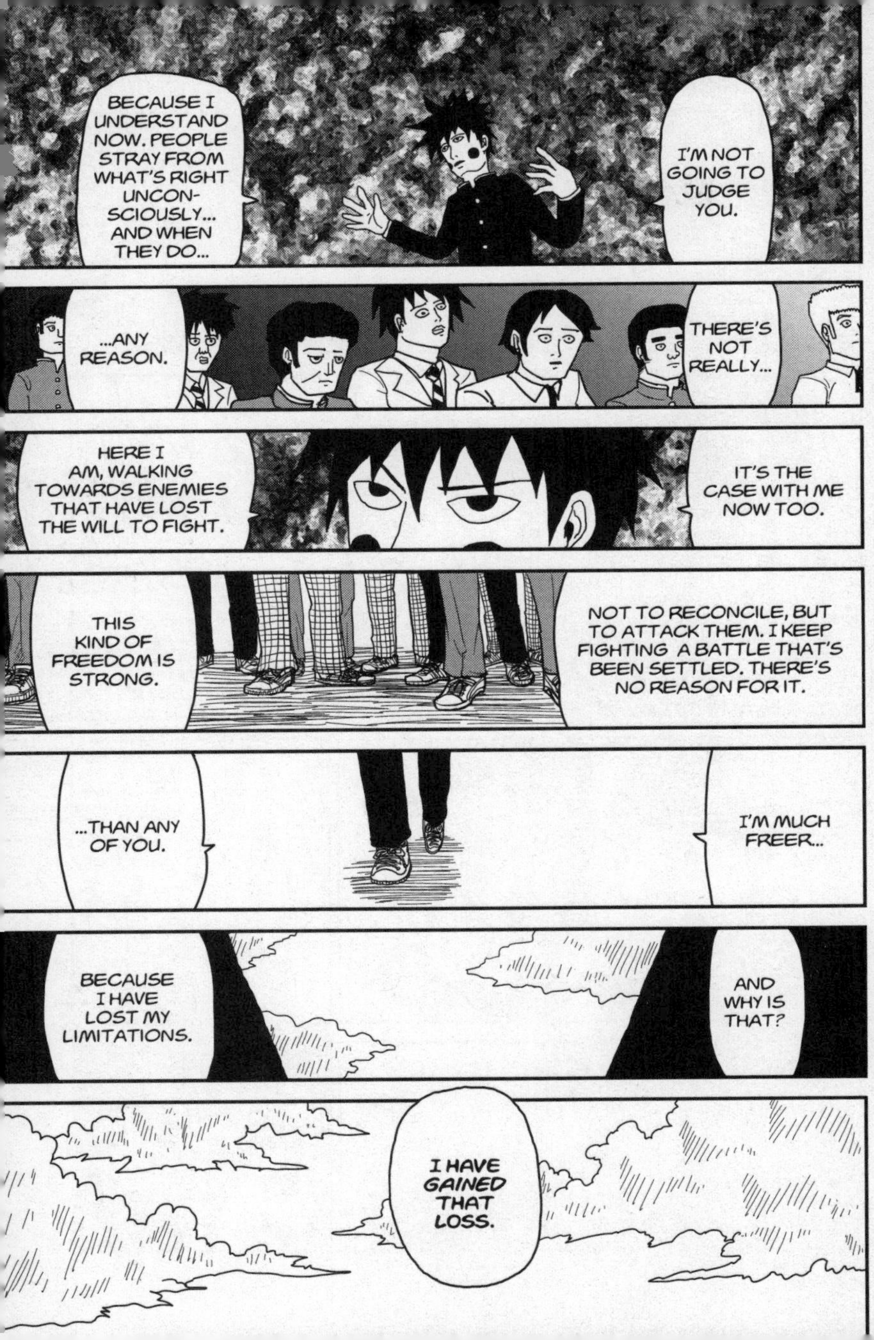
I'M NOT GOING TO JUDGE YOU.
BECAUSE I UNDERSTAND NOW. PEOPLE STRAY FROM WHAT'S RIGHT UNCONSCIOUSLY... AND WHEN THEY DO...
THERE'S NOT REALLY...
...ANY REASON.
IT'S THE CASE WITH ME NOW TOO.
HERE I AM, WALKING TOWARDS ENEMIES THAT HAVE LOST THE WILL TO FIGHT.
NOT TO RECONCILE, BUT TO ATTACK THEM. I KEEP FIGHTING A BATTLE THAT'S BEEN SETTLED. THERE'S NO REASON FOR IT.
THIS KIND OF FREEDOM IS STRONG.
I'M MUCH FREER...
...THAN ANY OF YOU.
AND WHY IS THAT?
BECAUSE I HAVE LOST MY LIMITATIONS.
I HAVE GAINED THAT LOSS.

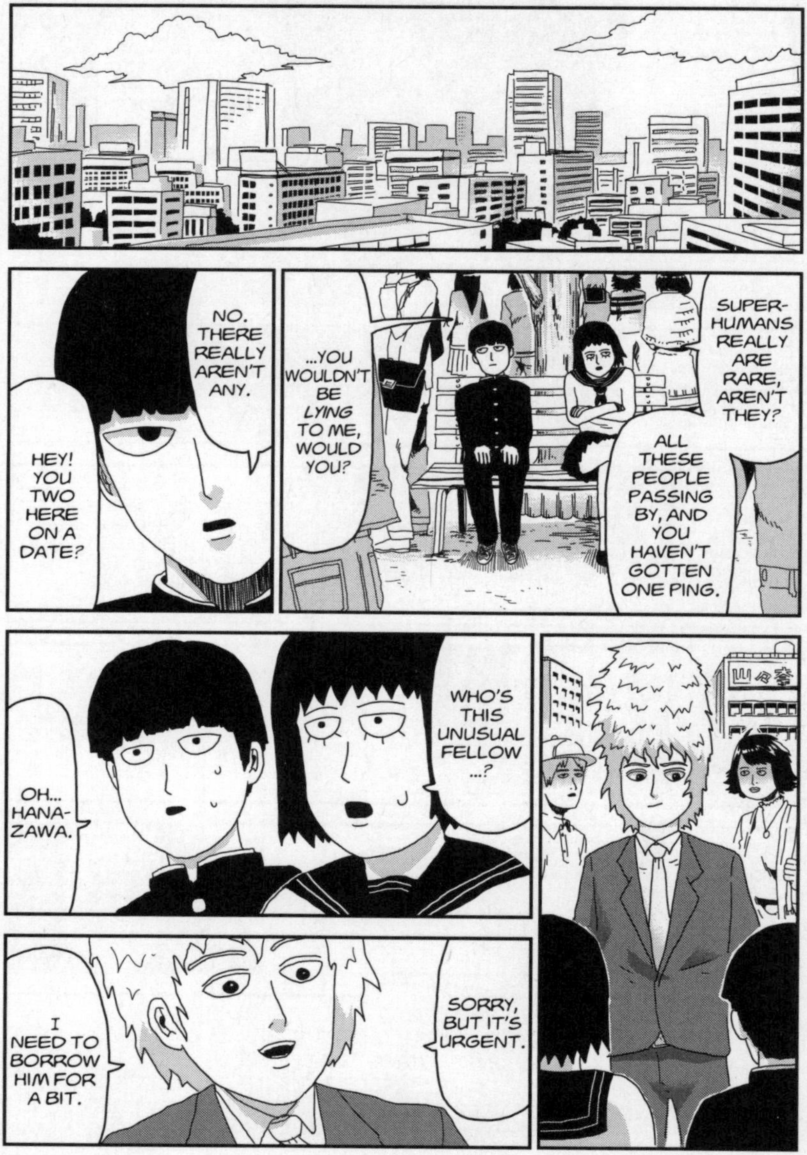
SUPER-HUMANS REALLY ARE RARE, AREN'T THEY?
ALL THESE PEOPLE PASSING BY, AND YOU HAVEN'T GOTTEN ONE PING.
...YOU WOULDN'T BE *LYING* TO ME, WOULD YOU?
NO. THERE REALLY AREN'T ANY.
HEY! YOU TWO HERE ON A DATE?
WHO'S THIS UNUSUAL FELLOW ...?
OH... HANA-ZAWA.
SORRY, BUT IT'S URGENT.
I NEED TO BORROW HIM FOR A BIT.

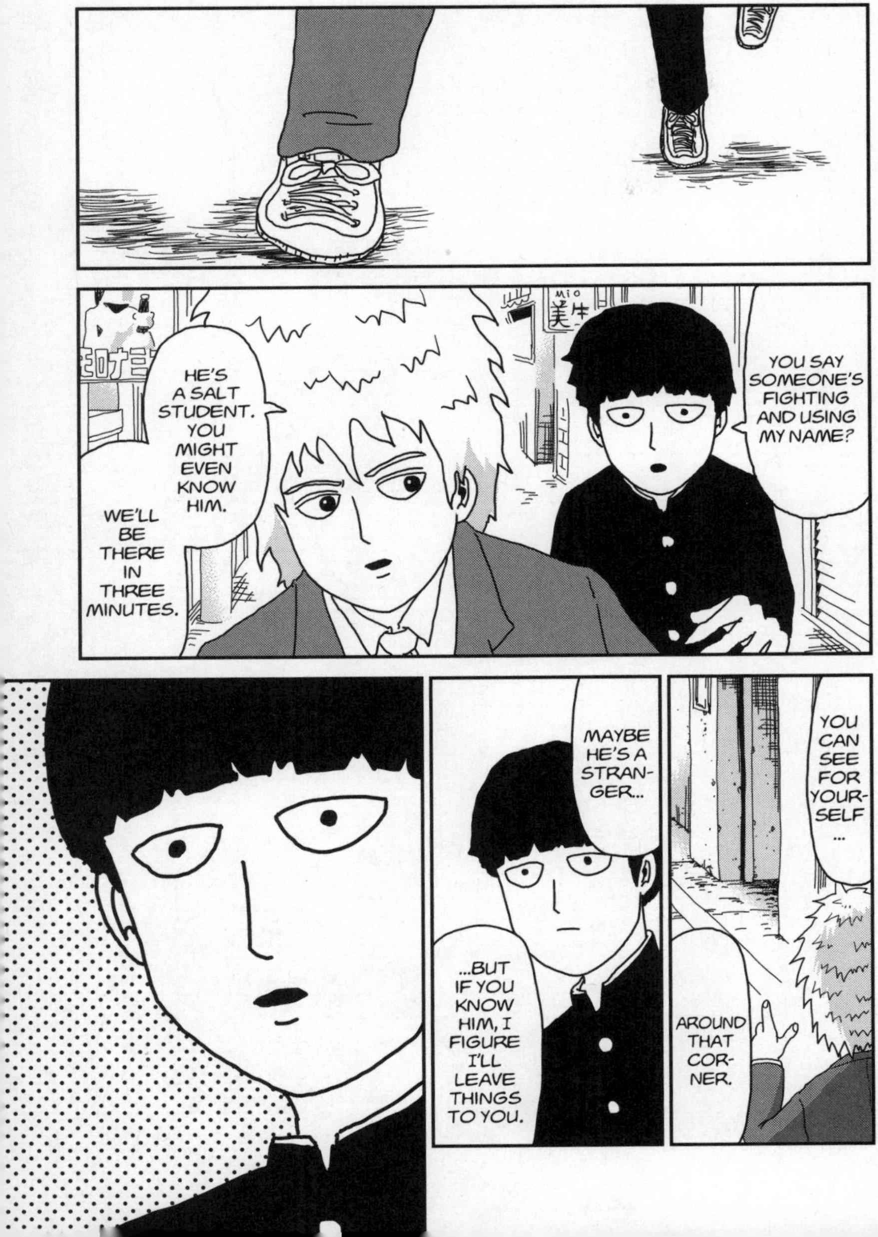
YOU SAY SOMEONE'S FIGHTING AND USING MY NAME?
HE'S A SALT STUDENT. YOU MIGHT EVEN KNOW HIM.
WE'LL BE THERE IN THREE MINUTES.
YOU CAN SEE FOR YOURSELF ...
AROUND THAT CORNER.
MAYBE HE'S A STRANGER...
...BUT IF YOU KNOW HIM, I FIGURE I'LL LEAVE THINGS TO YOU.

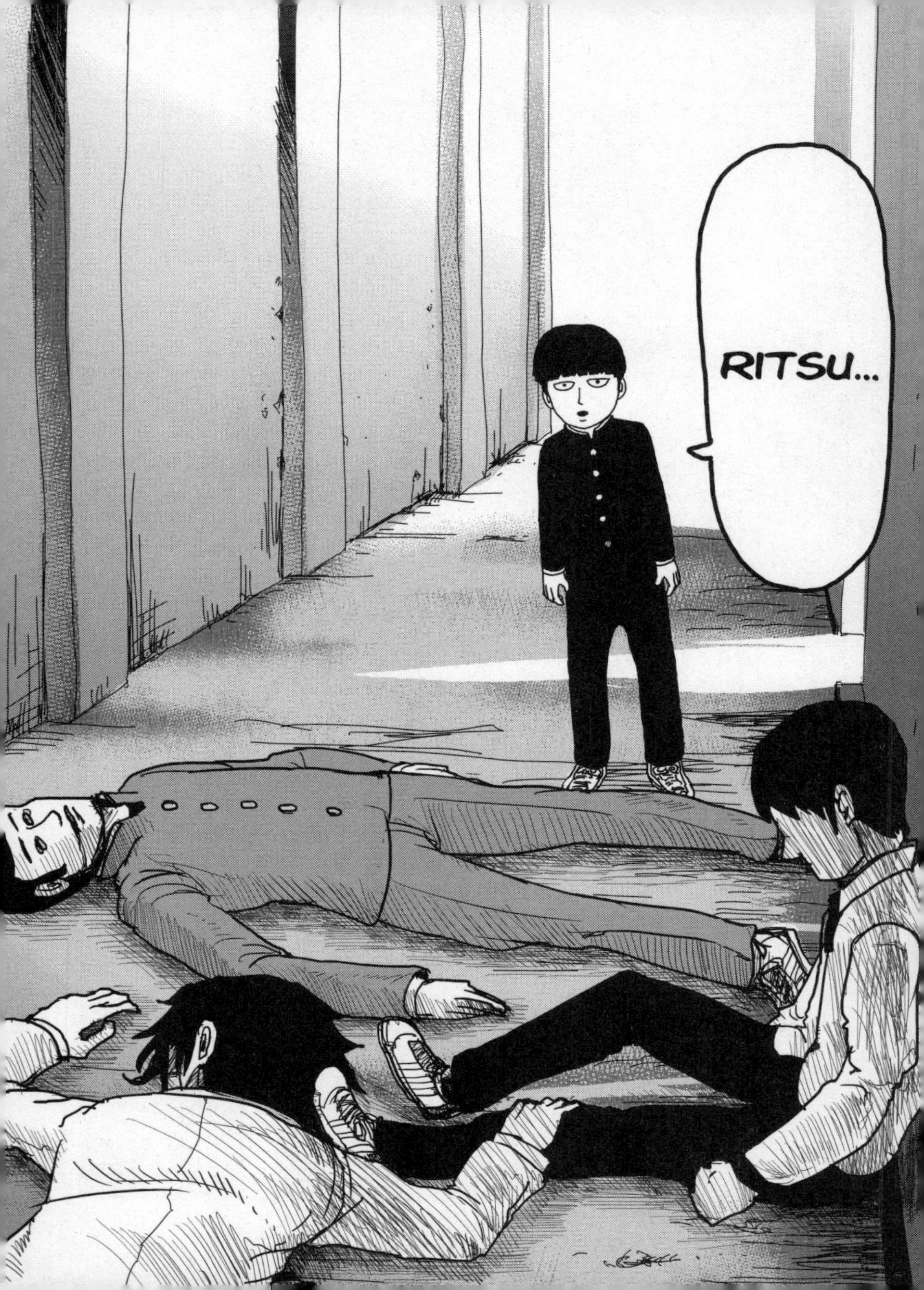
RITSU...

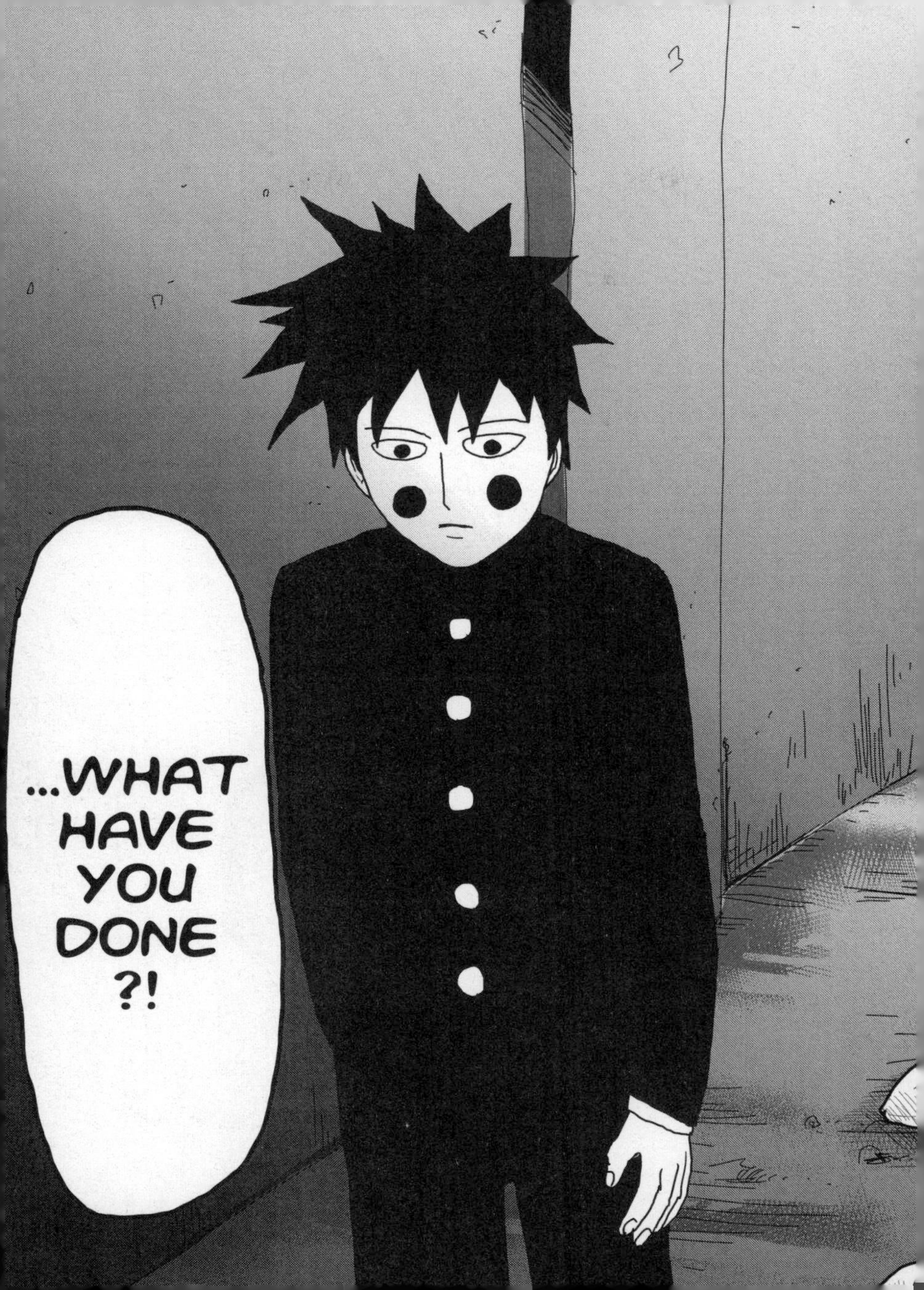
...WHAT HAVE YOU DONE ?!

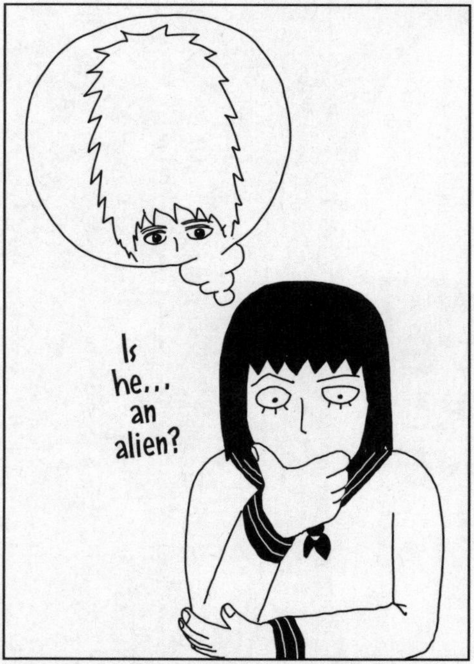
Is he... an alien?

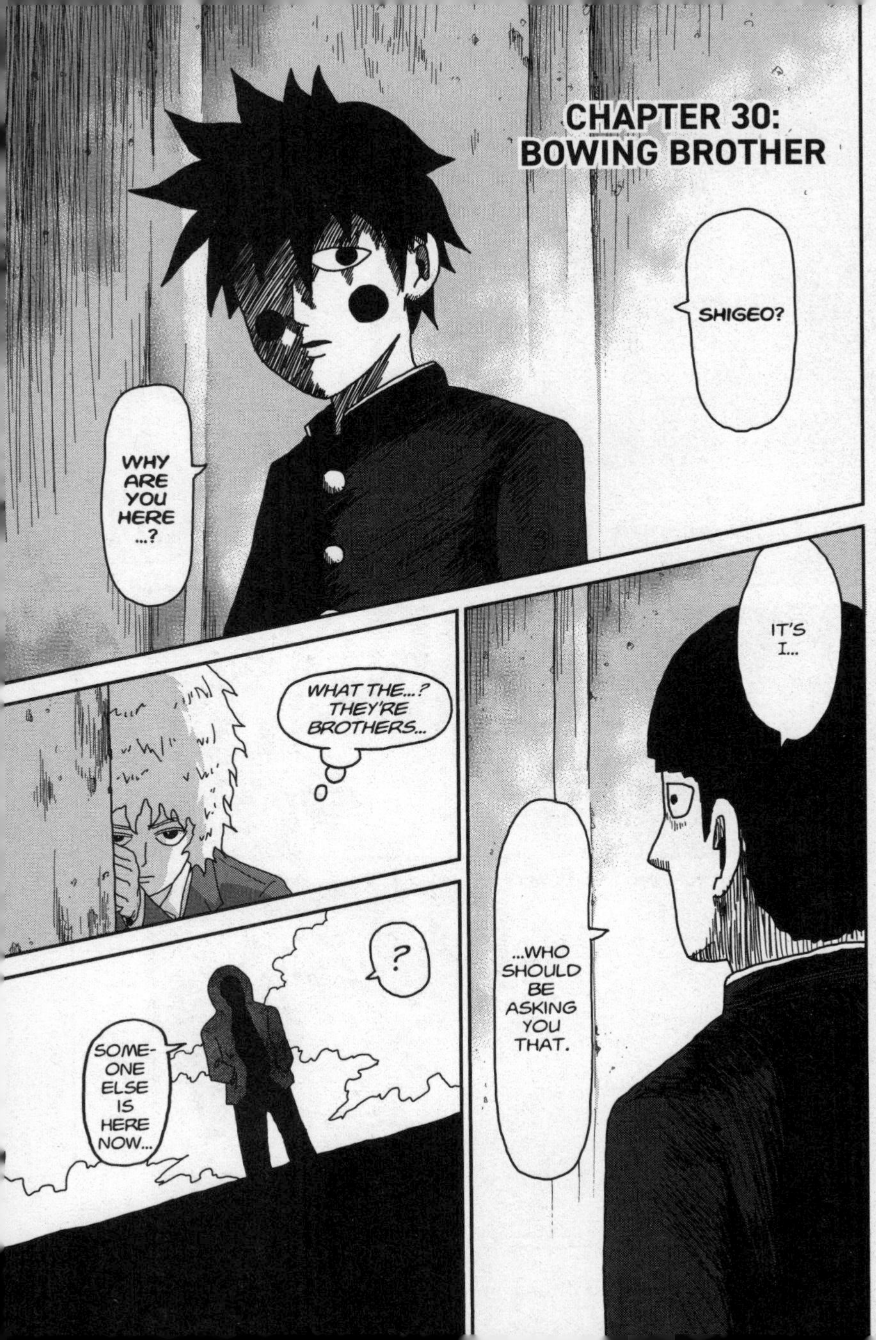
CHAPTER 30: BOWING BROTHER
SHIGEO?
WHY ARE YOU HERE ...?
IT'S I...
...WHO SHOULD BE ASKING YOU THAT.
WHAT THE...? THEY'RE BROTHERS...
?
SOME-ONE ELSE IS HERE NOW...

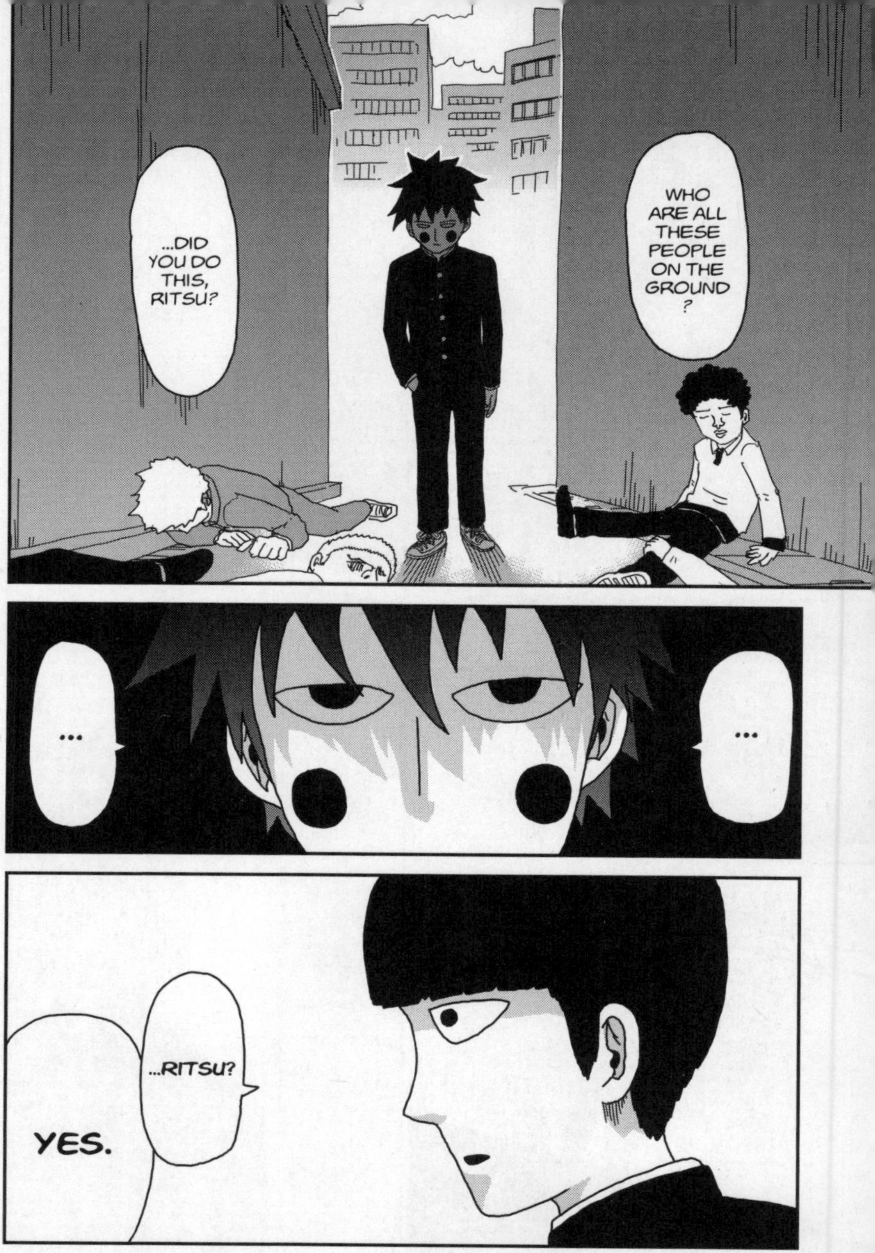
WHO ARE ALL THESE PEOPLE ON THE GROUND?
...DID YOU DO THIS, RITSU?
...
...
...RITSU?
YES.

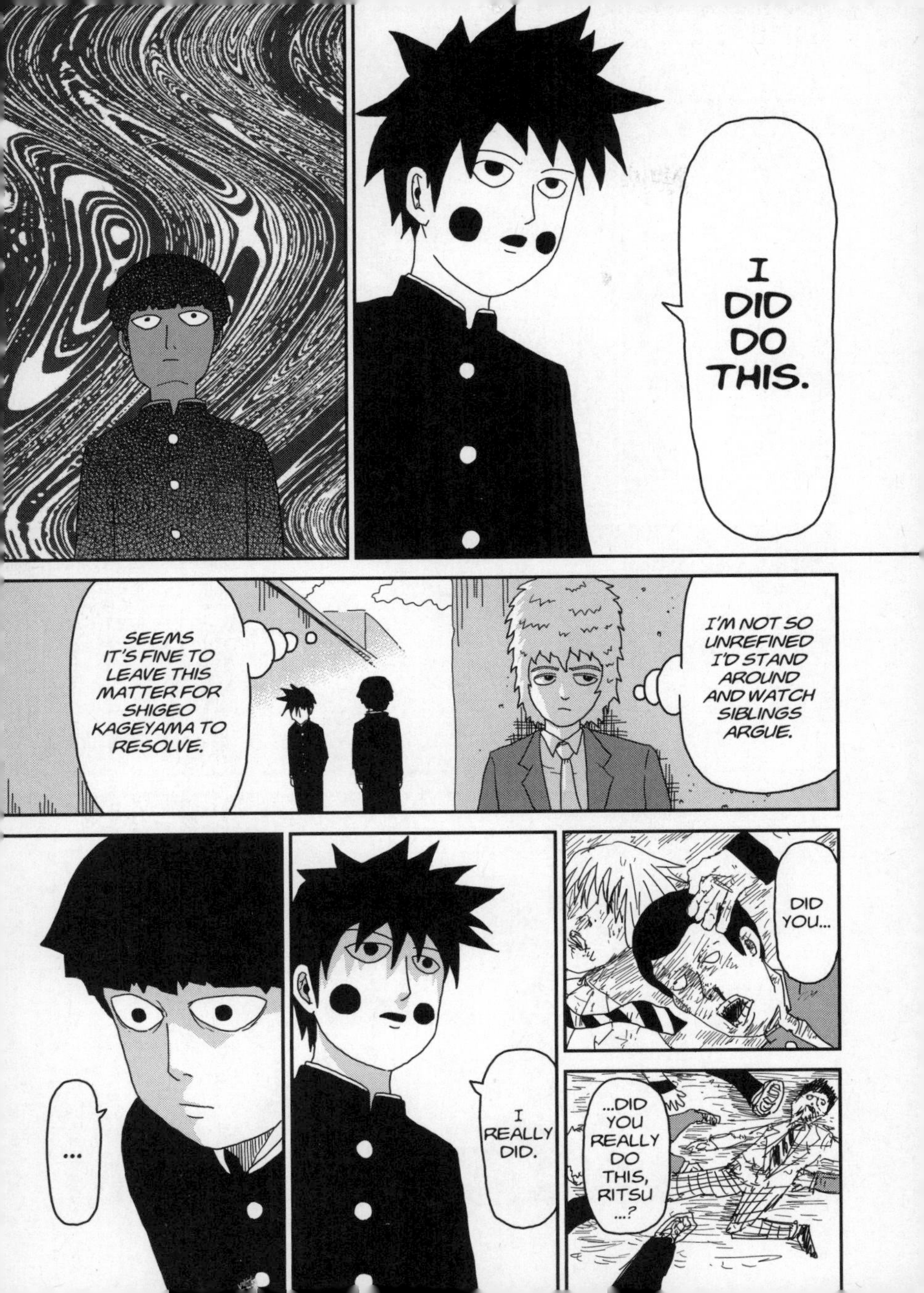
I DID DO THIS.
I'M NOT SO UNREFINED I'D STAND AROUND AND WATCH SIBLINGS ARGUE.
SEEMS IT'S FINE TO LEAVE THIS MATTER FOR SHIGEO KAGEYAMA TO RESOLVE.
DID YOU...
...DID YOU REALLY DO THIS, RITSU ...?
I REALLY DID.
...

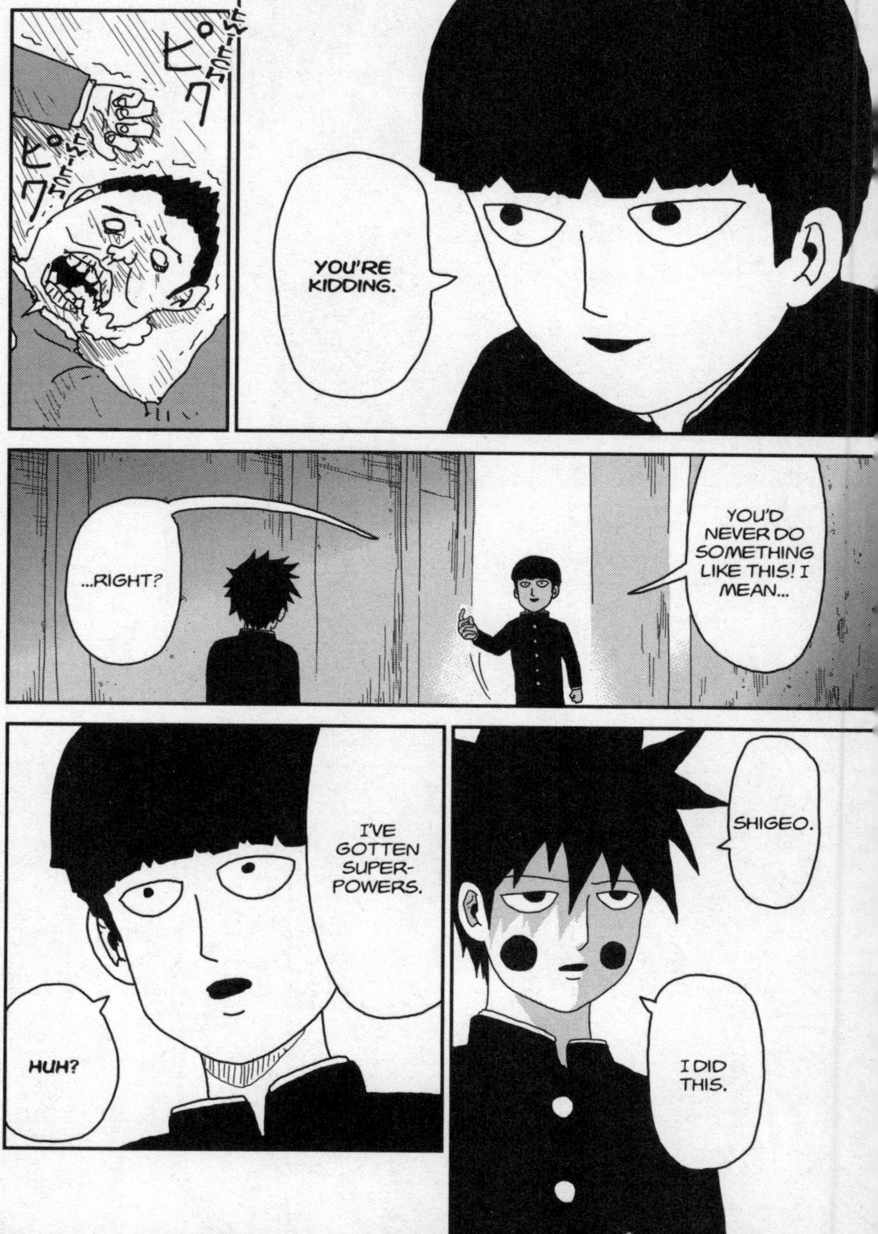
YOU'RE KIDDING.
ピク
TWITCH
ピク
TWITCH
YOU'D NEVER DO SOMETHING LIKE THIS! I MEAN...
...RIGHT?
SHIGEO.
I DID THIS.
I'VE GOTTEN SUPER-POWERS.
HUH?

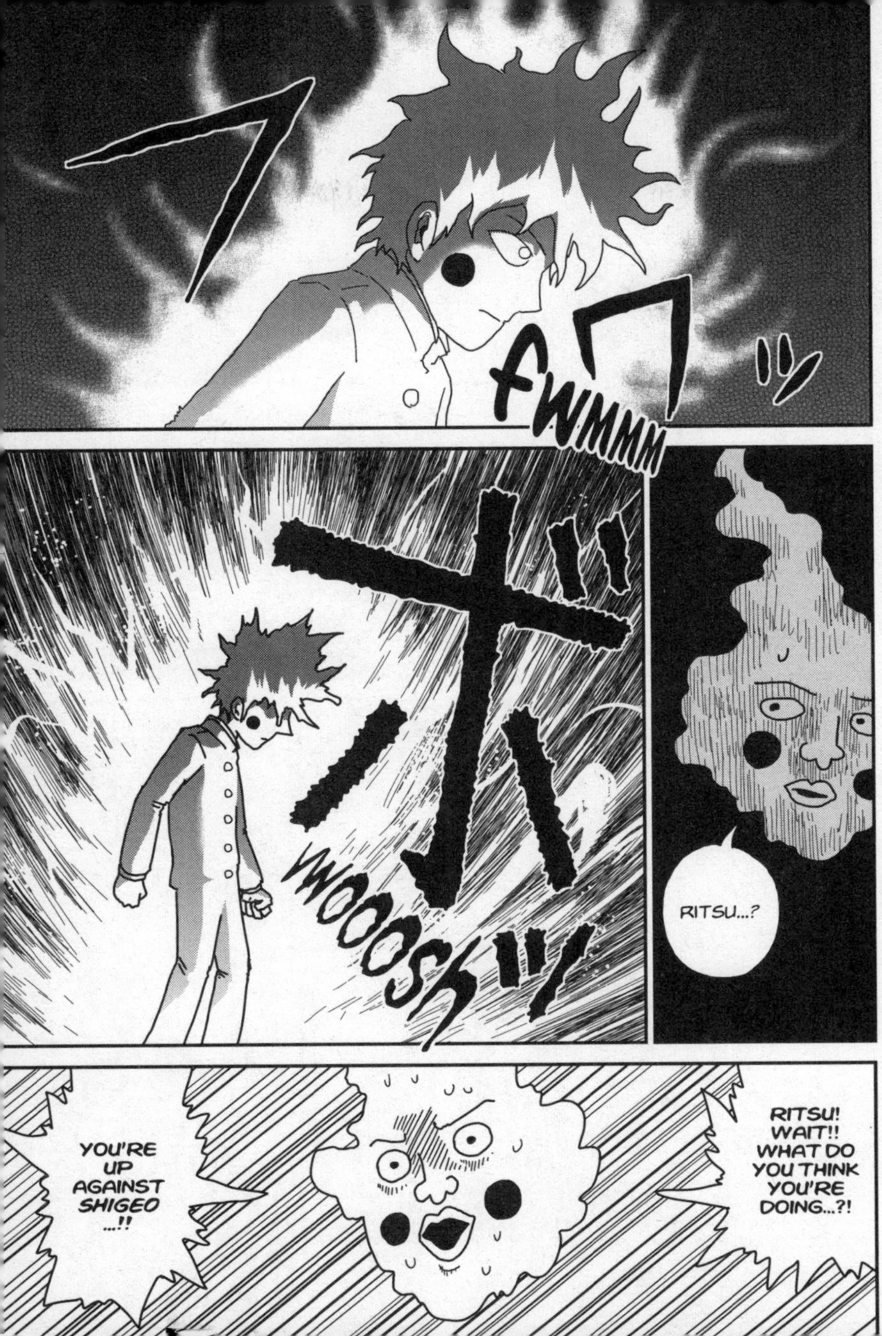
FWMMM
RITSU...?
WOOOSH
RITSU! WAIT!! WHAT DO YOU THINK YOU'RE DOING...?!
YOU'RE UP AGAINST SHIGEO ...!!

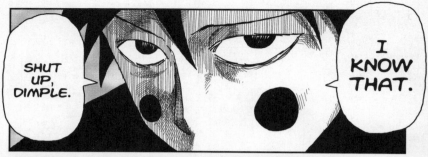

I KNOW THAT.
SHUT UP, DIMPLE.
CRAP...!
HE'S DRUNK WITH POWER!
THIS IS WHY I HATE KIDS!!
WELL, I'M NOT HANGING AROUND FOR A LOSING BATTLE! YOU CAN SETTLE THIS ON YOUR OWN!
ZZZMMM
DIMPLE?
HOW IS...?!
IT'S FINE.
I'VE GOT THE FEEL OF MY POWERS NOW.

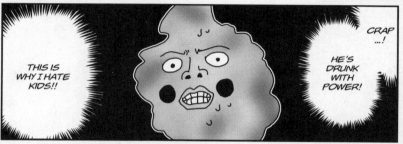

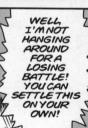

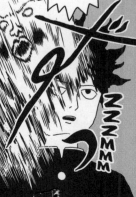

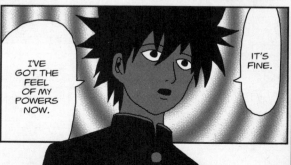

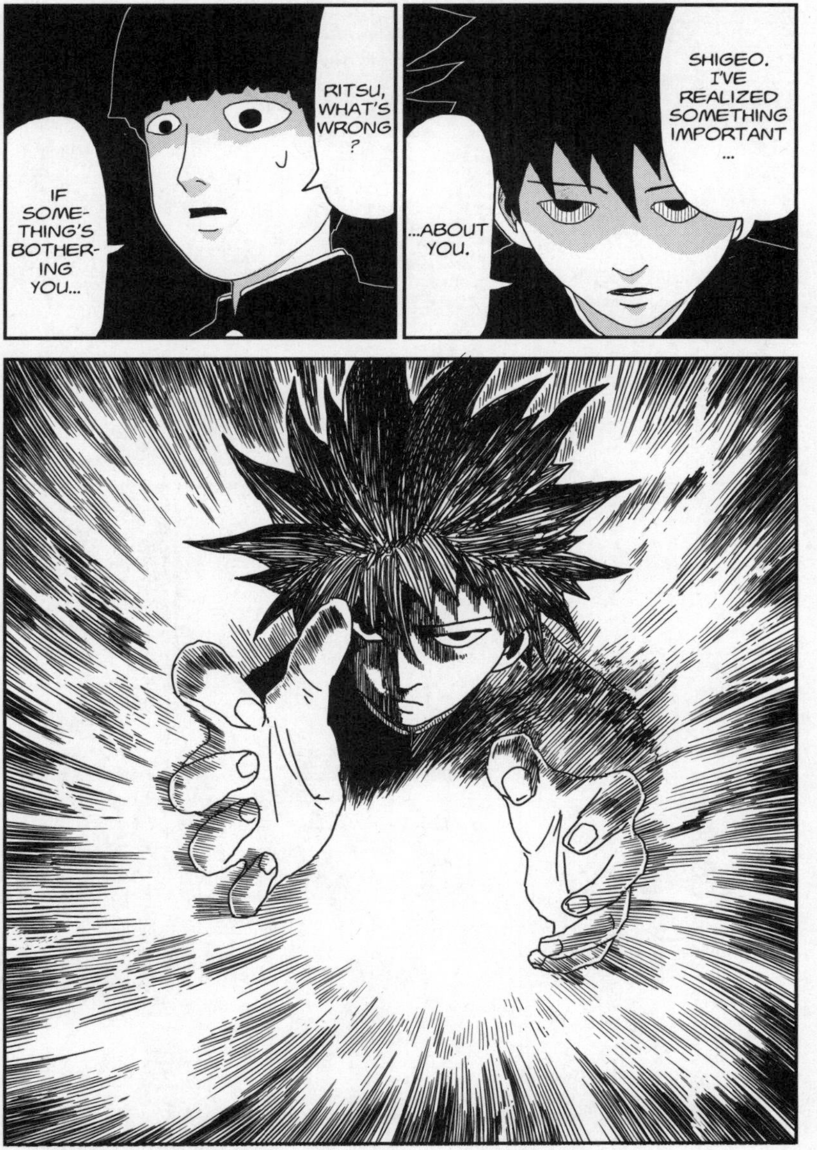
SHIGEO. I'VE REALIZED SOMETHING IMPORTANT...
...ABOUT YOU.
RITSU, WHAT'S WRONG?
IF SOMETHING'S BOTHERING YOU...

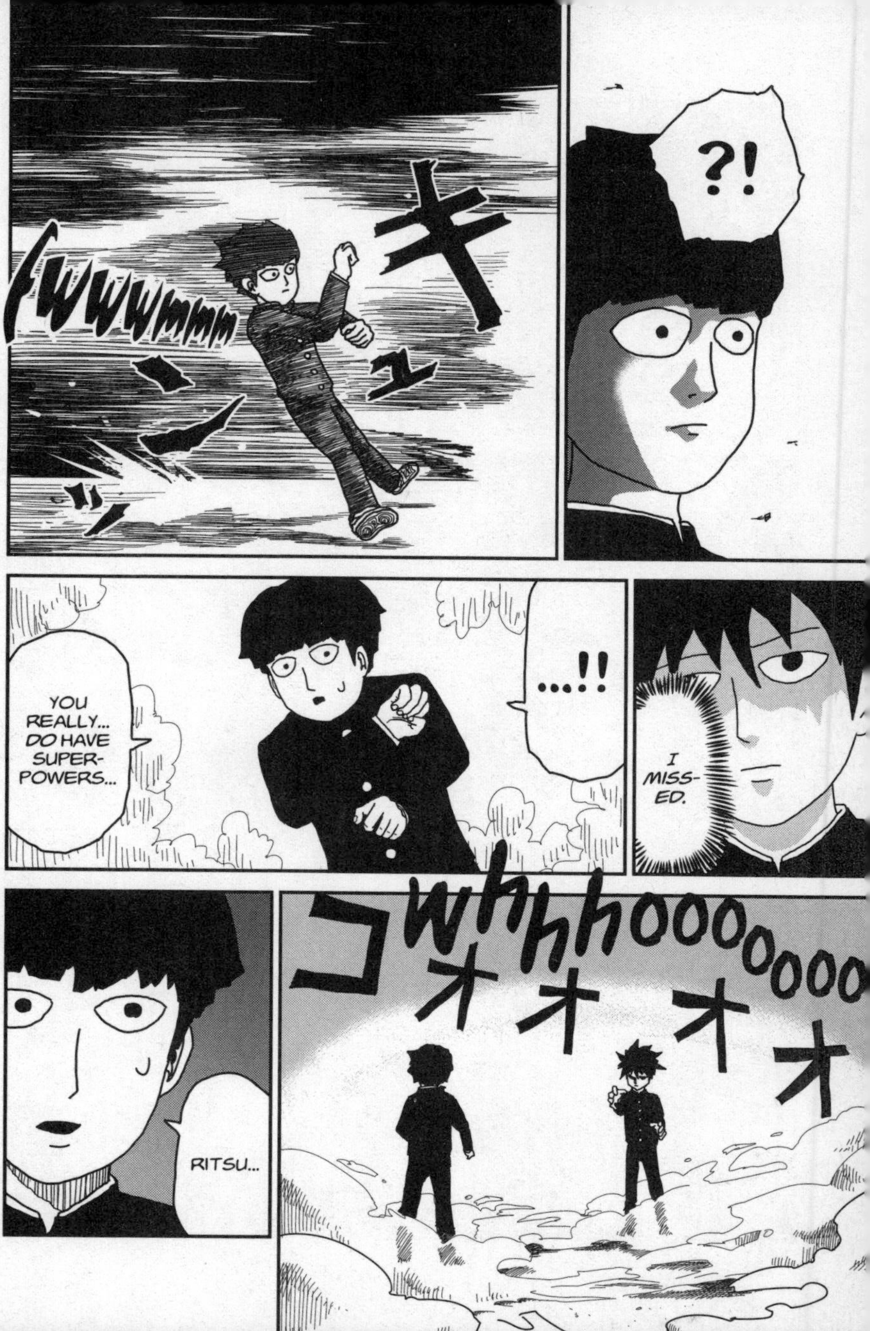
?!
fwwwmmm
キ
I MISS-ED.
...!!
YOU REALLY... DO HAVE SUPER-POWERS...
whhhooooooo
コオオオオ
RITSU...

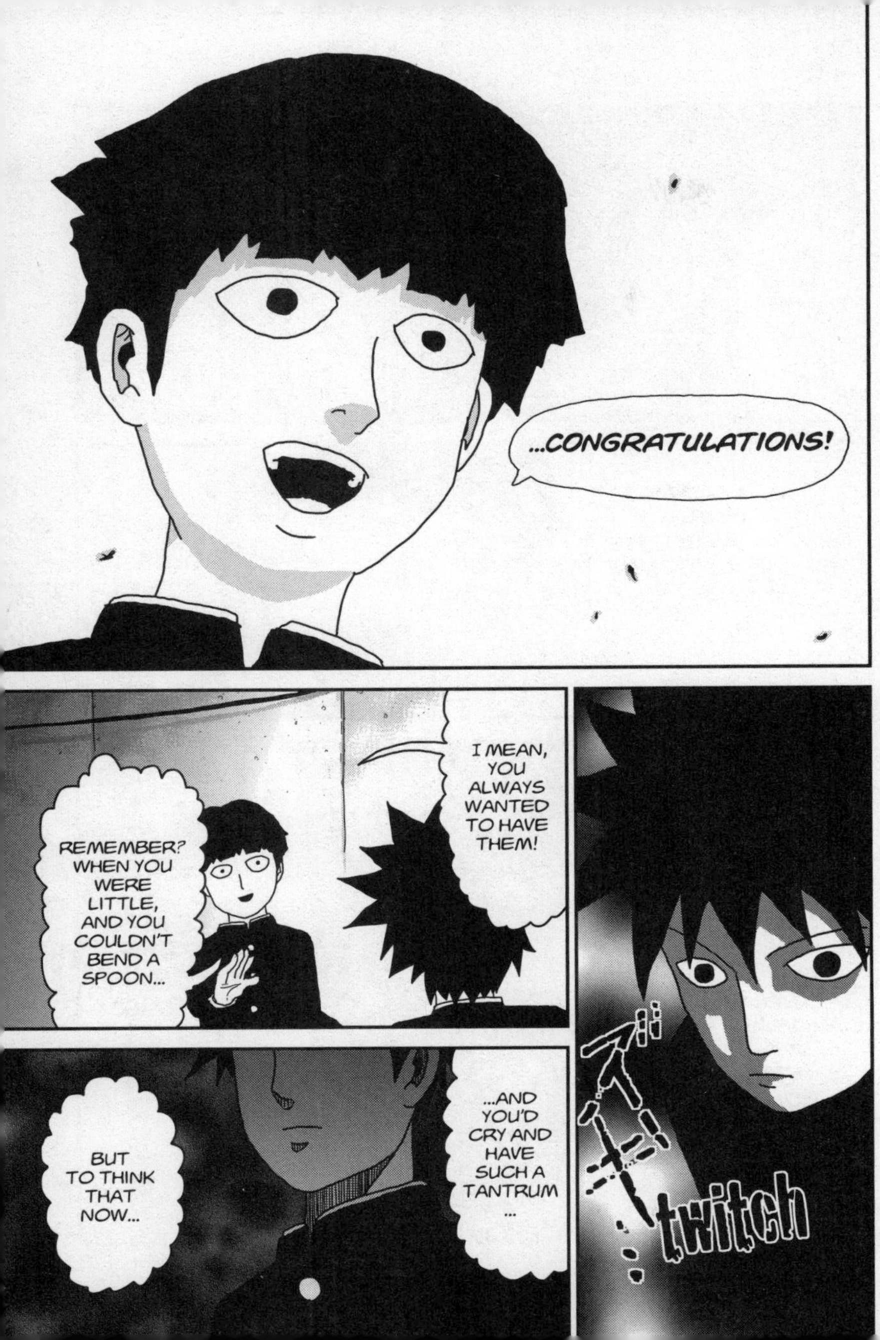
...CONGRATULATIONS!
twitch
I MEAN, YOU ALWAYS WANTED TO HAVE THEM!
REMEMBER? WHEN YOU WERE LITTLE, AND YOU COULDN'T BEND A SPOON...
...AND YOU'D CRY AND HAVE SUCH A TANTRUM ...
BUT TO THINK THAT NOW...

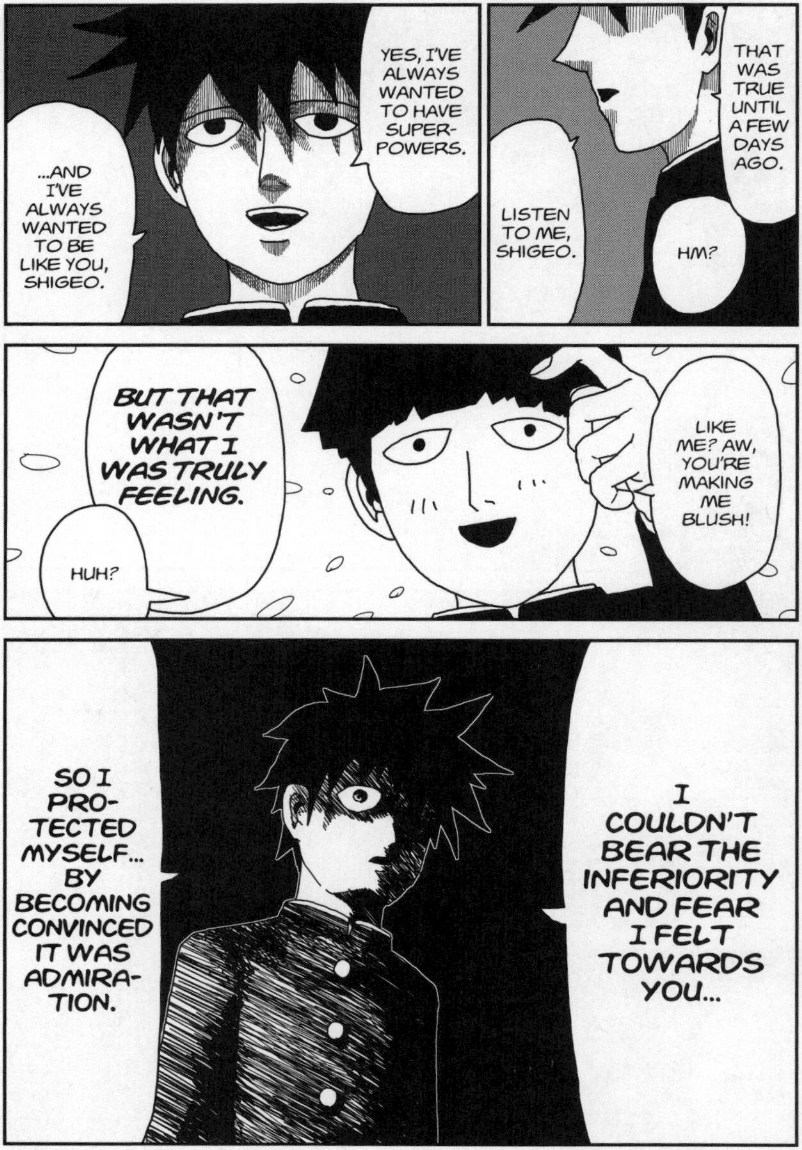
THAT WAS TRUE UNTIL A FEW DAYS AGO.
LISTEN TO ME, SHIGEO.
HM?
YES, I'VE ALWAYS WANTED TO HAVE SUPER-POWERS.
...AND I'VE ALWAYS WANTED TO BE LIKE YOU, SHIGEO.
LIKE ME? AW, YOU'RE MAKING ME BLUSH!
BUT THAT WASN'T WHAT I WAS TRULY FEELING.
HUH?
I COULDN'T BEAR THE INFERIORITY AND FEAR I FELT TOWARDS YOU...
SO I PRO-TECTED MYSELF... BY BECOMING CONVINCED IT WAS ADMIRA-TION.

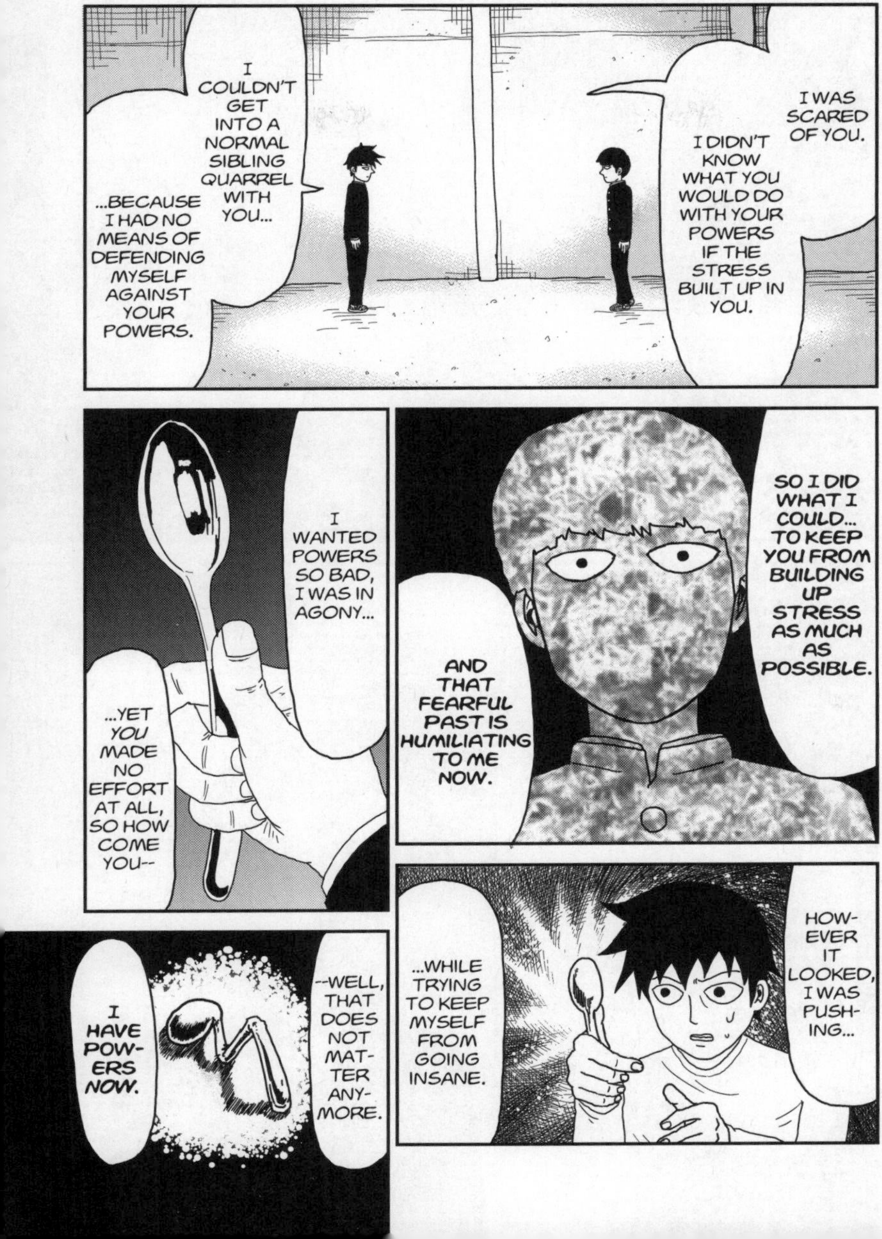
I WAS SCARED OF YOU.
I DIDN'T KNOW WHAT YOU WOULD DO WITH YOUR POWERS IF THE STRESS BUILT UP IN YOU.
I COULDN'T GET INTO A NORMAL SIBLING QUARREL WITH YOU...
...BECAUSE I HAD NO MEANS OF DEFENDING MYSELF AGAINST YOUR POWERS.
SO I DID WHAT I COULD... TO KEEP YOU FROM BUILDING UP STRESS AS MUCH AS POSSIBLE.
AND THAT FEARFUL PAST IS HUMILIATING TO ME NOW.
I WANTED POWERS SO BAD, I WAS IN AGONY...
...YET *YOU* MADE NO EFFORT AT ALL, SO HOW COME YOU--
HOW-EVER IT LOOKED, I WAS PUSH-ING...
...WHILE TRYING TO KEEP MYSELF FROM GOING INSANE.
--WELL, THAT DOES NOT MAT-TER ANY-MORE.
I HAVE POW-ERS NOW.

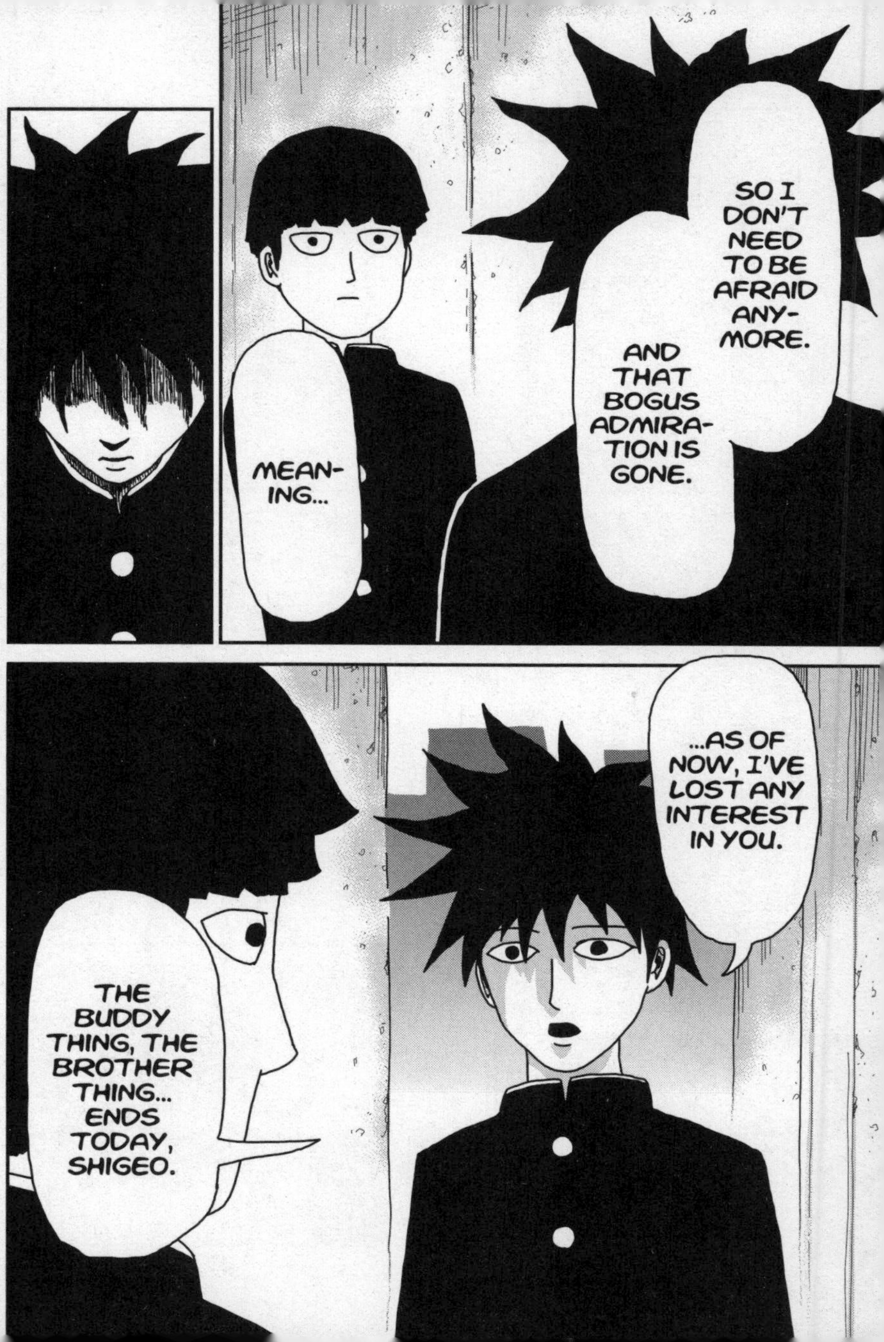
SO I DON'T NEED TO BE AFRAID ANY-MORE.
AND THAT BOGUS ADMIRA-TION IS GONE.
MEAN-ING...
...AS OF NOW, I'VE LOST ANY INTEREST IN YOU.
THE BUDDY THING, THE BROTHER THING... ENDS TODAY, SHIGEO.

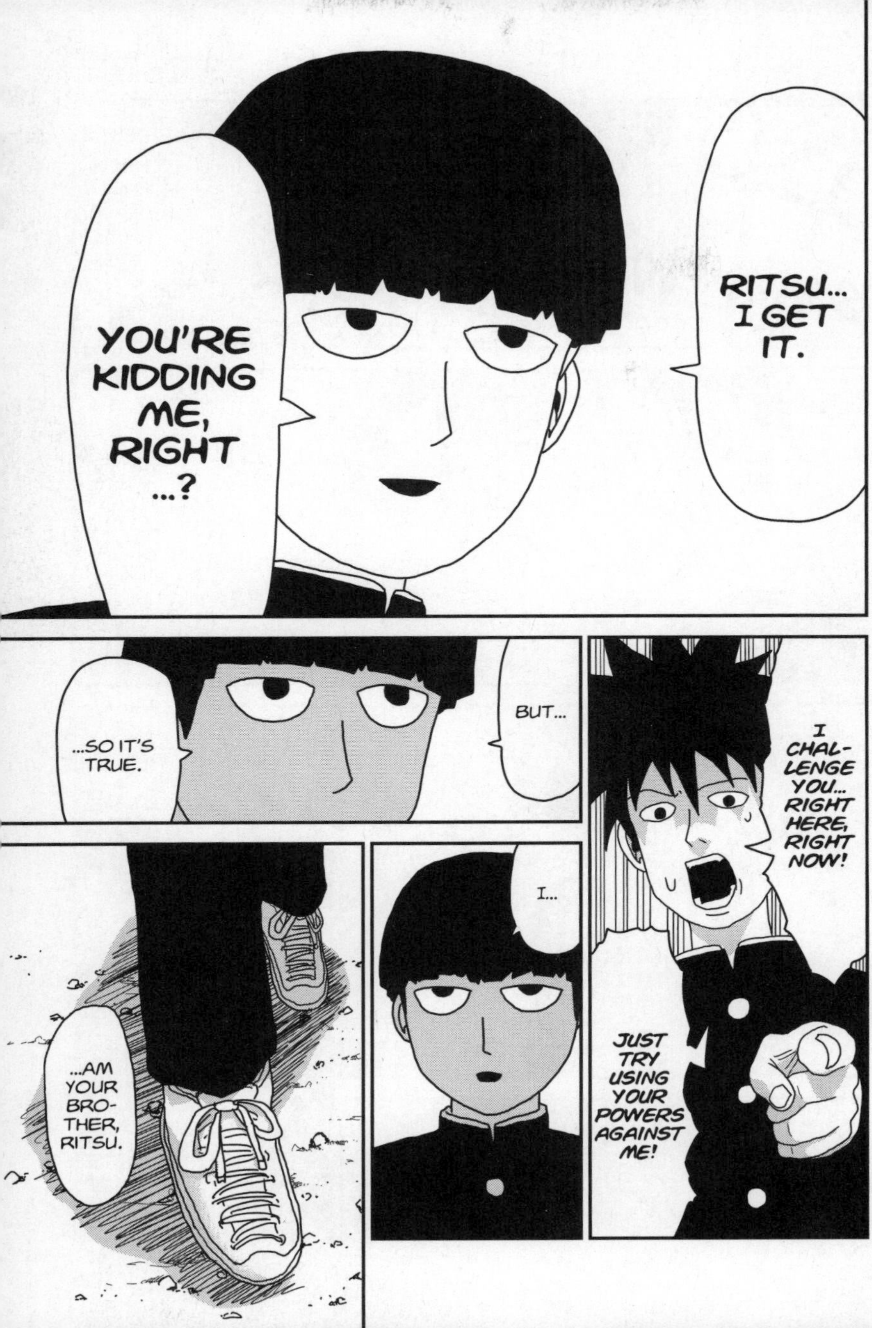
RITSU... I GET IT.
YOU'RE KIDDING ME, RIGHT ...?
I CHAL-LENGE YOU... RIGHT HERE, RIGHT NOW!
JUST TRY USING YOUR POWERS AGAINST ME!
BUT...
...SO IT'S TRUE.
I...
...AM YOUR BRO-THER, RITSU.

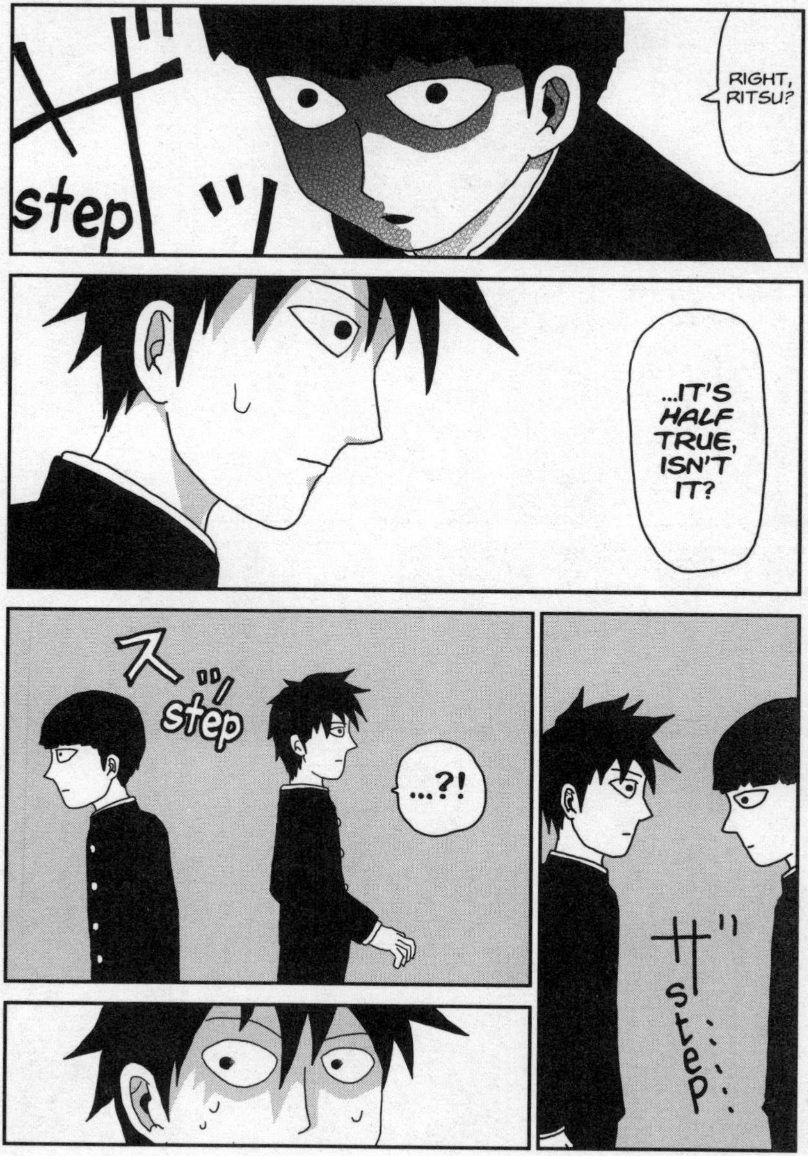
RIGHT, RITSU?
step
...IT'S *HALF* TRUE, ISN'T IT?
step....
step
...?!

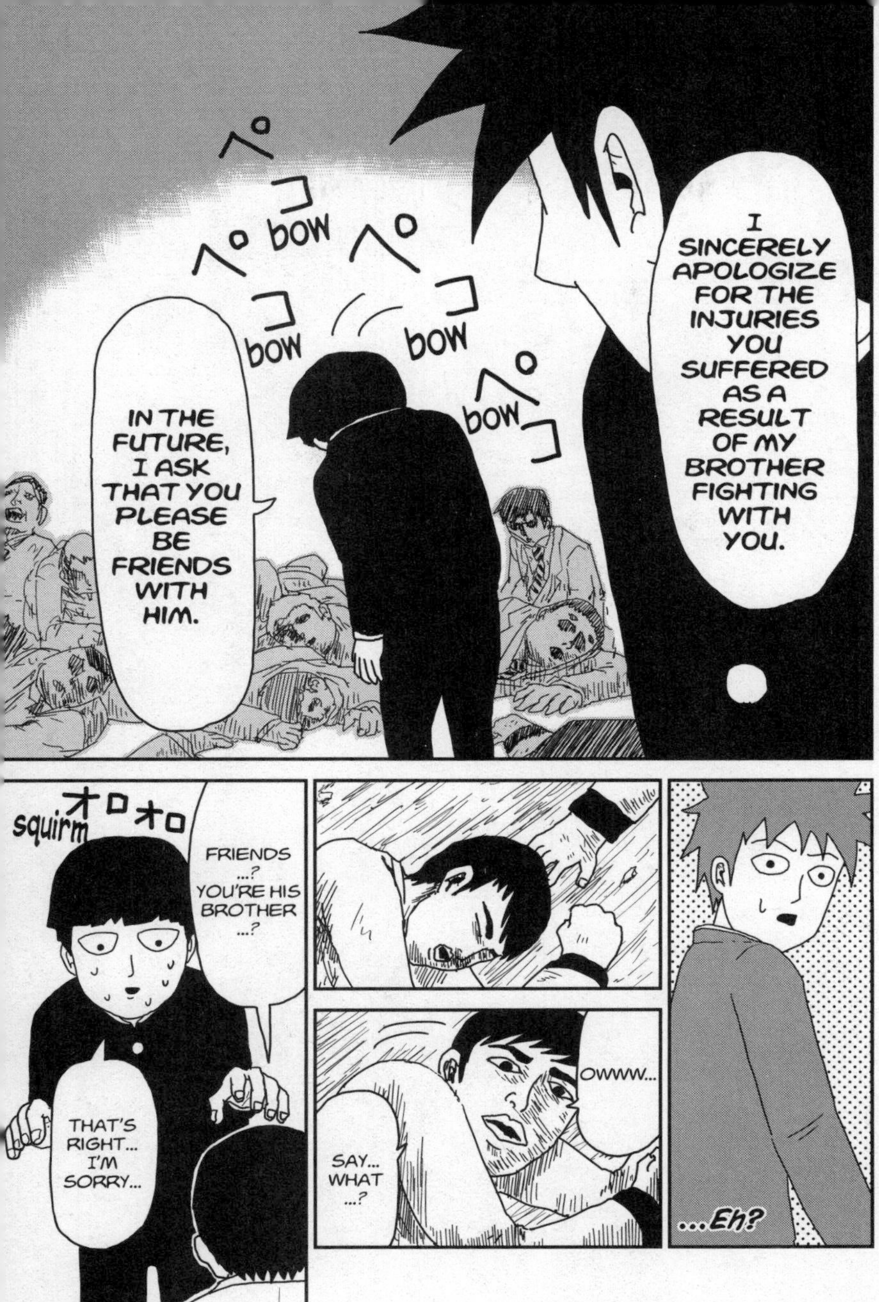
I SINCERELY APOLOGIZE FOR THE INJURIES YOU SUFFERED AS A RESULT OF MY BROTHER FIGHTING WITH YOU.
ペコ bow
ペコ bow
ペコ bow
ペコ bow
IN THE FUTURE, I ASK THAT YOU PLEASE BE FRIENDS WITH HIM.
...Eh?
OWWW...
SAY... WHAT ...?
オロオロ squirm
FRIENDS ...? YOU'RE HIS BROTHER ...?
THAT'S RIGHT... I'M SORRY...

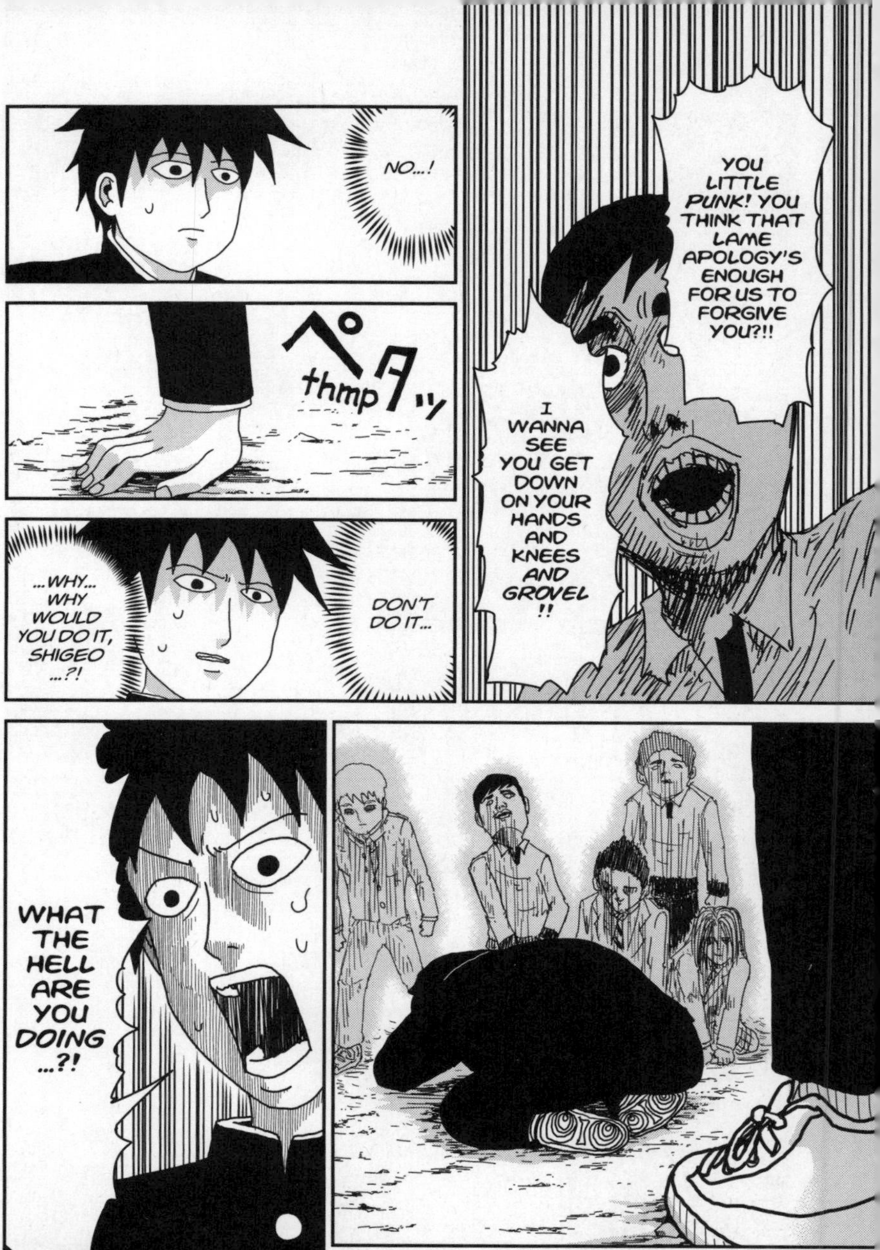
YOU LITTLE PUNK! YOU THINK THAT LAME APOLOGY'S ENOUGH FOR US TO FORGIVE YOU?!!
I WANNA SEE YOU GET DOWN ON YOUR HANDS AND KNEES AND GROVEL!!
NO...!
ペタッ
thmp
DON'T DO IT...
...WHY... WHY WOULD YOU DO IT, SHIGEO...?!
WHAT THE HELL ARE YOU DOING...?!

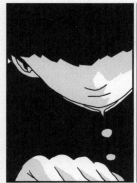

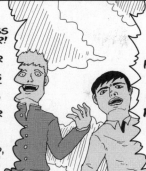

HA HA HA HA! FINALLY... SO THAT'S WHITE T POISON'S WEAKNESS...!
HIS WEAK-ASS BROTHER! NO MATTER HOW STRONG WHITE T MAY BE, IF WE GET OUR HANDS ON THIS LITTLE COWARD, WE WIN!
RITSU.
IT'S NO USE TRYING TO SHOVE ME ASIDE.
WE'RE BROTHERS.

PROGRESS TOWARD MOB'S EXPLOSION:
7%

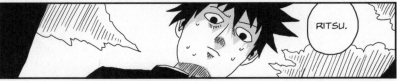

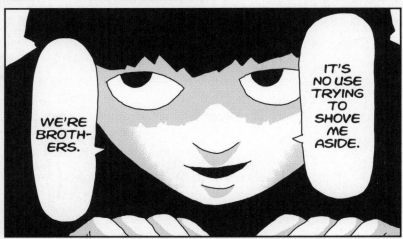

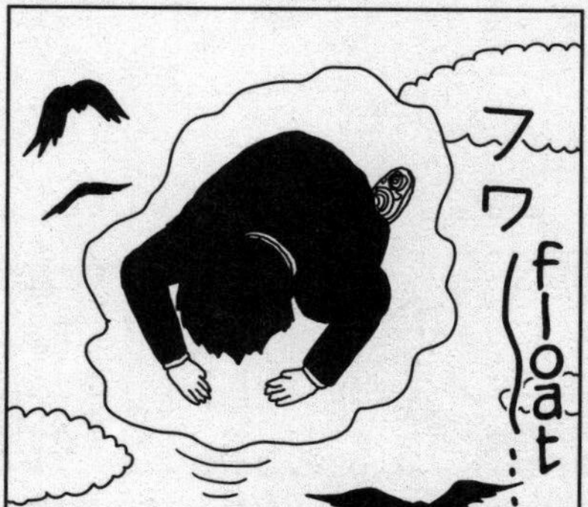
フワ…
float

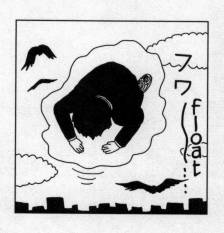

CHAPTER 31: MATURITY

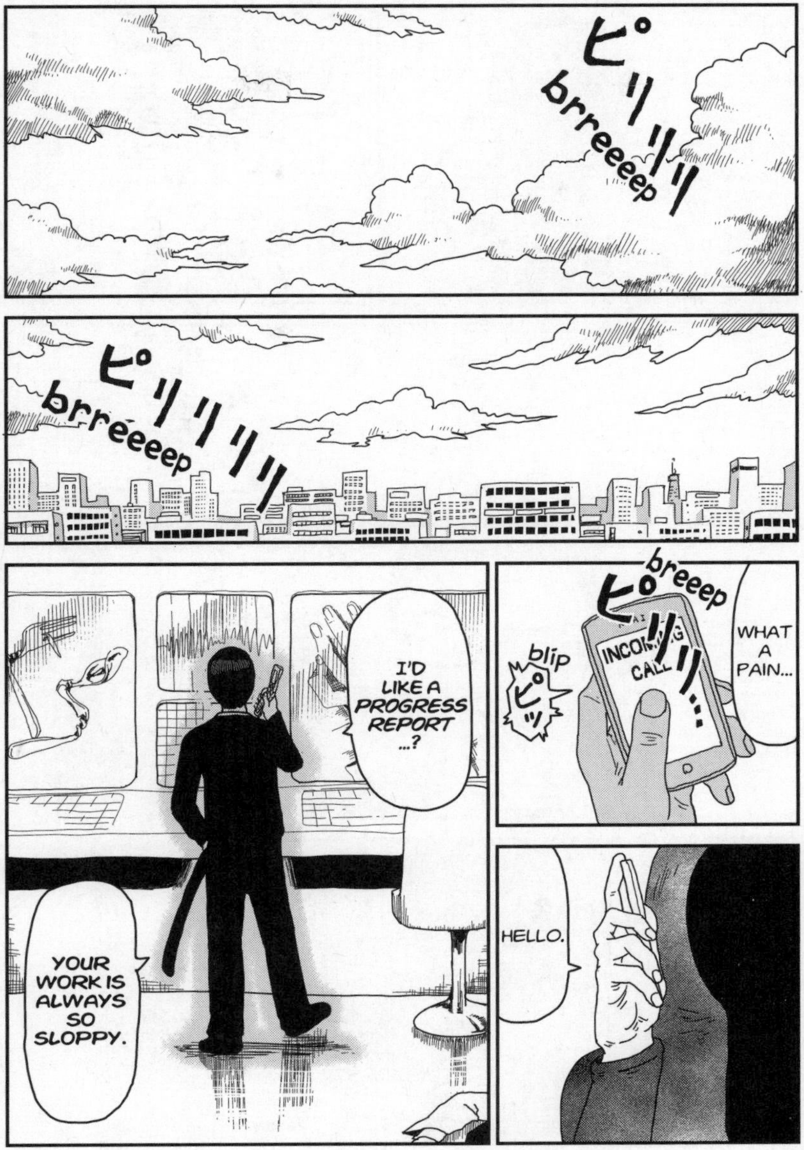
ピリリ
brreeeep
ピリリリ
brreeeep
ピリリ…
breeeep
WHAT A PAIN...
ピッ
blip
HELLO.
I'D LIKE A PROGRESS REPORT ...?
YOUR WORK IS ALWAYS SO SLOPPY.

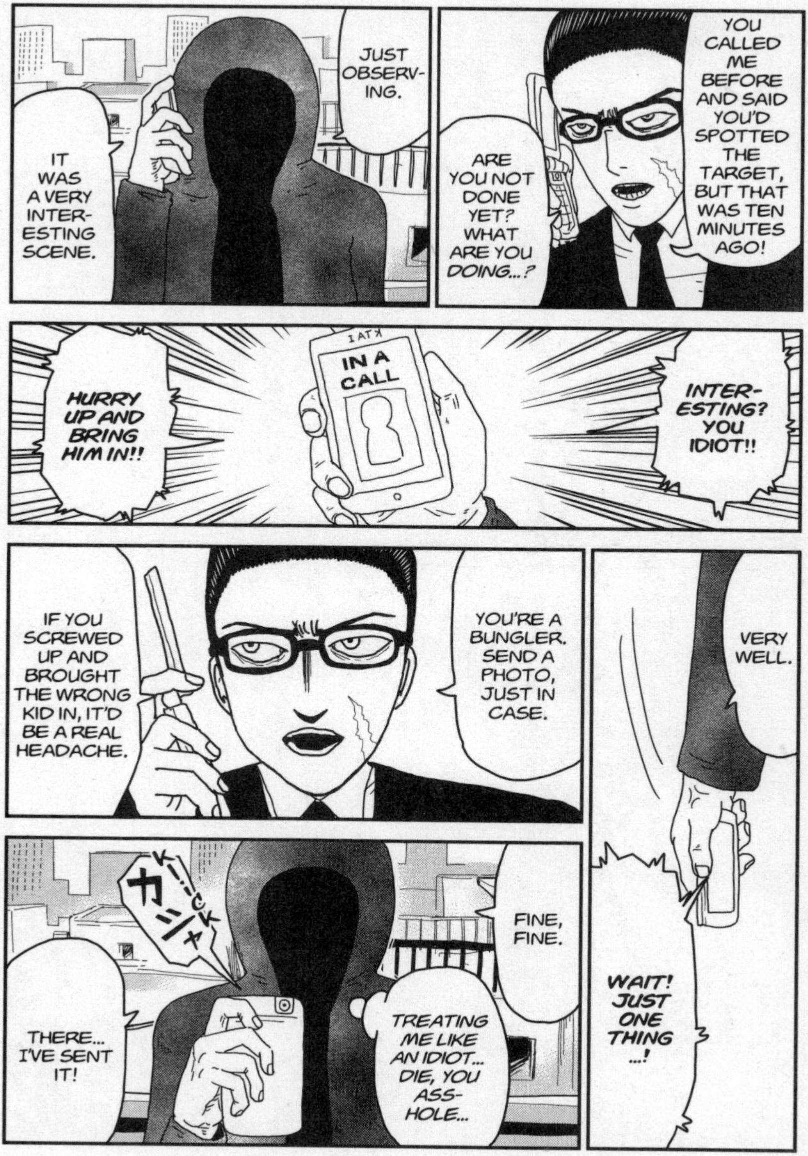
YOU CALLED ME BEFORE AND SAID YOU'D SPOTTED THE TARGET, BUT THAT WAS TEN MINUTES AGO!
ARE YOU NOT DONE YET? WHAT ARE YOU DOING...?
JUST OBSERVING.
IT WAS A VERY INTERESTING SCENE.
INTERESTING? YOU IDIOT!!
IN A CALL
HURRY UP AND BRING HIM IN!!
VERY WELL.
WAIT! JUST ONE THING...!
YOU'RE A BUNGLER. SEND A PHOTO, JUST IN CASE.
IF YOU SCREWED UP AND BROUGHT THE WRONG KID IN, IT'D BE A REAL HEADACHE.
FINE, FINE.
TREATING ME LIKE AN IDIOT... DIE, YOU ASSHOLE...
KLICK
カシャ
THERE... I'VE SENT IT!

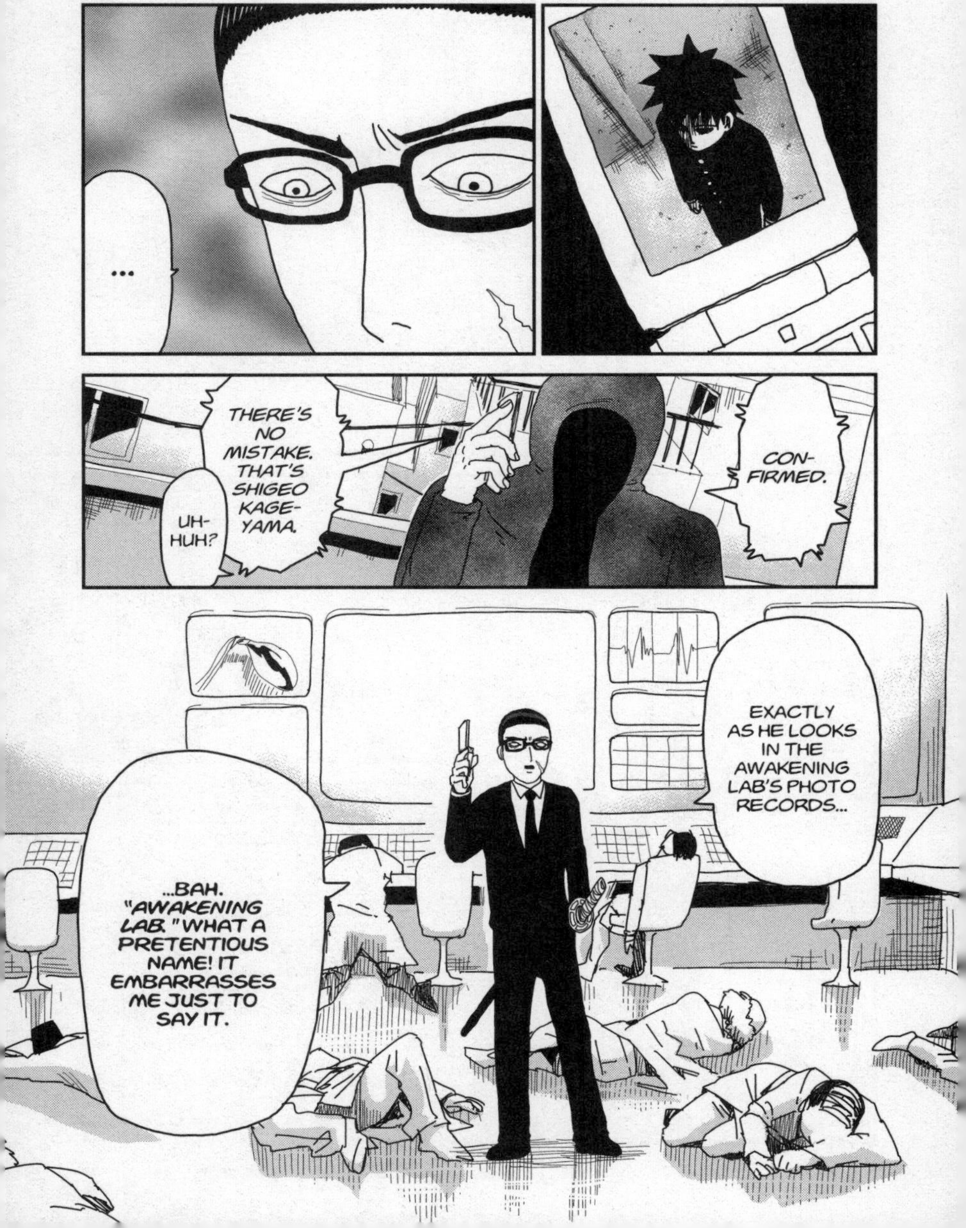
...
CON-FIRMED.
THERE'S NO MISTAKE. THAT'S SHIGEO KAGE-YAMA.
UH-HUH?
EXACTLY AS HE LOOKS IN THE AWAKENING LAB'S PHOTO RECORDS...
...BAH. "AWAKENING LAB." WHAT A PRETENTIOUS NAME! IT EMBARRASSES ME JUST TO SAY IT.

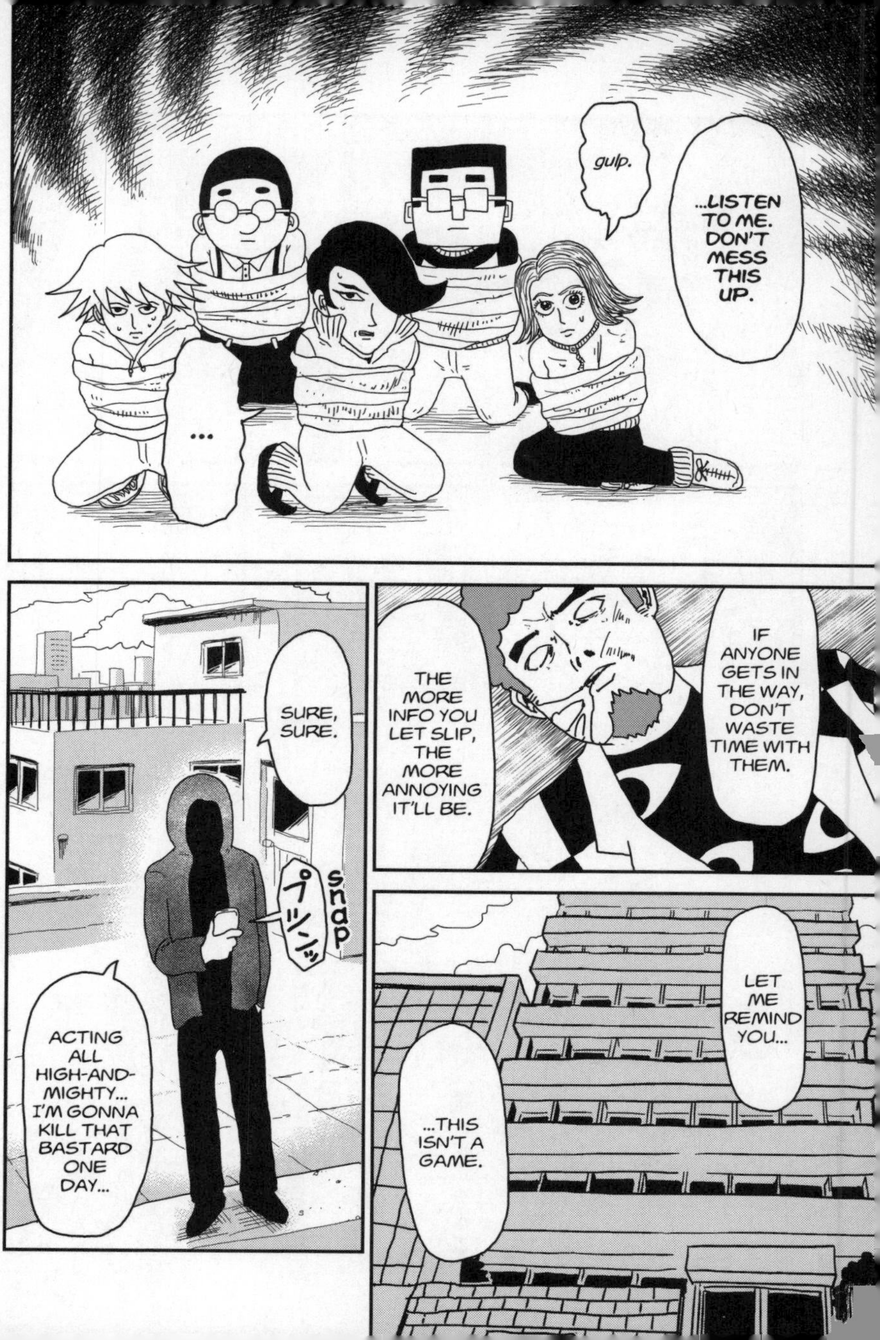
...LISTEN TO ME. DON'T MESS THIS UP.
gulp.
...
IF ANYONE GETS IN THE WAY, DON'T WASTE TIME WITH THEM.
THE MORE INFO YOU LET SLIP, THE MORE ANNOYING IT'LL BE.
LET ME REMIND YOU...
...THIS ISN'T A GAME.
SURE, SURE.
snap
ACTING ALL HIGH-AND-MIGHTY... I'M GONNA KILL THAT BASTARD ONE DAY...

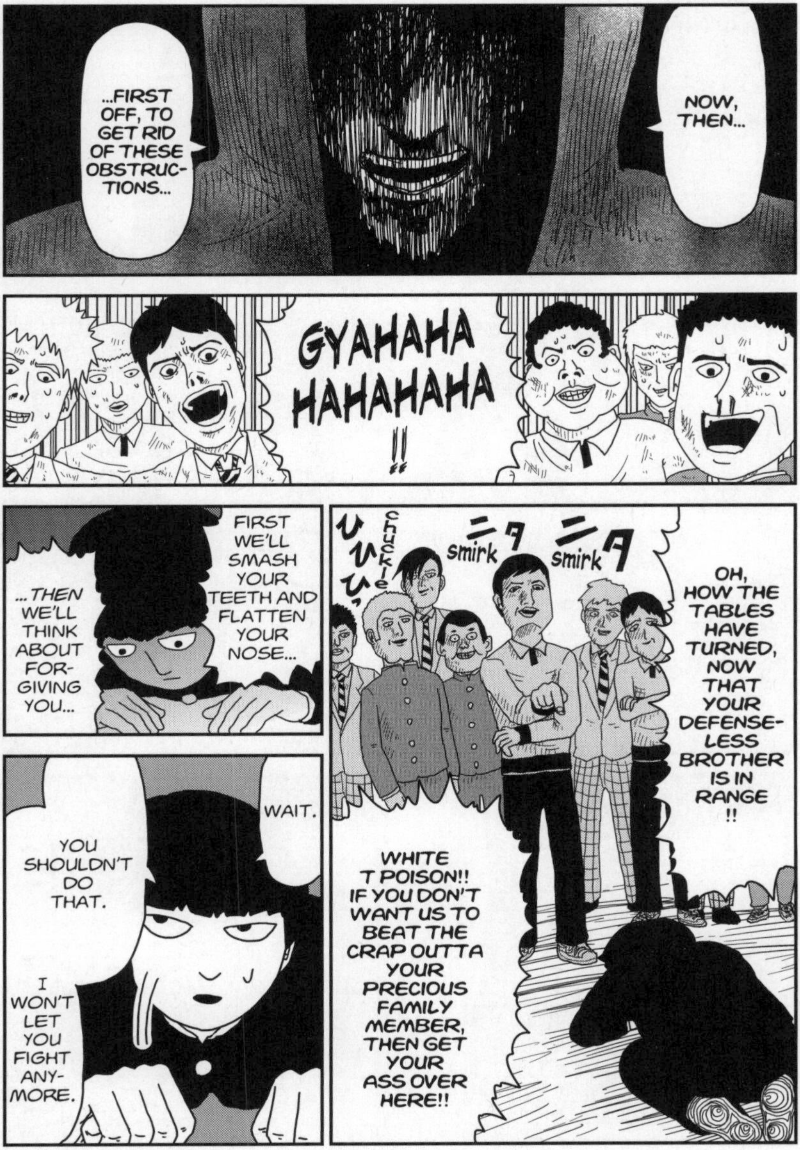
NOW, THEN...
...FIRST OFF, TO GET RID OF THESE OBSTRUC-TIONS...
GYAHAHA HAHAHAHA !!
OH, HOW THE TABLES HAVE TURNED, NOW THAT YOUR DEFENSE-LESS BROTHER IS IN RANGE !!
ニタ smirk
ニタ smirk
ひひひ chuckle
WHITE T POISON!! IF YOU DON'T WANT US TO BEAT THE CRAP OUTTA YOUR PRECIOUS FAMILY MEMBER, THEN GET YOUR ASS OVER HERE!!
FIRST WE'LL SMASH YOUR TEETH AND FLATTEN YOUR NOSE...
...THEN WE'LL THINK ABOUT FOR-GIVING YOU...
WAIT.
YOU SHOULDN'T DO THAT.
I WON'T LET YOU FIGHT ANY-MORE.

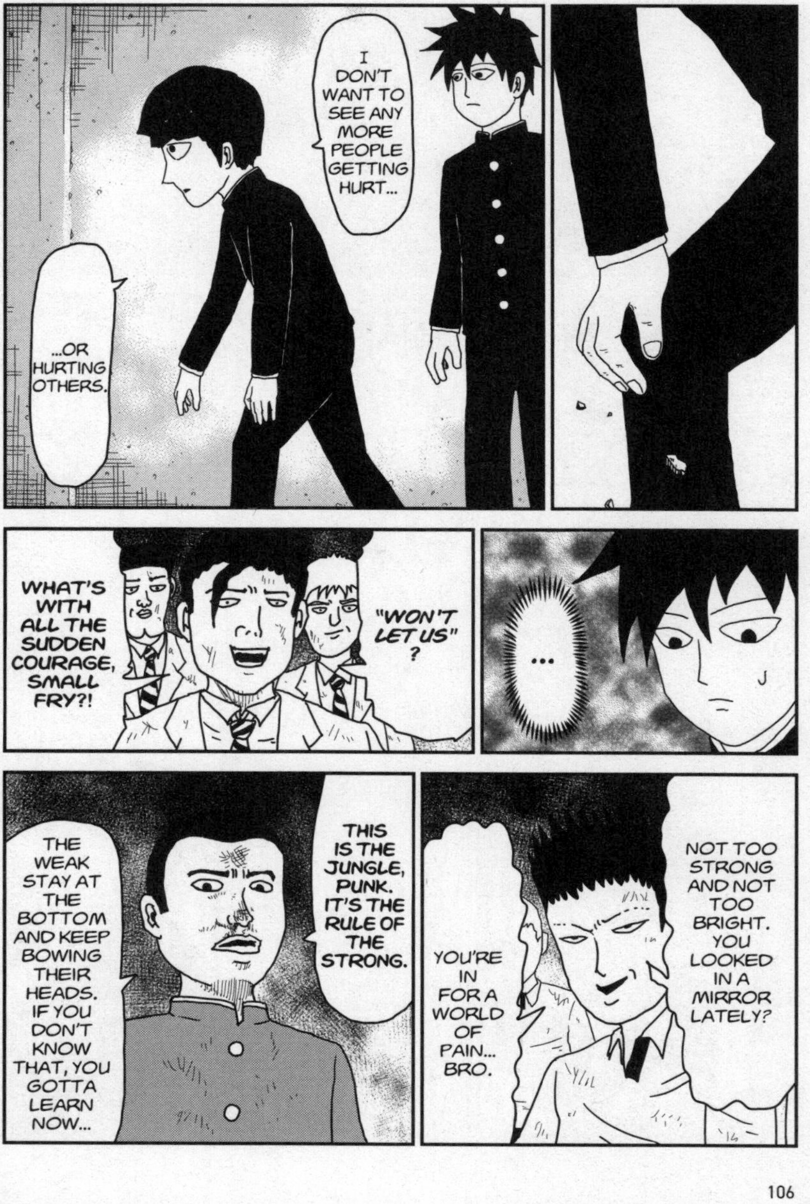
I DON'T WANT TO SEE ANY MORE PEOPLE GETTING HURT...
...OR HURTING OTHERS.
...
"WON'T LET US"?
WHAT'S WITH ALL THE SUDDEN COURAGE, SMALL FRY?!
NOT TOO STRONG AND NOT TOO BRIGHT. YOU LOOKED IN A MIRROR LATELY?
YOU'RE IN FOR A WORLD OF PAIN... BRO.
THIS IS THE JUNGLE, PUNK. IT'S THE RULE OF THE STRONG.
THE WEAK STAY AT THE BOTTOM AND KEEP BOWING THEIR HEADS. IF YOU DON'T KNOW THAT, YOU GOTTA LEARN NOW...

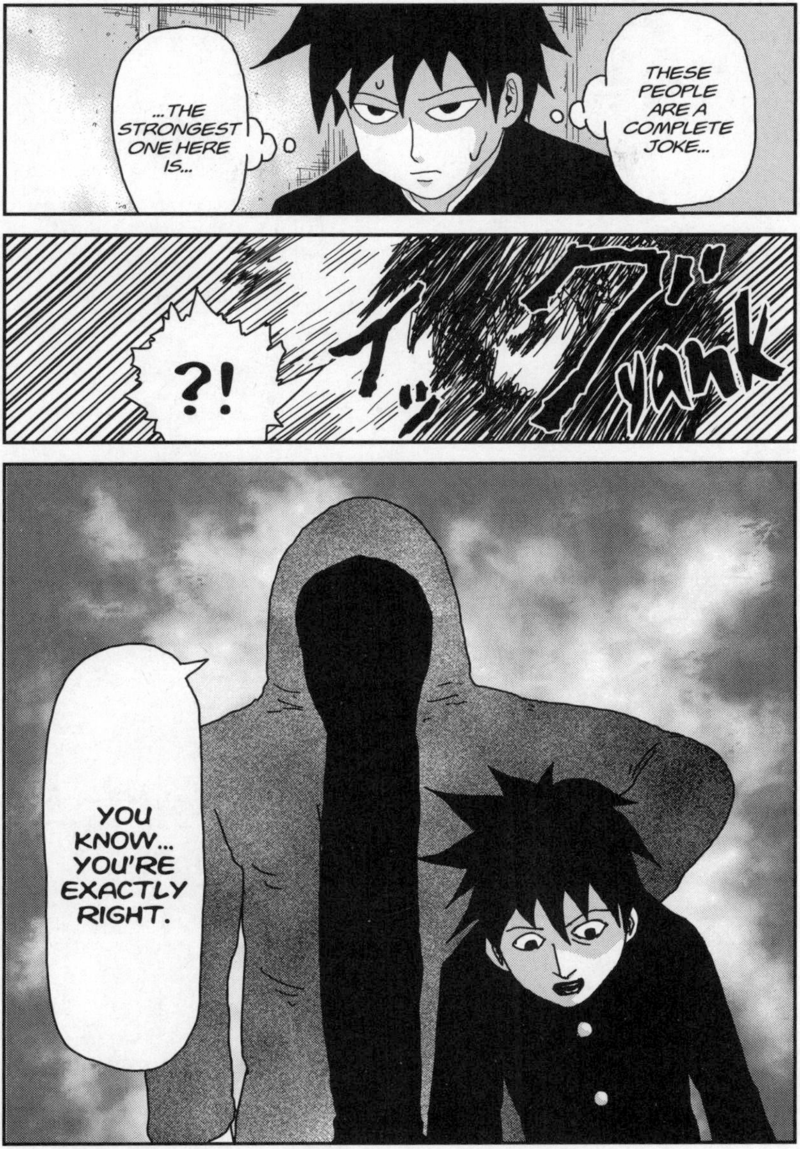
THESE PEOPLE ARE A COMPLETE JOKE...
...THE STRONGEST ONE HERE IS...
YANK
?!
YOU KNOW... YOU'RE EXACTLY RIGHT.

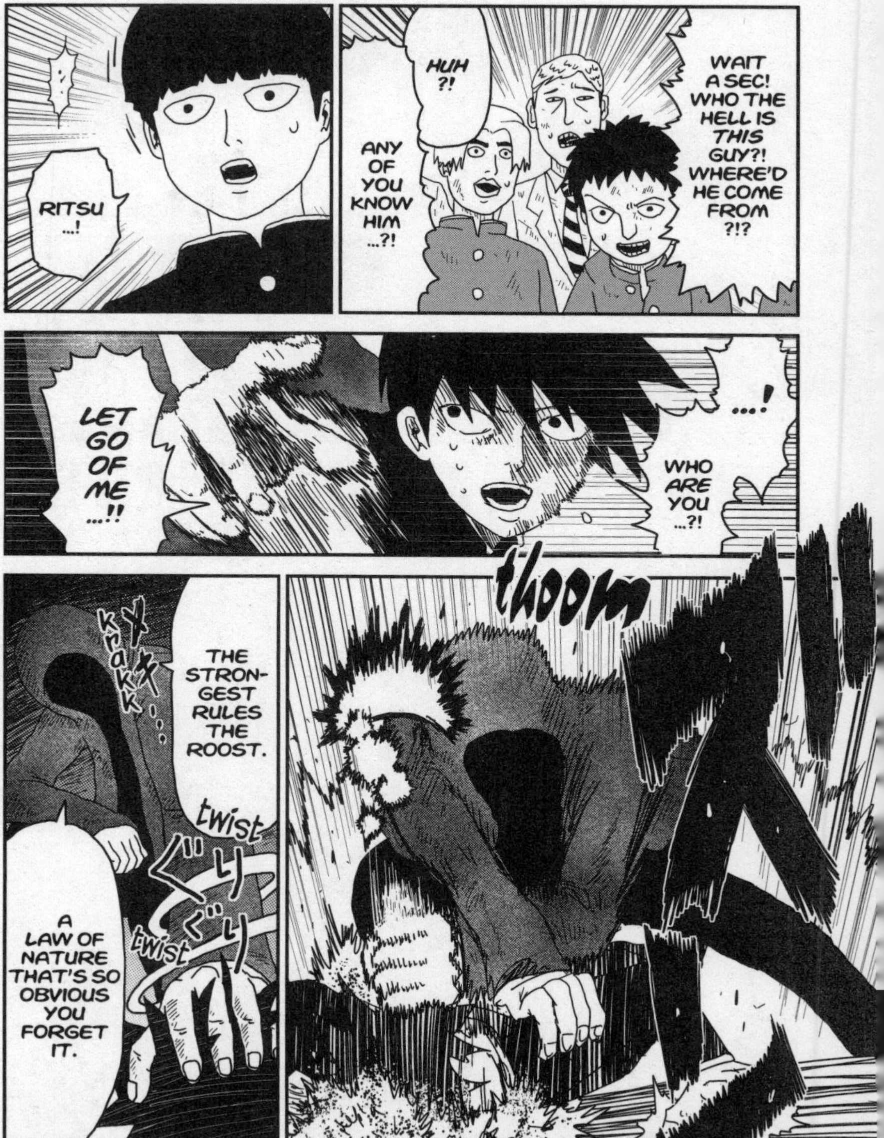
WAIT A SEC! WHO THE HELL IS THIS GUY?! WHERE'D HE COME FROM ?!?
HUH ?!
ANY OF YOU KNOW HIM ...?!
!?
RITSU ...!
...!
WHO ARE YOU ...?!
LET GO OF ME ...!!
thoom
THE STRONGEST RULES THE ROOST.
krakk...
twist
twist
A LAW OF NATURE THAT'S SO OBVIOUS YOU FORGET IT.

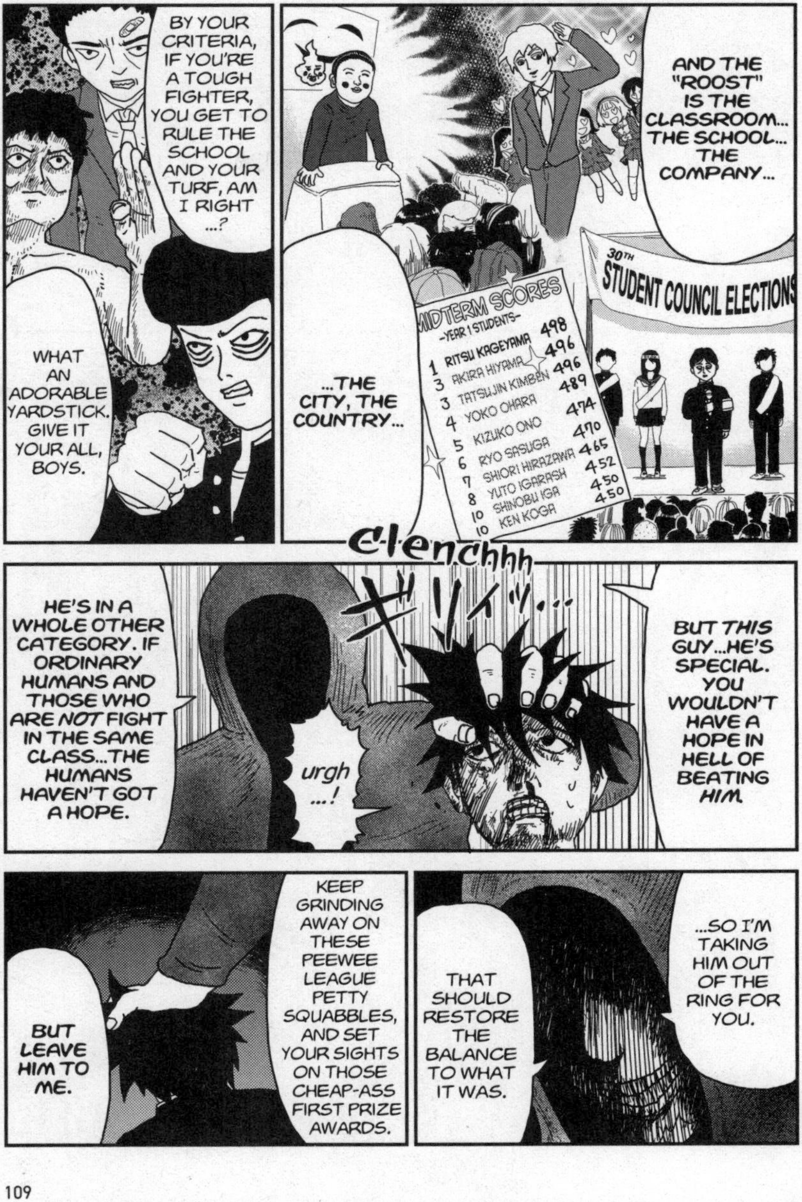
AND THE "ROOST" IS THE CLASSROOM... THE SCHOOL... THE COMPANY...
...THE CITY, THE COUNTRY...
MIDTERM SCORES
-YEAR 1 STUDENTS-
1 RITSU KAGEYAMA 498
3 AKIRA HIYAMA 496
3 TATSUJIN KIMBEN 496
4 YOKO OHARA 489
5 KIZUKO ONO 474
6 RYO SASUGA 470
7 SHIORI HIRAZAWA 465
8 YUTO IGARASH 452
10 SHINOBU IGA 450
10 KEN KOGA 450
30TH STUDENT COUNCIL ELECTIONS
BY YOUR CRITERIA, IF YOU'RE A TOUGH FIGHTER, YOU GET TO RULE THE SCHOOL AND YOUR TURF, AM I RIGHT ...?
WHAT AN ADORABLE YARDSTICK. GIVE IT YOUR ALL, BOYS.
Clenchhh
ギリィッ…
BUT THIS GUY...HE'S SPECIAL. YOU WOULDN'T HAVE A HOPE IN HELL OF BEATING HIM.
HE'S IN A WHOLE OTHER CATEGORY. IF ORDINARY HUMANS AND THOSE WHO ARE NOT FIGHT IN THE SAME CLASS...THE HUMANS HAVEN'T GOT A HOPE.
urgh ...!
...SO I'M TAKING HIM OUT OF THE RING FOR YOU.
THAT SHOULD RESTORE THE BALANCE TO WHAT IT WAS.
KEEP GRINDING AWAY ON THESE PEEWEE LEAGUE PETTY SQUABBLES, AND SET YOUR SIGHTS ON THOSE CHEAP-ASS FIRST PRIZE AWARDS.
BUT LEAVE HIM TO ME.

SASHES?

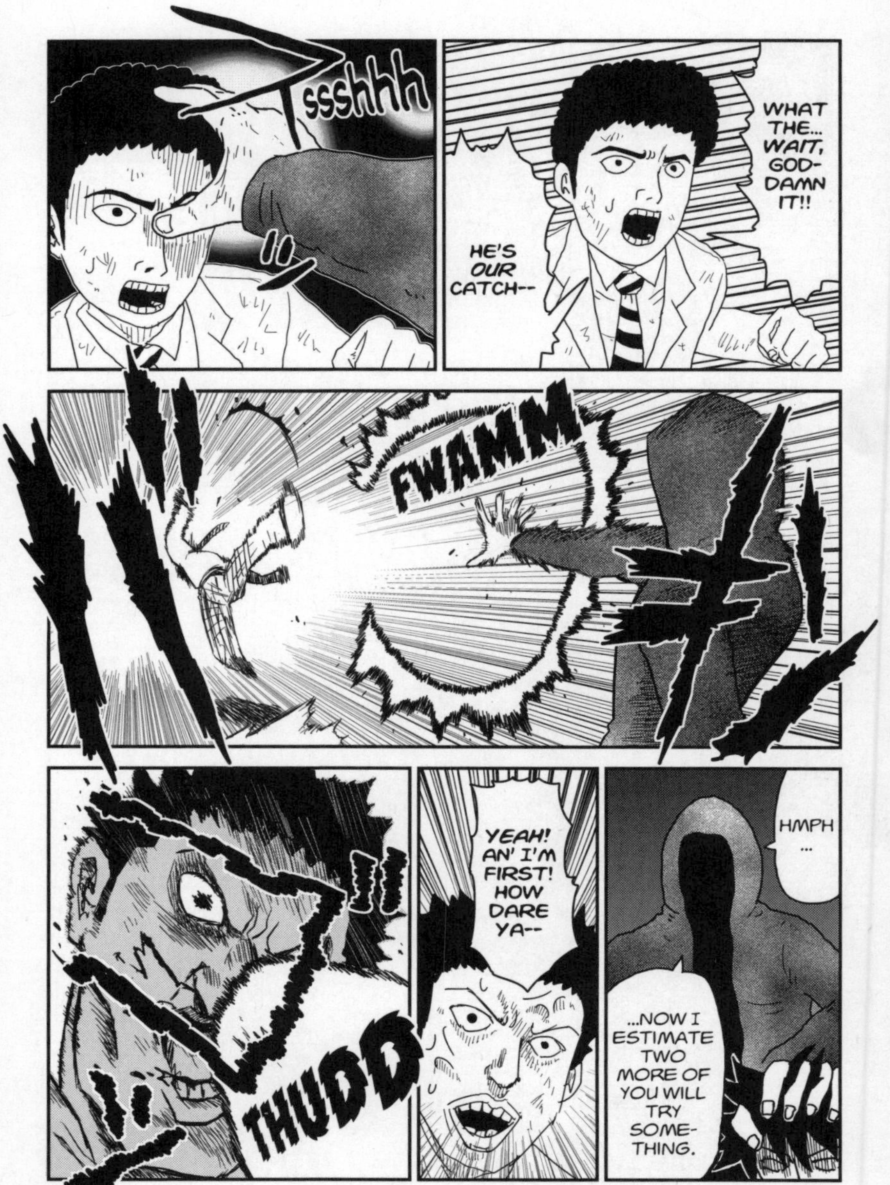
WHAT THE... WAIT, GOD-DAMN IT!!
HE'S OUR CATCH--
ssshhh
FWAMM
HMPH ...
...NOW I ESTIMATE TWO MORE OF YOU WILL TRY SOME-THING.
YEAH! AN' I'M FIRST! HOW DARE YA--
THUDD

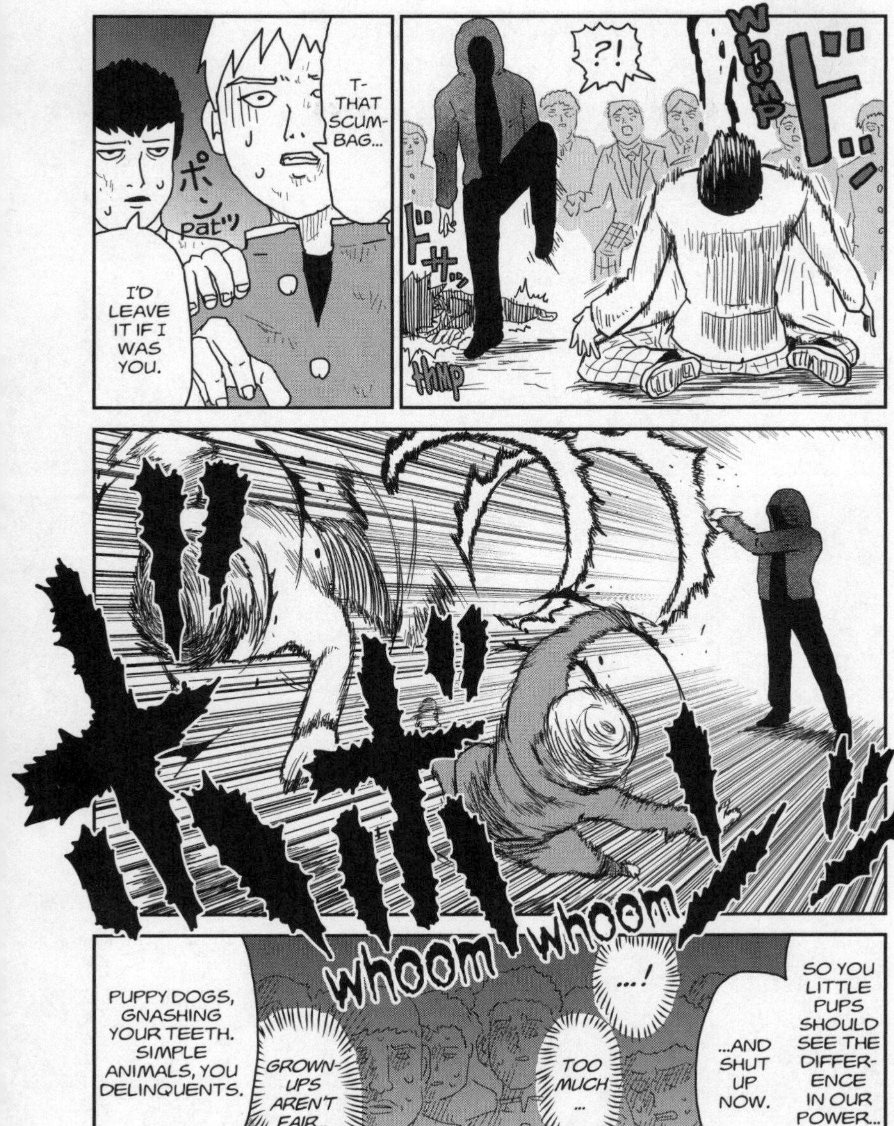
?!
WHUMP
ドド
ドサッ
T-THAT SCUMBAG...
ポン pat
I'D LEAVE IT IF I WAS YOU.
whoom whoom
SO YOU LITTLE PUPS SHOULD SEE THE DIFFERENCE IN OUR POWER...
...AND SHUT UP NOW.
...!
TOO MUCH ...
GROWN-UPS AREN'T FAIR..
PUPPY DOGS, GNASHING YOUR TEETH. SIMPLE ANIMALS, YOU DELINQUENTS.

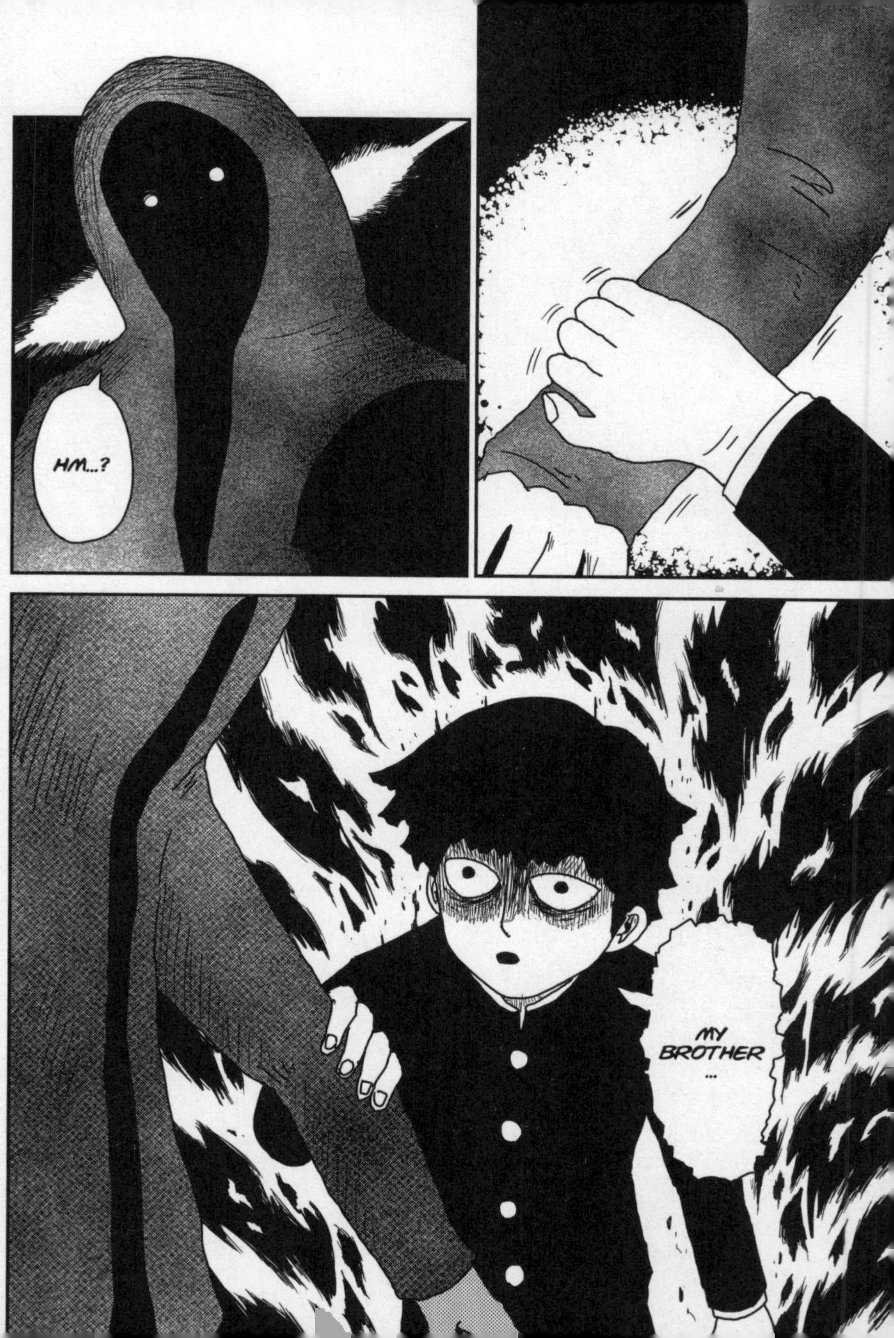
HM...?
MY BROTHER ...

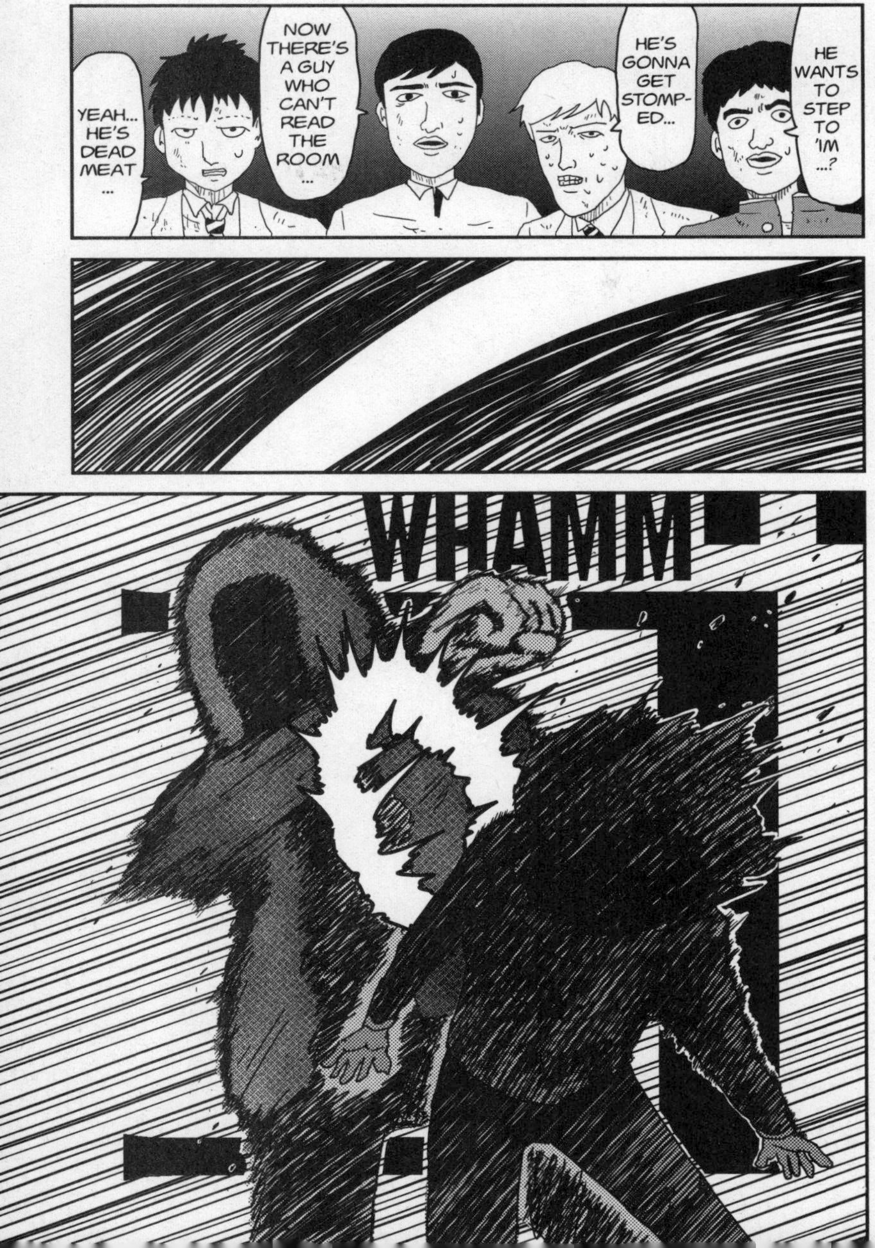
HE WANTS TO STEP TO 'IM ...?
HE'S GONNA GET STOMPED...
NOW THERE'S A GUY WHO CAN'T READ THE ROOM ...
YEAH... HE'S DEAD MEAT ...
WHAMM

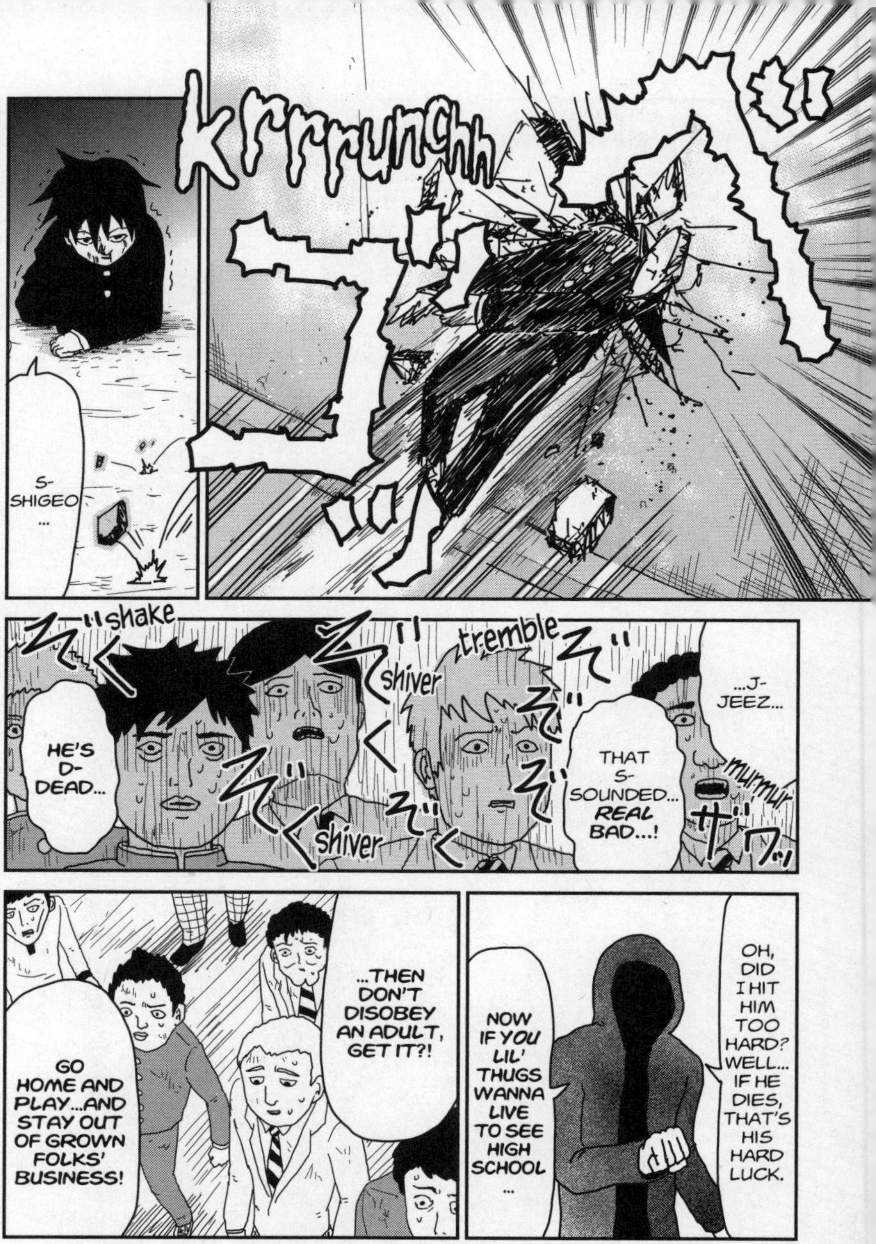
krrrunchh
S-SHIGEO ...
...J-JEEZ...
murmur
THAT S-SOUNDED... *REAL* BAD...!
tremble
shiver
shake
shiver
HE'S D-DEAD...
OH, DID I HIT HIM TOO HARD? WELL... IF HE DIES, THAT'S HIS HARD LUCK.
NOW IF *YOU* LIL' THUGS WANNA LIVE TO SEE HIGH SCHOOL ...
...THEN DON'T DISOBEY AN ADULT, GET IT?!
GO HOME AND PLAY...AND STAY OUT OF GROWN FOLKS' BUSINESS!

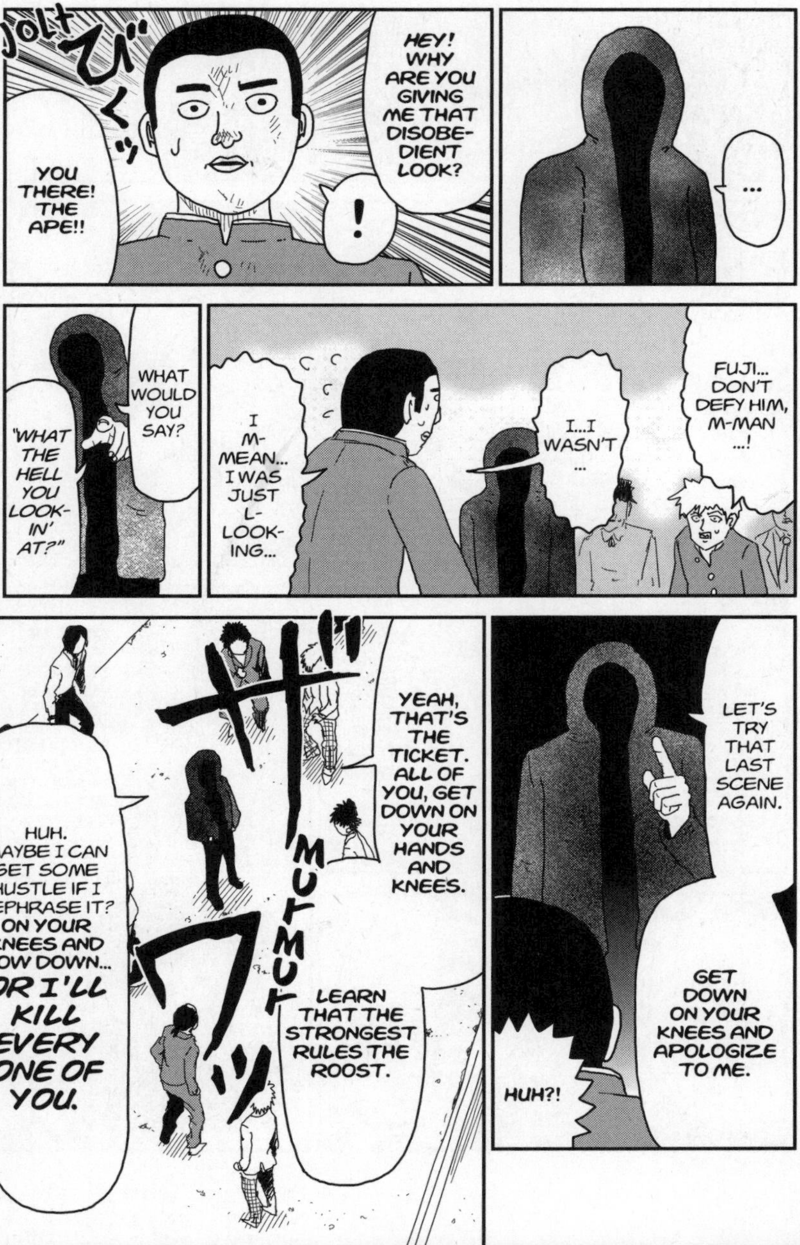
...
HEY! WHY ARE YOU GIVING ME THAT DISOBEDIENT LOOK?
JOLT
!
YOU THERE! THE APE!!
FUJI... DON'T DEFY HIM, M-MAN ...!
I...I WASN'T ...
I M-MEAN... I WAS JUST L-LOOKING...
WHAT WOULD YOU SAY?
"WHAT THE HELL YOU LOOKIN' AT?"
LET'S TRY THAT LAST SCENE AGAIN.
GET DOWN ON YOUR KNEES AND APOLOGIZE TO ME.
HUH?!
YEAH, THAT'S THE TICKET. ALL OF YOU, GET DOWN ON YOUR HANDS AND KNEES.
MUTMUT
LEARN THAT THE STRONGEST RULES THE ROOST.
HUH. MAYBE I CAN GET SOME HUSTLE IF I REPHRASE IT? ON YOUR KNEES AND BOW DOWN... OR I'LL KILL EVERY ONE OF YOU.

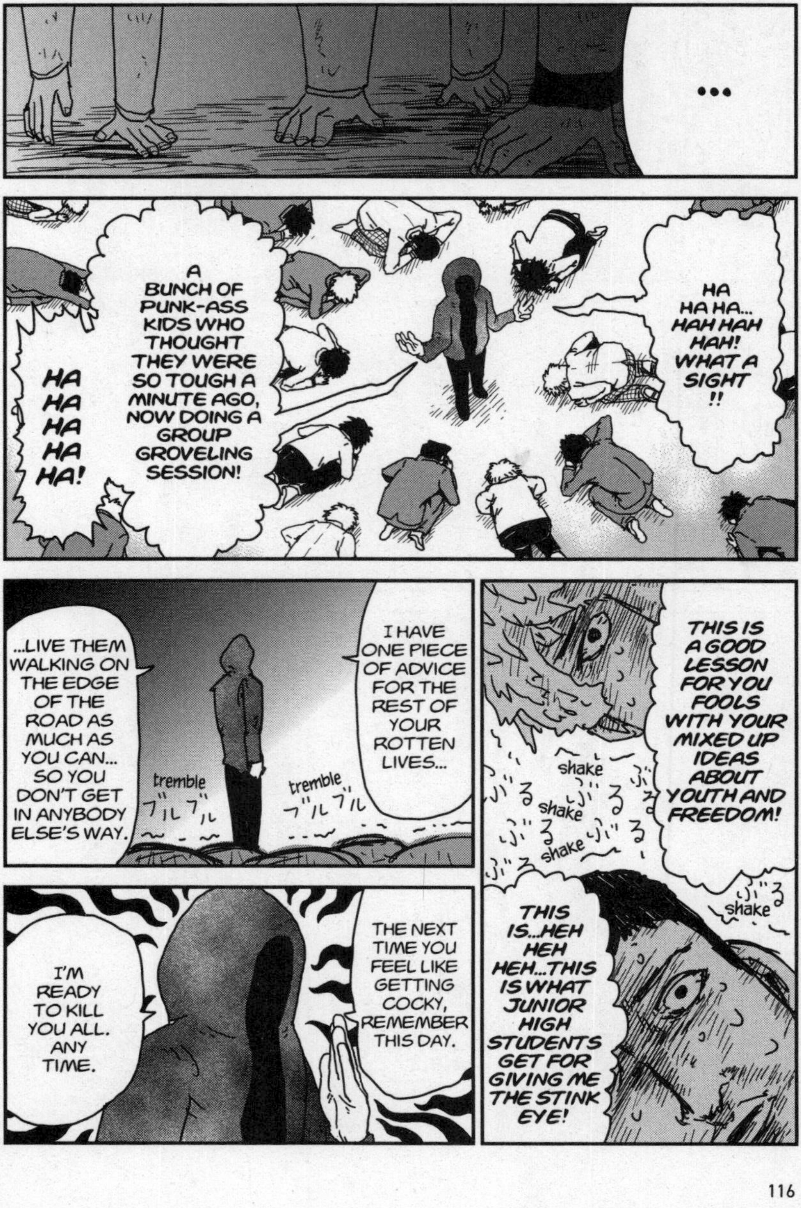

...
HA HA HA... HAH HAH HAH! WHAT A SIGHT!!
A BUNCH OF PUNK-ASS KIDS WHO THOUGHT THEY WERE SO TOUGH A MINUTE AGO, NOW DOING A GROUP GROVELING SESSION!
HA HA HA HA HA!
THIS IS A GOOD LESSON FOR YOU FOOLS WITH YOUR MIXED UP IDEAS ABOUT YOUTH AND FREEDOM!
shake ぶる
shake ぶる
shake ぶる
shake ぶる
THIS IS...HEH HEH...THIS IS WHAT JUNIOR HIGH STUDENTS GET FOR GIVING ME THE STINK EYE!
I HAVE ONE PIECE OF ADVICE FOR THE REST OF YOUR ROTTEN LIVES...
tremble ブルブル
...LIVE THEM WALKING ON THE EDGE OF THE ROAD AS MUCH AS YOU CAN... SO YOU DON'T GET IN ANYBODY ELSE'S WAY.
tremble ブルブル
THE NEXT TIME YOU FEEL LIKE GETTING COCKY, REMEMBER THIS DAY.
I'M READY TO KILL YOU ALL. ANY TIME.

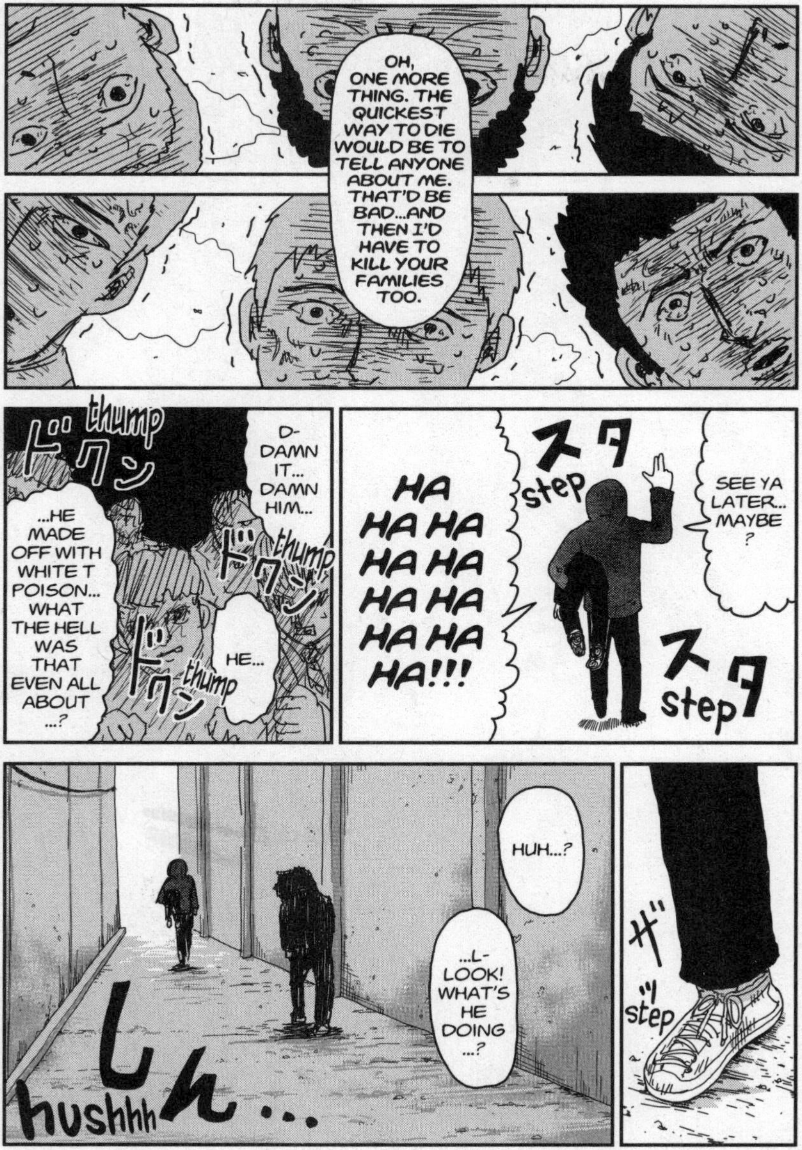
OH, ONE MORE THING. THE QUICKEST WAY TO DIE WOULD BE TO TELL ANYONE ABOUT ME. THAT'D BE BAD...AND THEN I'D HAVE TO KILL YOUR FAMILIES TOO.
SEE YA LATER... MAYBE?
スタ step
HA HA HA HA HA HA HA HA HA HA HA!!!
スタ step
D-DAMN IT... DAMN HIM...
ドクン thump
ドクン thump
HE...
ドクン thump
...HE MADE OFF WITH WHITE T POISON... WHAT THE HELL WAS THAT EVEN ALL ABOUT...?
ザッ step
HUH...?
...L-LOOK! WHAT'S HE DOING...?
しん... hushhh

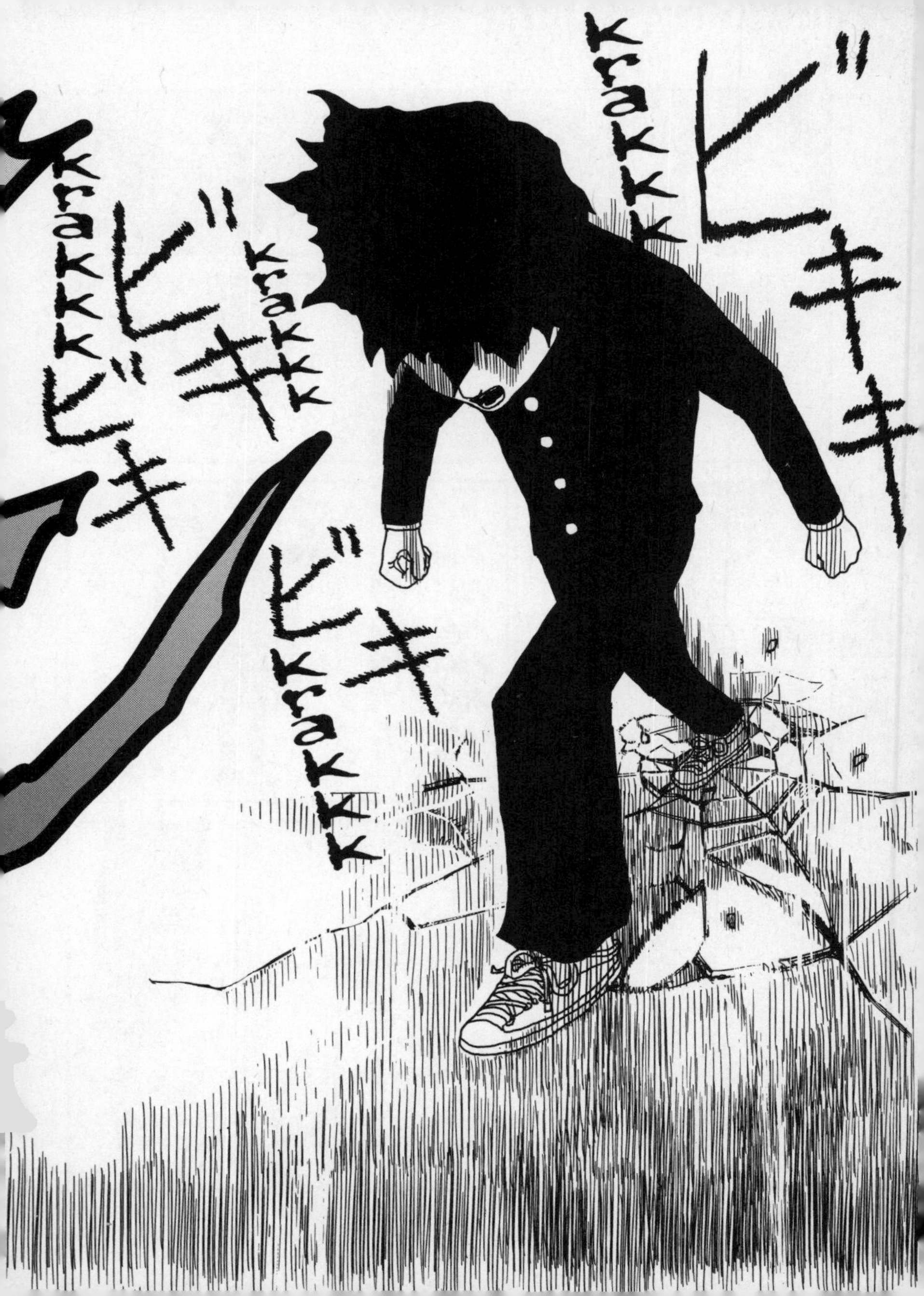
ビキキ
krakkk
ビキ
krakkk
ビビキ
krakkk
ビキ
krakkk

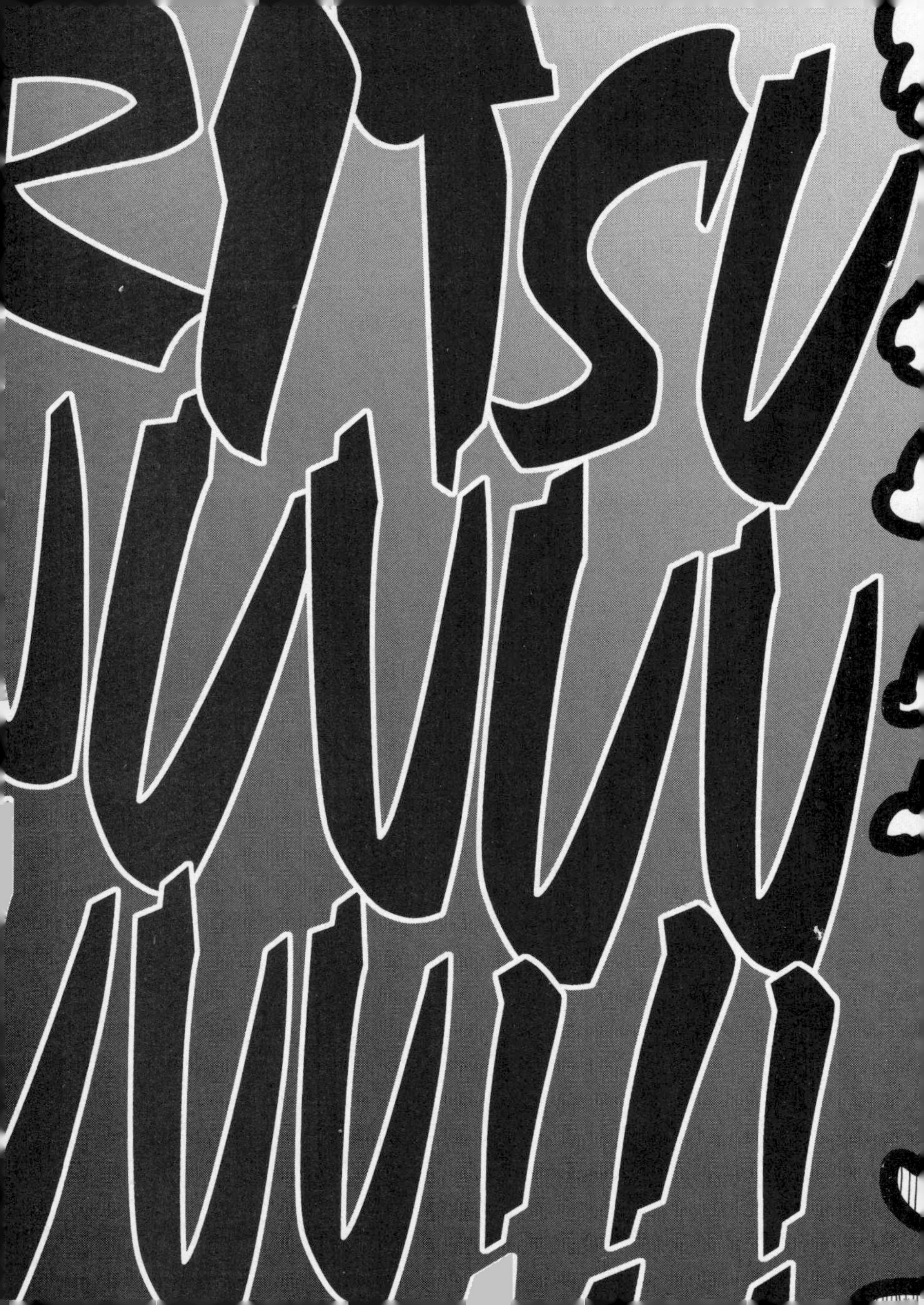

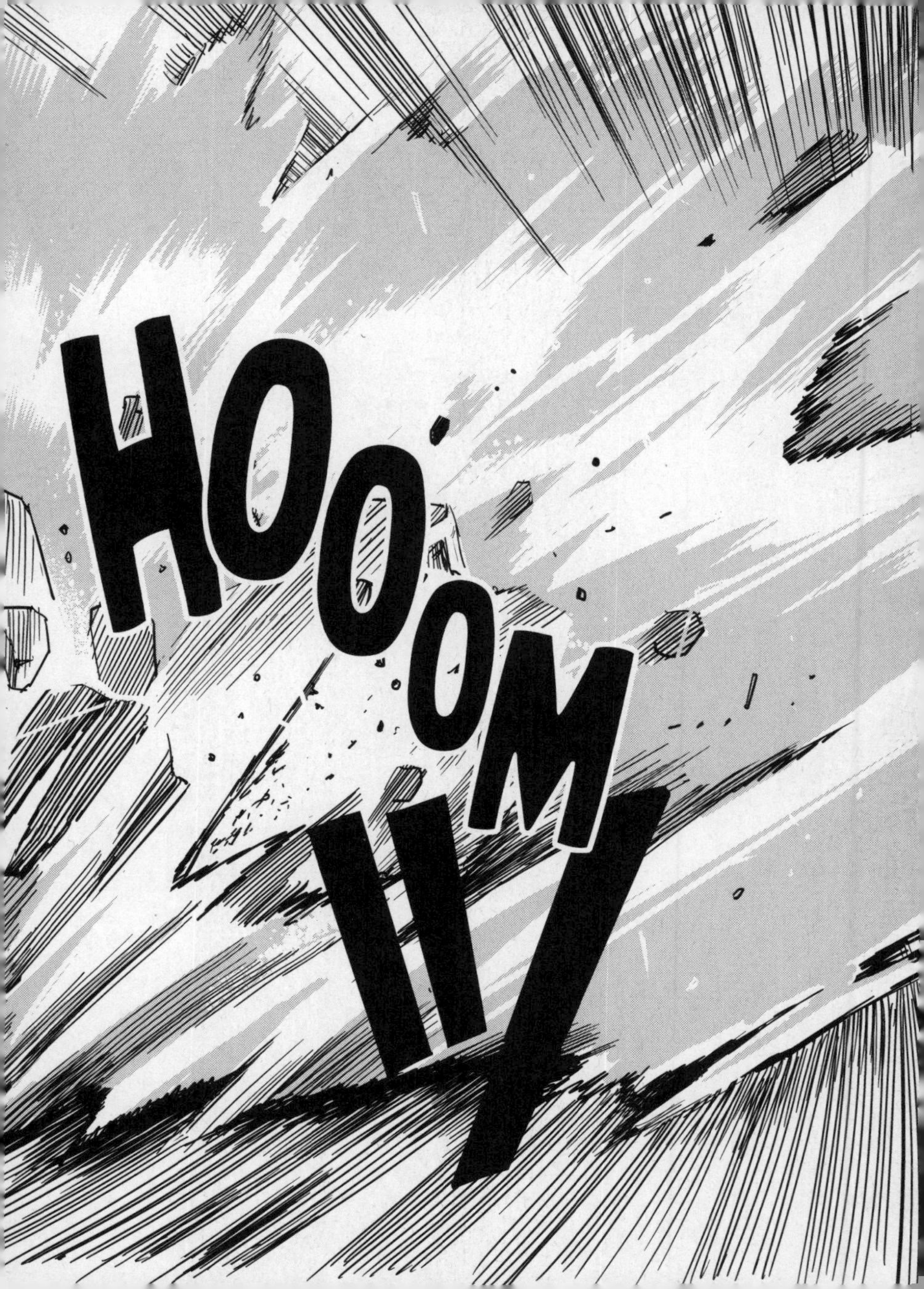
HOOOOM !!

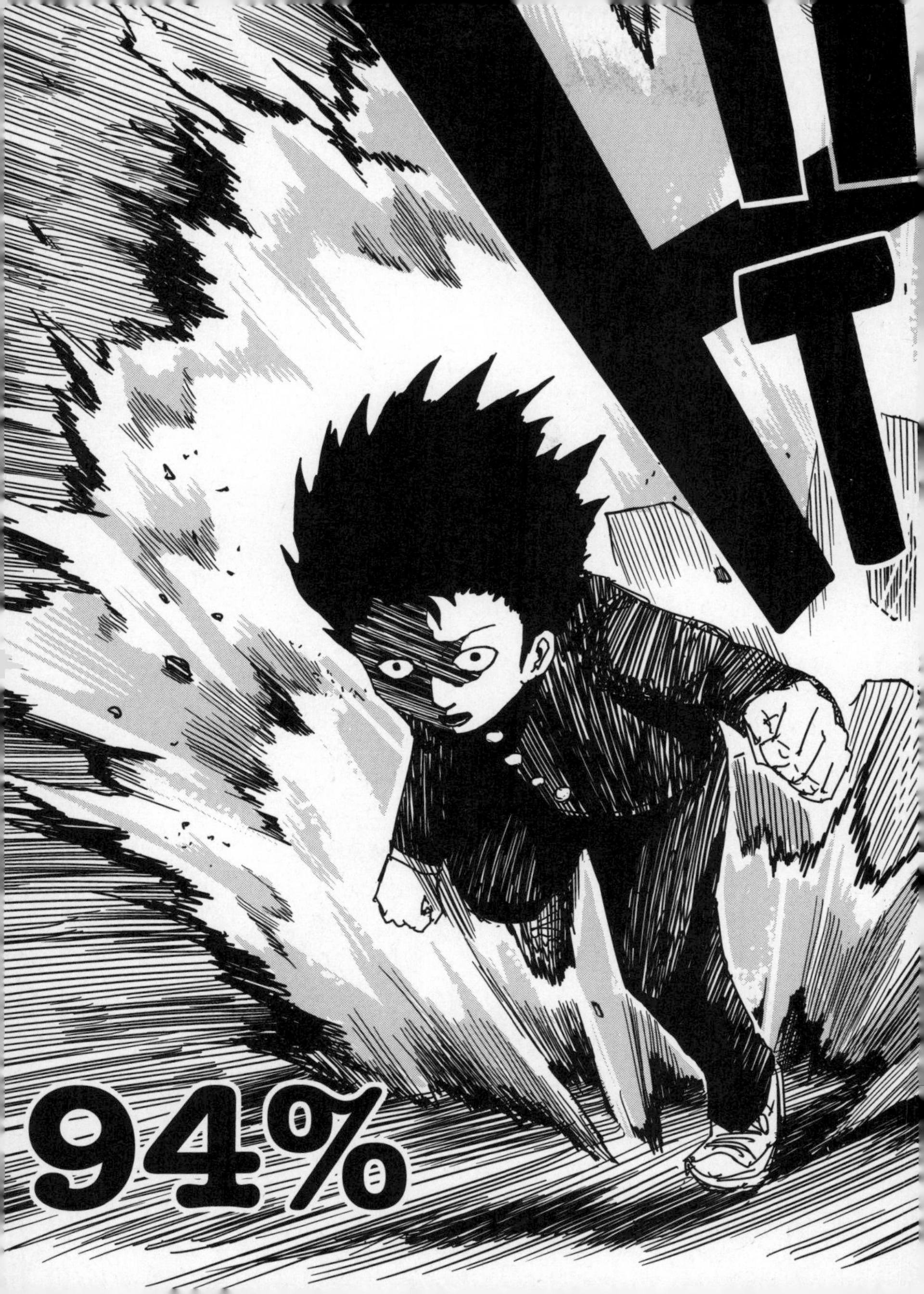
94%

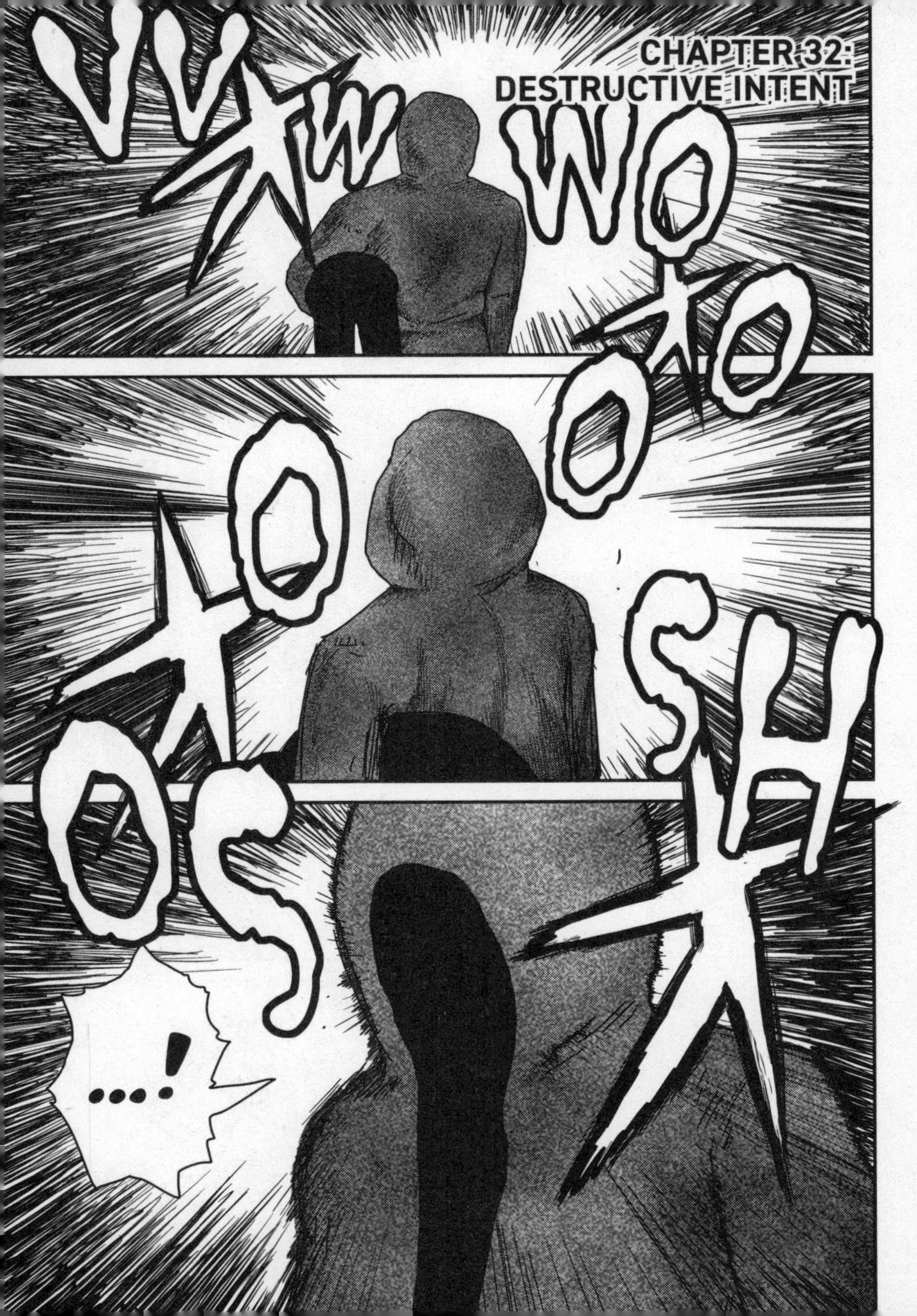

CHAPTER 32:
DESTRUCTIVE INTENT
VVWWOOOOOSSH
...!

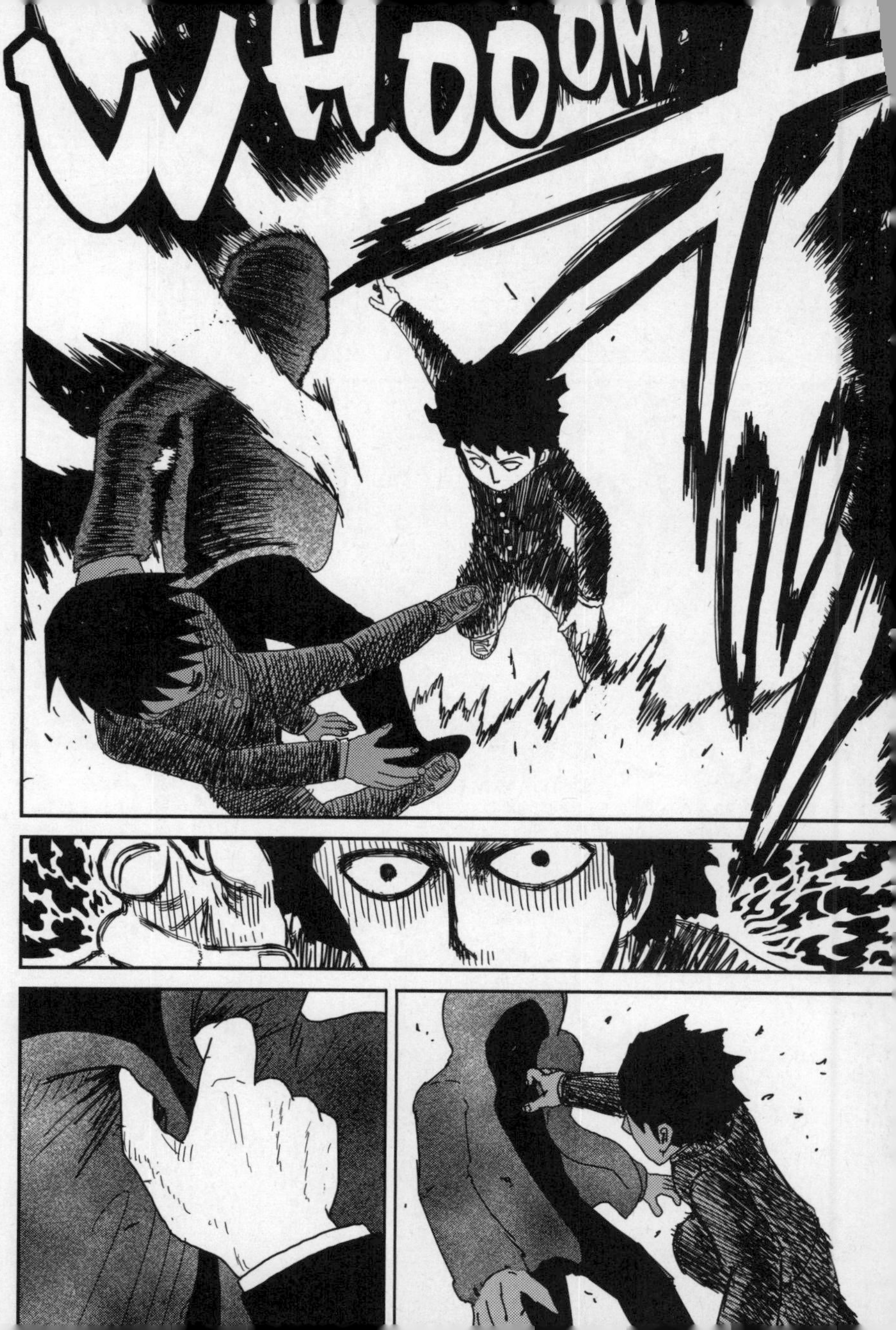
WHOOOM

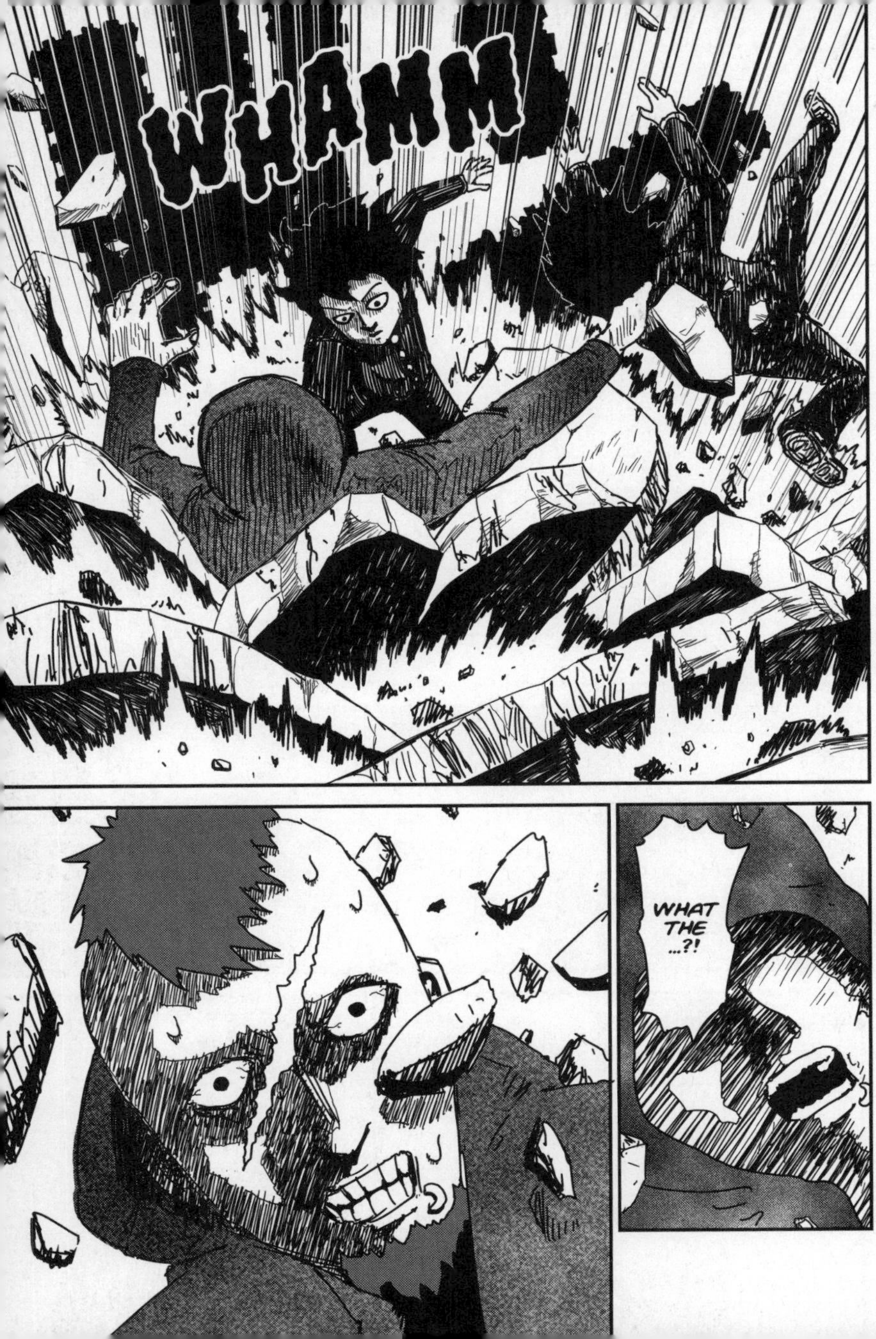
WHAMM
WHAT THE ...?!

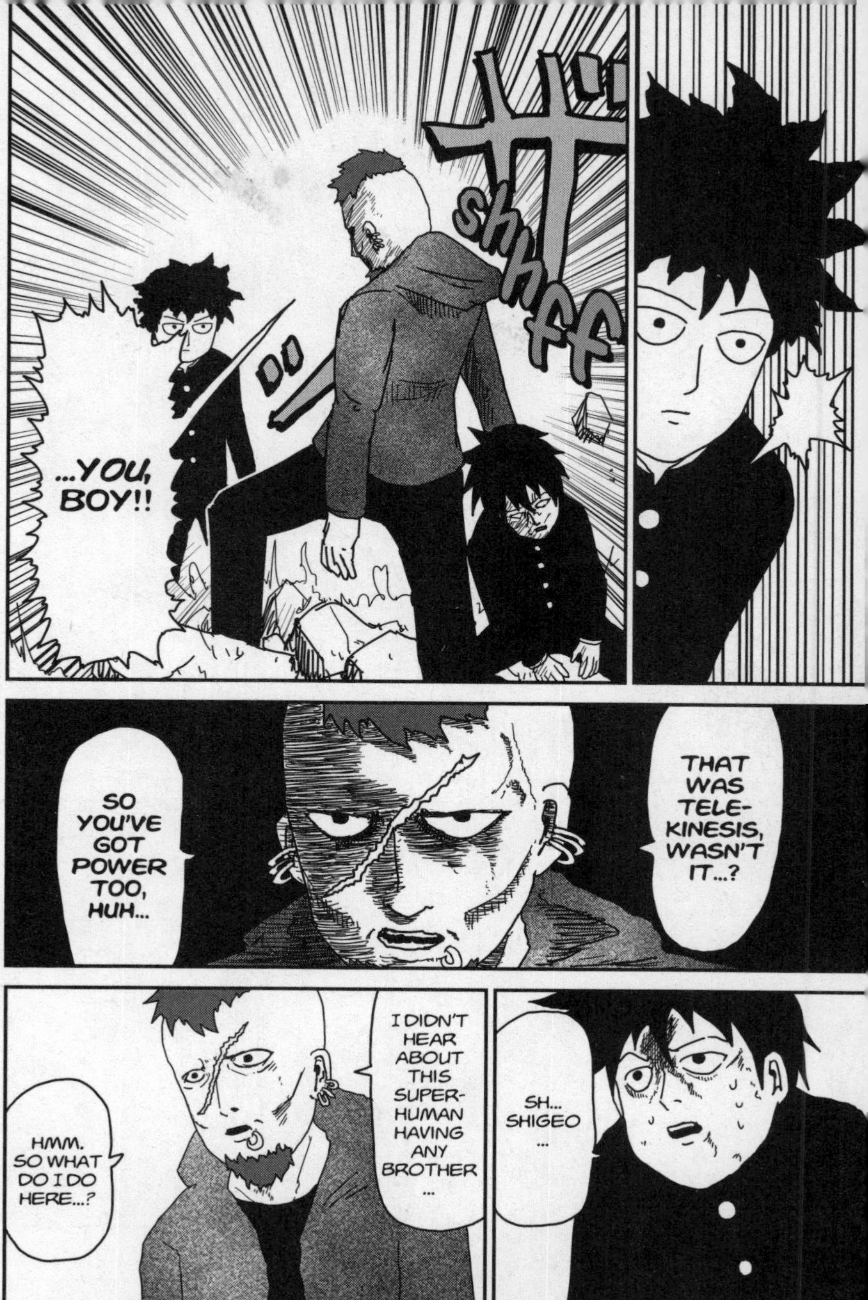
shhff
...YOU, BOY!!
THAT WAS TELE-KINESIS, WASN'T IT...?
SO YOU'VE GOT POWER TOO, HUH...
SH... SHIGEO ...
I DIDN'T HEAR ABOUT THIS SUPER-HUMAN HAVING ANY BROTHER ...
HMM. SO WHAT DO I DO HERE...?

grip

LET HIM GO?

IF YOU DON'T ...

LET GO OF MY BROTHER ...

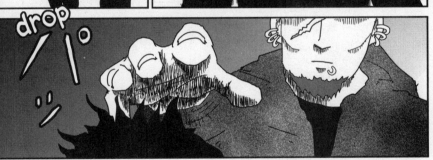

drop

YOU PUNK-ASS BRAT.

whudd

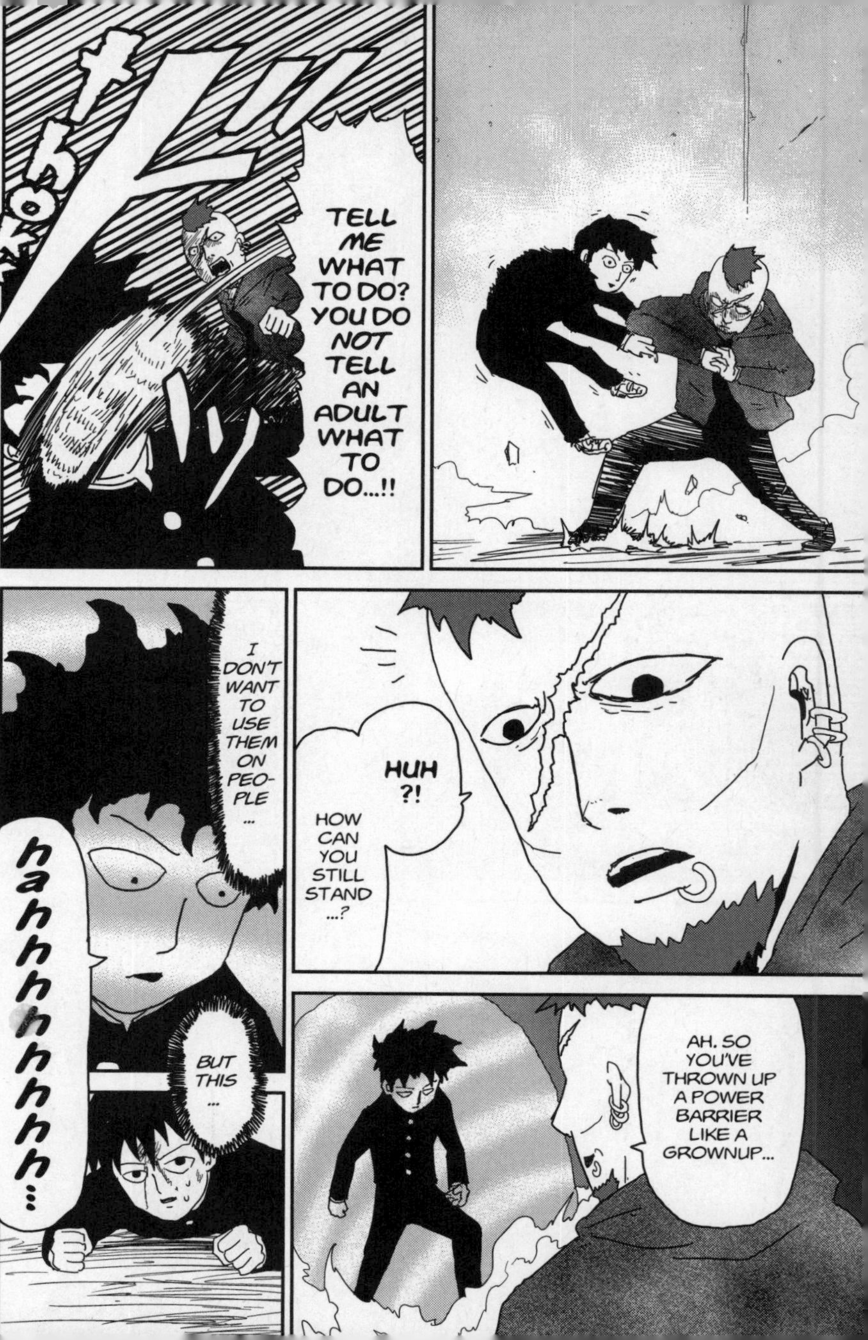
thokk
TELL ME WHAT TO DO? YOU DO NOT TELL AN ADULT WHAT TO DO...!!
HUH ?!
HOW CAN YOU STILL STAND ...?
AH. SO YOU'VE THROWN UP A POWER BARRIER LIKE A GROWNUP...
I DON'T WANT TO USE THEM ON PEO-PLE ...
BUT THIS ...
nnnnnnnnnnn...

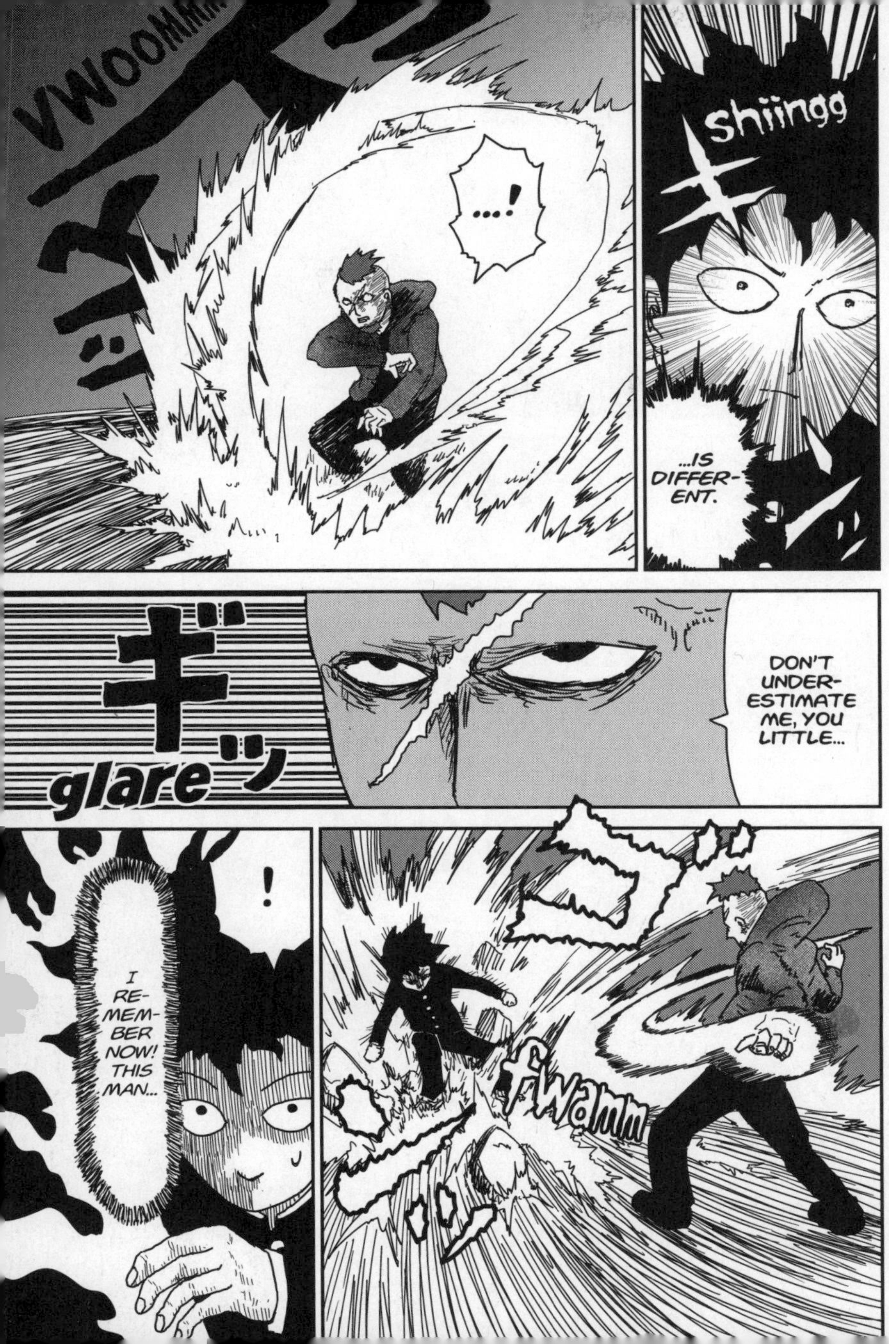
shiingg
...IS DIFFERENT.
VWOOMMM
...!
DON'T UNDERESTIMATE ME, YOU LITTLE...
glare
fwamm
!
I REMEMBER NOW! THIS MAN...

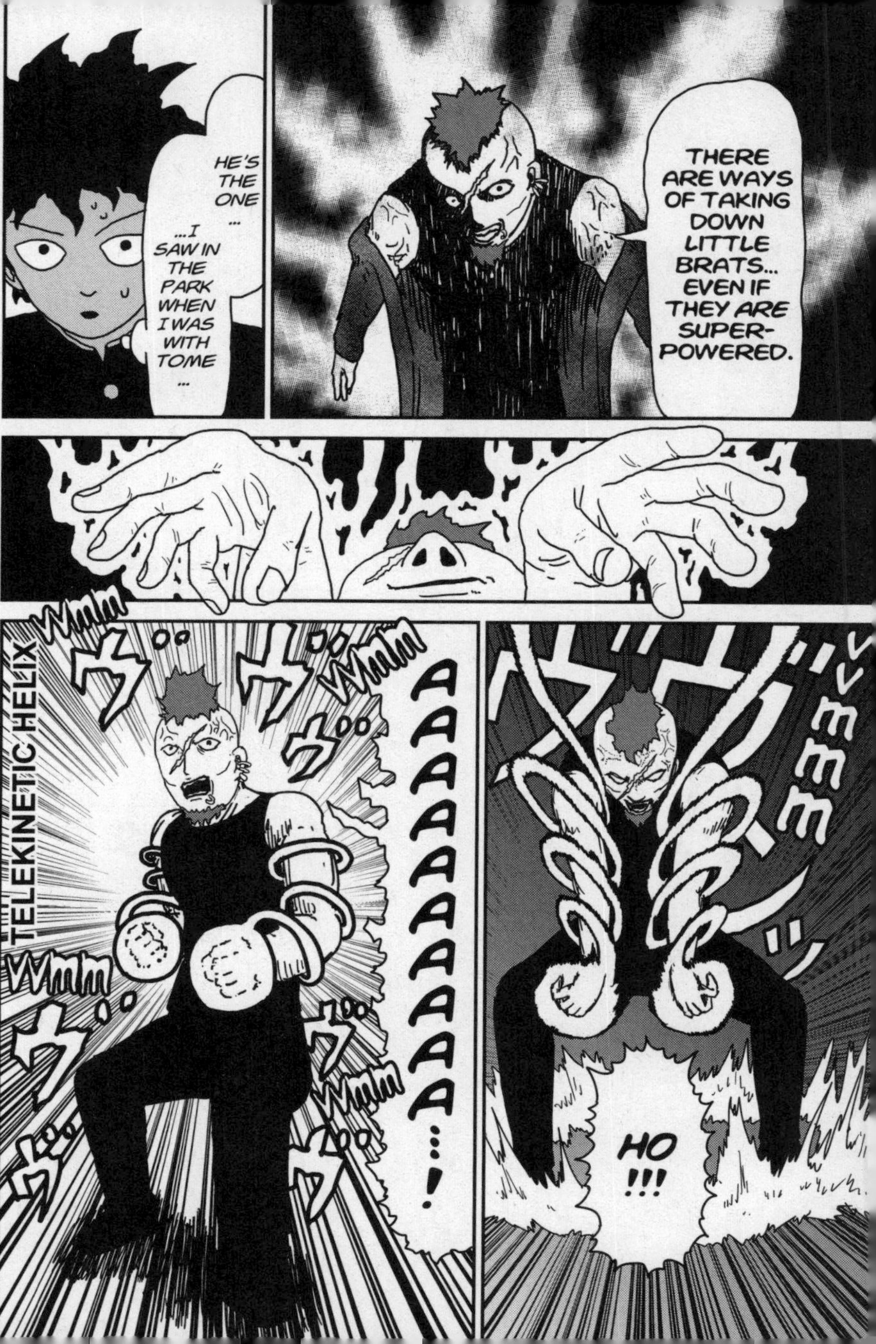
THERE ARE WAYS OF TAKING DOWN LITTLE BRATS... EVEN IF THEY ARE SUPER-POWERED.
HE'S THE ONE ...
...I SAW IN THE PARK WHEN I WAS WITH TOME ...
HO !!!
AAAAAAAAAAAAA...!
TELEKINETIC HELIX
Wmm
Wmm
Wmm
Wmm

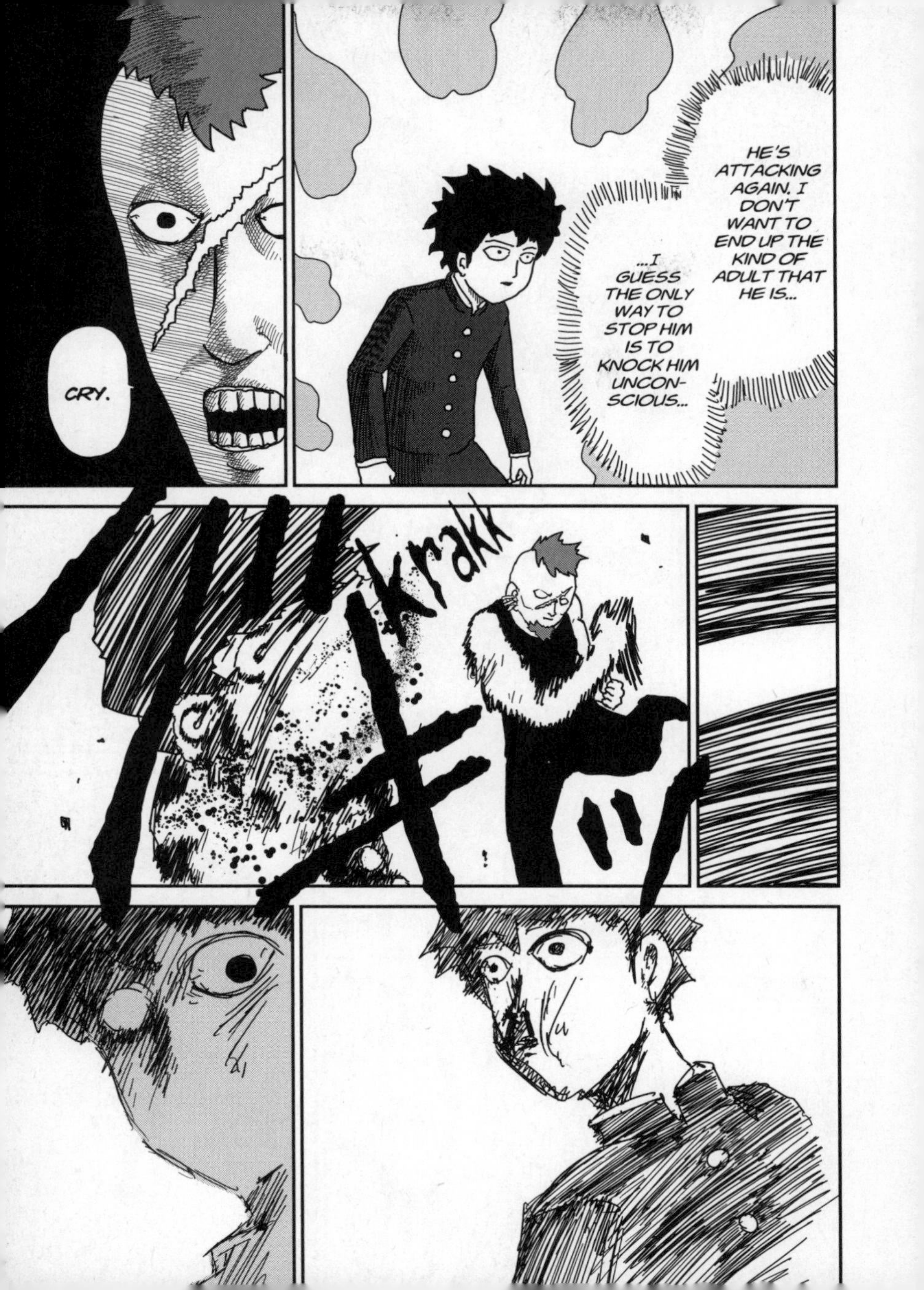
HE'S ATTACKING AGAIN. I DON'T WANT TO END UP THE KIND OF ADULT THAT HE IS...
...I GUESS THE ONLY WAY TO STOP HIM IS TO KNOCK HIM UNCON-SCIOUS...
CRY.
krakk

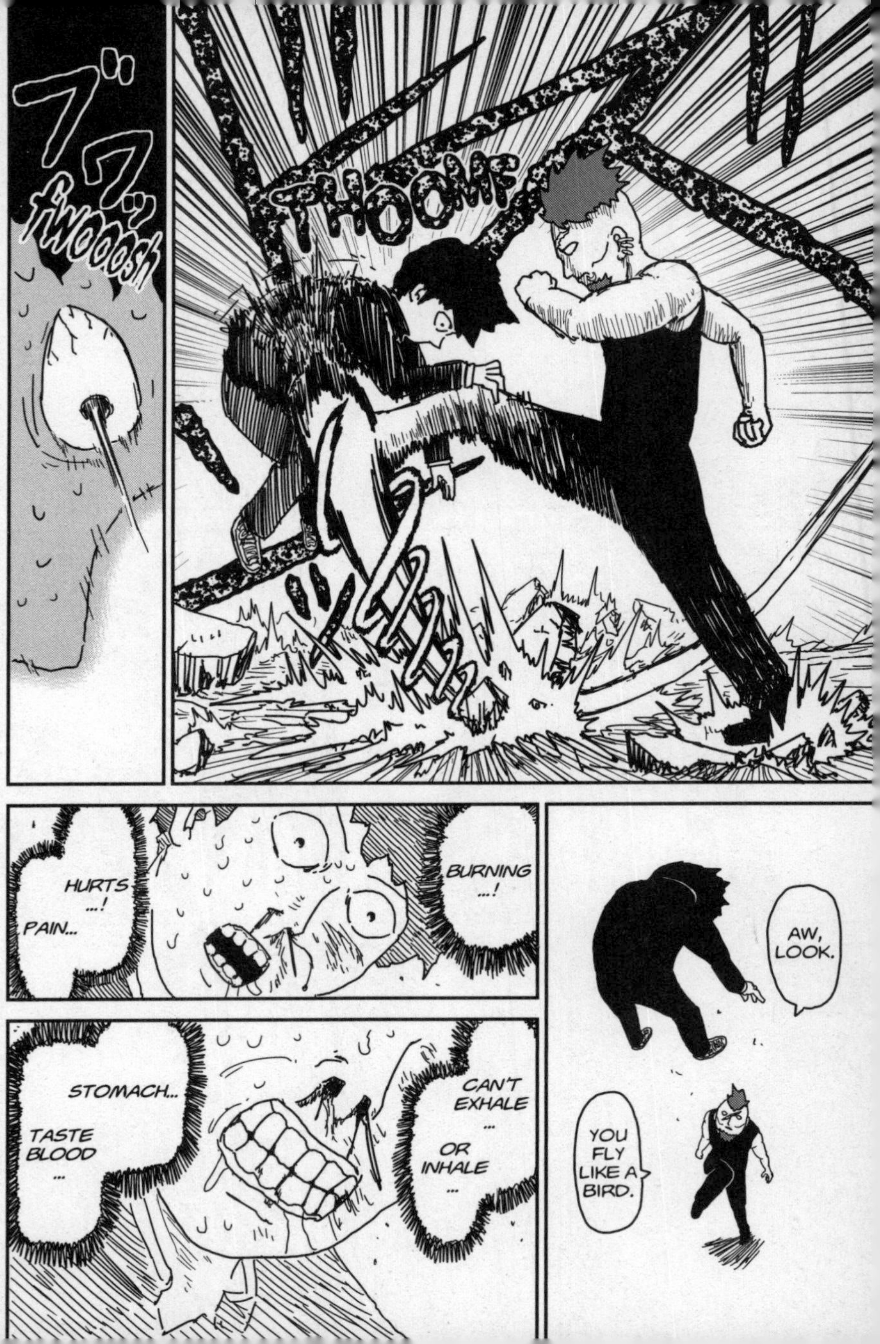
THOOMF
ブワッ
fwooosh
AW, LOOK.
YOU FLY LIKE A BIRD.
BURNING ...!
HURTS ...!
PAIN...
CAN'T EXHALE ...
OR INHALE ...
STOMACH...
TASTE BLOOD ...

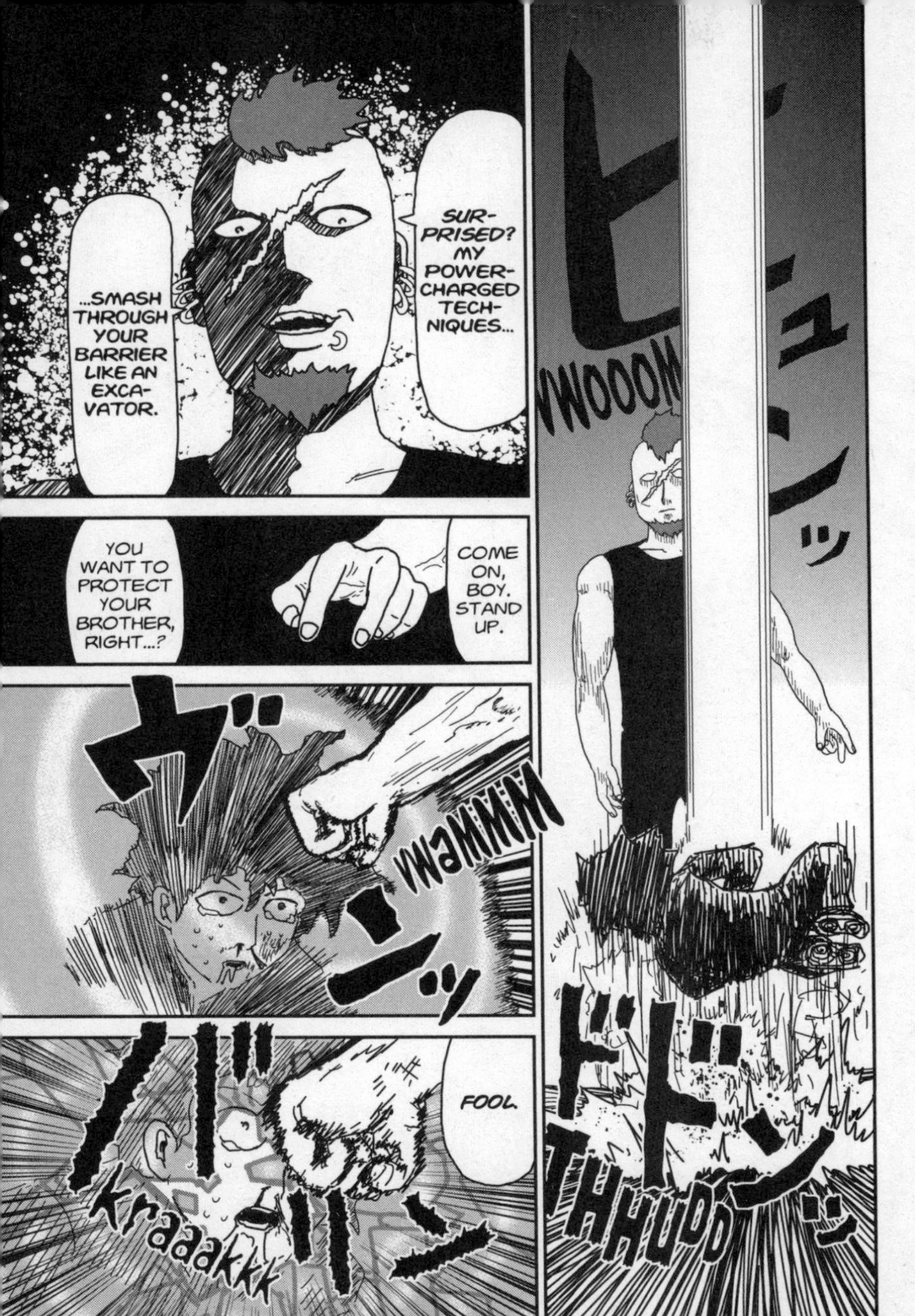
WWOOOM
THHUDD
SUR-PRISED? MY POWER-CHARGED TECH-NIQUES...
...SMASH THROUGH YOUR BARRIER LIKE AN EXCA-VATOR.
COME ON, BOY. STAND UP.
YOU WANT TO PROTECT YOUR BROTHER, RIGHT...?
WHAMMM
FOOL.
kraaakkk

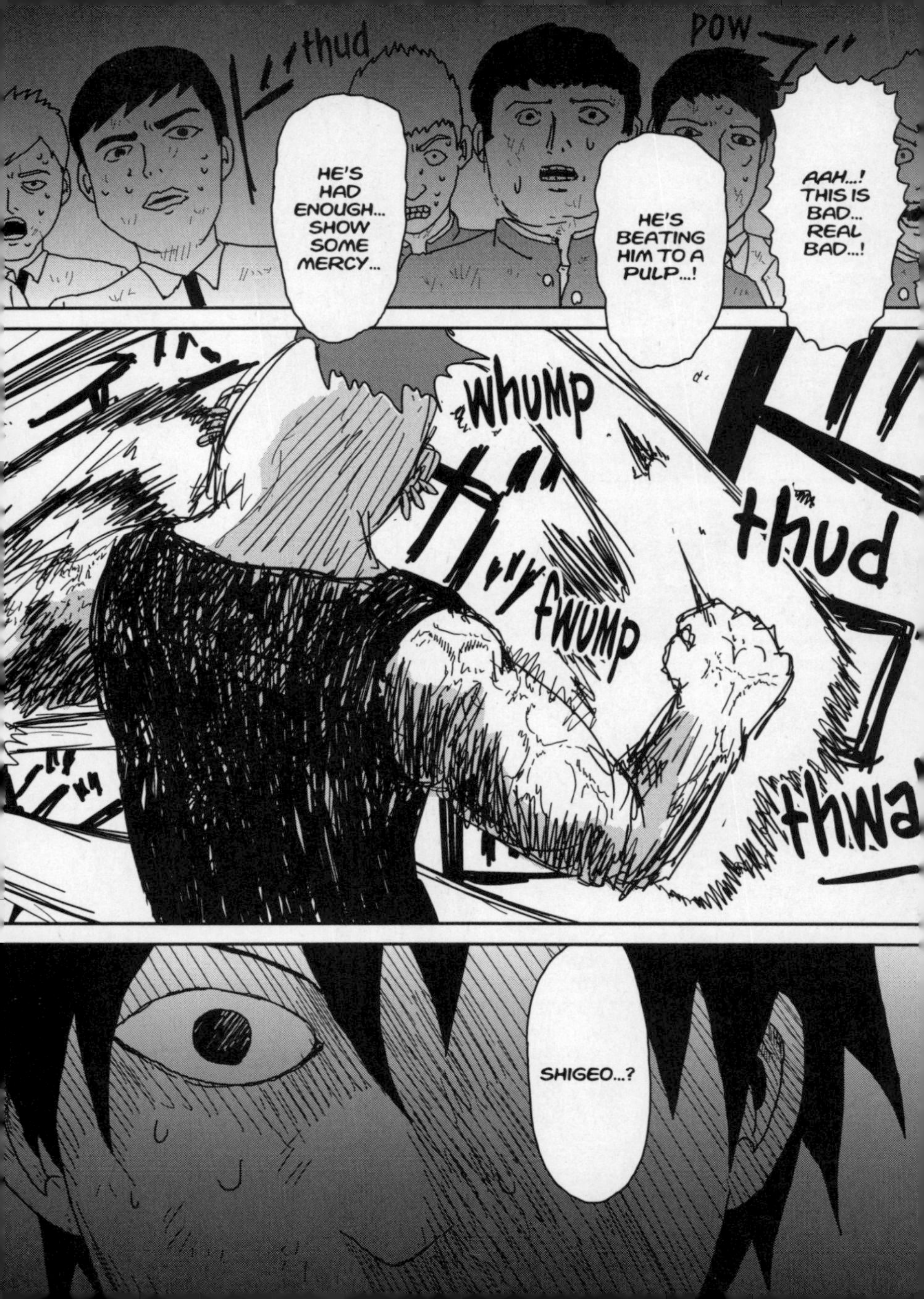
POW
AAH...! THIS IS BAD... REAL BAD...!
HE'S BEATING HIM TO A PULP...!
thud
HE'S HAD ENOUGH... SHOW SOME MERCY...
whump
thud
fwump
thwa
SHIGEO...?

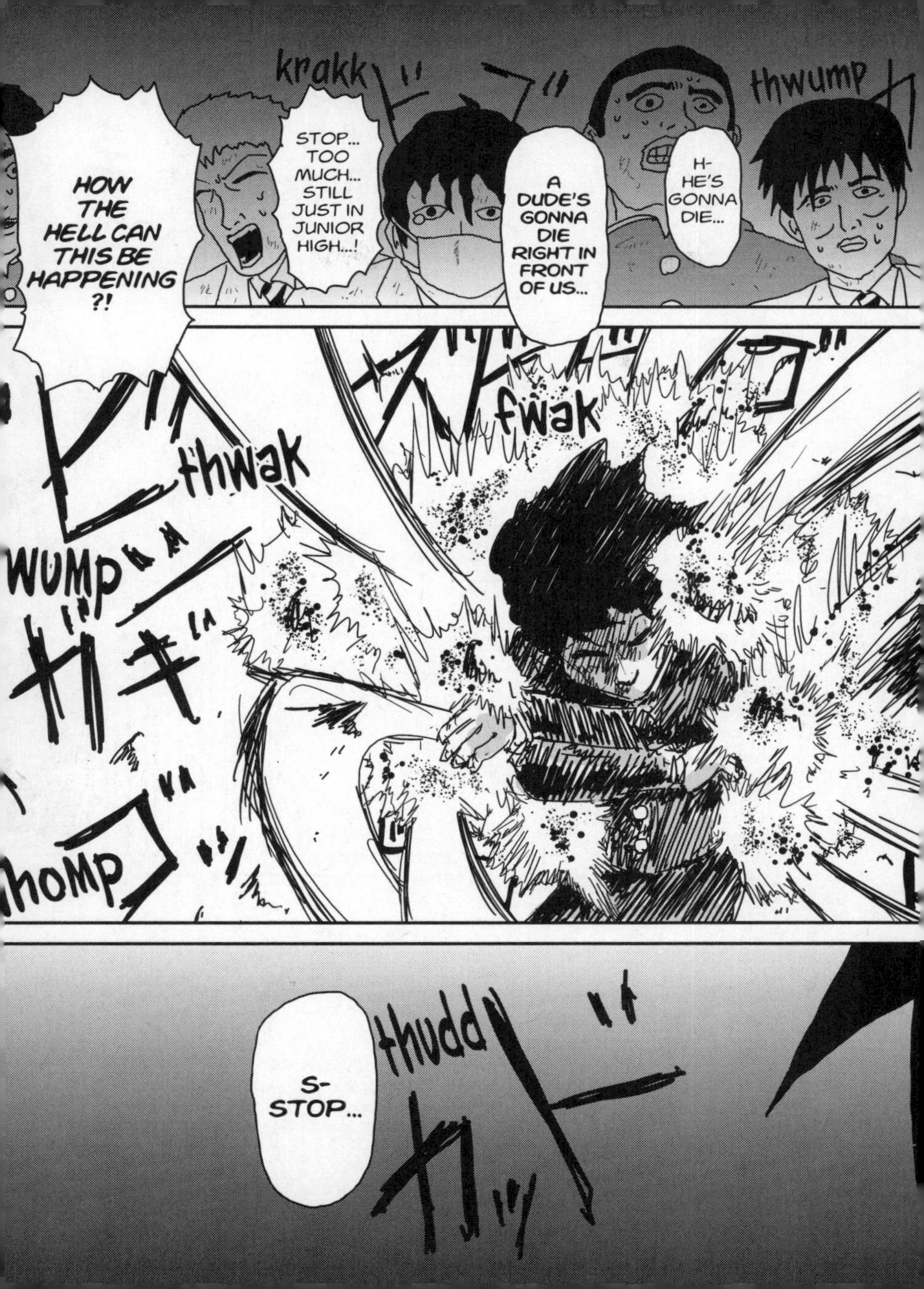
thwump
H-HE'S GONNA DIE...
A DUDE'S GONNA DIE RIGHT IN FRONT OF US...
krakk
STOP... TOO MUCH... STILL JUST IN JUNIOR HIGH...!
HOW THE HELL CAN THIS BE HAPPENING?!
fwak
thwak
wump
homp
thudd
S-STOP...

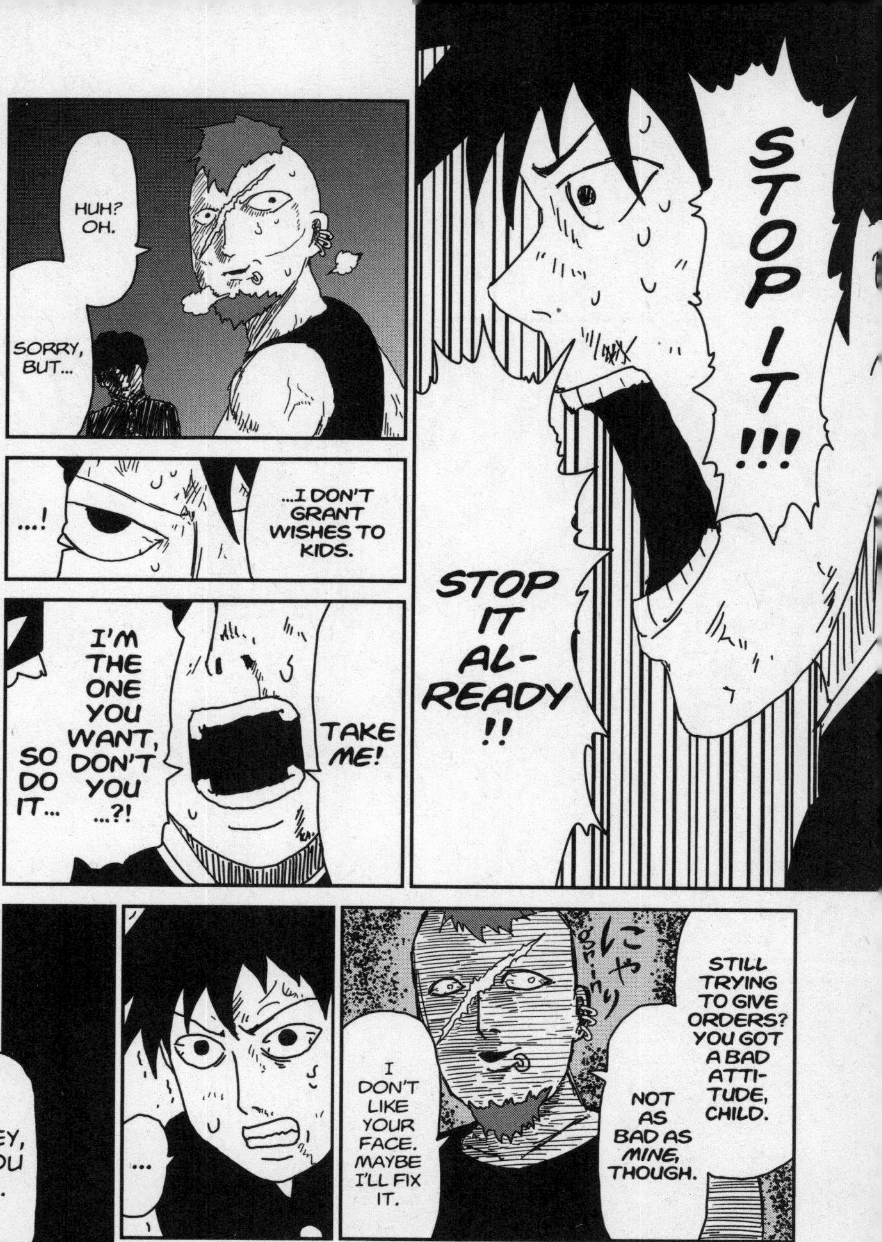
STOP IT!!!
STOP IT ALREADY!!
HUH? OH.
SORRY, BUT...
...I DON'T GRANT WISHES TO KIDS.
...!
TAKE ME!
I'M THE ONE YOU WANT, DON'T YOU...?!
SO DO IT...
STILL TRYING TO GIVE ORDERS? YOU GOT A BAD ATTITUDE, CHILD.
にやーり
NOT AS BAD AS MINE, THOUGH.
I DON'T LIKE YOUR FACE. MAYBE I'LL FIX IT.
...
HEY, YOU ...

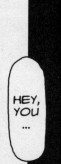

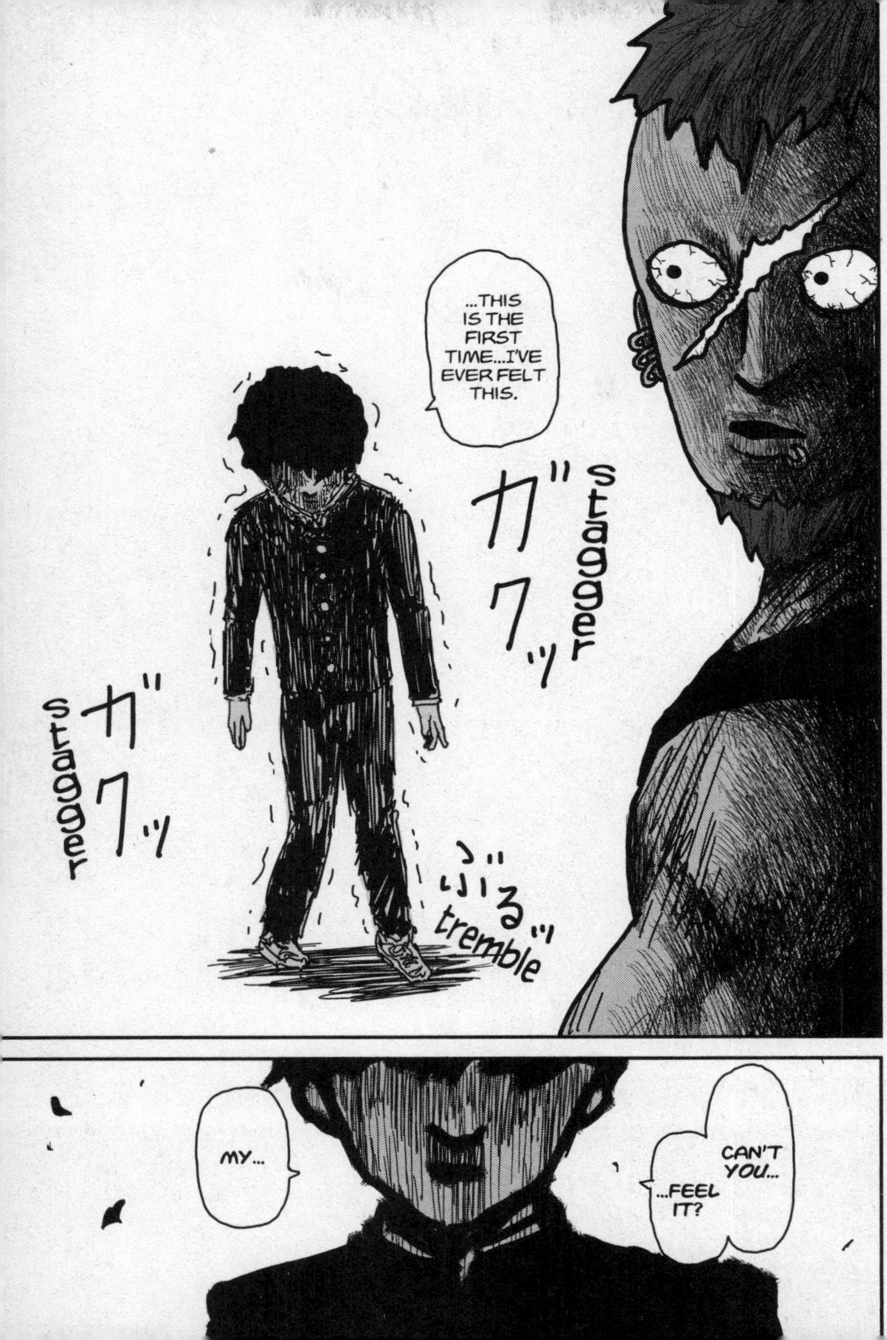
...THIS IS THE FIRST TIME...I'VE EVER FELT THIS.
ガクッ stagger
ガクッ stagger
ぶるっ tremble
CAN'T YOU... ...FEEL IT?
MY...

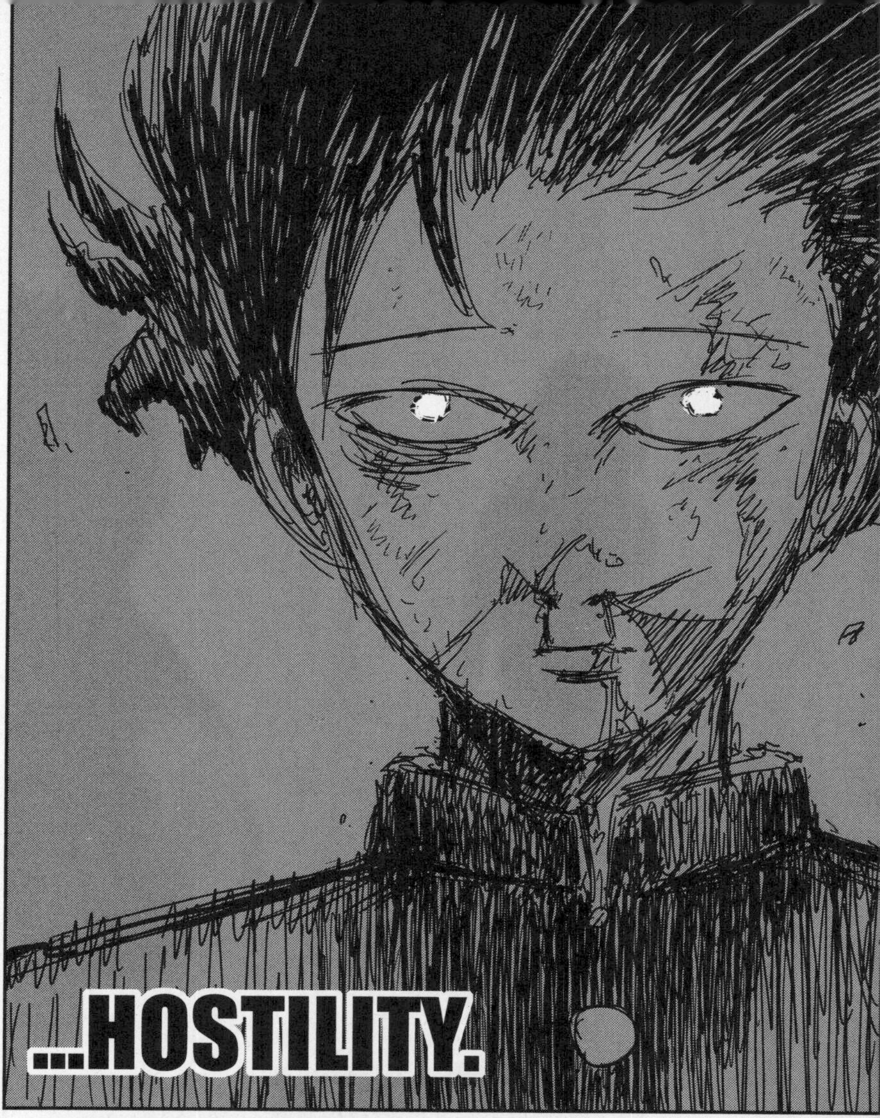
...HOSTILITY.

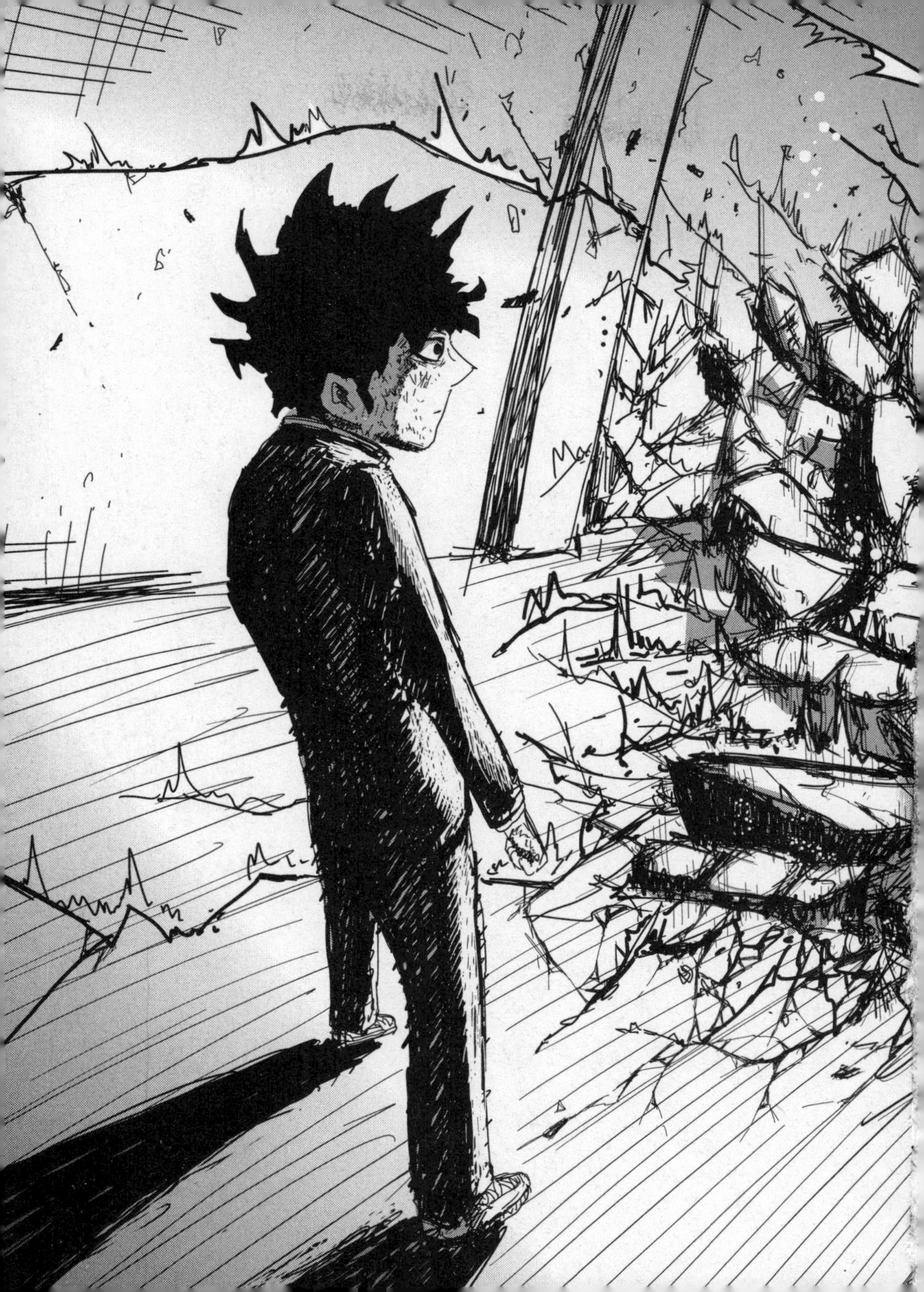

モブサイコ100

MOB PSYCHO 100

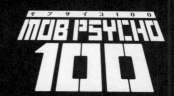

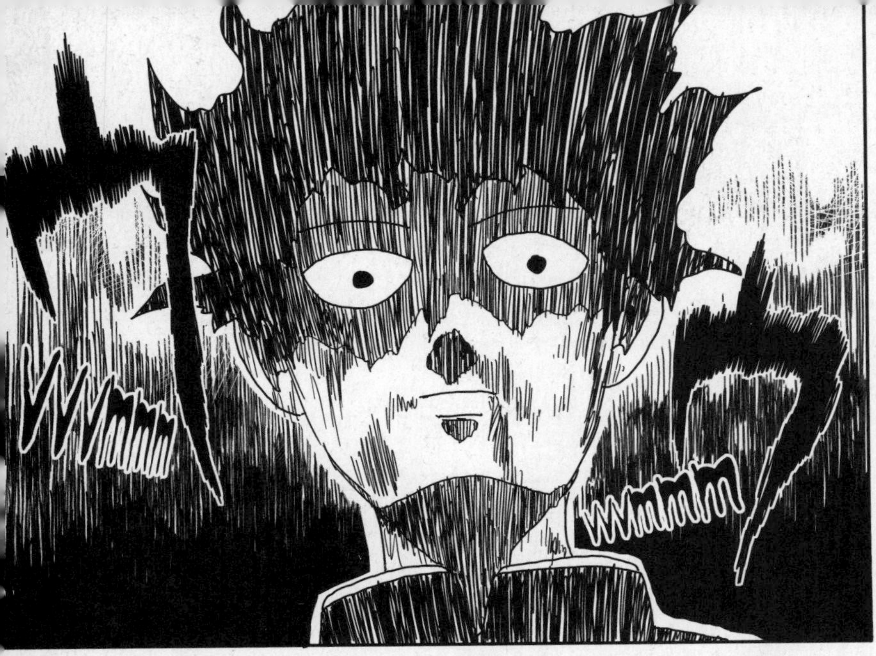

VVmmmm
VVVmmm

CHAPTER 33: A SECRET VS. A SECRET

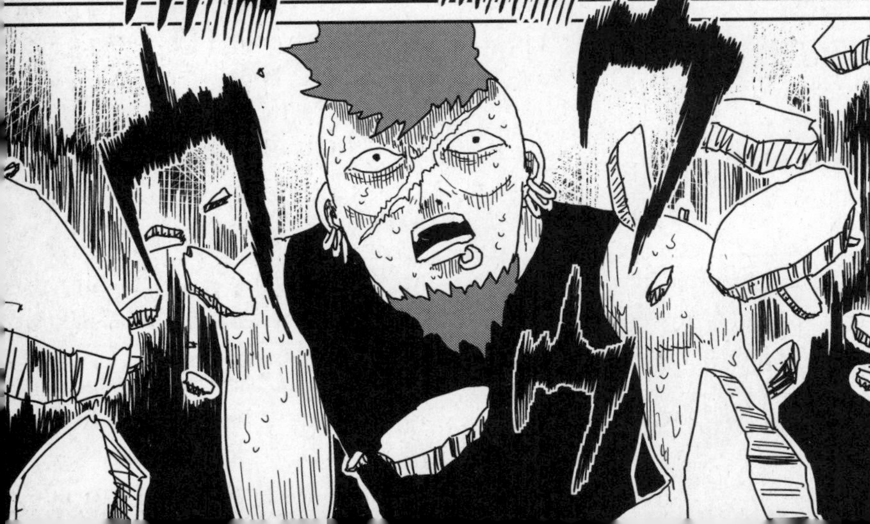

mmmm
VVVmmm

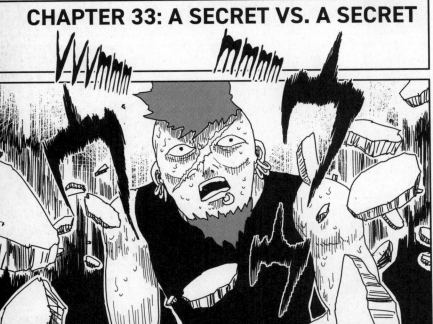

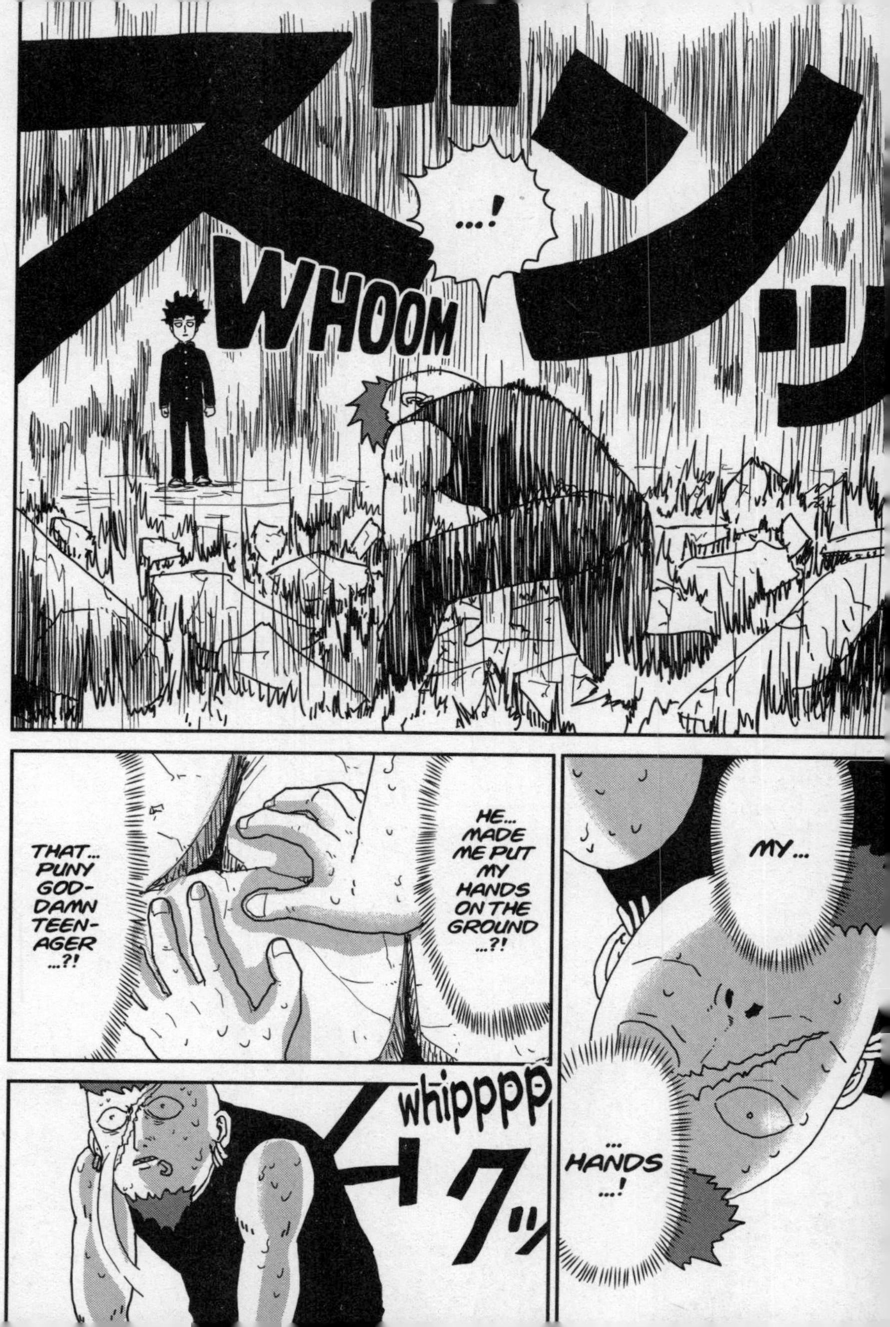
...!
WHOOM
MY...
...HANDS...!
HE... MADE ME PUT MY HANDS ON THE GROUND...?!
THAT... PUNY GOD-DAMN TEEN-AGER...?!
whipppp

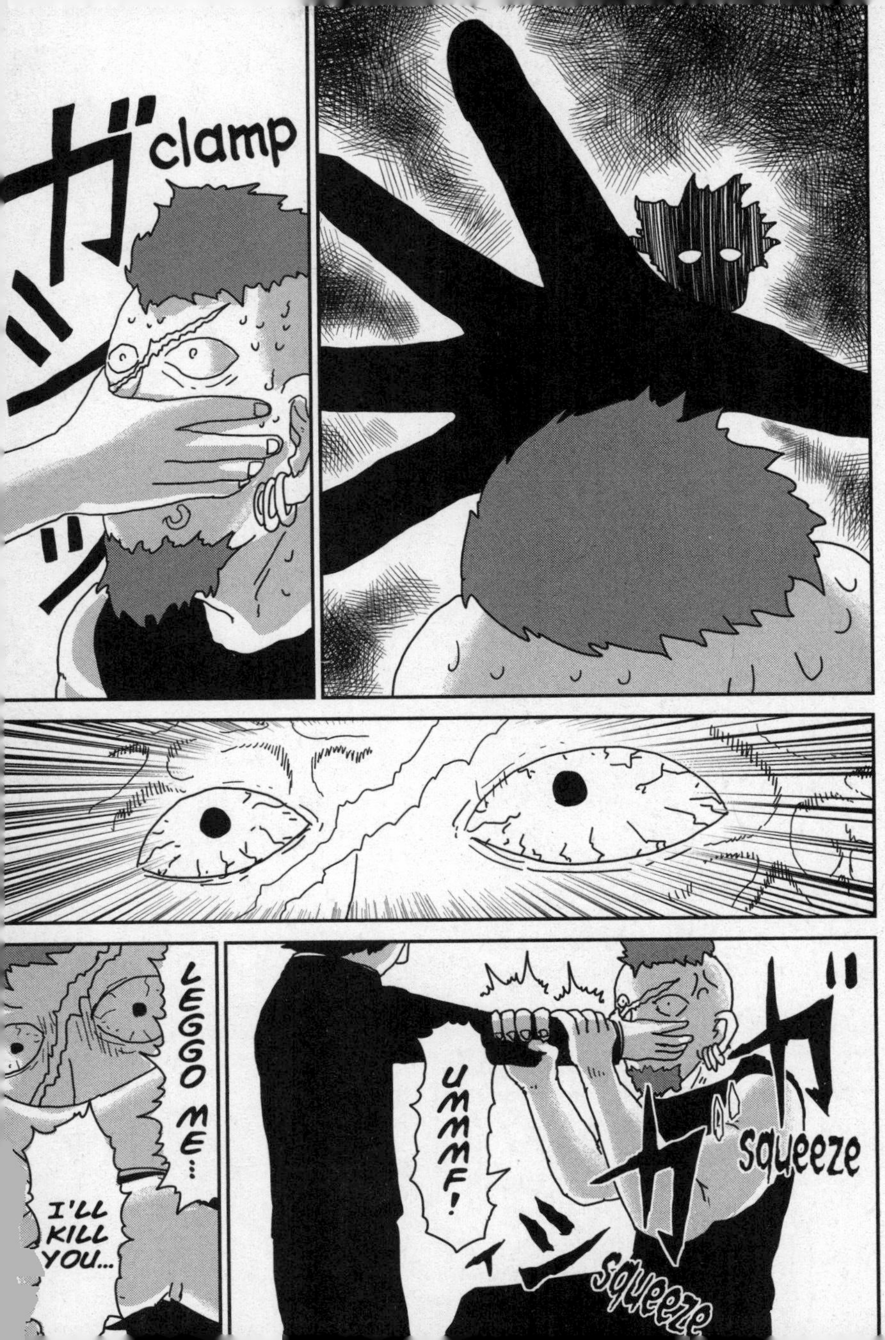
clamp
UMMMF!
squeeze
squeeze
LEGGO ME...
I'LL KILL YOU...

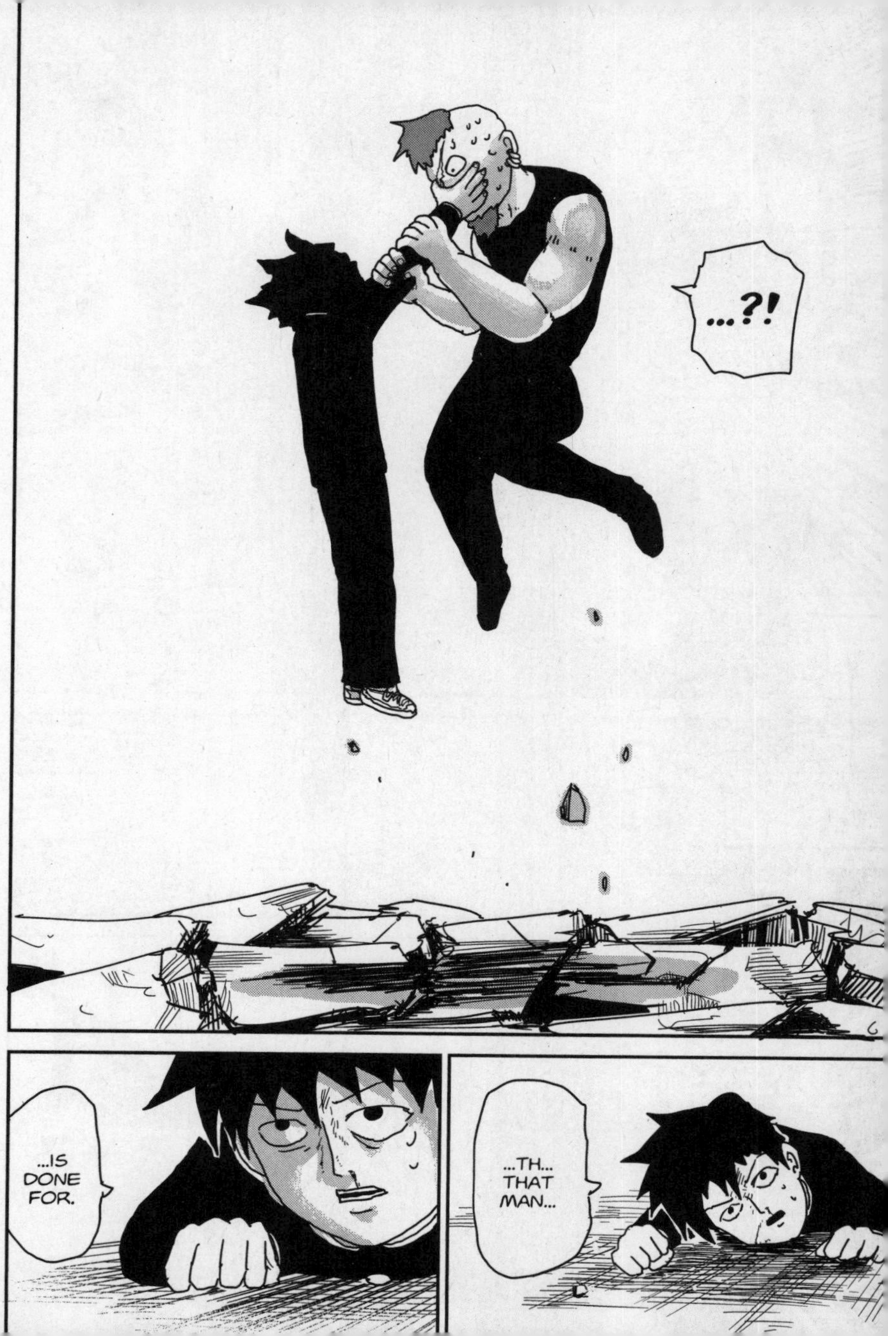
...?!
...TH... THAT MAN...
...IS DONE FOR.

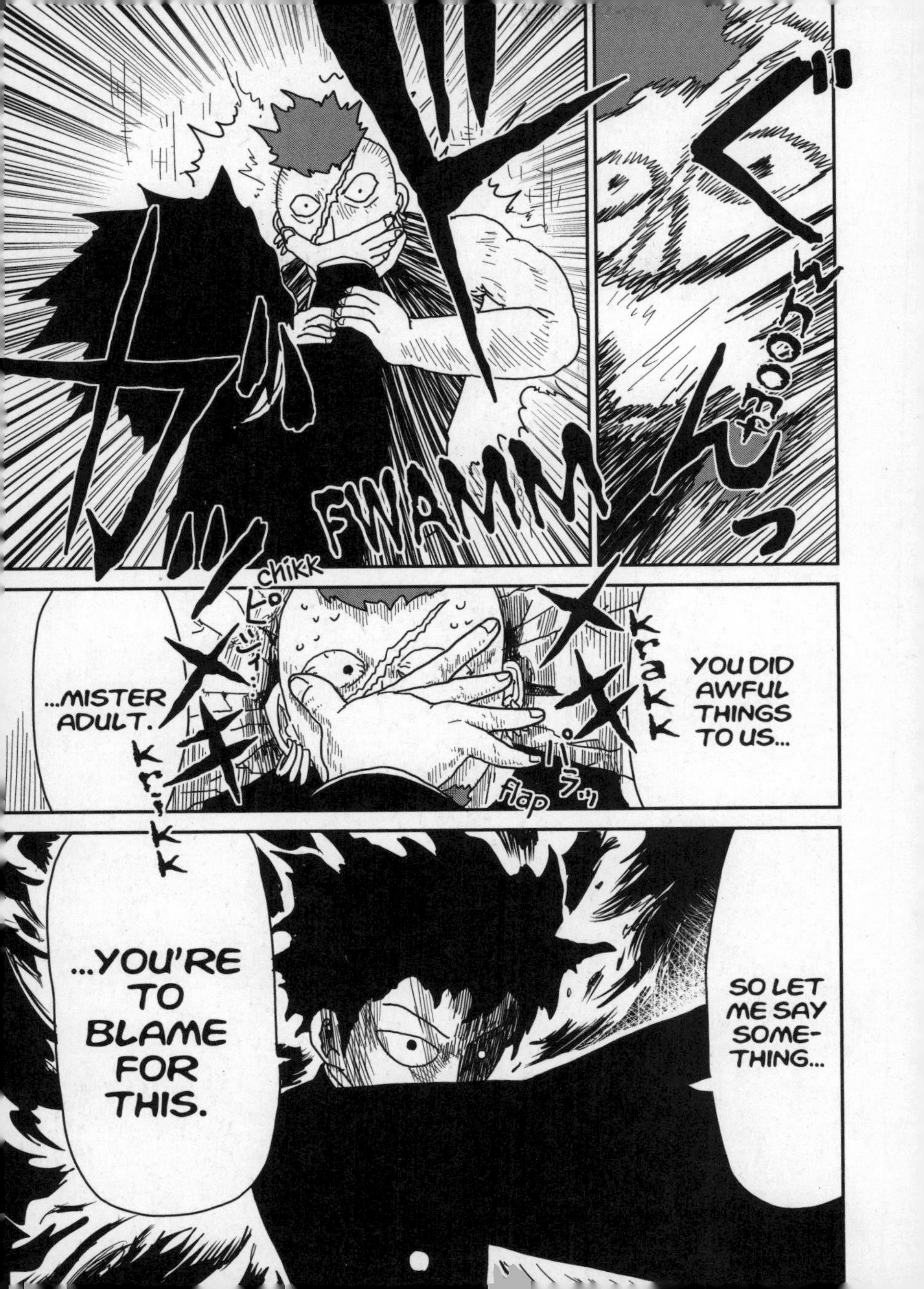
whoof
FWAMM
krakk
YOU DID AWFUL THINGS TO US...
flap
chikk
...MISTER ADULT.
krakk
SO LET ME SAY SOME-THING...
...YOU'RE TO BLAME FOR THIS.

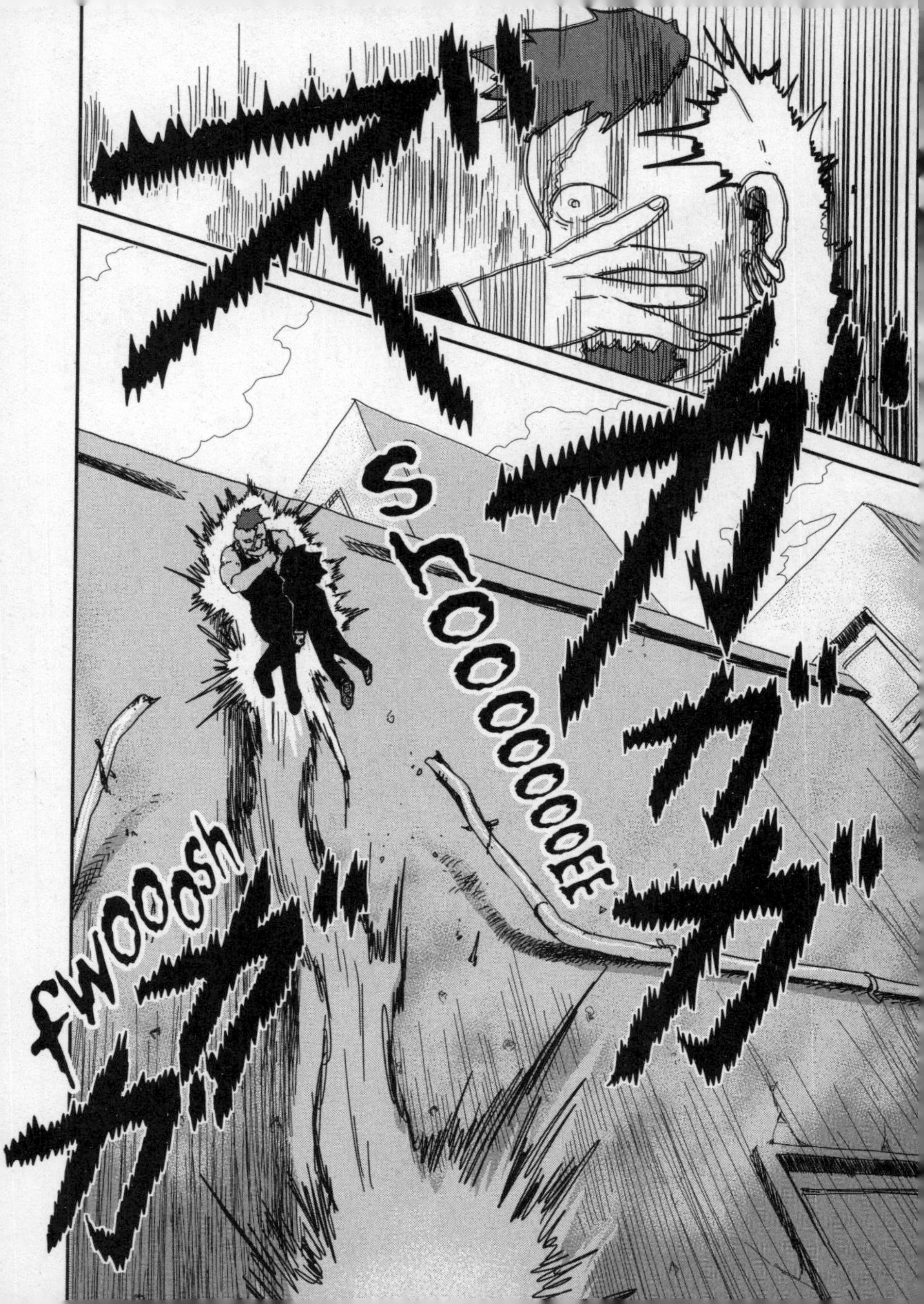
SHOOOOOOOFF
fwOOOsh

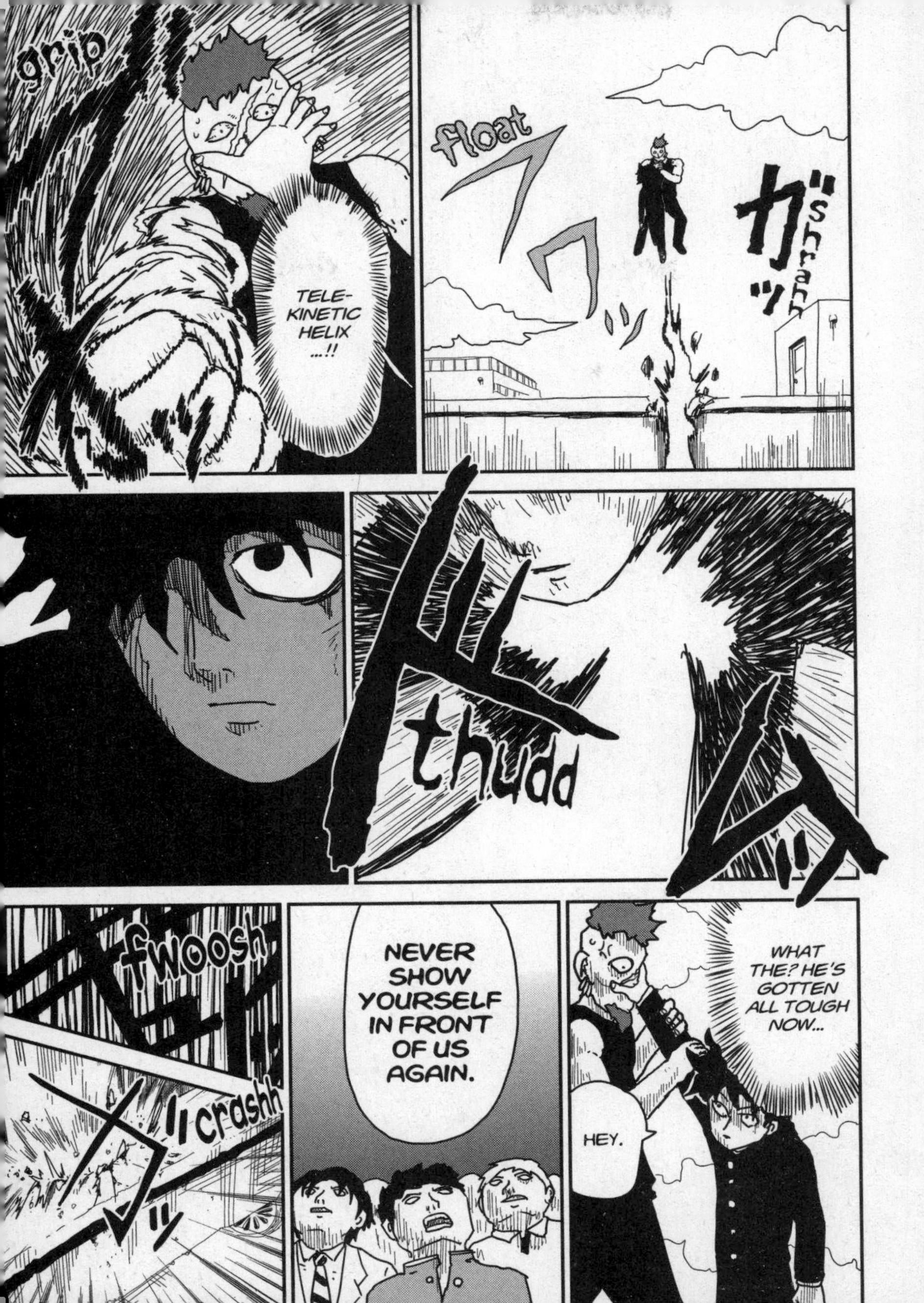
float
shrahh
grip
TELE-KINETIC HELIX ...!!
thudd
WHAT THE? HE'S GOTTEN ALL TOUGH NOW...
HEY.
NEVER SHOW YOURSELF IN FRONT OF US AGAIN.
fwoosh
crashh

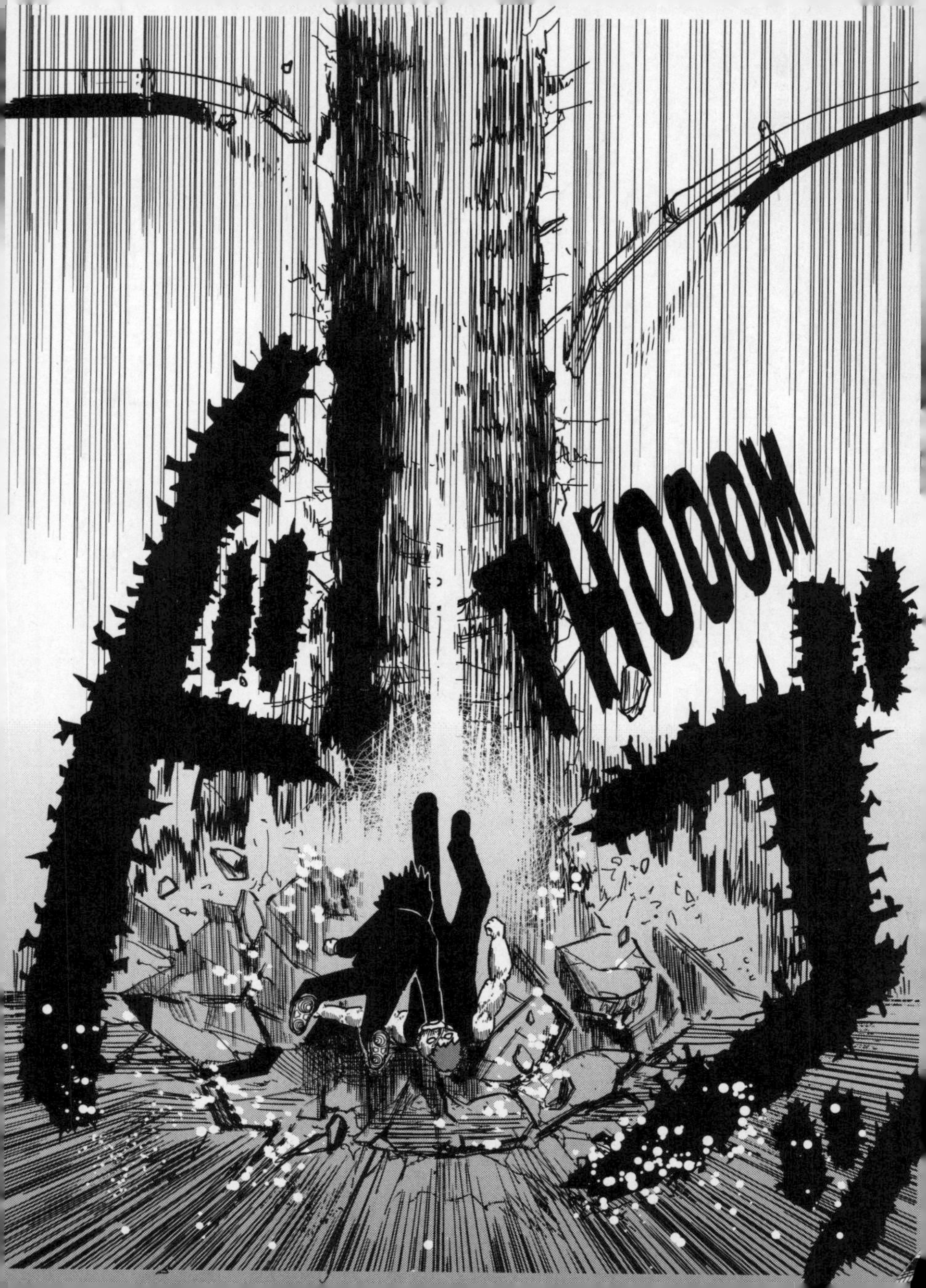
THOOOM

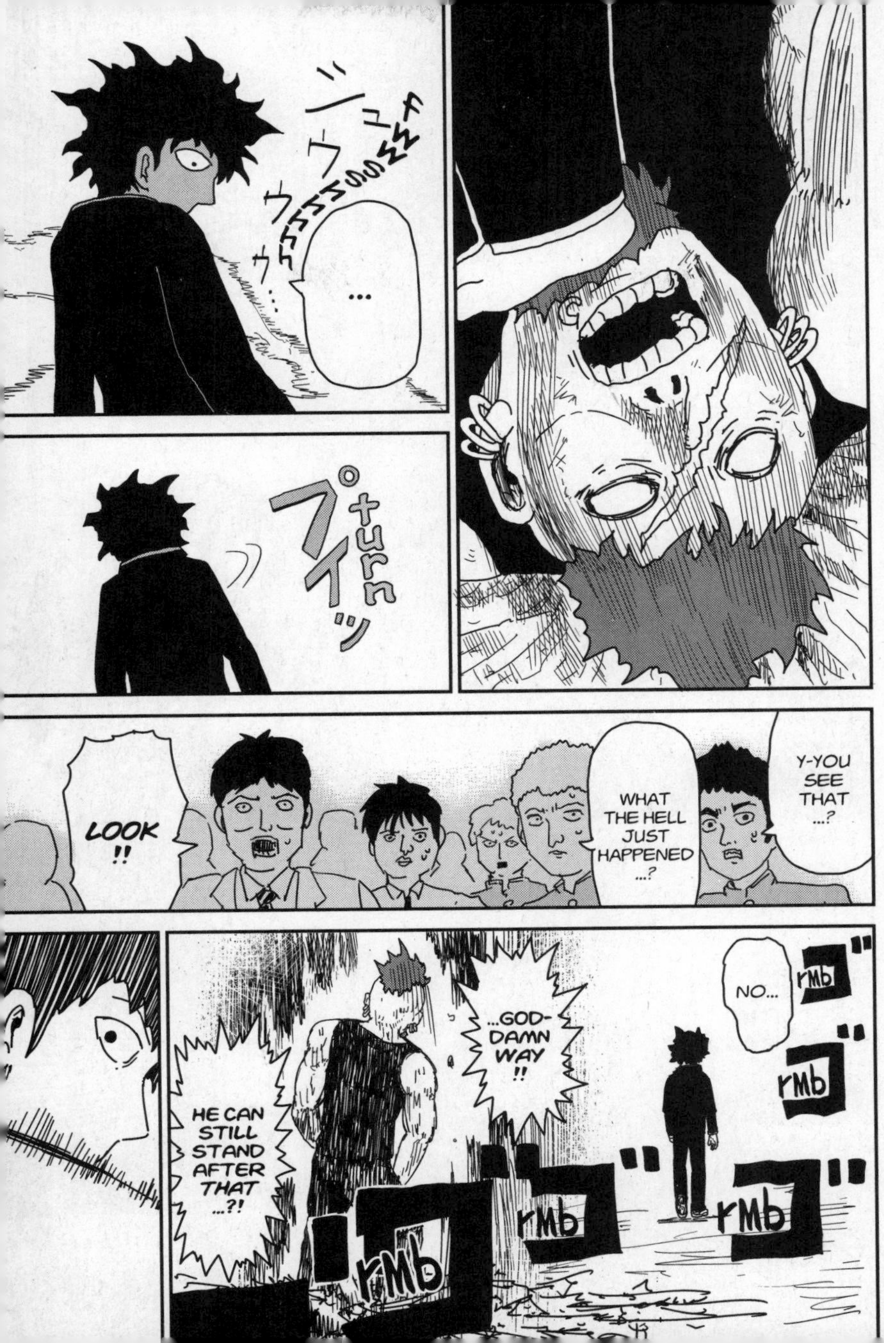

シュウウウウウ...
FWSSSSSS
...
プイッ
turn
Y-YOU SEE THAT ...?
WHAT THE HELL JUST HAPPENED ...?
LOOK !!
NO...
ゴ rMb
ゴ rMb
...GOD-DAMN WAY !!
ゴ rMb
ゴ rMb
HE CAN STILL STAND AFTER THAT ...?!
ゴ rMb

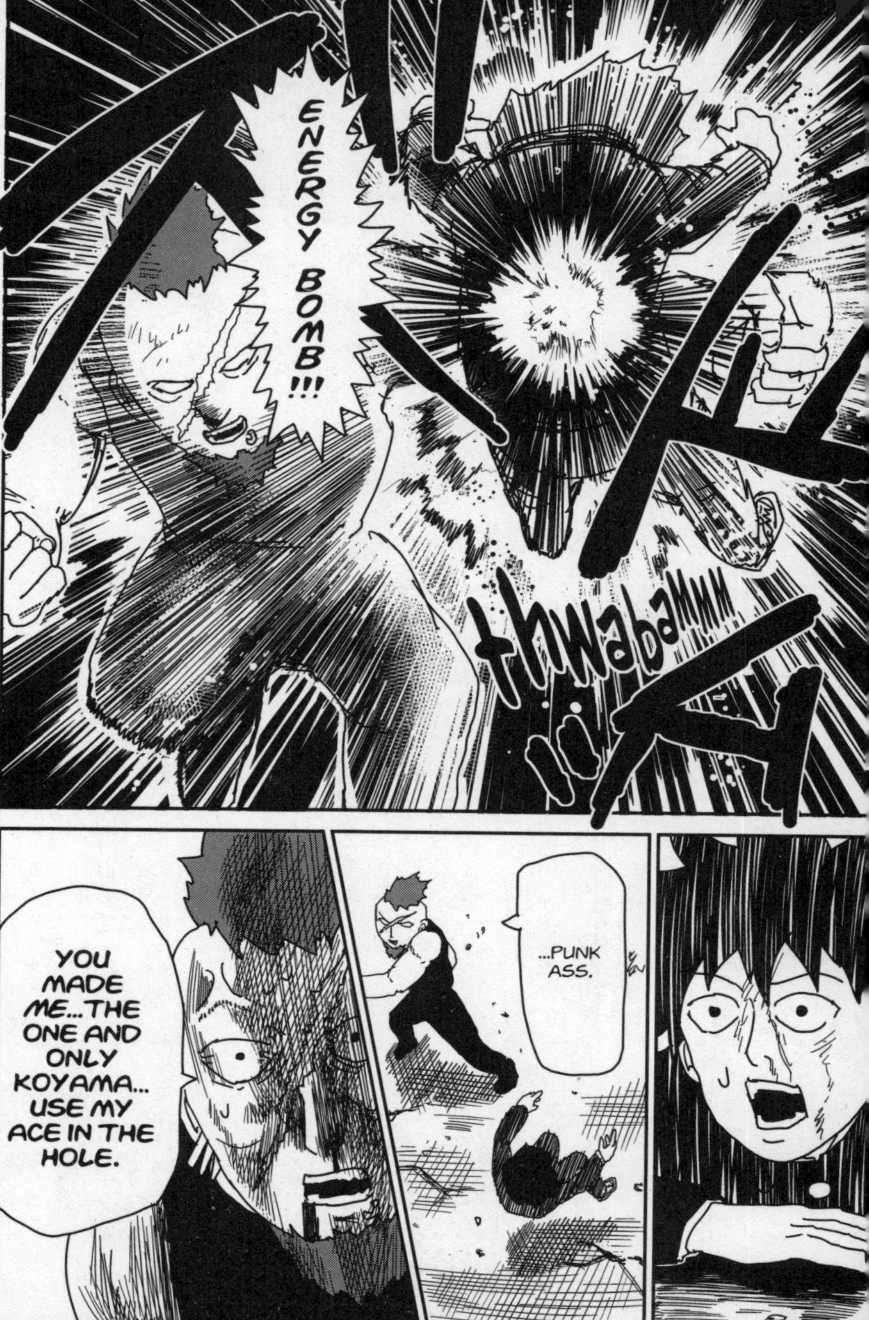
ENERGY BOMB!!!
thwabaMMMM
...PUNK ASS.
YOU MADE ME...THE ONE AND ONLY KOYAMA... USE MY ACE IN THE HOLE.

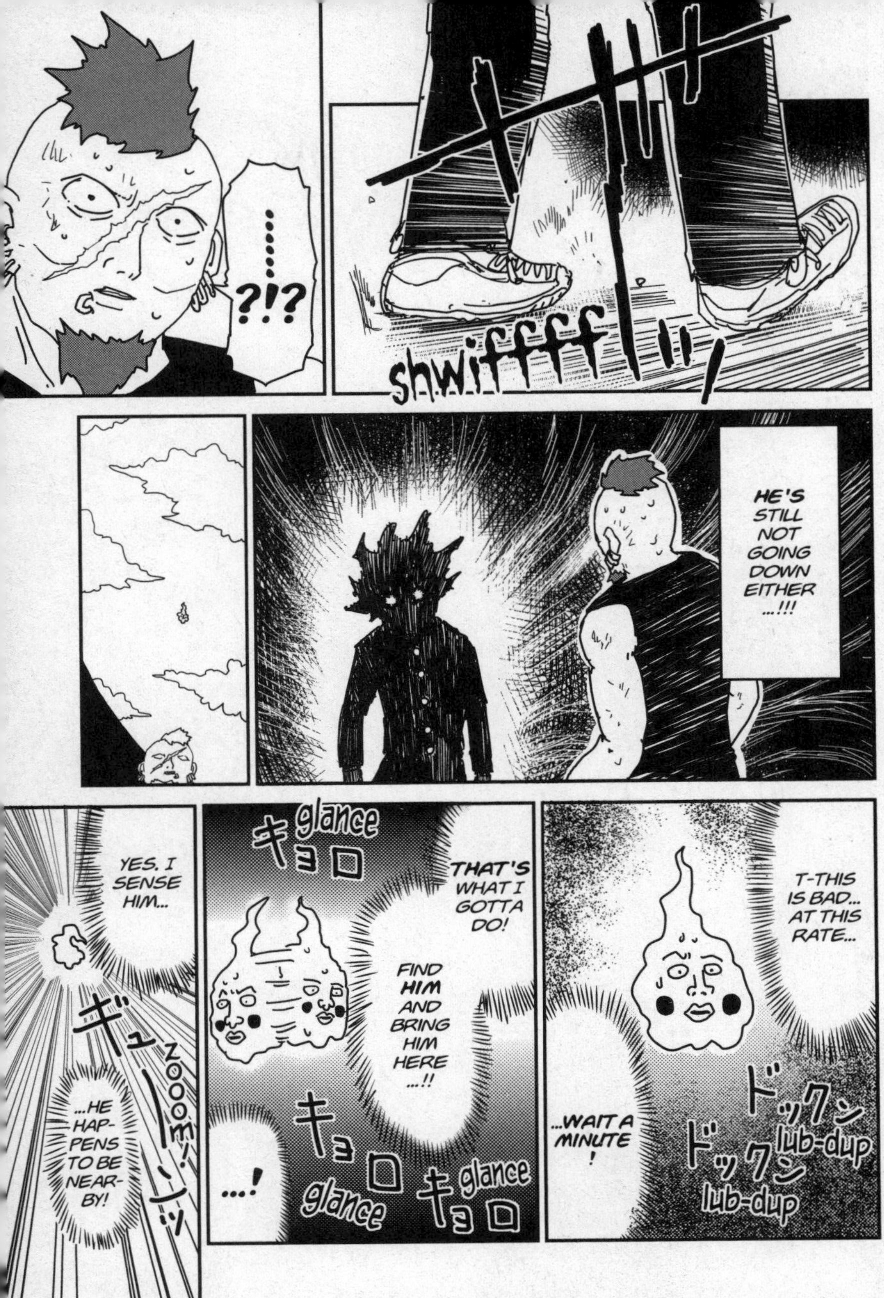
shwiffff
......
?!?
HE'S STILL NOT GOING DOWN EITHER ...!!!
T-THIS IS BAD... AT THIS RATE...
...WAIT A MINUTE!
ドックン lub-dup
ドックン lub-dup
キョロ glance
THAT'S WHAT I GOTTA DO!
FIND HIM AND BRING HIM HERE ...!!
キョロ glance
キョロ glance
...!
YES. I SENSE HIM...
ギューンッ ZOOOM!
...HE HAPPENS TO BE NEAR-BY!

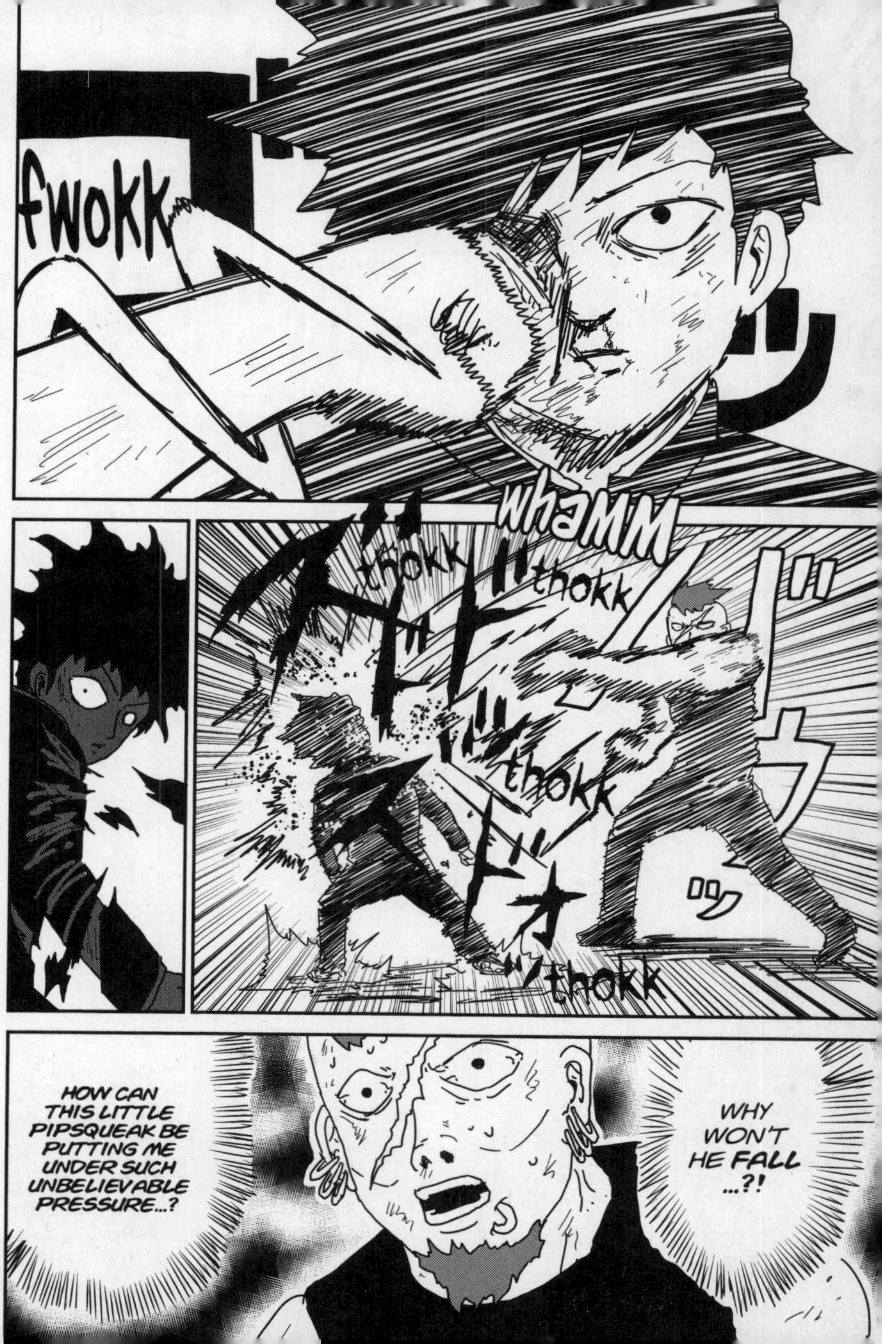
fwokk
whaMM
thokk
thokk
thokk
thokk
WHY WON'T HE FALL ...?!
HOW CAN THIS LITTLE PIPSQUEAK BE PUTTING ME UNDER SUCH UNBELIEVABLE PRESSURE...?

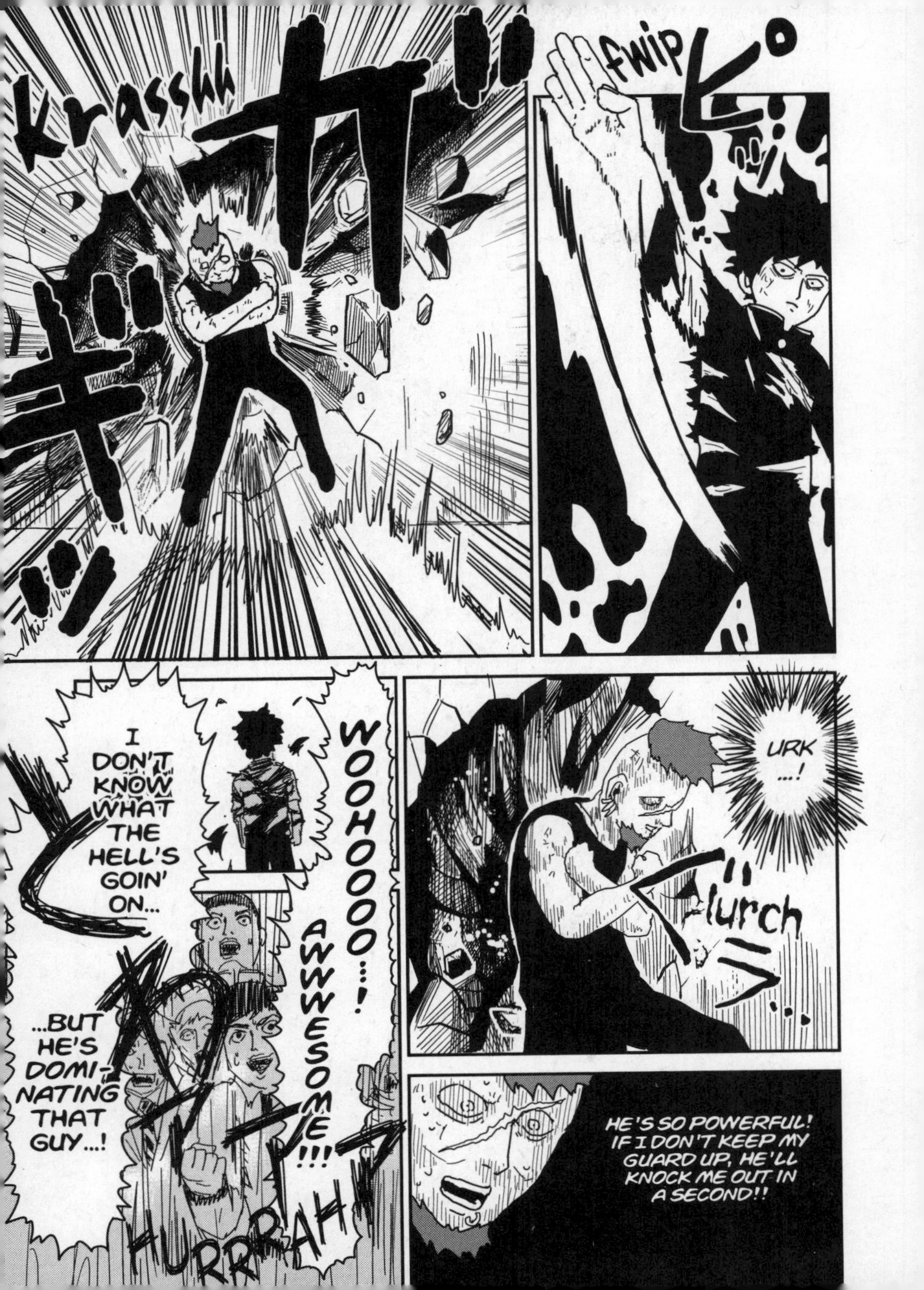
fwip
Krasshh
URK ...!
lurch
...
HE'S SO POWERFUL! IF I DON'T KEEP MY GUARD UP, HE'LL KNOCK ME OUT IN A SECOND!!
WOOHOOOOOO...! AWWWESOME!!!
I DON'T KNOW WHAT THE HELL'S GOIN' ON...
...BUT HE'S DOMINATING THAT GUY...!
HURRRAHH

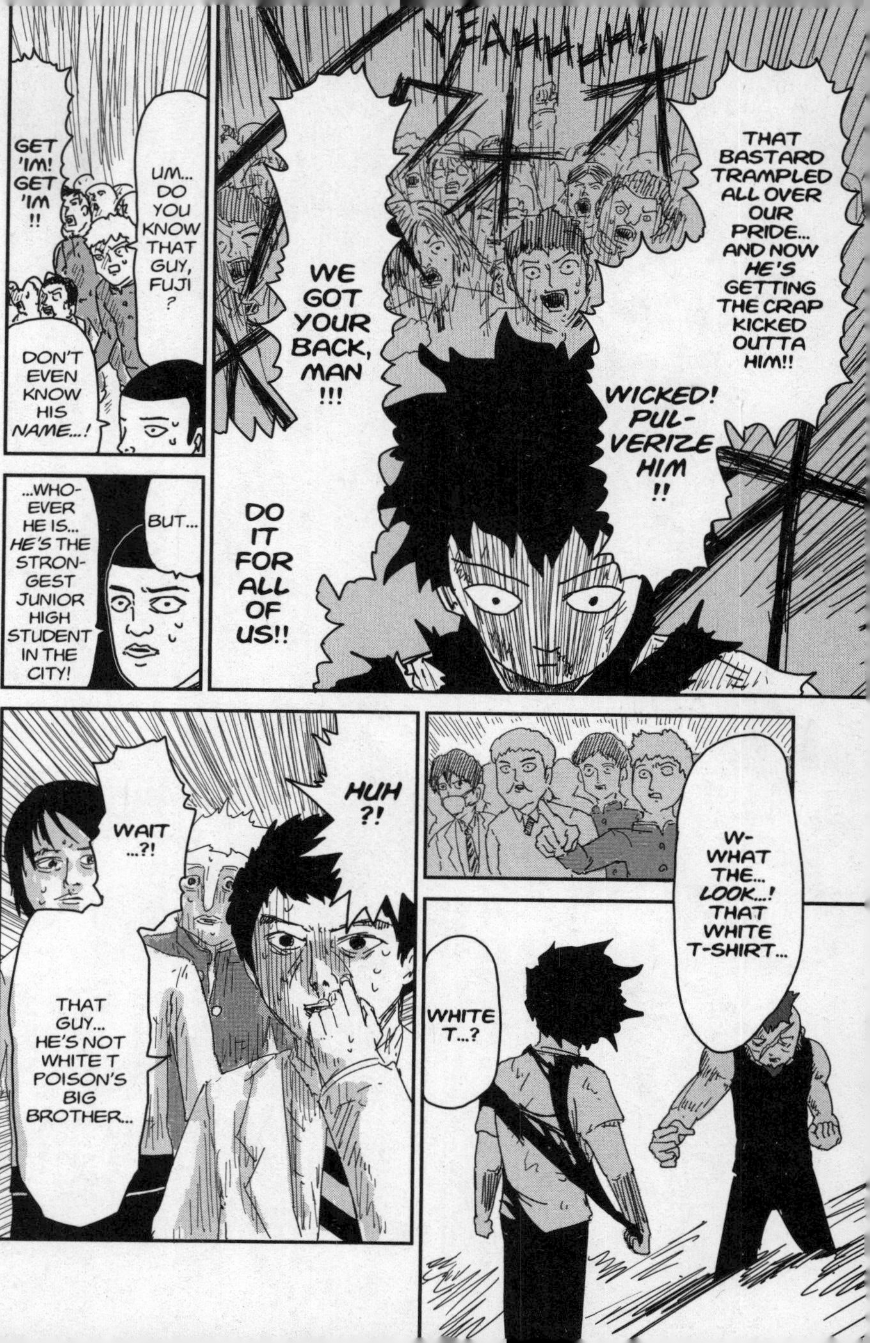
YEAHHHHH!
THAT BASTARD TRAMPLED ALL OVER OUR PRIDE... AND NOW HE'S GETTING THE CRAP KICKED OUTTA HIM!!
WICKED! PUL-VERIZE HIM!!
WE GOT YOUR BACK, MAN!!!
DO IT FOR ALL OF US!!
UM... DO YOU KNOW THAT GUY, FUJI?
GET 'IM! GET 'IM!!
DON'T EVEN KNOW HIS NAME...!
BUT...
...WHO-EVER HE IS... HE'S THE STRON-GEST JUNIOR HIGH STUDENT IN THE CITY!
W-WHAT THE... LOOK...! THAT WHITE T-SHIRT...
WHITE T...?
HUH?!
WAIT...?!
THAT GUY... HE'S NOT WHITE T POISON'S BIG BROTHER...

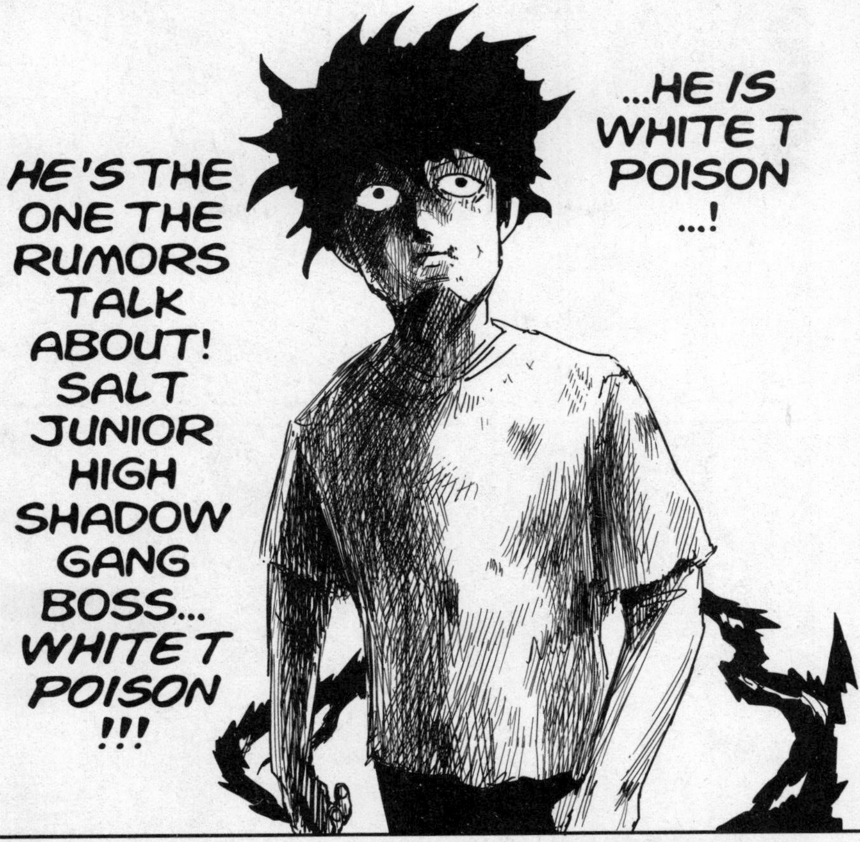
...HE IS WHITE T POISON ...!
HE'S THE ONE THE RUMORS TALK ABOUT! SALT JUNIOR HIGH SHADOW GANG BOSS... WHITE T POISON !!!
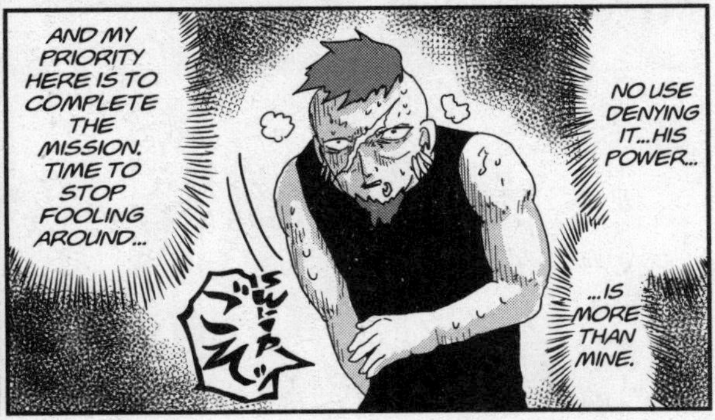
NO USE DENYING IT...HIS POWER...
...IS MORE THAN MINE.
AND MY PRIORITY HERE IS TO COMPLETE THE MISSION. TIME TO STOP FOOLING AROUND...
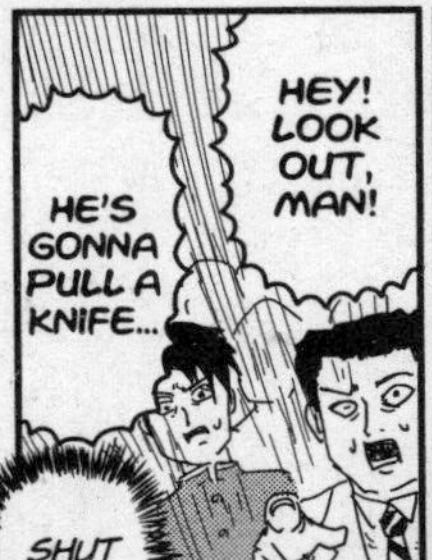
HEY! LOOK OUT, MAN!
HE'S GONNA PULL A KNIFE...
SHUT UP, YOU DUMB BRATS...

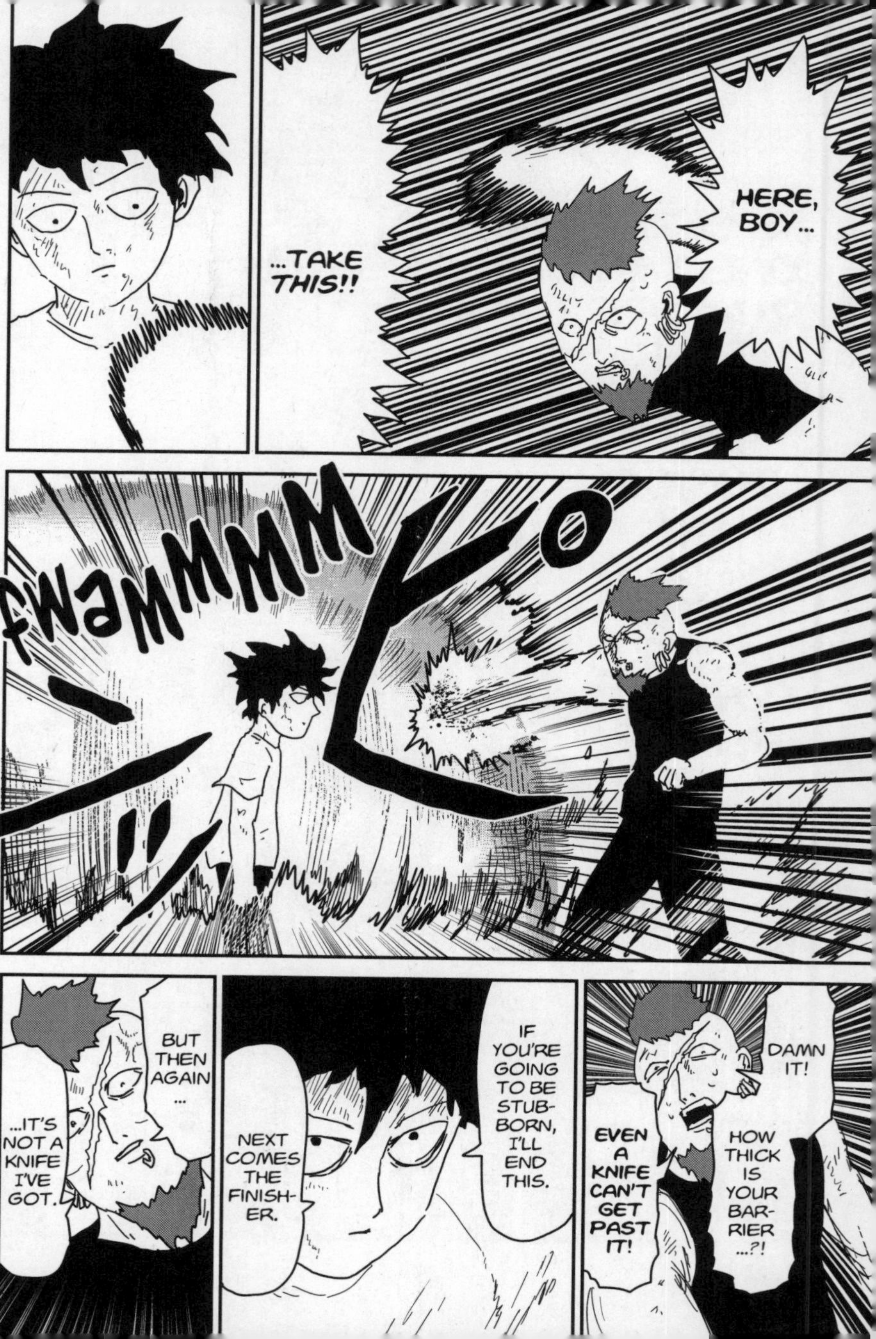
HERE, BOY...
...TAKE THIS!!
FWAMMMM!!
DAMN IT!
HOW THICK IS YOUR BAR-RIER ...?!
EVEN A KNIFE CAN'T GET PAST IT!
IF YOU'RE GOING TO BE STUB-BORN, I'LL END THIS.
NEXT COMES THE FINISH-ER.
BUT THEN AGAIN ...
...IT'S NOT A KNIFE I'VE GOT.

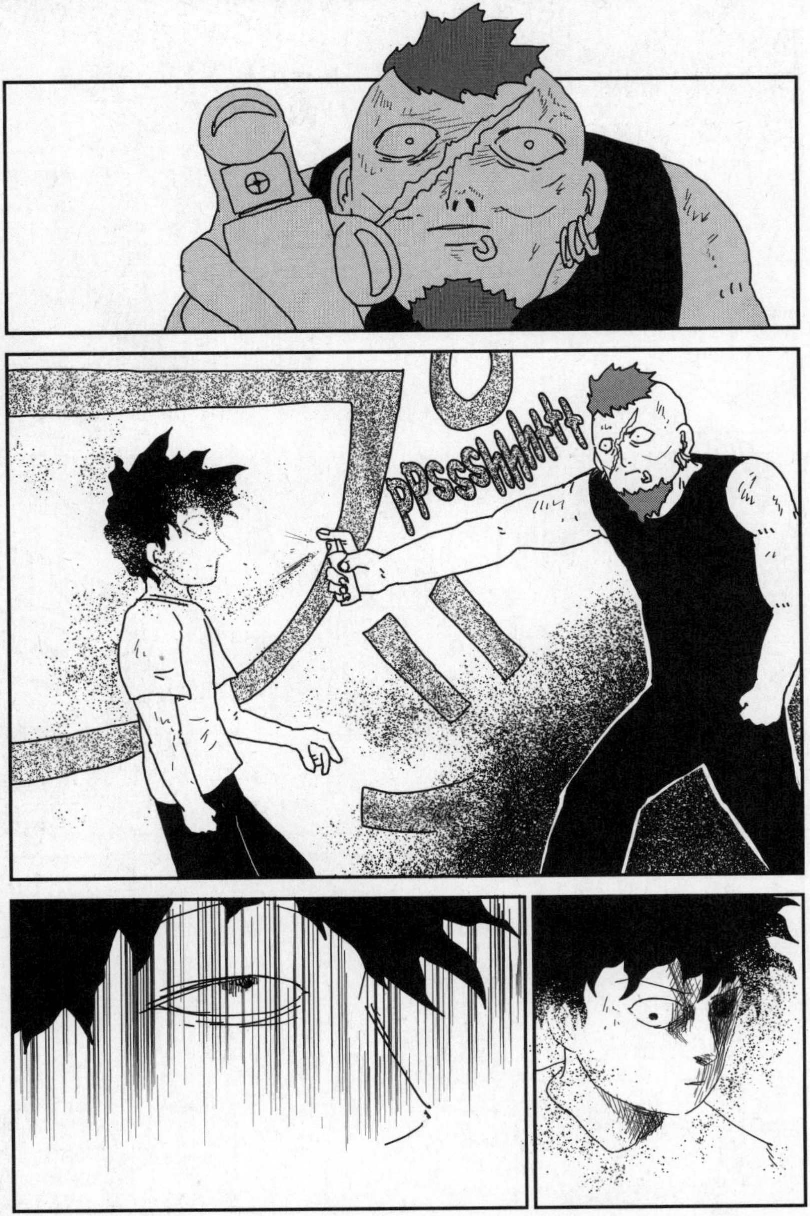
ppssshhhttt

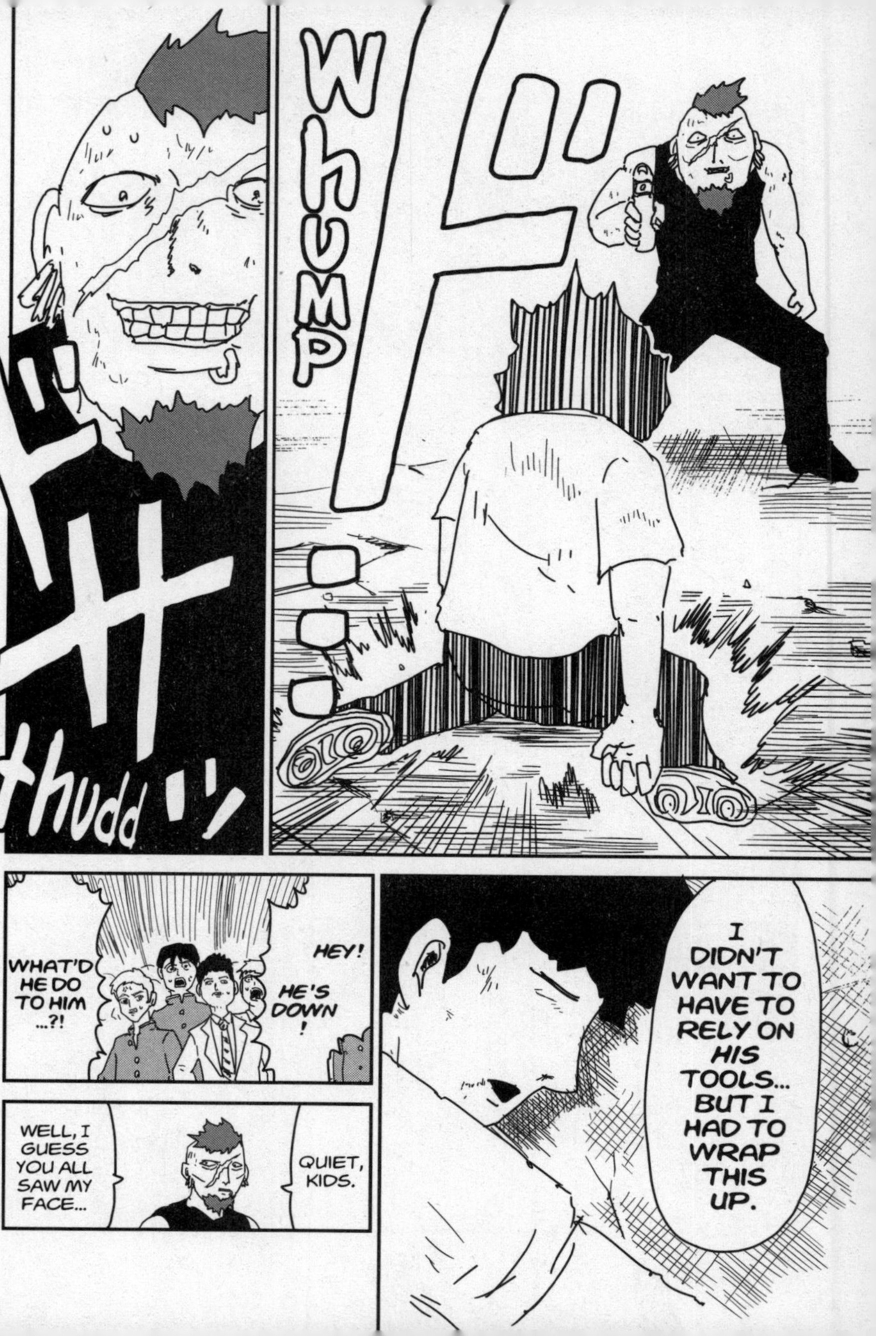
ド
WHUMP
...
ドサ
thudd ッ
I DIDN'T WANT TO HAVE TO RELY ON HIS TOOLS... BUT I HAD TO WRAP THIS UP.
HEY!
HE'S DOWN!
WHAT'D HE DO TO HIM ...?!
QUIET, KIDS.
WELL, I GUESS YOU ALL SAW MY FACE...

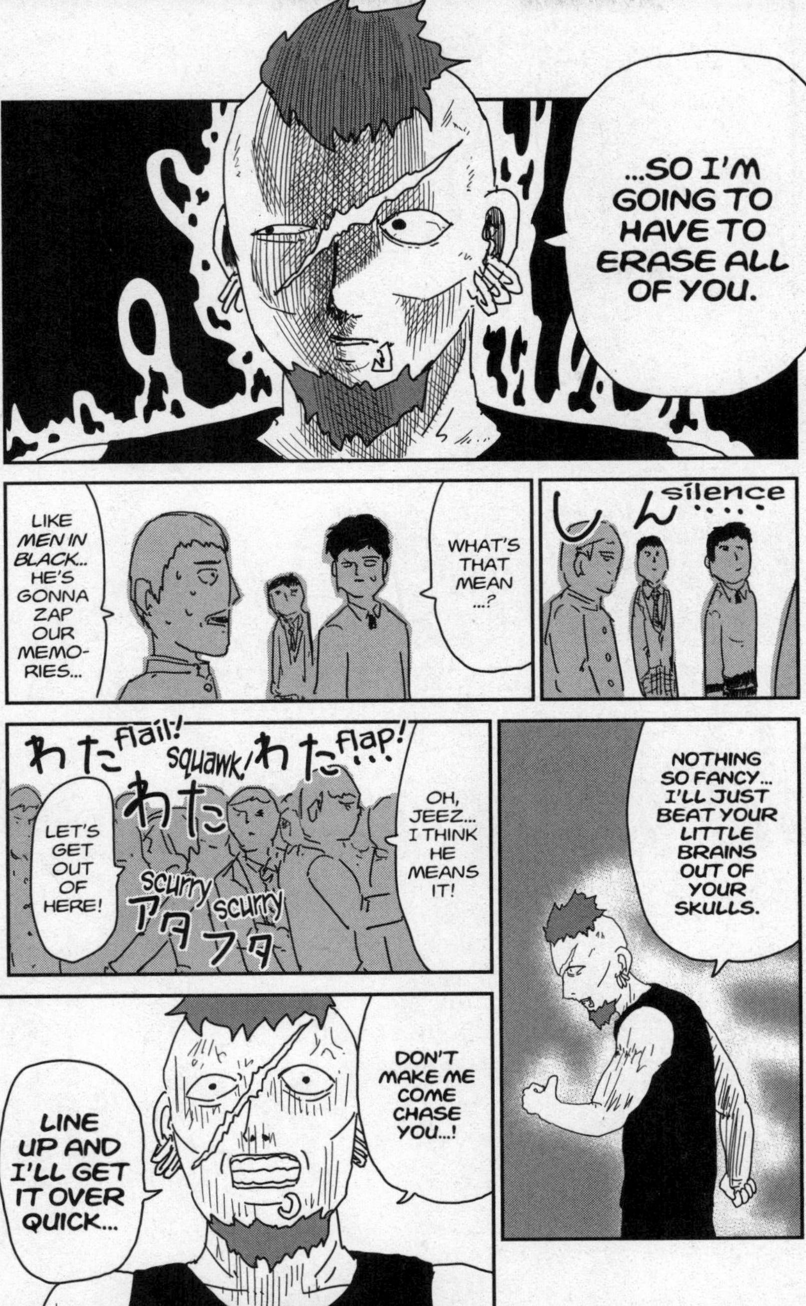
...SO I'M GOING TO HAVE TO ERASE ALL OF YOU.
しん silence...
WHAT'S THAT MEAN ...?
LIKE MEN IN BLACK... HE'S GONNA ZAP OUR MEMORIES...
NOTHING SO FANCY... I'LL JUST BEAT YOUR LITTLE BRAINS OUT OF YOUR SKULLS.
わた flap!...
squawk!
わた flail!
わた
OH, JEEZ... I THINK HE MEANS IT!
LET'S GET OUT OF HERE!
アタフタ scurry scurry
DON'T MAKE ME COME CHASE YOU...!
LINE UP AND I'LL GET IT OVER QUICK...

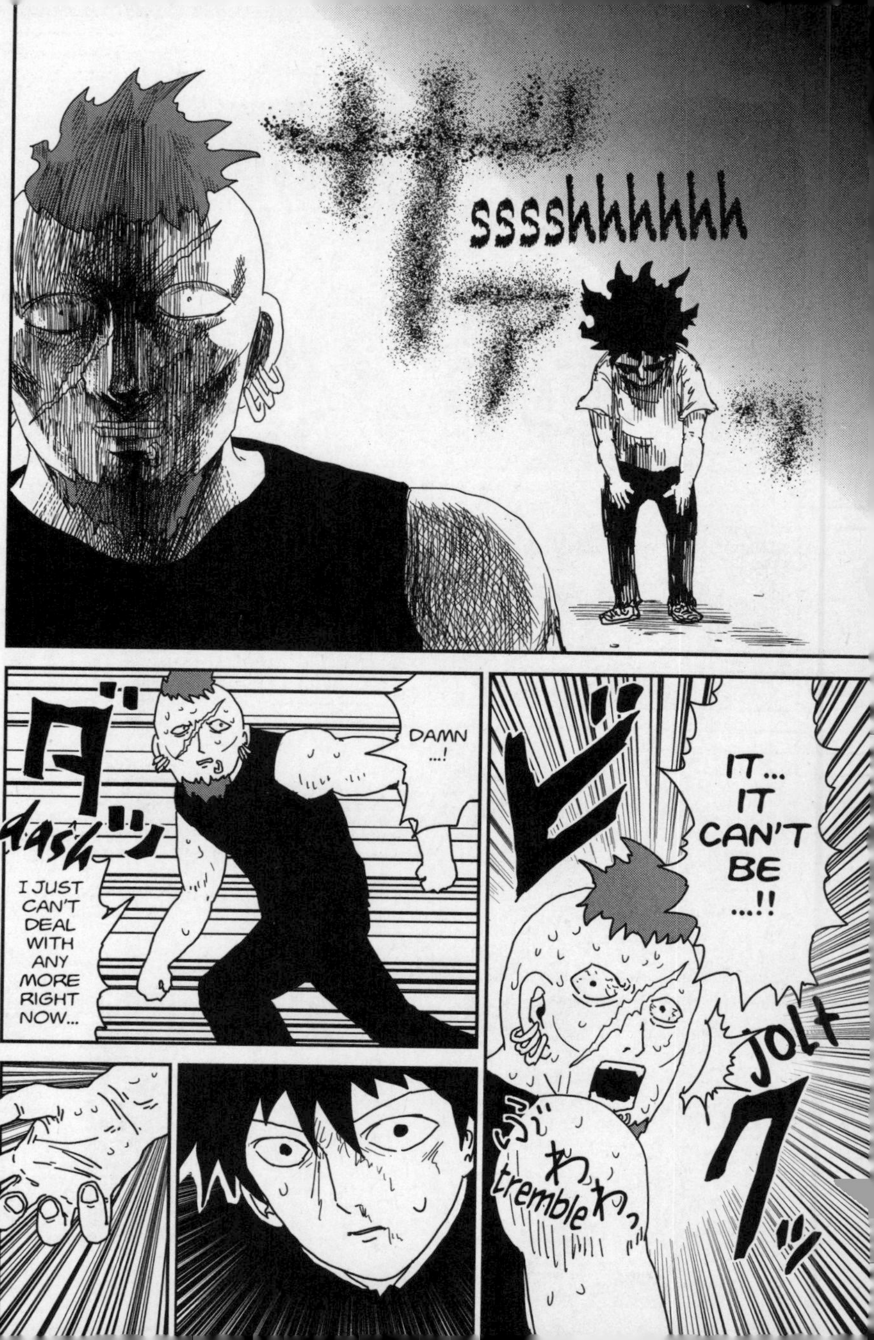
sssshhhhhh
IT... IT CAN'T BE ...!!
JOLT
tremble
dash
DAMN ...!
I JUST CAN'T DEAL WITH ANY MORE RIGHT NOW...

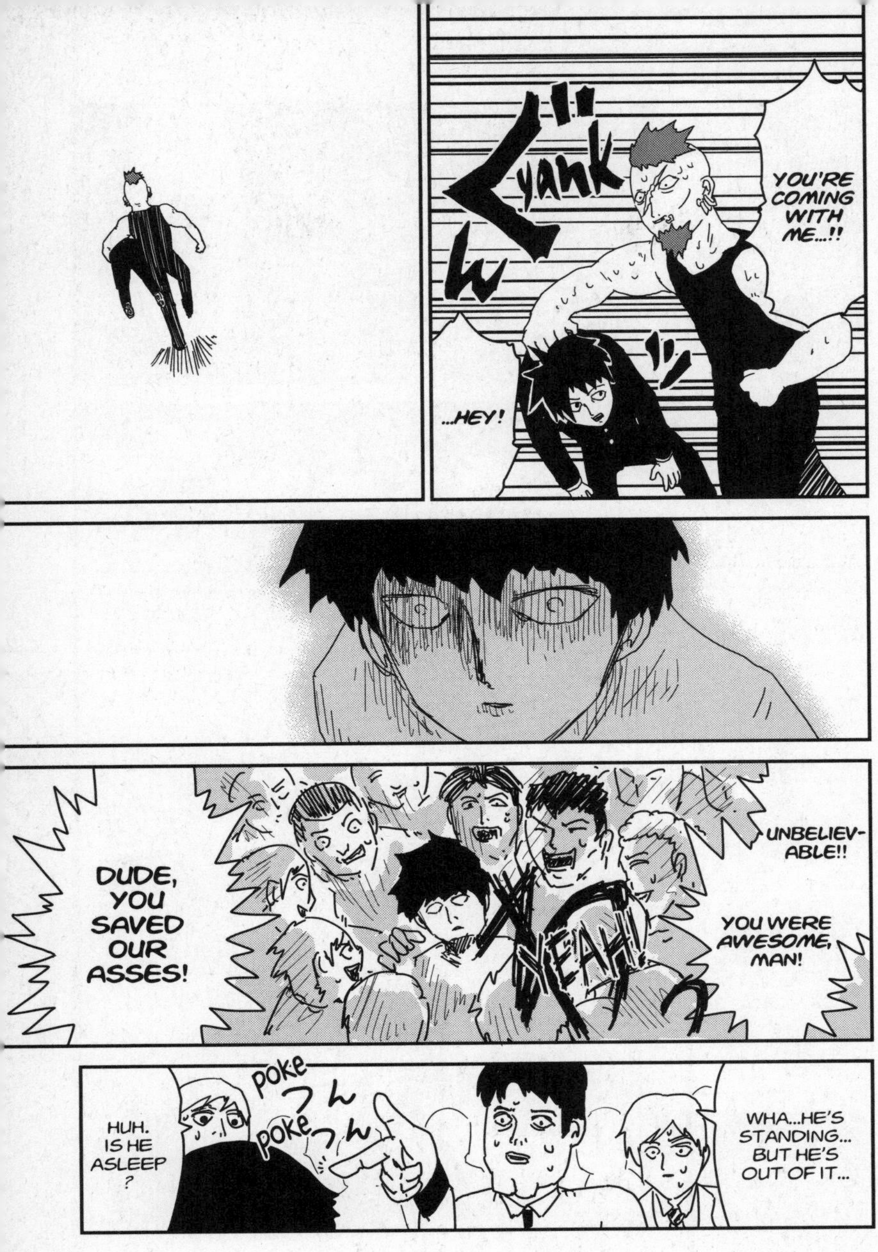
YOU'RE COMING WITH ME...!!
yank
...HEY!
UNBELIEV-ABLE!!
YOU WERE AWESOME, MAN!
YEAH!
DUDE, YOU SAVED OUR ASSES!
WHA...HE'S STANDING... BUT HE'S OUT OF IT...
poke
poke
HUH. IS HE ASLEEP ?

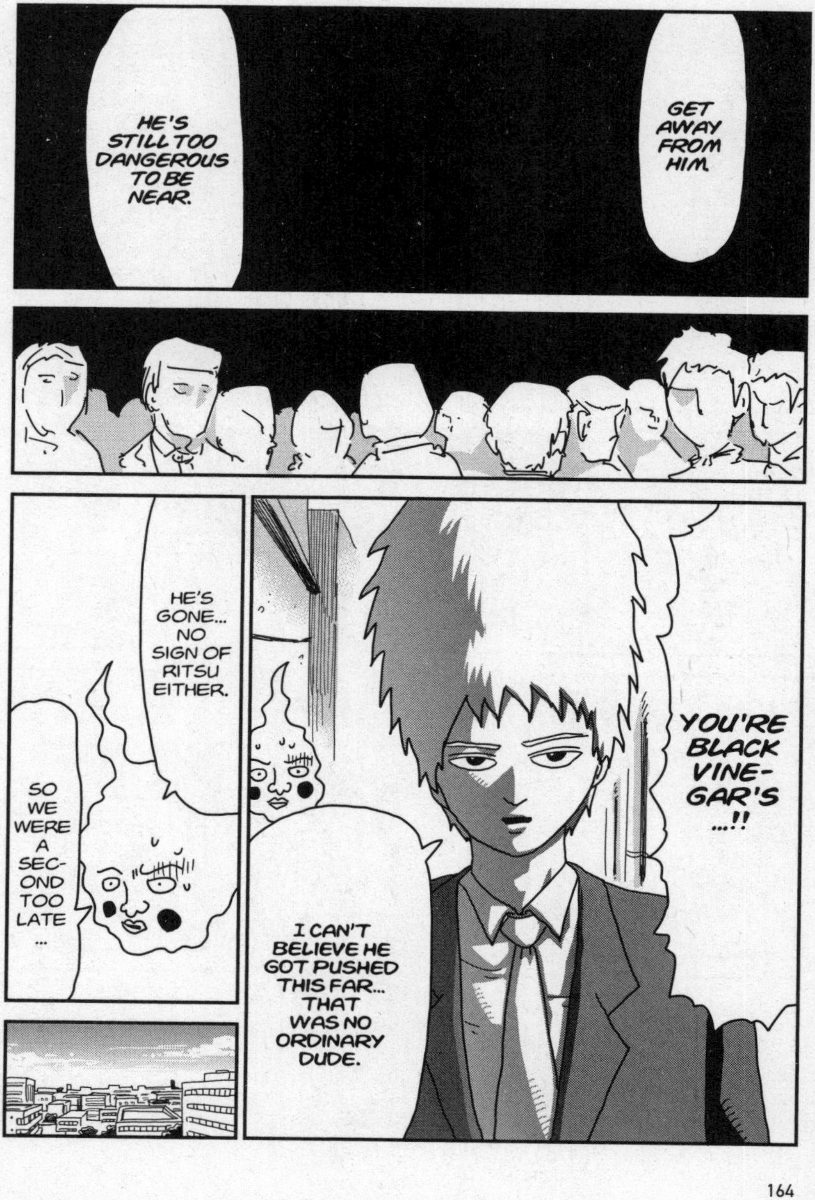
GET AWAY FROM HIM.
HE'S STILL TOO DANGEROUS TO BE NEAR.
YOU'RE BLACK VINE-GAR'S ...!!
I CAN'T BELIEVE HE GOT PUSHED THIS FAR... THAT WAS NO ORDINARY DUDE.
HE'S GONE... NO SIGN OF RITSU EITHER.
SO WE WERE A SEC-OND TOO LATE ...

CHAPTER 34: "CLAW"

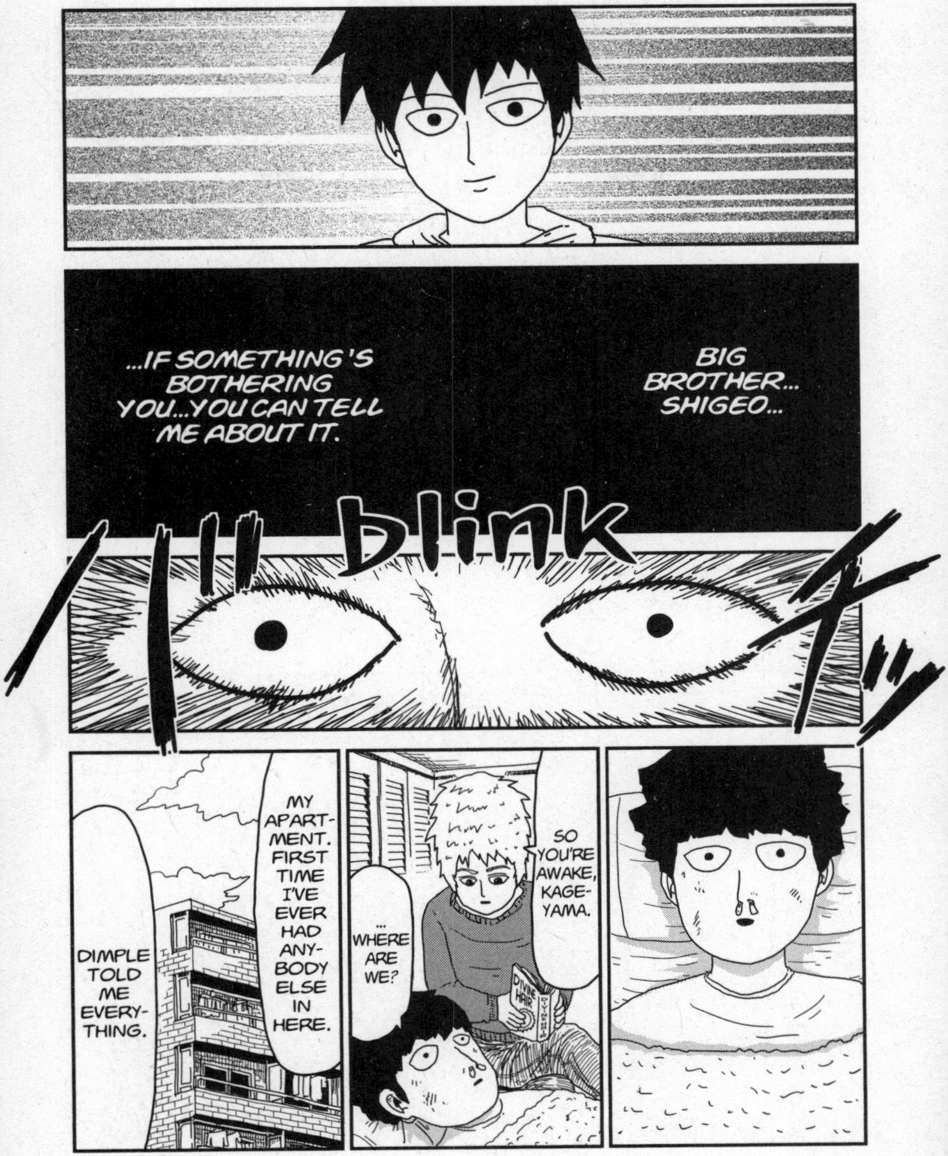

BIG BROTHER... SHIGEO...
...IF SOMETHING'S BOTHERING YOU...YOU CAN TELL ME ABOUT IT.
blink
SO YOU'RE AWAKE, KAGE-YAMA.
...WHERE ARE WE?
DIVINE HAIR
MY APART-MENT. FIRST TIME I'VE EVER HAD ANY-BODY ELSE IN HERE.
DIMPLE TOLD ME EVERY-THING.

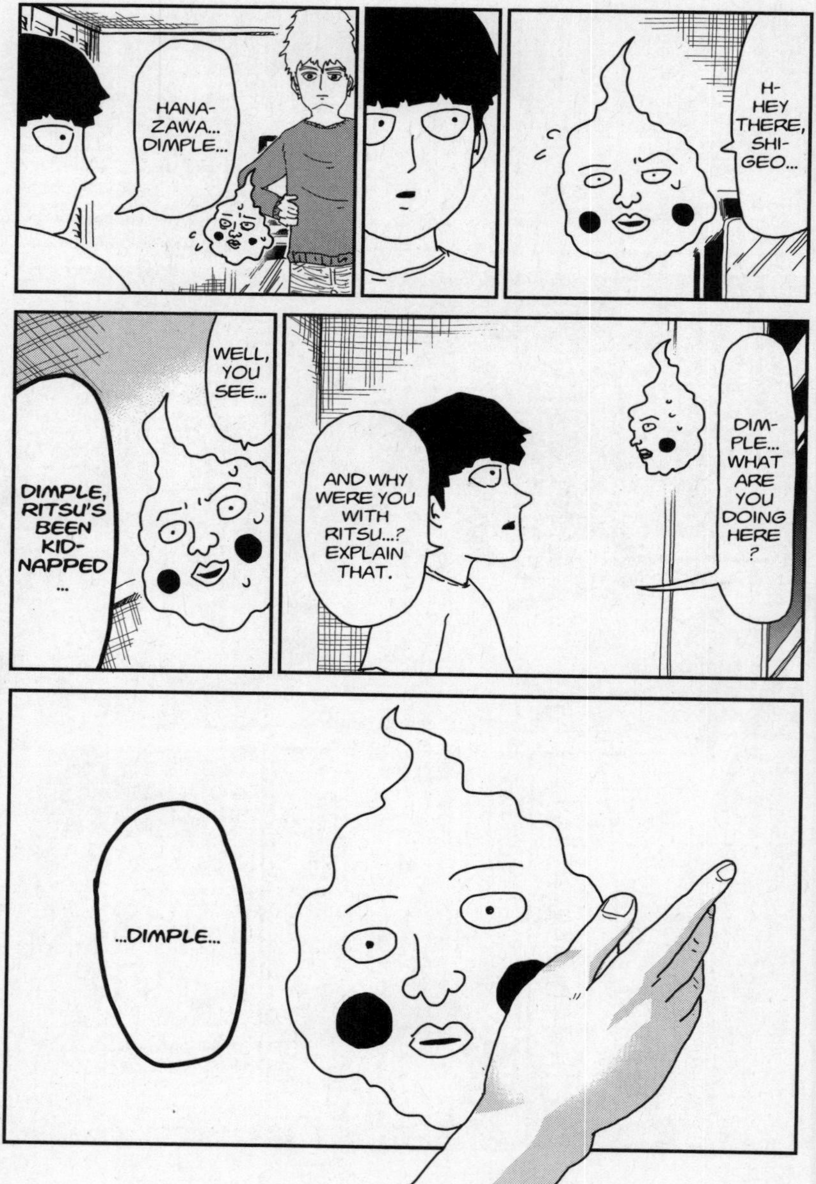

H-HEY THERE, SHI-GEO...
HANA-ZAWA... DIMPLE...
DIM-PLE... WHAT ARE YOU DOING HERE ?
AND WHY WERE YOU WITH RITSU...? EXPLAIN THAT.
WELL, YOU SEE...
DIMPLE, RITSU'S BEEN KID-NAPPED ...
...DIMPLE...

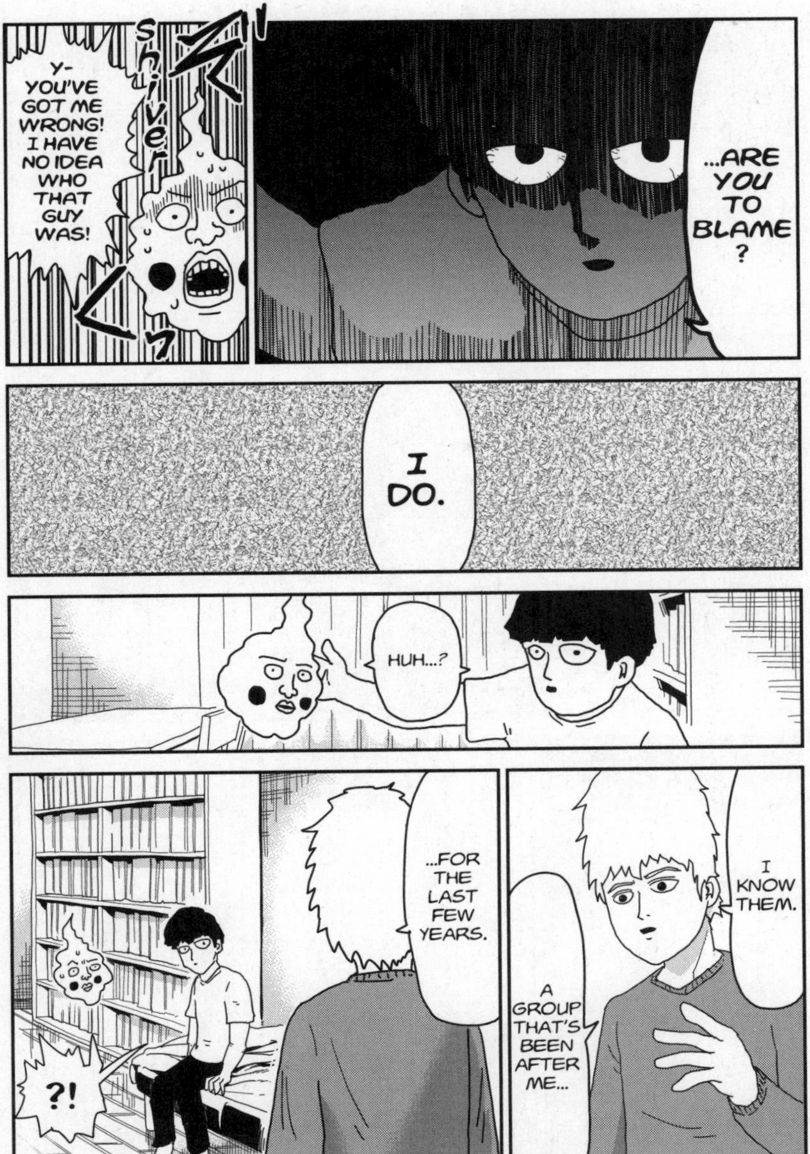
...ARE YOU TO BLAME?
shiver
Y- YOU'VE GOT ME WRONG! I HAVE NO IDEA WHO THAT GUY WAS!
I DO.
HUH...?
I KNOW THEM.
A GROUP THAT'S BEEN AFTER ME...
...FOR THE LAST FEW YEARS.
?!

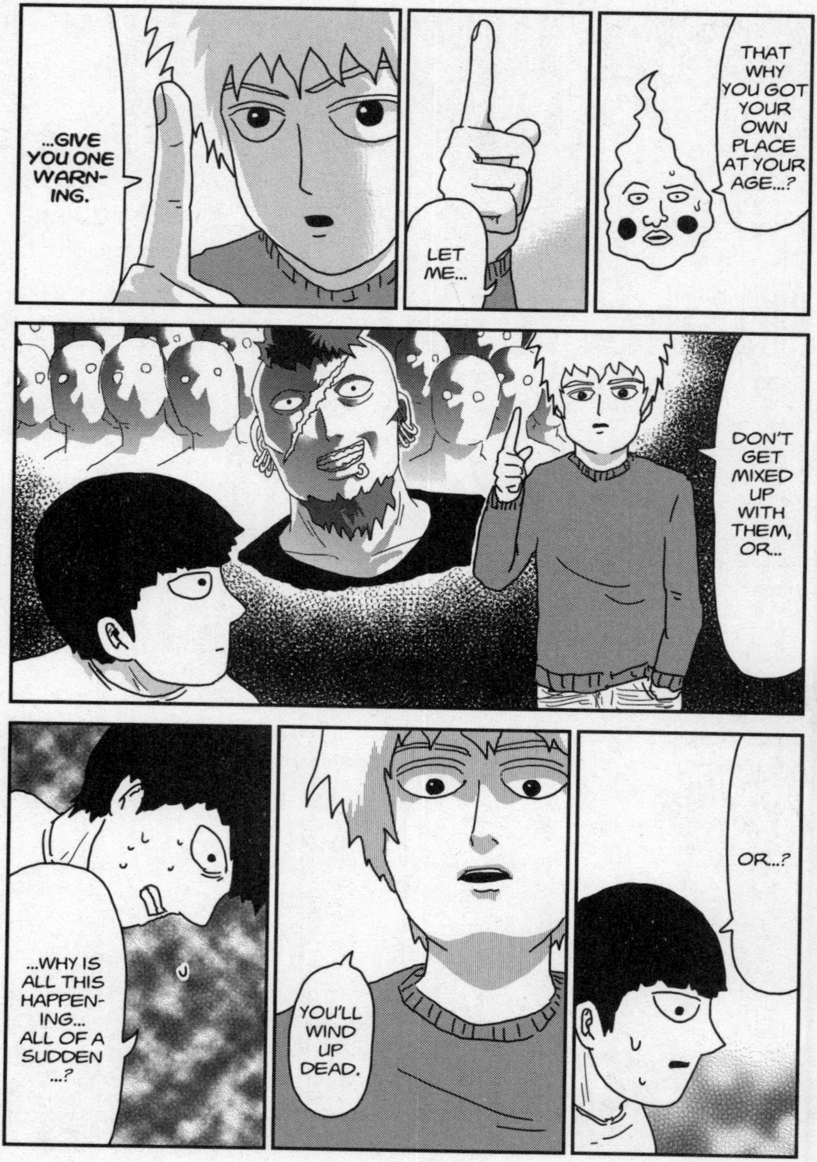
THAT WHY YOU GOT YOUR OWN PLACE AT YOUR AGE...?
LET ME...
...GIVE YOU ONE WARNING.
DON'T GET MIXED UP WITH THEM, OR...
OR...?
YOU'LL WIND UP DEAD.
...WHY IS ALL THIS HAPPENING... ALL OF A SUDDEN...?

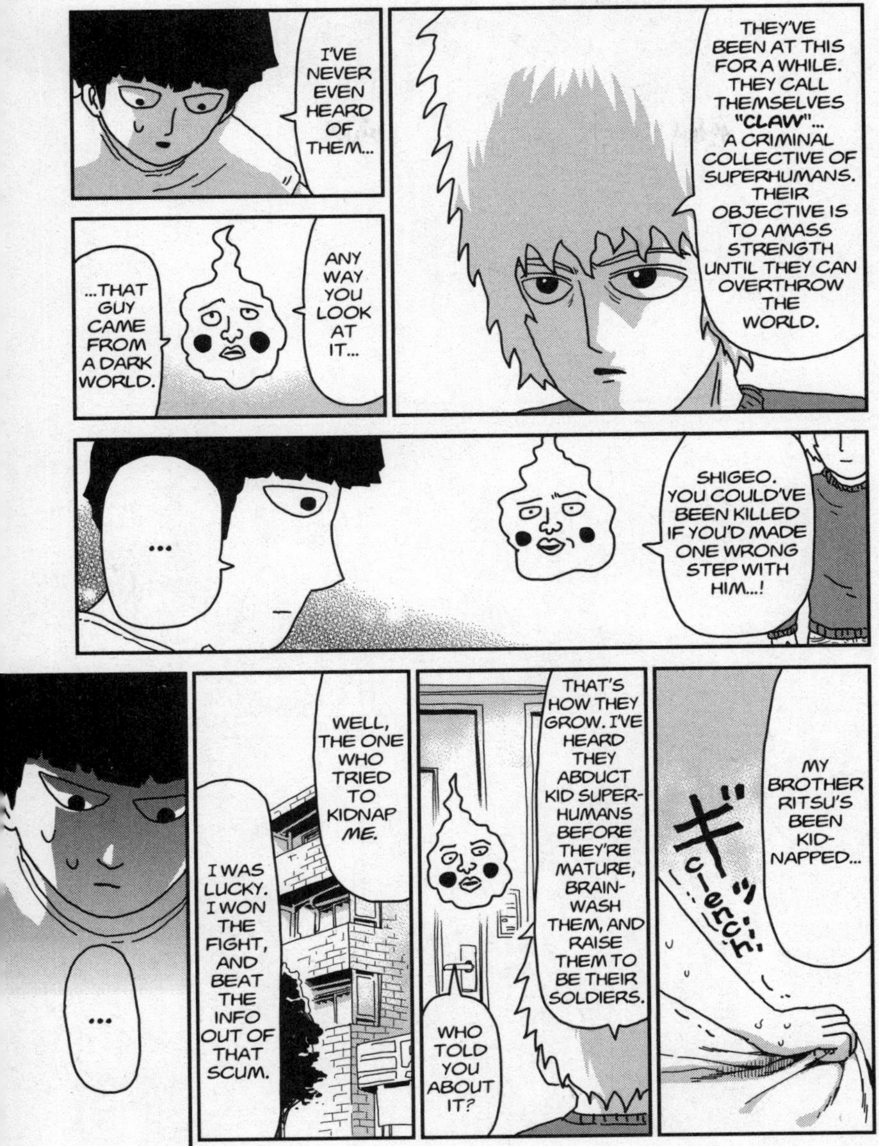
THEY'VE BEEN AT THIS FOR A WHILE. THEY CALL THEMSELVES "CLAW"... A CRIMINAL COLLECTIVE OF SUPERHUMANS. THEIR OBJECTIVE IS TO AMASS STRENGTH UNTIL THEY CAN OVERTHROW THE WORLD.
I'VE NEVER EVEN HEARD OF THEM...
ANY WAY YOU LOOK AT IT...
...THAT GUY CAME FROM A DARK WORLD.
SHIGEO. YOU COULD'VE BEEN KILLED IF YOU'D MADE ONE WRONG STEP WITH HIM...!
...
MY BROTHER RITSU'S BEEN KID-NAPPED...
clench
THAT'S HOW THEY GROW. I'VE HEARD THEY ABDUCT KID SUPER-HUMANS BEFORE THEY'RE MATURE, BRAIN-WASH THEM, AND RAISE THEM TO BE THEIR SOLDIERS.
WHO TOLD YOU ABOUT IT?
WELL, THE ONE WHO TRIED TO KIDNAP ME.
I WAS LUCKY. I WON THE FIGHT, AND BEAT THE INFO OUT OF THAT SCUM.
...

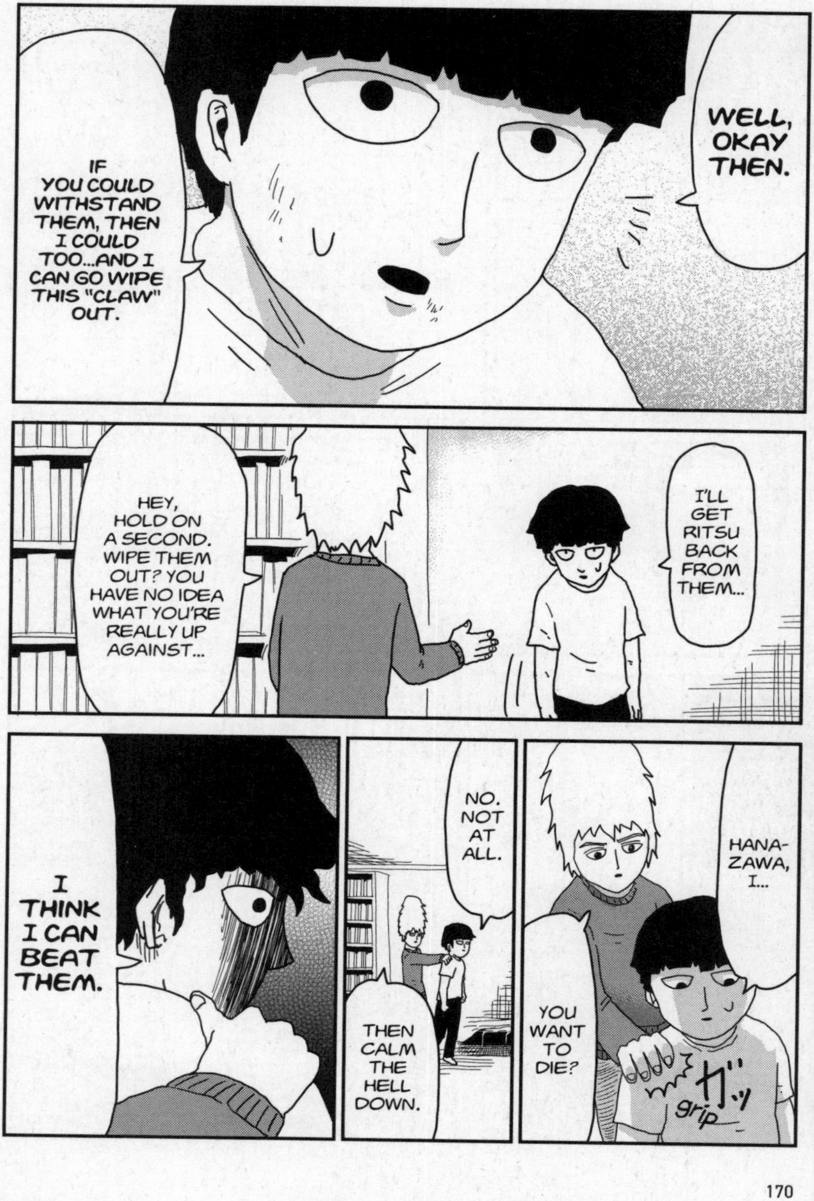
WELL, OKAY THEN.
IF YOU COULD WITHSTAND THEM, THEN I COULD TOO...AND I CAN GO WIPE THIS "CLAW" OUT.
I'LL GET RITSU BACK FROM THEM...
HEY, HOLD ON A SECOND. WIPE THEM OUT? YOU HAVE NO IDEA WHAT YOU'RE REALLY UP AGAINST...
HANA-ZAWA, I...
grip
YOU WANT TO DIE?
NO. NOT AT ALL.
THEN CALM THE HELL DOWN.
I THINK I CAN BEAT THEM.

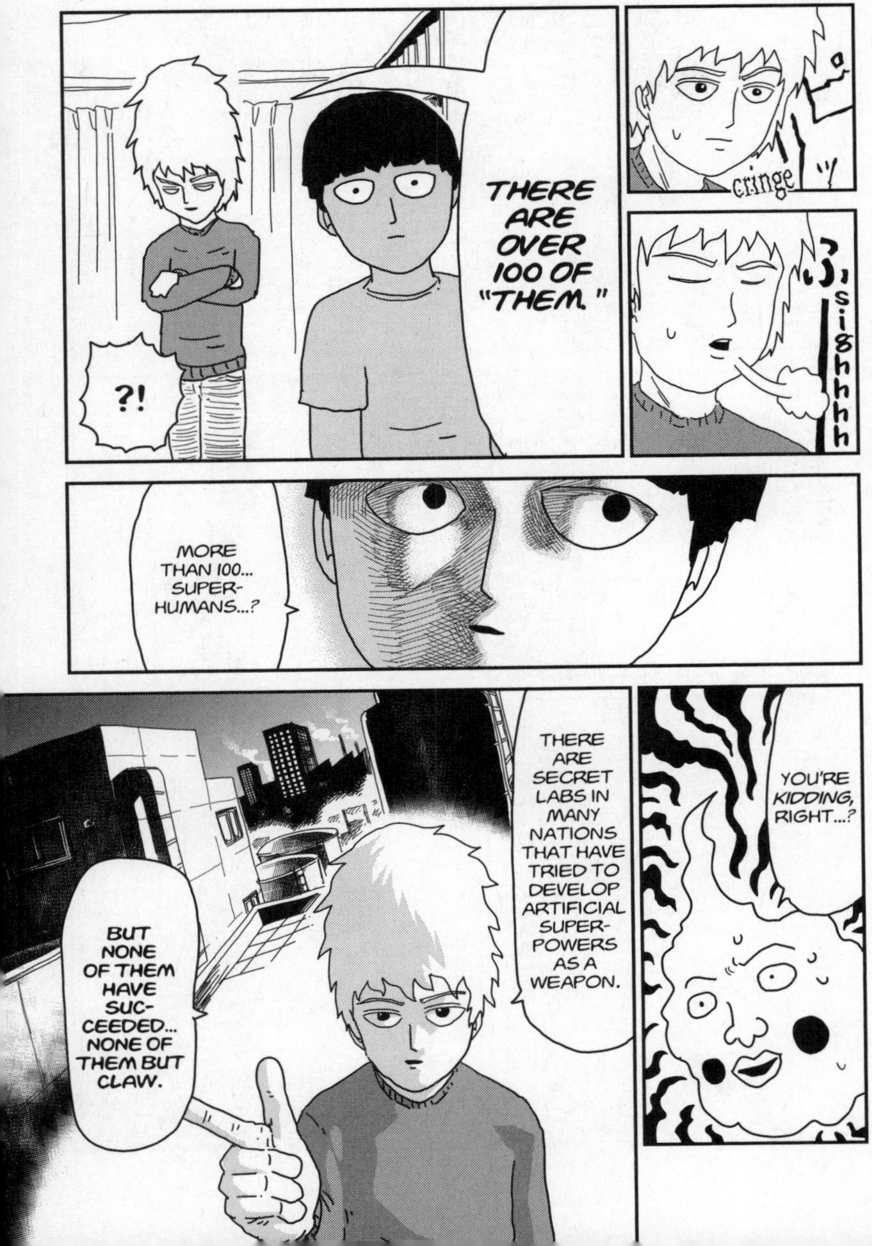
ツ
cringe
ふ
sighhhh
THERE ARE OVER 100 OF "THEM."
?!
MORE THAN 100... SUPER-HUMANS...?
YOU'RE KIDDING, RIGHT...?
THERE ARE SECRET LABS IN MANY NATIONS THAT HAVE TRIED TO DEVELOP ARTIFICIAL SUPER-POWERS AS A WEAPON.
BUT NONE OF THEM HAVE SUC-CEEDED... NONE OF THEM BUT CLAW.

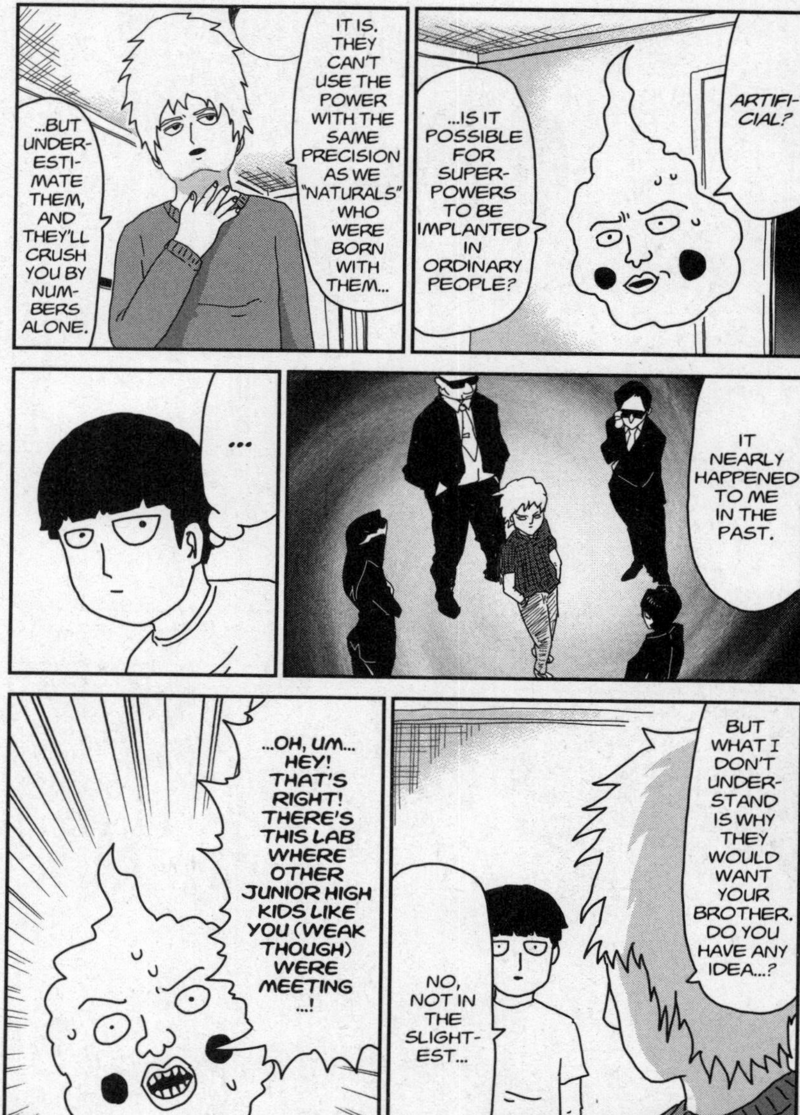
ARTIFICIAL?
...IS IT POSSIBLE FOR SUPERPOWERS TO BE IMPLANTED IN ORDINARY PEOPLE?
IT IS. THEY CAN'T USE THE POWER WITH THE SAME PRECISION AS WE "NATURALS" WHO WERE BORN WITH THEM...
...BUT UNDERESTIMATE THEM, AND THEY'LL CRUSH YOU BY NUMBERS ALONE.
IT NEARLY HAPPENED TO ME IN THE PAST.
...
BUT WHAT I DON'T UNDERSTAND IS WHY THEY WOULD WANT YOUR BROTHER. DO YOU HAVE ANY IDEA...?
NO, NOT IN THE SLIGHTEST...
...OH, UM... HEY! THAT'S RIGHT! THERE'S THIS LAB WHERE OTHER JUNIOR HIGH KIDS LIKE YOU (WEAK THOUGH) WERE MEETING ...!

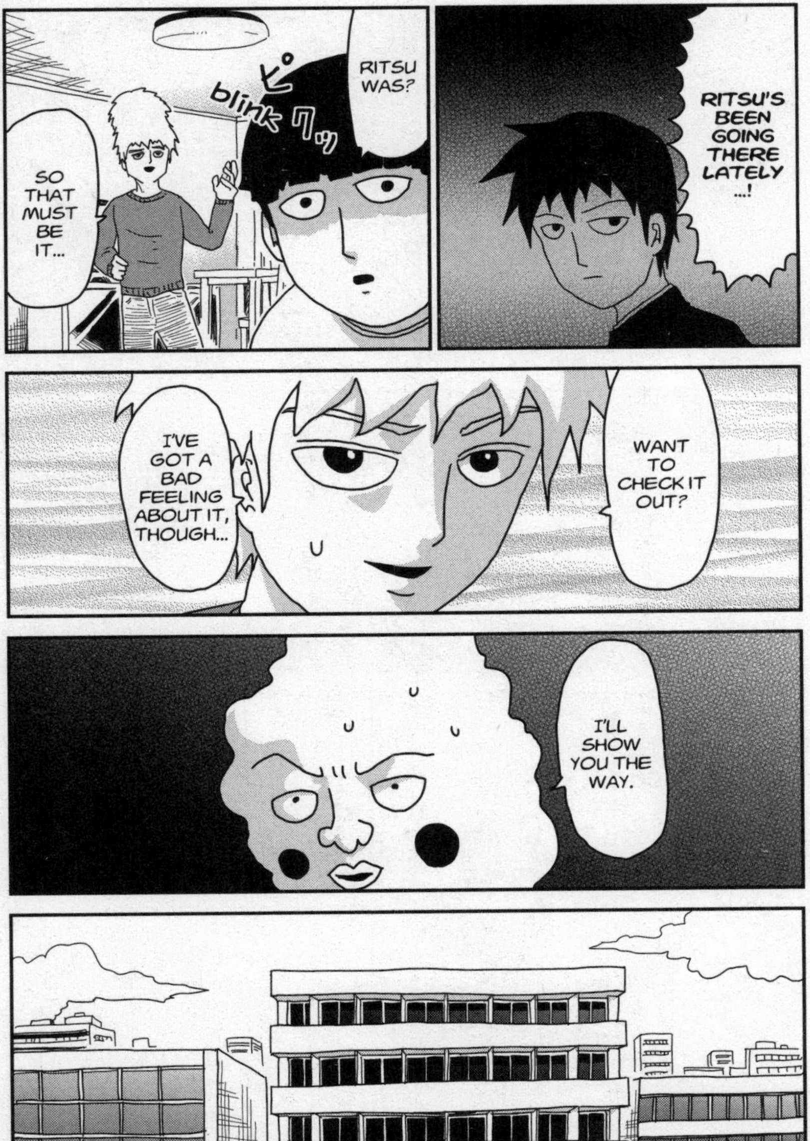
RITSU'S BEEN GOING THERE LATELY ...!
RITSU WAS?
ピクッ
blink
SO THAT MUST BE IT...
WANT TO CHECK IT OUT?
I'VE GOT A BAD FEELING ABOUT IT, THOUGH...
I'LL SHOW YOU THE WAY.

HARSH... THESE WERE ORDINARY PEOPLE ...
THEY'RE ALIVE. OUT COLD, THOUGH...
KAGE-YAMA, CALL AN AMBULANCE.
YES...
...WAIT. LET'S LOOK AROUND A BIT MORE FIRST.
UM ...
IF THEY TIED HIM UP, IT WAS TO TALK.
KAGE-YAMA, GO GET SOME WATER.
UM...

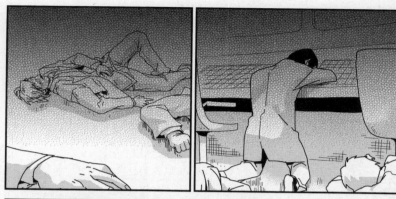

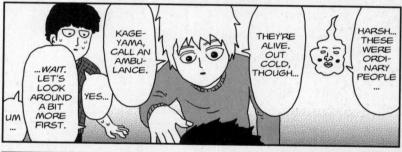

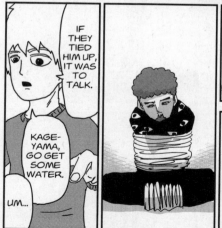

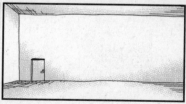

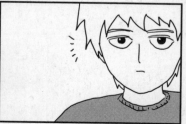

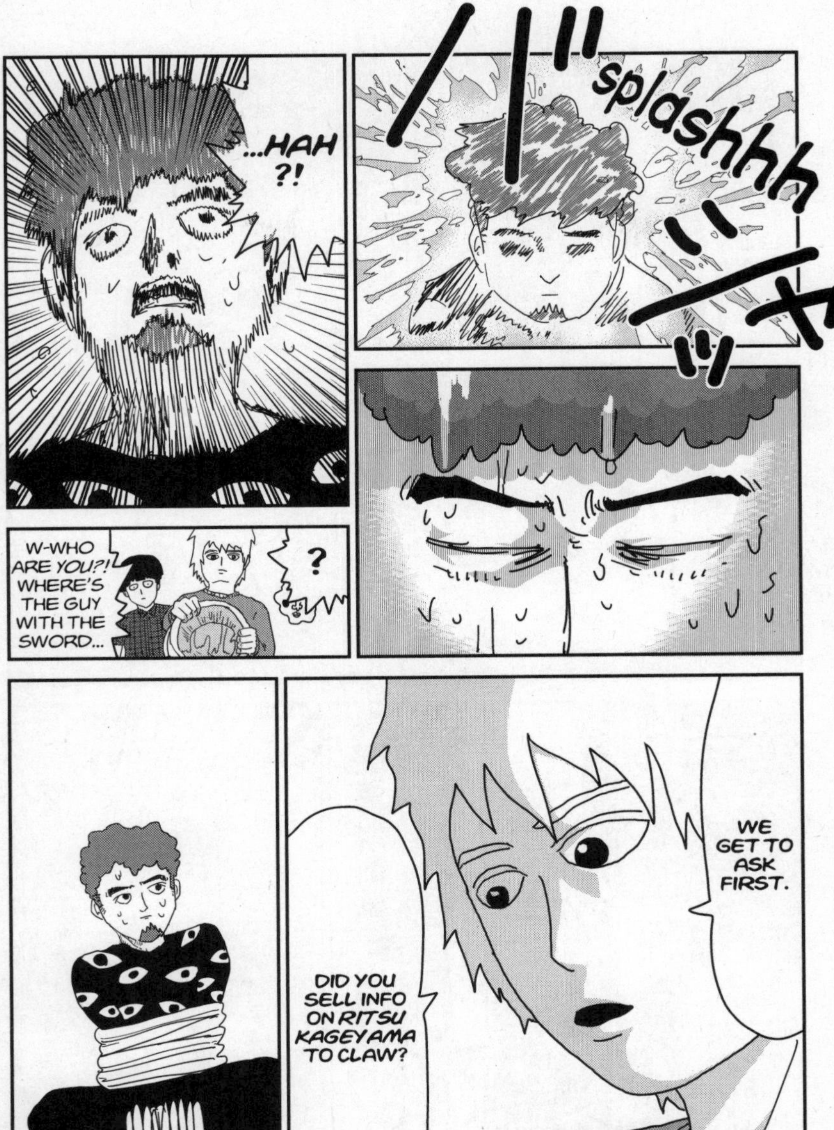
バシャッ
splashhh
...HAH ?!
?
W-WHO ARE *YOU?!* WHERE'S THE GUY WITH THE SWORD...
WE GET TO ASK FIRST.
DID YOU SELL INFO ON *RITSU KAGEYAMA* TO CLAW?

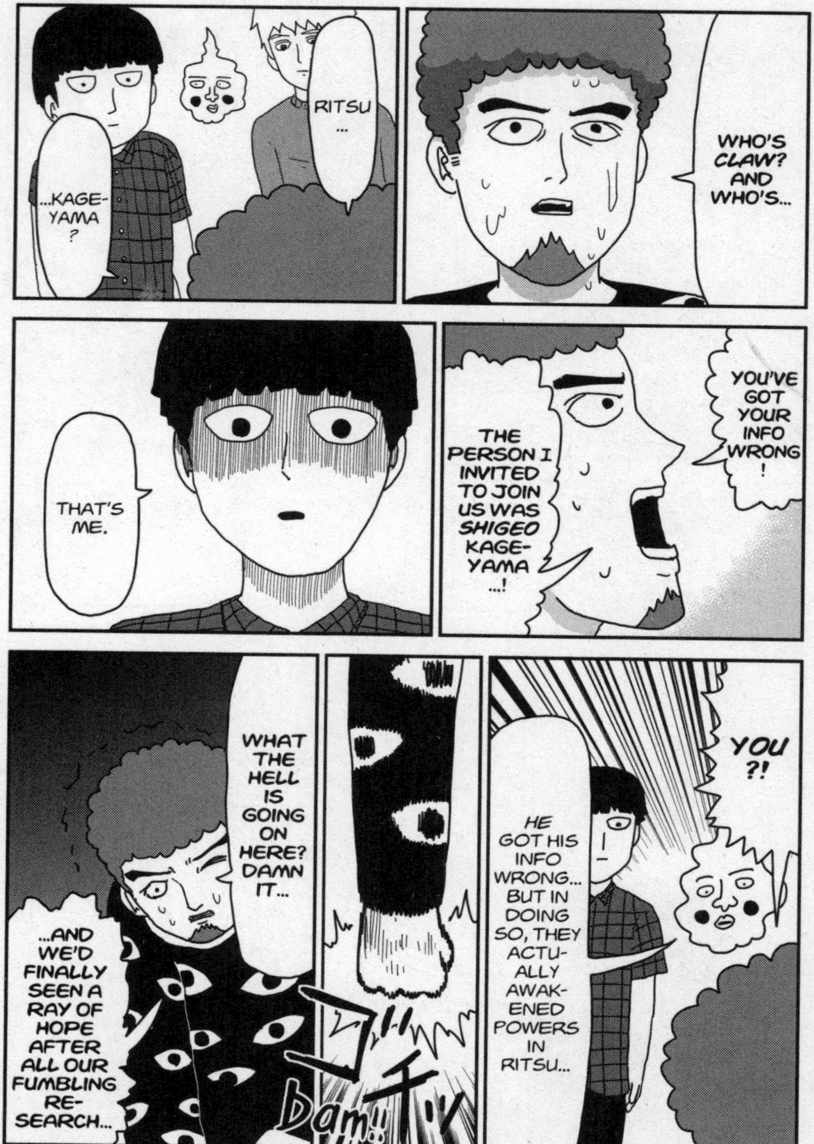

WHO'S CLAW? AND WHO'S...
RITSU ...
...KAGE-YAMA ?
YOU'VE GOT YOUR INFO WRONG !
THE PERSON I INVITED TO JOIN US WAS SHIGEO KAGE-YAMA ...!
THAT'S ME.
YOU ?!
HE GOT HIS INFO WRONG... BUT IN DOING SO, THEY ACTU-ALLY AWAK-ENED POWERS IN RITSU...
Dam!!
WHAT THE HELL IS GOING ON HERE? DAMN IT...
...AND WE'D FINALLY SEEN A RAY OF HOPE AFTER ALL OUR FUMBLING RE-SEARCH...

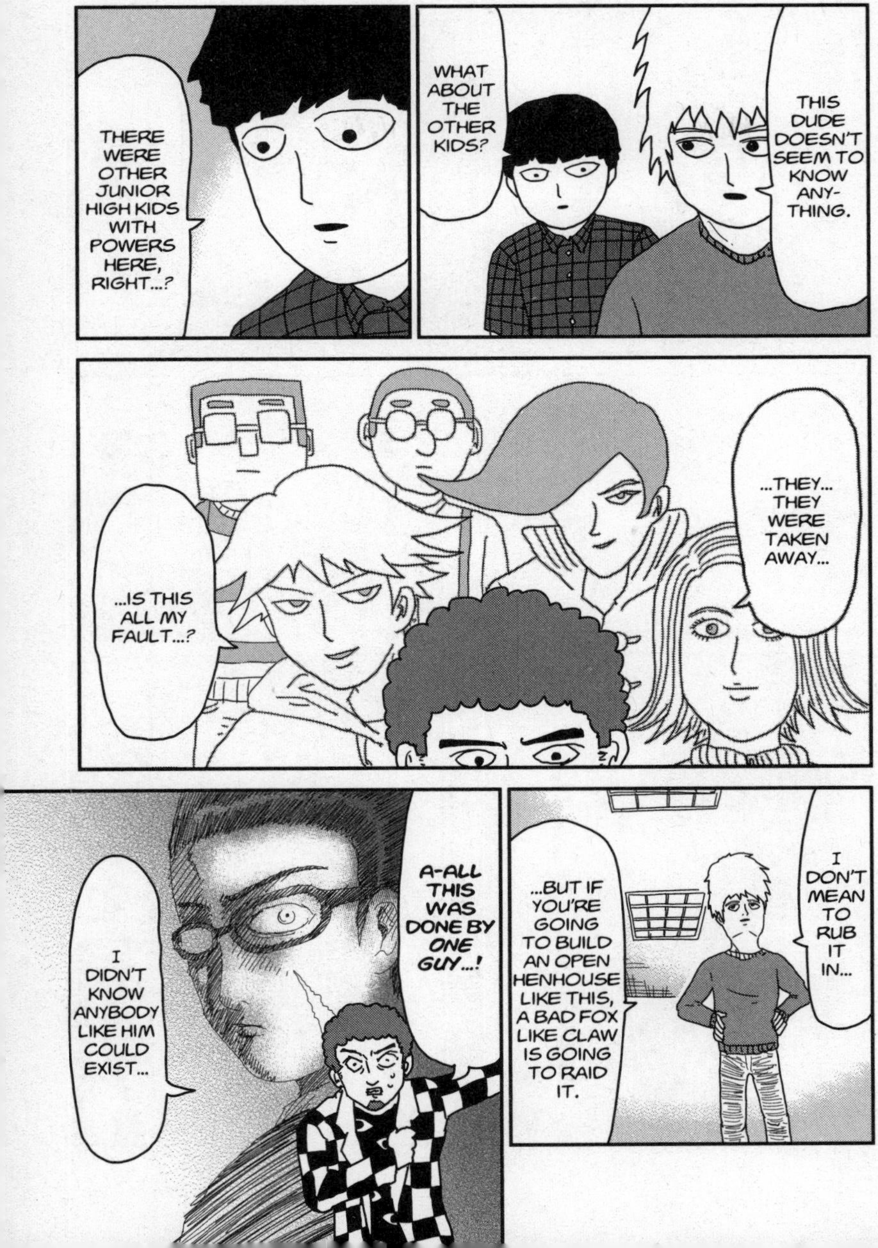

THIS DUDE DOESN'T SEEM TO KNOW ANYTHING.
WHAT ABOUT THE OTHER KIDS?
THERE WERE OTHER JUNIOR HIGH KIDS WITH POWERS HERE, RIGHT...?
...THEY... THEY WERE TAKEN AWAY...
...IS THIS ALL MY FAULT...?
I DON'T MEAN TO RUB IT IN...
...BUT IF YOU'RE GOING TO BUILD AN OPEN HENHOUSE LIKE THIS, A BAD FOX LIKE CLAW IS GOING TO RAID IT.
A-ALL THIS WAS DONE BY ONE GUY...!
I DIDN'T KNOW ANYBODY LIKE HIM COULD EXIST...

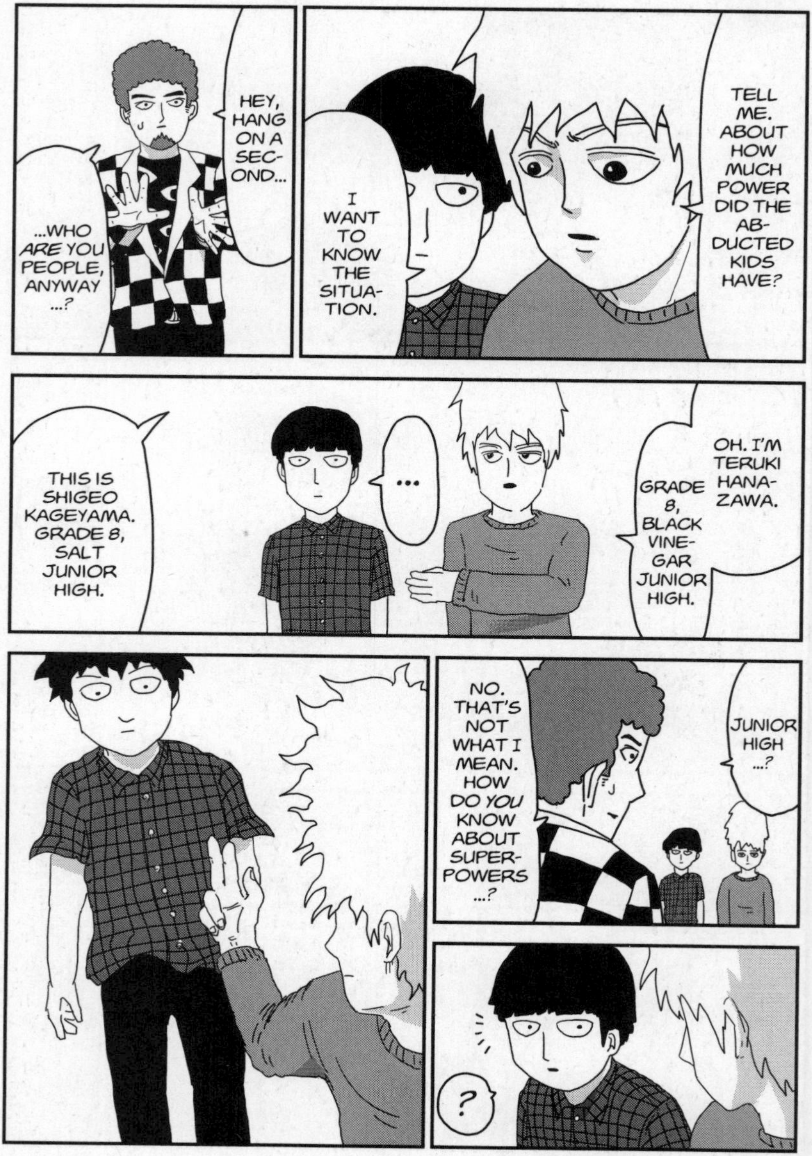
TELL ME. ABOUT HOW MUCH POWER DID THE ABDUCTED KIDS HAVE?
I WANT TO KNOW THE SITUATION.
HEY, HANG ON A SECOND...
...WHO *ARE* YOU PEOPLE, ANYWAY ...?
OH. I'M TERUKI HANAZAWA.
GRADE 8, BLACK VINEGAR JUNIOR HIGH.
...
THIS IS SHIGEO KAGEYAMA. GRADE 8, SALT JUNIOR HIGH.
JUNIOR HIGH ...?
NO. THAT'S NOT WHAT I MEAN. HOW DO *YOU* KNOW ABOUT SUPERPOWERS ...?
?

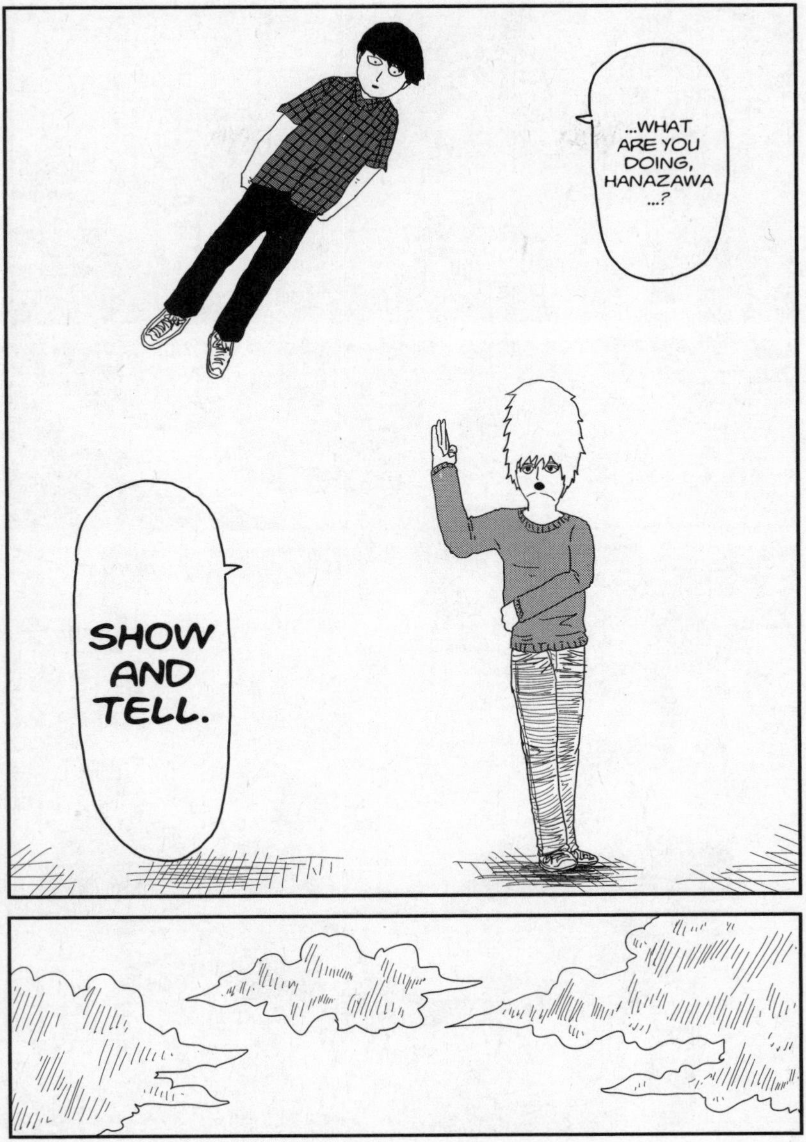
...WHAT ARE YOU DOING, HANAZAWA ...?
SHOW AND TELL.

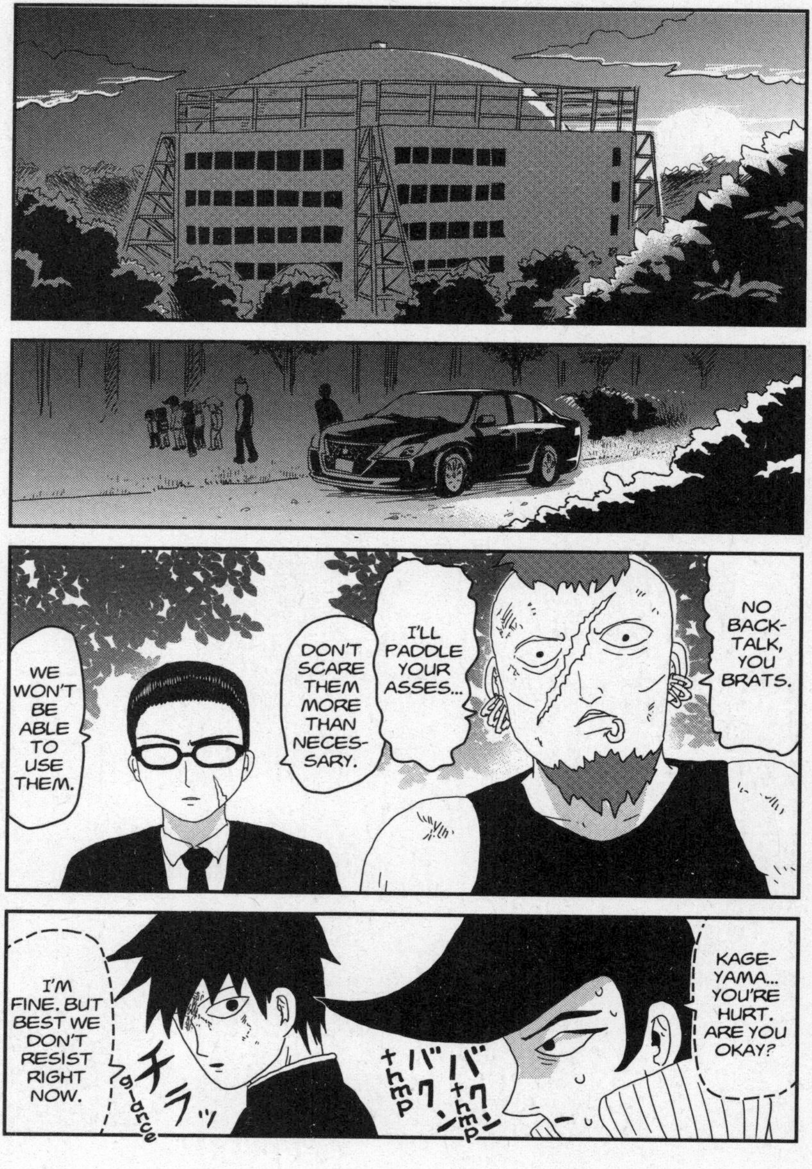
NO BACK-TALK, YOU BRATS.
I'LL PADDLE YOUR ASSES...
DON'T SCARE THEM MORE THAN NECES-SARY.
WE WON'T BE ABLE TO USE THEM.
KAGE-YAMA... YOU'RE HURT. ARE YOU OKAY?
バクン thmp
バクン thmp
チラッ glance
I'M FINE. BUT BEST WE DON'T RESIST RIGHT NOW.

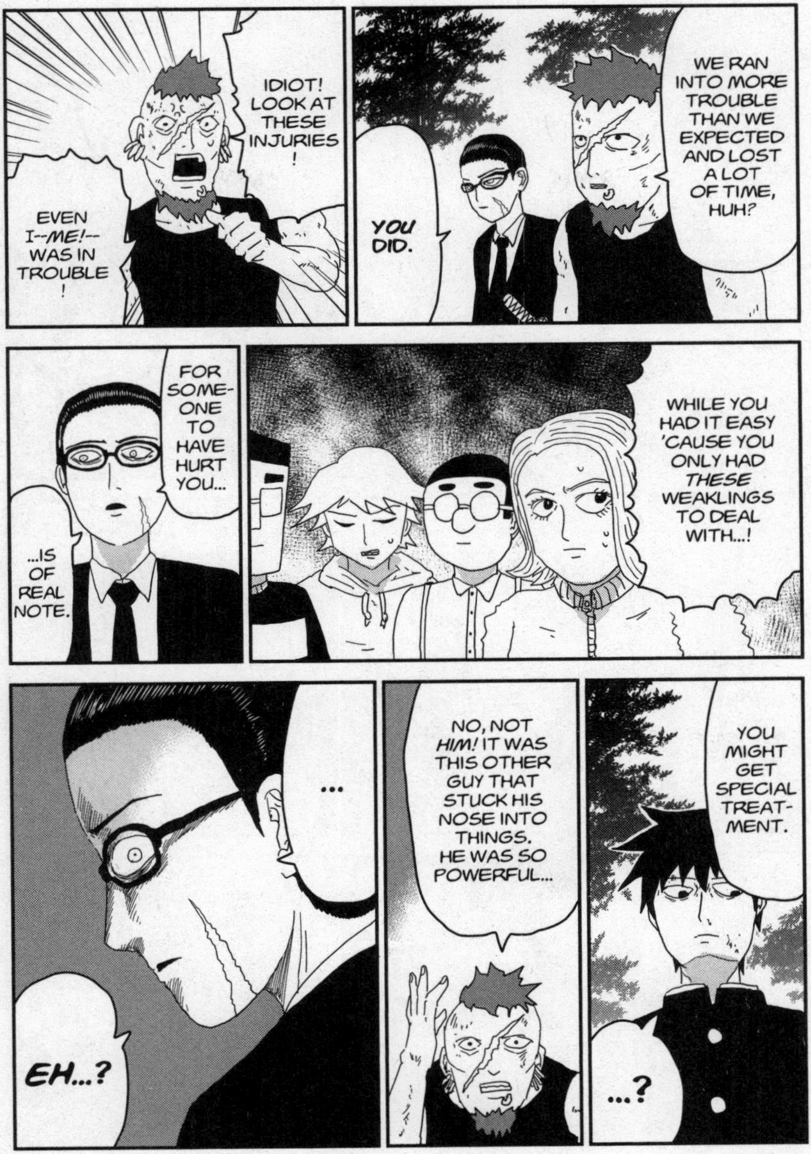
WE RAN INTO MORE TROUBLE THAN WE EXPECTED AND LOST A LOT OF TIME, HUH?
YOU DID.
IDIOT! LOOK AT THESE INJURIES!
EVEN I--ME!--WAS IN TROUBLE!
WHILE YOU HAD IT EASY 'CAUSE YOU ONLY HAD THESE WEAKLINGS TO DEAL WITH...!
FOR SOMEONE TO HAVE HURT YOU...
...IS OF REAL NOTE.
YOU MIGHT GET SPECIAL TREATMENT.
...?
NO, NOT HIM! IT WAS THIS OTHER GUY THAT STUCK HIS NOSE INTO THINGS. HE WAS SO POWERFUL...
...
EH...?

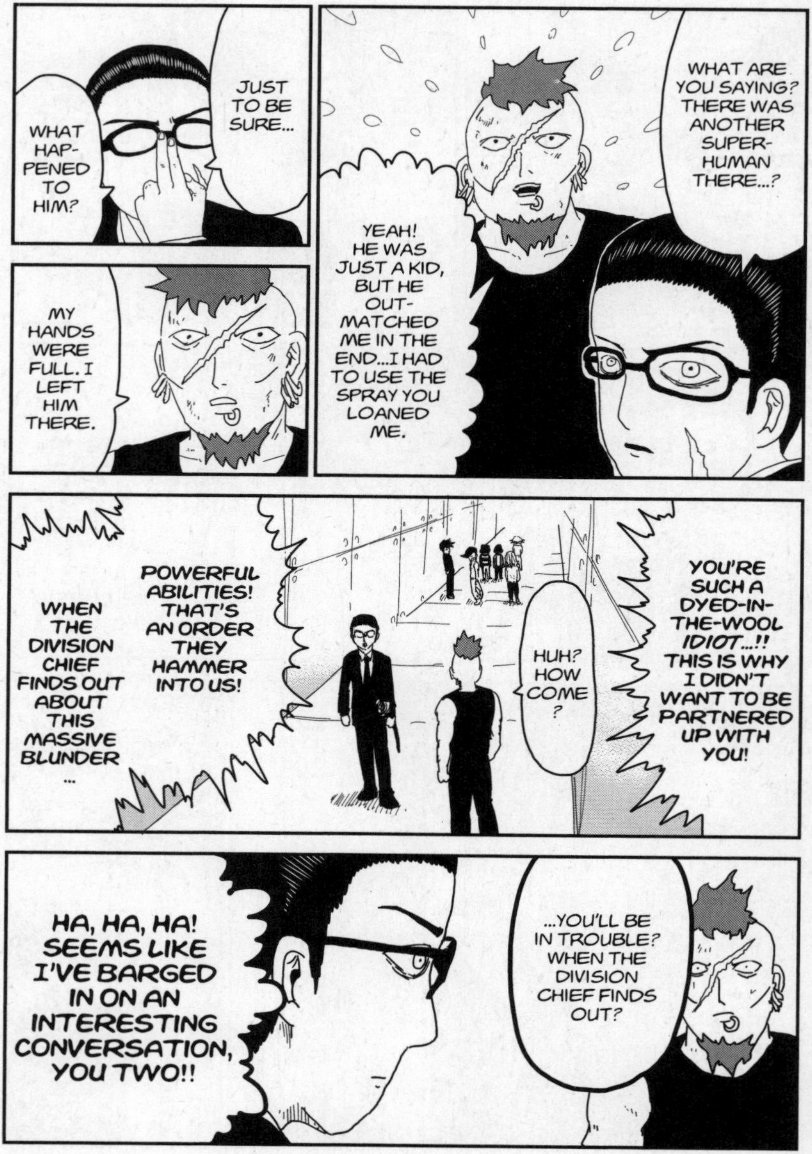
WHAT ARE YOU SAYING? THERE WAS ANOTHER SUPER-HUMAN THERE...?
YEAH! HE WAS JUST A KID, BUT HE OUT-MATCHED ME IN THE END...I HAD TO USE THE SPRAY YOU LOANED ME.
JUST TO BE SURE...
WHAT HAP-PENED TO HIM?
MY HANDS WERE FULL. I LEFT HIM THERE.
YOU'RE SUCH A DYED-IN-THE-WOOL IDIOT...!! THIS IS WHY I DIDN'T WANT TO BE PARTNERED UP WITH YOU!
HUH? HOW COME?
POWERFUL ABILITIES! THAT'S AN ORDER THEY HAMMER INTO US!
WHEN THE DIVISION CHIEF FINDS OUT ABOUT THIS MASSIVE BLUNDER...
...YOU'LL BE IN TROUBLE? WHEN THE DIVISION CHIEF FINDS OUT?
HA, HA, HA! SEEMS LIKE I'VE BARGED IN ON AN INTERESTING CONVERSATION, YOU TWO!!

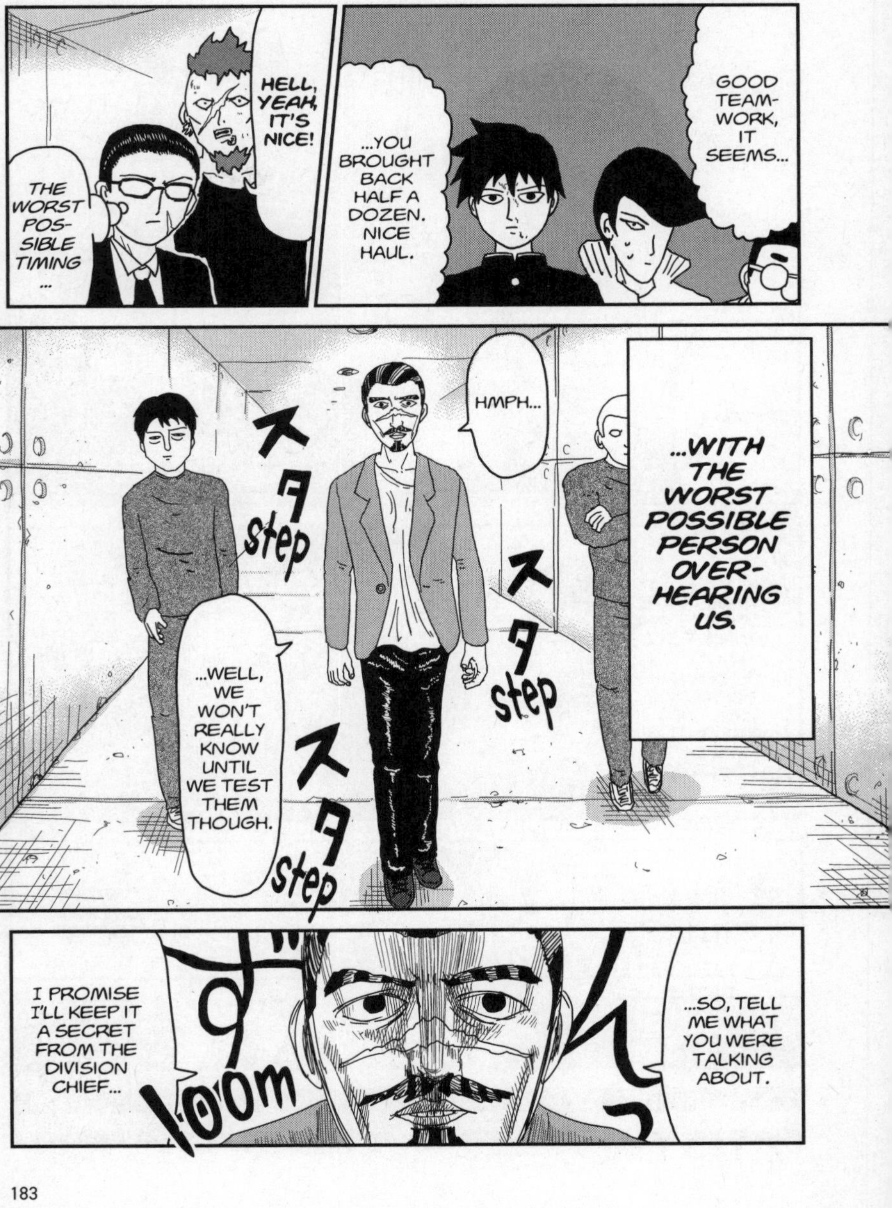
GOOD TEAMWORK, IT SEEMS...
...YOU BROUGHT BACK HALF A DOZEN. NICE HAUL.
HELL, YEAH, IT'S NICE!
THE WORST POSSIBLE TIMING...
...WITH THE WORST POSSIBLE PERSON OVERHEARING US.
HMPH...
スタ step
スタ step
スタ step
...WELL, WE WON'T REALLY KNOW UNTIL WE TEST THEM THOUGH.
...SO, TELL ME WHAT YOU WERE TALKING ABOUT.
I PROMISE I'LL KEEP IT A SECRET FROM THE DIVISION CHIEF...
loom

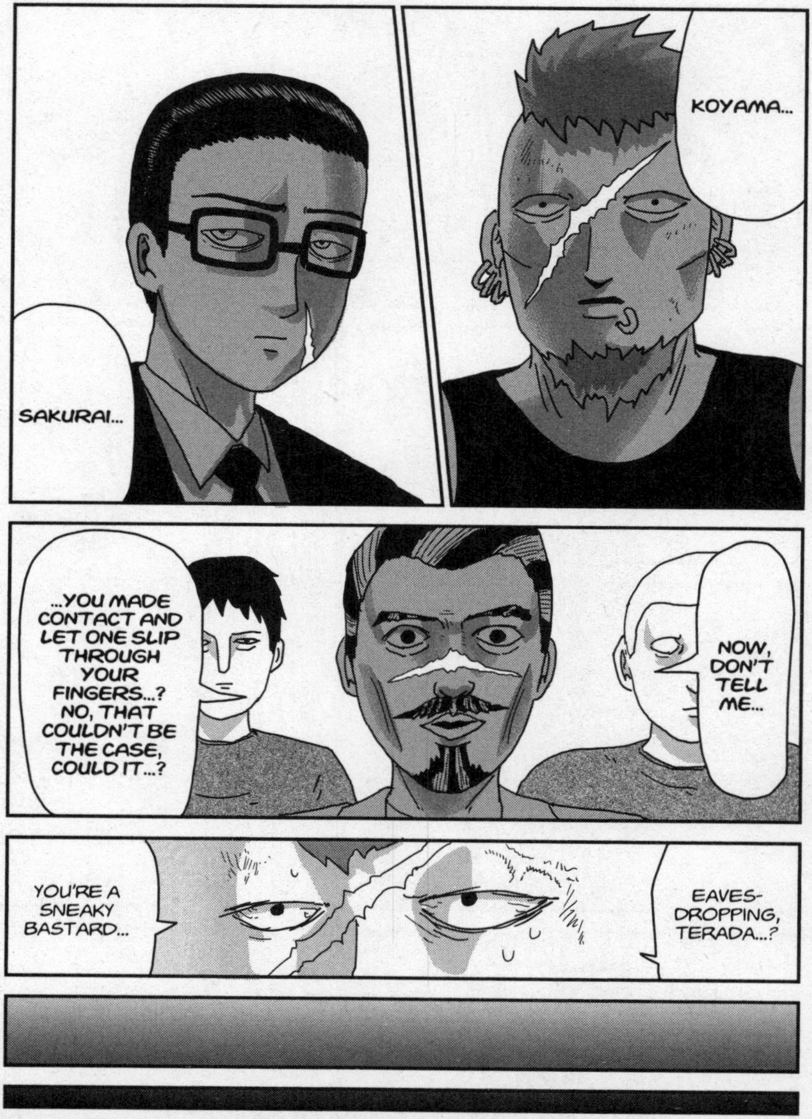
KOYAMA...
SAKURAI...
NOW, DON'T TELL ME...
...YOU MADE CONTACT AND LET ONE SLIP THROUGH YOUR FINGERS...? NO, THAT COULDN'T BE THE CASE, COULD IT...?
EAVES-DROPPING, TERADA...?
YOU'RE A SNEAKY BASTARD...

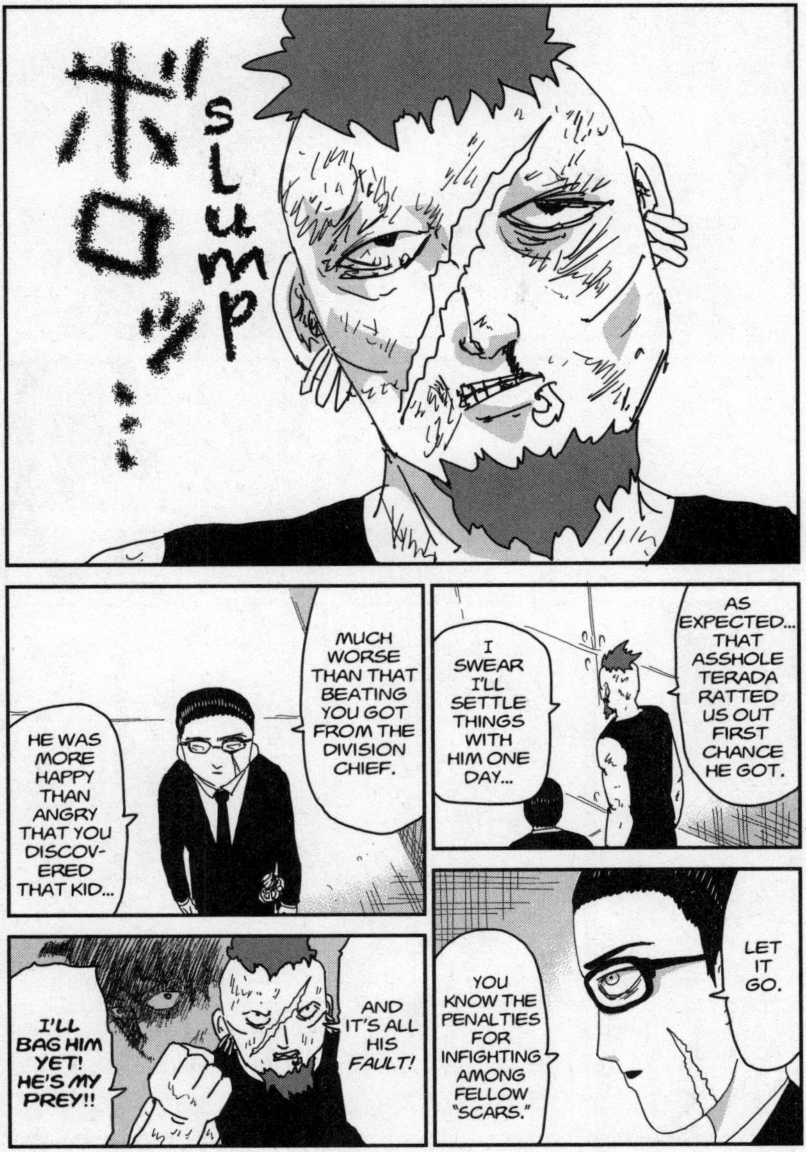
ボロッ…
SLUMP
AS EXPECTED... THAT ASSHOLE TERADA RATTED US OUT FIRST CHANCE HE GOT.
I SWEAR I'LL SETTLE THINGS WITH HIM ONE DAY...
MUCH WORSE THAN THAT BEATING YOU GOT FROM THE DIVISION CHIEF.
HE WAS MORE HAPPY THAN ANGRY THAT YOU DISCOVERED THAT KID...
LET IT GO.
YOU KNOW THE PENALTIES FOR INFIGHTING AMONG FELLOW "SCARS."
AND IT'S ALL HIS *FAULT!*
I'LL BAG HIM YET! HE'S MY PREY!!

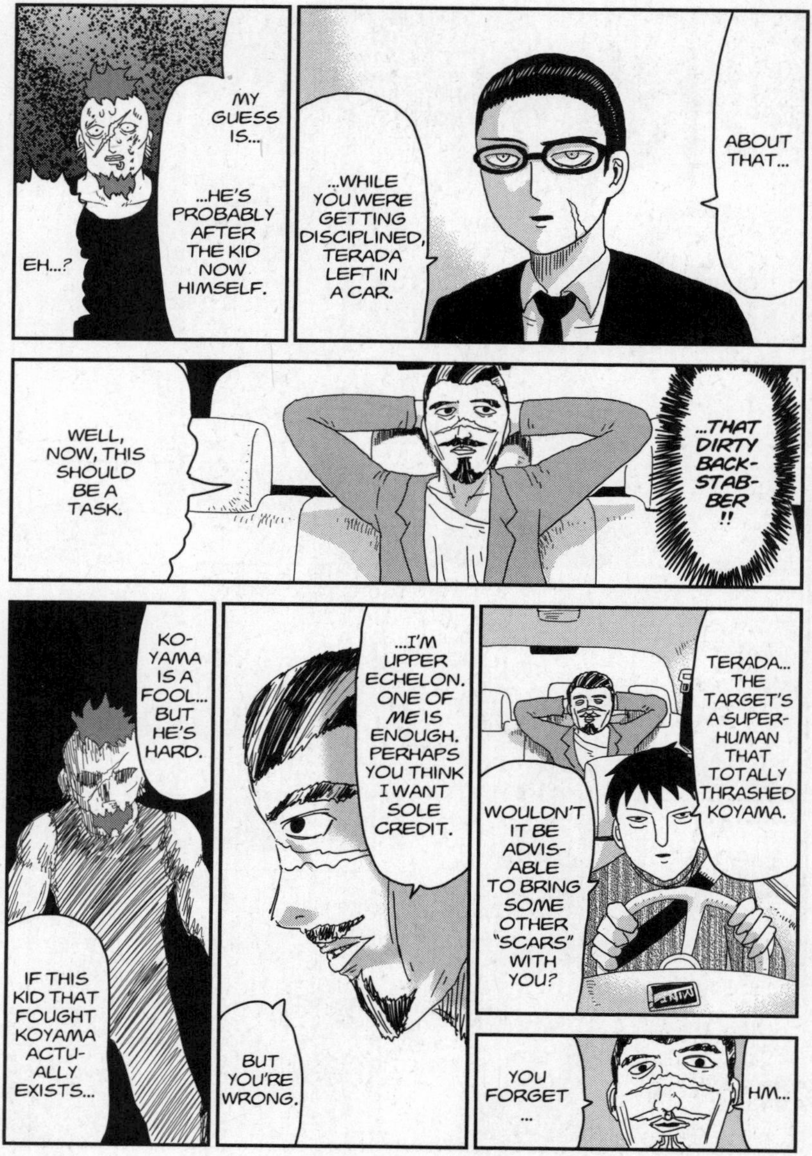
ABOUT THAT...
...WHILE YOU WERE GETTING DISCIPLINED, TERADA LEFT IN A CAR.
MY GUESS IS...
...HE'S PROBABLY AFTER THE KID NOW HIMSELF.
EH...?
...THAT DIRTY BACKSTABBER!!
WELL, NOW, THIS SHOULD BE A TASK.
TERADA... THE TARGET'S A SUPERHUMAN THAT TOTALLY THRASHED KOYAMA.
WOULDN'T IT BE ADVISABLE TO BRING SOME OTHER "SCARS" WITH YOU?
HM...
YOU FORGET...
...I'M UPPER ECHELON. ONE OF *ME* IS ENOUGH. PERHAPS YOU THINK I WANT SOLE CREDIT.
BUT YOU'RE WRONG.
KOYAMA IS A FOOL... BUT HE'S HARD.
IF THIS KID THAT FOUGHT KOYAMA ACTUALLY EXISTS...

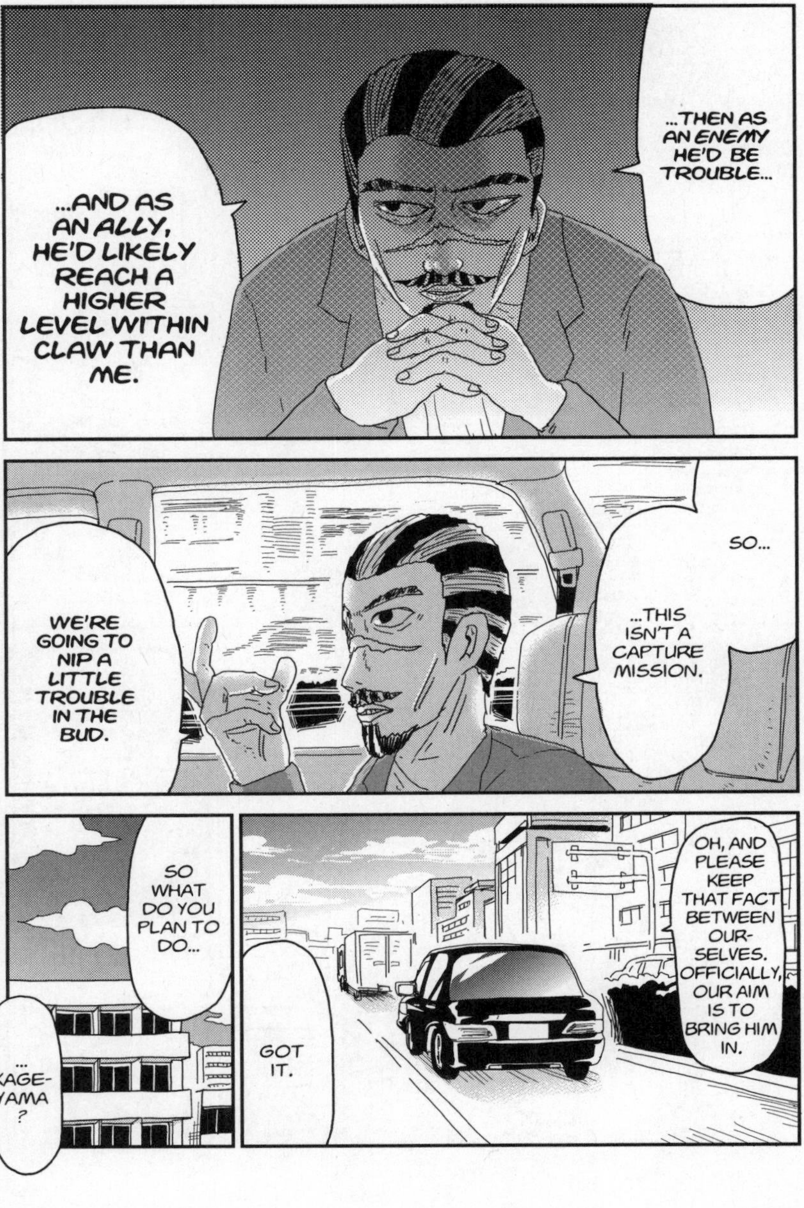
...THEN AS AN *ENEMY* HE'D BE TROUBLE...
...AND AS AN *ALLY*, HE'D LIKELY REACH A HIGHER LEVEL WITHIN CLAW THAN ME.
SO...
...THIS ISN'T A CAPTURE MISSION.
WE'RE GOING TO NIP A LITTLE TROUBLE IN THE BUD.
OH, AND PLEASE KEEP THAT FACT BETWEEN OUR-SELVES. OFFICIALLY, OUR AIM IS TO BRING HIM IN.
GOT IT.
SO WHAT DO YOU PLAN TO DO...
...KAGE-YAMA?

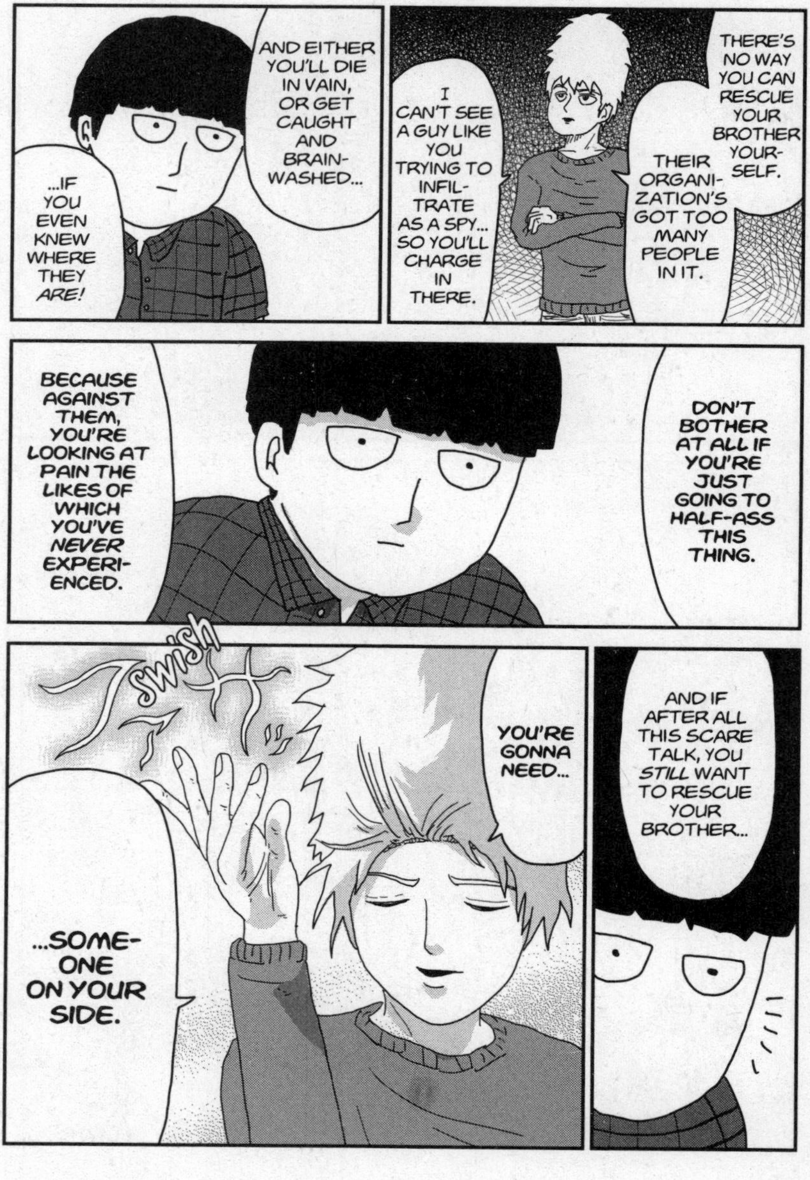
THERE'S NO WAY YOU CAN RESCUE YOUR BROTHER YOURSELF.
THEIR ORGANIZATION'S GOT TOO MANY PEOPLE IN IT.
I CAN'T SEE A GUY LIKE YOU TRYING TO INFILTRATE AS A SPY... SO YOU'LL CHARGE IN THERE.
AND EITHER YOU'LL DIE IN VAIN, OR GET CAUGHT AND BRAINWASHED...
...IF YOU EVEN KNEW WHERE THEY *ARE!*
DON'T BOTHER AT ALL IF YOU'RE JUST GOING TO HALF-ASS THIS THING.
BECAUSE AGAINST THEM, YOU'RE LOOKING AT PAIN THE LIKES OF WHICH YOU'VE *NEVER* EXPERIENCED.
AND IF AFTER ALL THIS SCARE TALK, YOU *STILL* WANT TO RESCUE YOUR BROTHER...
YOU'RE GONNA NEED...
SWISH
...SOMEONE ON YOUR SIDE.

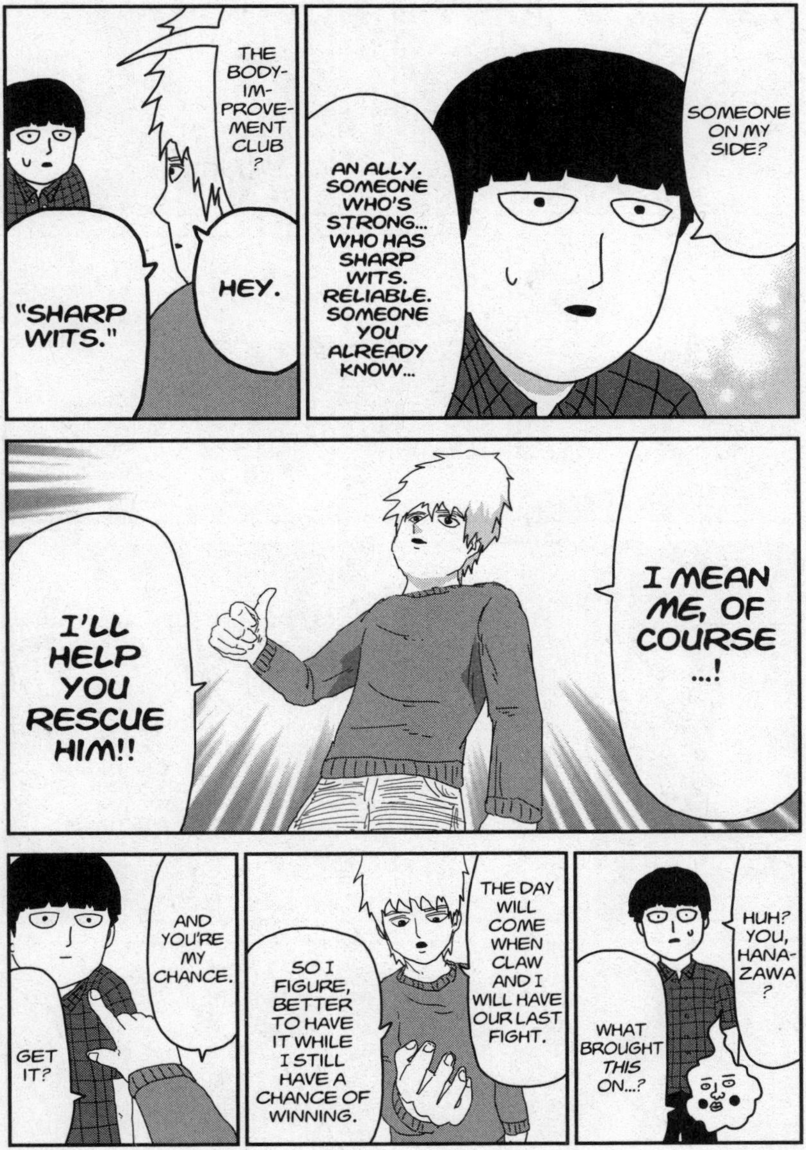
SOMEONE ON MY SIDE?
AN ALLY. SOMEONE WHO'S STRONG... WHO HAS SHARP WITS. RELIABLE. SOMEONE YOU ALREADY KNOW...
THE BODY-IMPROVEMENT CLUB?
HEY.
"SHARP WITS."
I MEAN ME, OF COURSE...!
I'LL HELP YOU RESCUE HIM!!
HUH? YOU, HANAZAWA?
WHAT BROUGHT THIS ON...?
THE DAY WILL COME WHEN CLAW AND I WILL HAVE OUR LAST FIGHT.
SO I FIGURE, BETTER TO HAVE IT WHILE I STILL HAVE A CHANCE OF WINNING.
AND YOU'RE MY CHANCE.
GET IT?

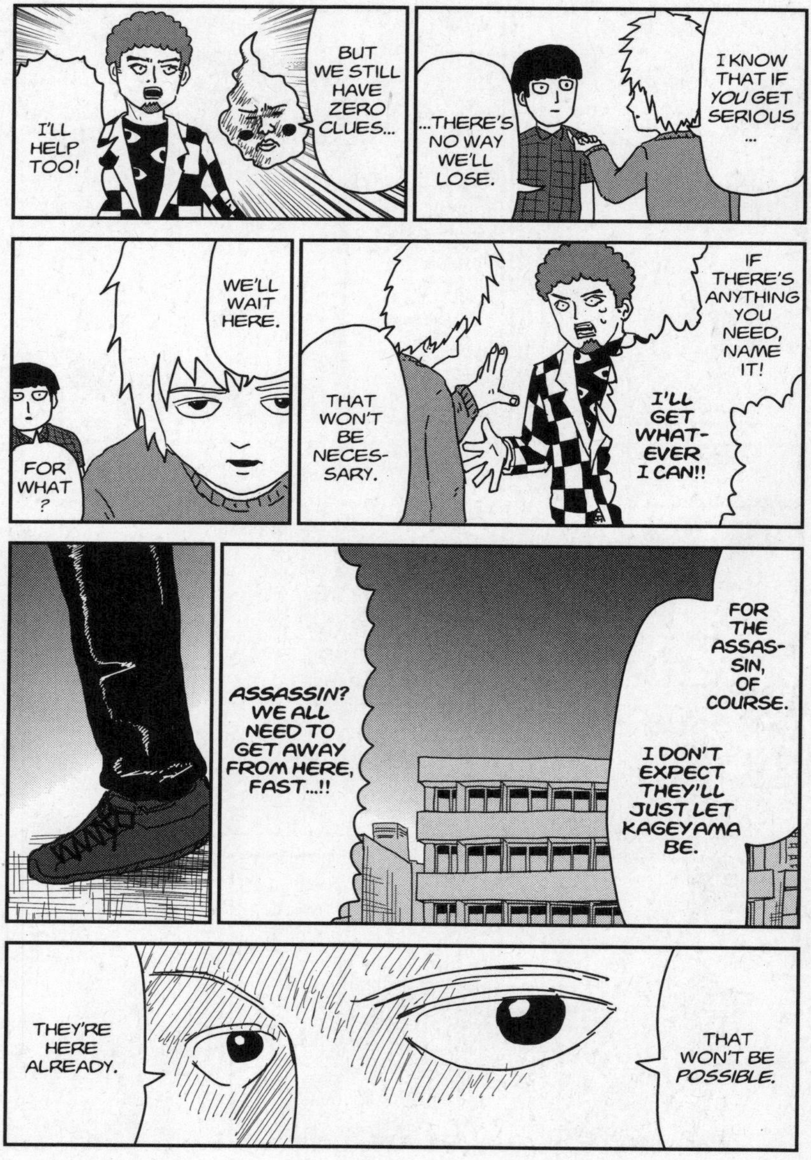
I KNOW THAT IF YOU GET SERIOUS ...
...THERE'S NO WAY WE'LL LOSE.
BUT WE STILL HAVE ZERO CLUES...
I'LL HELP TOO!
IF THERE'S ANYTHING YOU NEED, NAME IT!
I'LL GET WHAT-EVER I CAN!!
THAT WON'T BE NECES-SARY.
WE'LL WAIT HERE.
FOR WHAT?
FOR THE ASSAS-SIN, OF COURSE.
I DON'T EXPECT THEY'LL JUST LET KAGEYAMA BE.
ASSASSIN? WE ALL NEED TO GET AWAY FROM HERE, FAST...!!
THAT WON'T BE POSSIBLE.
THEY'RE HERE ALREADY.

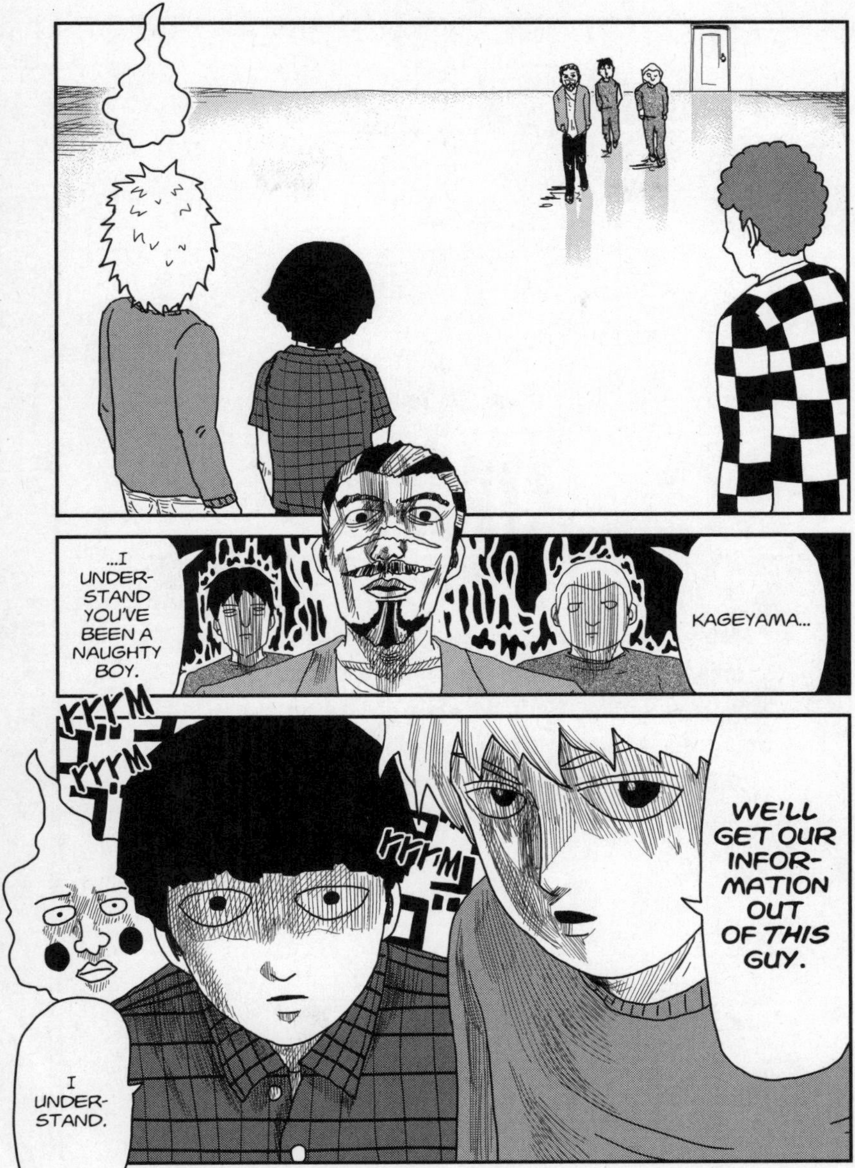
KAGEYAMA...
...I UNDERSTAND YOU'VE BEEN A NAUGHTY BOY.
WE'LL GET OUR INFORMATION OUT OF THIS GUY.
RRRRM
RRRRM
RRRRM
RRRRM
I UNDERSTAND.

CONTINUED IN VOL. 5
OF *MOB PSYCHO 100*!

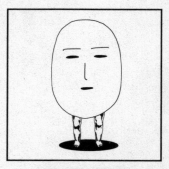

ONE

Mob's nickname is short for "mob character" which means "minor role" in Japanese, and that's why it was given to him. He is the main character, but he is a background figure. He is a background figure, but he is the main character. Perhaps it is the same in life.

president and publisher
MIKE RICHARDSON

editor
CARL GUSTAV HORN

designer
SARAH TERRY

digital art technician
SAMANTHA HUMMER

English-language version produced by Dark Horse Comics

MOB PSYCHO 100

MOB PSYCHO 100 Volume 4 by ONE © 2013 ONE. All rights reserved. Original Japanese edition published by SHOGAKUKAN. English translation rights arranged with SHOGAKUKAN through Tuttle-Mori Agency, Inc., Tokyo. This English-language edition © 2020 by Dark Horse Comics LLC. All other material © 2020 by Dark Horse Comics LLC. Dark Horse Manga™ is a trademark of Dark Horse Comics LLC. All rights reserved. No portion of this publication may be reproduced or transmitted, in any form or by any means, without the express written permission of Dark Horse Comics LLC. Names, characters, places, and incidents featured in this publication either are the product of the author's imagination or are used fictitiously. Any resemblance to actual persons (living or dead), events, institutions, or locales, without satiric intent, is coincidental.

Published by Dark Horse Manga
A division of Dark Horse Comics LLC
10956 SE Main Street, Milwaukie, OR 97222

DarkHorse.com

To find a comics shop in your area, visit comicshoplocator.com.

First edition: March 2020 | ISBN 978-1-50671-369-4

1 3 5 7 9 10 8 6 4 2

Printed in the United States of America

NEIL HANKERSON Executive Vice President **TOM WEDDLE** Chief Financial Officer **RANDY STRADLEY** Vice President of Publishing **NICK McWHORTER** Chief Business Development Officer **DALE LAFOUNTAIN** Vice President of Information Technology **MATT PARKINSON** Vice President of Marketing **CARA NIECE** Vice President of Production and Scheduling **MARK BERNARDI** Vice President of Book Trade and Digital Sales **KEN LIZZI** General Counsel **DAVE MARSHALL** Editor in Chief **DAVEY ESTRADA** Editorial Director **CHRIS WARNER** Senior Books Editor **CARY GRAZZINI** Director of Specialty Projects **LIA RIBACCHI** Art Director **VANESSA TODD-HOLMES** Director of Print Purchasing **MATT DRYER** Director of Digital Art and Prepress **MICHAEL GOMBOS** Director of International Publishing and Licensing **KARI YADRO** Director of Custom Programs **KARI TORSON** Director of International Licensing **SEAN BRICE** Director of Trade Sales

REPENT, SINNERS! THEY'RE BACK!

Miss the anime?
Try the *Panty & Stocking with Garterbelt* manga! Nine ALL-NEW
stories of your favorite filthy fallen angels, written and drawn by TAGRO,
with a special afterword by *Kill La Kill* director Hiroyuki Imaishi!
978-1-61655-735-5 | $9.99

AVAILABLE AT YOUR LOCAL COMICS SHOP OR BOOKSTORE | To find a comics shop in your area, visit comicshoplocator.com
For more information or to order direct: On the web: DarkHorse.com E-mail: mailorder@darkhorse.com
Phone: 1-800-862-0052 Mon.–Fri. 9 a.m. to 5 p.m. Pacific Time.
Panty & Stocking with Garterbelt © GAINAX/GEEKS. © TAGRO. Dark Horse Manga™ is a trademark of Dark Horse Comics LLC. All rights reserved. (BL 7065)

QUITE POSSIBLY THE MOST *fabulous* EVANGELION MANGA EVER.

"IT'S A TRULY LAUGH-OUT-LOUD BOOK THAT *EVANGELION* FANS SHOULD BE SURE TO PICK UP. **RECOMMENDED.**"—CHE GILSON, OTAKU USA

DON'T BE CONCERNED THAT THERE'S NO REI OR ASUKA ON THIS COVER. THERE'S PLENTY OF THEM INSIDE. OH, YEAH, AND THAT SHINJI DUDE, TOO.

VOLUME 1
978-1-50670-151-6 • $11.99

VOLUME 2
978-1-50670-375-6 • $11.99

AVAILABLE AT YOUR LOCAL COMICS SHOP OR BOOKSTORE
To find a comics shop in your area, visit comicshoplocator.com • For more information or to order direct • On the web: Dark Horse.com • E-mail: mailorder@darkhorse.com • Phone: 1-800-862-0052 Mon.–Fri. 9 AM to 5 PM Pacific Time.

Neon Genesis Evangelion: Legend of the Piko Piko Middle School Students • Illustration by YUSHI KAWATA and YUKITO. © khara

I AM A HERO

OMNIBUS SERIES FROM DARK HORSE MANGA

"THE GREATEST ZOMBIE MANGA EVER."
—Jason Thompson
(Manga: The Complete Guide)

Shogakukan partners with Dark Horse to bring Kengo Hanazawa's hit zombie-survival manga to the English language! A mentally unhinged manga artist witnesses the start of a zombie outbreak in Tokyo, and he's certain of only two things: he's destined to be a hero, and he possesses something very rare in Japan—an actual firearm! This realistically drawn international bestseller takes us from initial small battles for survival to a huge, body-horror epidemic that threatens all of humanity! Could Hideo find other heroes out in the world, or is humankind doomed? These special omnibus volumes will collect two of the original Japanese books into each Dark Horse edition.

OMNIBUS VOLUME ONE
ISBN 978-1-61655-920-5
$19.99

OMNIBUS VOLUME TWO
ISBN 978-1-50670-019-9
$19.99

OMNIBUS VOLUME THREE
ISBN 978-1-50670-145-5
$19.99

OMNIBUS VOLUME FOUR
ISBN 978-1-50670-349-7
$19.99

OMNIBUS VOLUME FIVE
ISBN 978-1-50670-350-3
$19.99

OMNIBUS VOLUME SIX
ISBN 978-1-50670-396-1
$19.99

OMNIBUS VOLUME SEVEN
ISBN 978-1-50670-702-0
$19.99

OMNIBUS VOLUME EIGHT
ISBN 978-1-50670-750-1
$19.99

OMNIBUS VOLUME NINE
ISBN 978-1-50670-830-0
$19.99

AVAILABLE AT UNINFECTED LOCATIONS EVERYWHERE!

SOMETHING'S WRONG HERE . . .

You sense it, somehow. You suspect this story doesn't really go the way it should. You're suspicious! But a smooth talker like Reigen would know what to say at this point. *"Just flip the book around and start reading it the other way instead."* Aha! So this was really the last page of the book. You're saved! Thank you, Reigen-sensei! *"Now, about my fee . . . "*

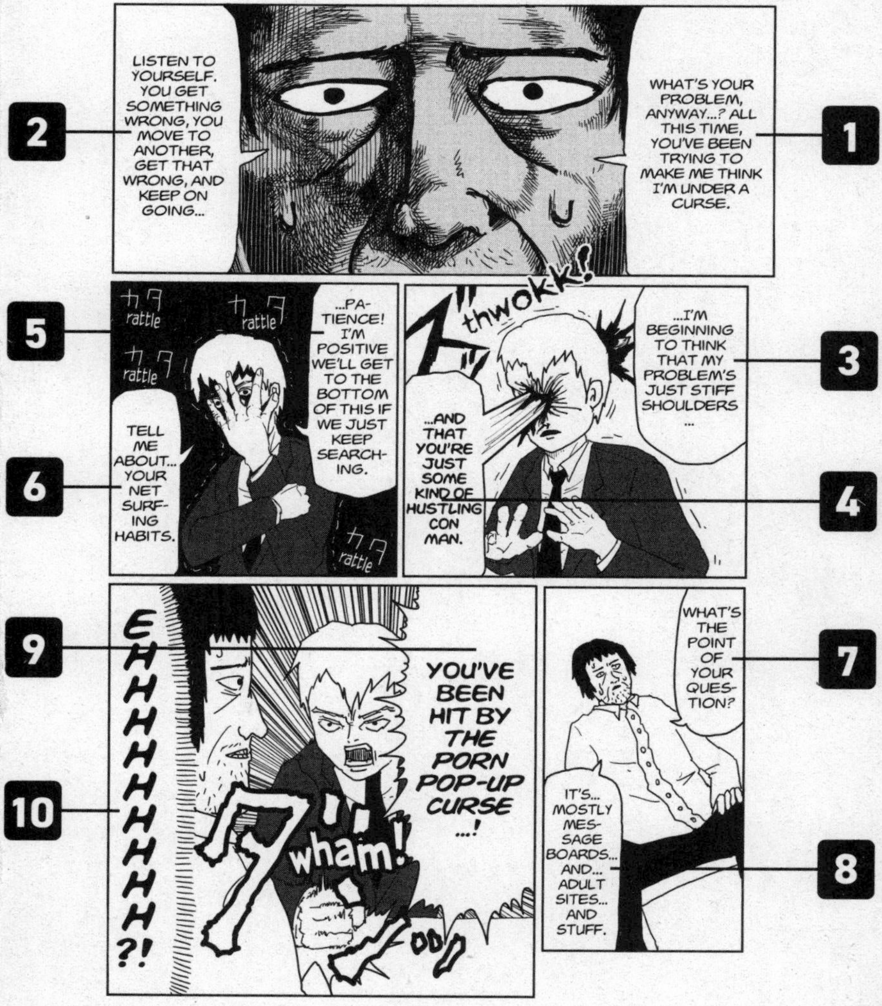
1
WHAT'S YOUR PROBLEM, ANYWAY...? ALL THIS TIME, YOU'VE BEEN TRYING TO MAKE ME THINK I'M UNDER A CURSE.
2
LISTEN TO YOURSELF. YOU GET SOMETHING WRONG, YOU MOVE TO ANOTHER, GET THAT WRONG, AND KEEP ON GOING...
thwokk!
3
...I'M BEGINNING TO THINK THAT MY PROBLEM'S JUST STIFF SHOULDERS ...
4
...AND THAT YOU'RE JUST SOME KIND OF HUSTLING CON MAN.
rattle
rattle
rattle
5
...PA-TIENCE! I'M POSITIVE WE'LL GET TO THE BOTTOM OF THIS IF WE JUST KEEP SEARCH-ING.
6
TELL ME ABOUT... YOUR NET SURF-ING HABITS.
rattle
7
WHAT'S THE POINT OF YOUR QUES-TION?
8
IT'S... MOSTLY MES-SAGE BOARDS... AND... ADULT SITES... AND STUFF.
9
YOU'VE BEEN HIT BY THE PORN POP-UP CURSE ...!
wham!
10
EHHHHHHHHHHHHH?!

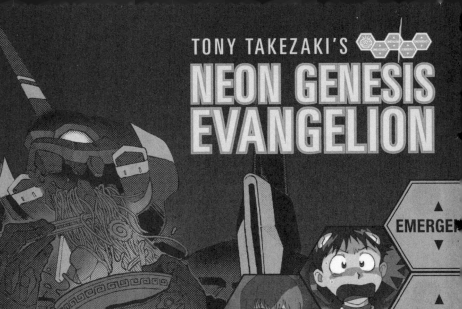

TONY TAKEZAKI'S
NEON GENESIS
EVANGELION

EMERGEN ▲ ▼

EMERGEN ▲ ▼

EMERGEN ▲ ▼

EMERGENCY ▲ ▼

HUNGRY FOR MORE *EVANGELION*?

Place a takeout order for this manga, containing twenty-three servings of satire in both color and black and white from prankster Tony Takezaki, voted a fan favorite in Japan! It's a meal instead of a snack! 978-1-61655-736-2 | $12.99

AVAILABLE AT YOUR LOCAL COMICS SHOP OR BOOKSTORE | TO FIND A COMICS SHOP IN YOUR AREA, VISIT COMICSHOPLOCATOR.COM
For more information or to order direct: On the web: DarkHorse.com E-mail: mailorder@darkhorse.com
Phone: 1-800-862-0052 Mon.–Fri. 9 a.m. to 5 p.m. Pacific Time.

TONY TAKEZAKI NO EVANGELION. Illustration by TONY TAKEZAKI. Edited by KADOKAWA SHOTEN. Dark Horse Manga™ is a trademark of Dark Horse Comics LLC. All rights reserved. (BL 7046)

DRIFTERS

KOHTA HIRANO

Heroes from Earth's history are deposited in an enchanted land where humans subjugate the nonhuman races. This wild, action-packed series features historical characters such as Joan of Arc, Hannibal, and Rasputin being used as chess pieces in a bloody, endless battle!

From Kohta Hirano, creator of the smash-hit *Hellsing*, *Drifters* is an all-out fantasy slugfest of epic proportion!

VOLUME ONE	**VOLUME TWO**	**VOLUME THREE**
978-1-59582-769-2 | $13.99	978-1-59582-933-7 | $12.99	978-1-61655-339-5 | $12.99

VOLUME FOUR	**VOLUME FIVE**	**VOLUME SIX**
978-1-61655-574-0 | $13.99	978-1-50670-379-4 | $13.99	978-1-50671-546-9 | $14.99

AVAILABLE AT YOUR LOCAL COMICS SHOP OR BOOKSTORE
TO FIND A COMICS SHOP IN YOUR AREA, visit comicshoplocator.com
For more information or to order direct: On the web: DarkHorse.com • E-mail: mailorder@darkhorse.com

DARK HORSE MANGA

Drifters © Kouta Hirano. Originally published in Japan in 2010 by Shonen Gahosha Co., Ltd., Tokyo. English translation rights arranged with Shonen Gahosha Co., Ltd., Tokyo through Tohan Corporation, Tokyo. (BL 7092)

FROM THE CREATOR OF TRIGUN AND GUNGRAVE!

YASUHIRO NIGHTOW

³BLOOD BLOCKADE BATTLEFRONT

Three years ago, a gateway between Earth and the Beyond opened over New York City. In one terrible night, New York was destroyed and rebuilt, trapping New Yorkers and extradimensional creatures alike in an impenetrable bubble. New York is now Hellsalem's Lot, a paranormal melting pot where magic and madness dwell alongside the mundane, where human vermin gather to exploit otherworldly assets for earthly profit. Now someone is threatening to breach the bubble and release Hellsalem's horrors, but the mysterious super-agents of Libra fight to prevent the unthinkable.

Trigun creator Yasuhiro Nightow returns with *Blood Blockade Battlefront*, an action-packed supernatural science-fiction steamroller as only Nightow can conjure.

VOLUME ONE
ISBN 978-1-59582-718-0 | $12.99

VOLUME TWO
ISBN 978-1-59582-912-2 | $12.99

VOLUME THREE
ISBN 978-1-59582-913-9 | $10.99

VOLUME FOUR
ISBN 978-1-61655-223-7 | $12.99

VOLUME FIVE
ISBN 978-1-61655-224-4 | $12.99

VOLUME SIX
ISBN 978-1-61655-557-3 | $12.99

VOLUME SEVEN
ISBN 978-1-61655-568-9 | $12.99

VOLUME EIGHT
ISBN 978-1-61655-583-2 | $12.99

VOLUME NINE
ISBN 978-1-50670-705-1 | $12.99

VOLUME TEN
ISBN 978-1-50670-704-4 | $12.99

AVAILABLE AT YOUR LOCAL COMICS SHOP OR BOOKSTORE
To find a comics shop in your area, visit comicshoplocator.com • For more information or to order direct: On the web: DarkHorse.com | E-mail: mailorder@darkhorse.com
Phone: 1-800-862-0052 Mon.–Fri. 9 a.m. to 5 p.m. Pacific Time.
Kekkai Sensen © Yasuhiro Nightow. All rights reserved. Original Japanese edition published by SHUEISHA, Inc., Tokyo. English translation rights in the United States and Canada arranged by SHUEISHA, Inc. (BL7099)